Blackstone's
POLICE MANUAL

EVIDENCE AND PROCEDURE

Blackstone's
POLICE MANUAL

EVIDENCE AND PROCEDURE

2000 edition

Glenn Hutton BA, MPhil, FIPD
and
David Johnston LLB, LLM, Barrister

BLACKSTONE
PRESS LIMITED

First published in Great Britain 1998 by Blackstone Press Limited,
Aldine Place, London W12 8AA. Telephone (020) 8740 2277
www.blackstonepress.com

© Glenn Hutton and David Johnston, 1998

First edition 1998
Second edition 1999

ISBN: 1 85431 914 0

British Library Cataloguing in Publication Data
A CIP catalogue record for this book is available from the British Library.

Typeset by Style Photosetting Ltd, Mayfield, East Sussex
Printed by Ashford Colour Press, Gosport, Hampshire

CONTENTS

CONTENTS

CONTENTS

CONTENTS

CONTENTS

PREFACE

Since publication of the first edition of this Manual we have received some excellent suggestions from both operational officers and trainers for improving both the content and presentation style. These improvements have been incorporated, where appropriate, but we are not complacent to the fact that the Manual can be further developed. Together with Blackstone Press, we constantly seek feedback for this development to continue.

As always with the law there have been continuous changes to primary and secondary legislation and a considerable number of case decisions which have impacted on how the police and other criminal justice practitioners conduct their criminal investigations.

By far the most significant legislative intervention in the criminal justice process has been the Crime and Disorder Act 1998. This Act is part of the government's manifesto to be 'Tough on crime, tough on the causes of crime'. Although commencement of the majority of the Act is not expected until sometime in 2000, a number of the provisions, especially those which apply to youth offending, are subject to 18 month pilot studies by a number of police forces. Consequently, the main provisions of the Act have been included in the Manual and are contained in two new chapters: Youth Justice and Youth Crime and Disorder.

As the Blackstone's Police Manual series are designed for use by all police officers, to ensure their adequacy as a legal reference the *Evidence and Procedure* Manual has been extended to include a separate chapter relating solely to Bail (Chapter 5) and a new chapter on Sentencing (Chapter 9).

Similarly to the first edition, the Manual is fully indexed and cross-referenced and in an effort to assist practitioners in their workplace includes a number of relevant appendices: The Code for Crown Prosecutors; CPS National Casework Guidelines: Visual Identification; Codes of Practice in relation to Disclosure; PACE Codes of Practice — Code C (Detention, Treatment and Questioning); Code D (Identification) and Code E (Tape Recording of Interviews). A new addition to the appendices has been the inclusion of a number of PACE related flow charts.

For police officers intending to sit the police promotion qualifying examinations for sergeant and inspector rank (OSPRE), if the law is not in the latest edition of the manual it is not in the examination. In this second edition readers will find that in certain chapters a continuous vertical line has been inserted down the left-hand margin of the text. The text so marked denotes that this part of the Manual will not be tested in the OSPRE examinations, i.e., it is not in the syllabus. This applies to: Chapter 1 (Sources of Law); Chapter 2 (The Courts); Chapter 3 (Parties in

PREFACE

Criminal Cases); Chapter 7 (Youth Justice); Chapter 8 (Youth Crime and Disorder — with the exception of 'Removal of Truants to Designated Premises, etc.); and Chapter 9 (Sentencing — with the exception of 'Release of Short-term Prisoners Subject to Home Curfew').

While every care has been taken to ensure the accuracy of the contents of this Manual, neither the authors nor the publishers can accept any responsibility for any actions taken, or not taken, on the basis of the information contained in this Manual.

ACKNOWLEDGEMENTS

Similarly with the first edition of the Manual we have continued to be helped and supported by people too numerous to mention and especially two of our colleagues within National Police Training, Examinations and Assessment, Santokh Sidhu and Charlie Eyre.

We would like to thank four specific people who have provided considerable feedback on both this and the previous edition but also on what might be usefully included within this second edition. These are: Paul Murphy (Greater Manchester Police), George Cooper (Northamptonshire Police), Stuart Fairclough (Metropolitan Police) and David Anson.

Thanks also to the Crown Prosecution Service for permission to include: The Code for Crown Prosecutors and the CPS National Casework Guidelines: Visual Identification.

Finally to Alistair, Richard and Mandy — a big thank you, but to Heather a special thanks for her support, faith and, in many instances, her charity on realistic deadlines.

TABLE OF CASES

TABLE OF CASES

TABLE OF STATUTES

TABLE OF STATUTES

TABLE OF STATUTES

TABLE OF STATUTES

TABLE OF STATUTORY INSTRUMENTS
AND CODES OF PRACTICE

TABLE OF STATUTORY INSTRUMENTS AND CODES OF PRACTICE

PART ONE

THE CRIMINAL JUSTICE SYSTEM

CHAPTER ONE

SOURCES OF LAW

1.1 Introduction

As with most branches of the law in England and Wales, the sources of criminal law are found partly in common law and partly in statute law.

1.2 Common Law

Common law originated from the customs of the early communities, which were unified and developed in the Royal Courts during the three centuries following the Norman Conquest.

There is no authoritative text of the common law (although *Stephen's Digest* is one of the most often cited) and, as a whole, its sources lie in the principles of the law declared by the judges in the course of deciding particular cases. It should be noted that the common law can only be declared authoritatively by the judge(s) of the superior courts (i.e. from the High Court) and then only to the extent that it is necessary to do so for the purpose of deciding a particular case. For this reason, the development of the common law has always been dependent upon the incidence of cases arising for decision, and the particular facts of those cases.

Those decisions are the *authoritative sources* of certain offences and powers, in exactly the same way as an Act (such as the Theft Act 1968) and will be relevant irrespective of how ancient the case is — if anything, the older a case authority is, the more persuasive it is, having stood the test of time. A good example of this would be the decision in *Doodeward* v *Spence* (1907) 6 CLR 406 where it was held that a human body could not be 'property' for the purposes of theft (**see Crime, chapter 12**). Reviewing this decision in 1998, Lord Justice Rose said that he was reluctant to interfere with a decision which had stood the test of time for so long and left the issue for Parliament.

In relation to certain offences which originate in the common law, e.g. murder, theft, rape, robbery and arson, precise definitions were evolved because the severity of the punishment rendered this necessary. As most were punishable by death, the burden of proof on the prosecution (as to which **see chapter 11**) was also very high — and has remained so ever since. Other offences of similar origin, however, e.g. conspiracy and attempts to commit crime, are notable for the lack of precision in their formulation (**see Crime, chapter 3**), and are still being used to bring new sets of facts within the ambit of the criminal law, as in the decisions of *Shaw* v *DPP* [1962] AC 220 and *Knuller (Publishing, Printing and Promotions) Ltd* v *DPP* [1973] AC 435 on conspiracy to corrupt public morals.

1.3   Legislation

Statutes, in the form of Acts of Parliament, have always been regarded as supplementary to the common law. It is true that the major part of criminal law and procedure is now in statutory form, but it is equally true that the principles of common law, notably in relation to criminal liability generally, homicide and the rules of evidence and procedure at a criminal trial, have not lessened in importance.

Statutes are enacted by Parliament and it is the duty of the court, as and when the occasion arises, to interpret and give effect to the intention of Parliament as expressed in the words of the statute. The courts have the same task in relation to delegated legislation, i.e. in the form of Orders in Council, statutory instruments and bye-laws made by Ministers, heads of Government Departments, local authorities and other bodies under powers delegated to them by Parliament. In looking at the intentions of Parliament, the courts may now consider the content of any debates within either House as reported in *Hansard* (*Pepper* v *Hart* [1993] AC 593).

The only distinction, for practical purposes, between statutes and delegated legislation is that, while the validity of the former cannot be questioned in a court, the latter are valid only within the limits of the powers conferred by the enabling statute, and in the case of bye-laws they must also be reasonable. Consequently, the courts have the power, though rarely exercised, to hold that delegated legislation is invalid because the terms of the statute under which it is made have not been complied with.

A statute is construed so far as possible in conformity with the common law, because of the presumption against the alteration of general common law principles. Where the two cannot be reconciled, the statute prevails.

The Interpretation Act 1978 (which is the main authority for interpreting the effect of statutes), s. 18 provides:

> *Where an act or omission constitutes an offence under two or more Acts, or both under an Act and at common law, the offender shall, unless the contrary intention appears, be liable to be prosecuted and punished under either or any of those Acts or at common law, but shall not be liable to be punished more than once for the same offence.*

1.4   Judicial Precedents

The decision in a criminal trial as to the guilt or innocence of the defendant is a matter for the jury (or the magistrate(s); **see chapter 2**) although this decision will only be left to them when the trial judge is satisfied that a verdict of guilty would be proper in law on the facts, and that there is evidence which, if believed, would justify such a verdict.

Juries decide questions of *fact*; judges decide questions of *law* (and, confusingly, magistrates decide both *fact and law*), **see para. 2.6.2.**

Matters of law are solely for the judge who frequently has to rule on these during the course of a trial. Ultimately, the judge directs the jury on the law in summing up. In a trial by jury these rulings and directions alone are important in the development and illustration of the law.

1.4.1 The Courts and Decided Cases

The system of courts in England and Wales is a hierarchy, the various courts being related to one another as superior and inferior. An inferior court is generally bound by the decision and directions of a superior court. For example, judges of the Divisional Court and Crown Courts are bound by the decisions of the Court of Appeal. The Appeal Court is in turn bound by the decisions of the House of Lords, which is also bound — to an extent — by decisions of the European Court of Justice. It should be noted that, although the Crown Court is superior to a magistrates' court and enjoys wider powers (**see para. 2.10**), it is still a 'lower' court and its decisions are not generally binding on other courts.

When it is said that a decision is binding, or more fully, a binding and authoritative precedent, what is meant is that the *principle of law* on which the decision was based, or the reason for the decision, is binding. This principle of the law is known as the *ratio decidendi* of the case. An example of this would be the decision that, once the prosecution have proved that a defendant was carrying a weapon that is 'offensive' *per se*, there is no need to prove any intention to use that weapon offensively (*Ohlson* v *Hylton* [1975] 1 WLR 724). (For the law on weapons generally, **see General Police Duties, chapter 6.**)

The *ratio decidendi* consists only of the principle(s) of law essential to a decision. A judge, or court as a whole, may sometimes go beyond the facts of a particular case and give an *opinion* on some connected matter, which is intended to be of guidance in future cases. Such an opinion is known as an *obiter dictum*, and may be persuasive, but not binding, on other courts in a future case. Such *obiter dicta* are often made where an important point has arisen from the arguments in an appeal case but that point has not been directly raised by the defendant.

In some cases, particularly those which go to the House of Lords, the *dissenting* judgment — that is, the speech of a judge who does not agree with his/her fellow judges on the bench — can also be very instructive and it is not uncommon for those judgments to become law through Acts of Parliament at a later date (see, for example, Lord Mustill's speech in the 'Spanner trial' involving sado-masochism (*R* v *Brown* [1993] 2 All ER 75, at 101)).

Where a case decision becomes authoritative or binding, it is a 'reported' (**see para. 1.4.2**) or 'decided' case. Such cases are often referred to as *stated cases*, a description which is inaccurate and also misleading as stated cases are a very specific form of appeal to the Queen's Bench Divisional Court (**see chapter 2**).

In addition to the above, the Human Rights Act 1998 will have considerable implications for the criminal law. The government has announced that the provisions of the 1998 Act will be enacted on 2 October 2000. The domestic law of England and Wales will need to take account of the European Convention for the Protection of Human Rights and Fundamental Freedoms and case decisions emanating from the European Court of Human Rights. These matters will be concerned with the inclusion of the substantive rights within the Convention:

- the right to life (Article 2);

- freedom from torture (Article 3);

- freedom from slavery (Article 4);

- freedom from arbitrary arrest and detention (Article 5);

- the right to a fair trial (Article 6);

- freedom from retrospective penalties (Article 7);

- the right to respect for privacy and family life (Article 8);

- freedom of thought, conscience and religion (Article 9);

- right to free speech (Article 10);

- freedom of assembly and association (Article 11);

- the right to marry and found a family (Article 12);

- freedom from discrimination (Article 14);

- restriction on the political activities of aliens (Article 16);

- prohibition of abuse of rights (Article 17);

- limitation on use of restrictions on rights (Article 18);

- the right to peaceful enjoyment of property (First Protocol, Article 1);

- the right to education (First Protocol, Article 2);

- the right to free elections (First Protocol, Article 3).

The European Convention for the Protection of Human Rights and Fundamental Freedoms has been in existence since 1950 and is ratified by over 40 countries within Europe. The United Kingdom, although one of the earlier members to ratify the Convention, considered sufficient safeguards existed within the common law and that there was no need to incorporate it into domestic law.

1.4.2 Law Reports

The authority of judicial precedents dates from the beginning of modern law reporting in the eighteenth century. Until 1865, there were numerous private reports, each series published under the name of the reporter, and which are still occasionally referred to today. Since 1865, the Incorporated Council of Law Reporting in England and Wales has published the series known as 'The Law Reports'. These are cited according to the court (e.g. Appeal Court; Queen's Bench Divisional Court) in which the case was heard and the year in which the case is reported (e.g. *R v Brown* [1994] 1 AC 212; *R v Bryant* [1979] QB 108).

These reports are now supplemented by various commercial series, of which the best known are:

- Criminal Appeal Reports (e.g. *R v Bray* (1988) 88 Cr App R 354);

- Justice of the Peace Reports (e.g. *R v Britzman* (1983) 147 JP 531);

- All England Law Reports (e.g. *R v Bryce* [1992] 4 All ER 567);

- Weekly Law Reports (e.g. *R v Khan* [1996] 3 WLR 162);

- Criminal Law Review (e.g. *R v Deakin* [1972] Crim LR 781).

The examples shown in parenthesis are how cases are usually referenced (cited) in law texts. The numbers which follow the date in a reported case are simply the *volume*, and then the *page* where the report begins, or the page where the relevant speech of the judge can be found. Many important cases can be found in a number of different reports, though decisions of the House of Lords are usually to be found in the Appeal Cases (AC).

When researching a legal reference it is worth remembering that many authors in criminal law texts refer simply to the surname or family name of the defendant (e.g. *Deakin*) and not '*R v Deakin*'.

In addition to the above reports, cases are also published in some newspapers, e.g. *The Times* and the *Independent*. All the reports are made by barristers and may be cited in court as and when necessary.

Other reports of cases which may appear in newspapers for their general news value are *not* 'reported' cases and this often causes frustration when trying to look up a particular case that has appeared in the press.

CHAPTER TWO

THE COURTS

2.1 | Introduction

The nature of an offence will determine in which court a case is heard. Offences can be tried in either the magistrates' court or the Crown Court. Cases tried in the magistrates' court are tried by either a stipendiary magistrate, who is a qualified lawyer, or a panel of lay magistrates (**see para. 2.8**). In the magistrates' court the magistrates decide on questions of law and fact. Cases tried in the Crown Court are presided over by a judge, who is a qualified lawyer; he/she decides on any points of law while questions of fact are decided by a jury (**see para. 2.10**). All cases will start with the defendant appearing at the magistrates' court who will either deal with the matter themselves or commit the case to the Crown Court for trial or, on occasions, for sentence.

Which court the accused goes before will depend on the offences charged and the seriousness of the offence. The nature of the particular court is also important in terms of sentencing. A magistrates' court can only ever give a maximum aggregate prison sentence of 12 months and there are also limits on the size of the fine that can be given. The Crown Court has much wider powers of sentencing, which is another factor when deciding which of the two courts will deal with the case.

2.2 | Categories of Trial

Offences are categorised in three groups:

- summary offences
- indictable offences
- either way offences.

2.2.1 | Summary Offences

These offences tend to be considered as less 'serious' in the eyes of the law (although not in the eyes of the victim!) and can only be tried in the magistrates' court, where the penalties are less severe. When an offender is charged with several offences, some of which go to the Crown Court, these lesser offences are not generally pursued and are 'left on file'.

2.2.2 Indictable Offences

These offences are considered to be the more serious offences and must be dealt with in the Crown Court whether the person pleads guilty or not. The accused will still first appear at the magistrates' court for preliminary matters (e.g. bail), and the case will then be committed to the Crown Court to be heard.

2.2.3 Either Way Offences

Offences that fall within this category can be dealt with either in the magistrates' court or the Crown Court. The defendant can elect the trial court. If the defendant elects to be tried in the Crown Court, the case is automatically committed to the Crown Court. Where the defence ask to be dealt with in the magistrates' court then it is for the magistrates to decide whether this is appropriate.

The prosecution at this stage are given an opportunity to indicate in which court they wish the case to be heard. Much will depend on how complicated the case is in terms of facts or law and the seriousness of the offence. The case can be committed to the Crown Court either at this stage or, if the magistrates feel they cannot pass a sufficient sentence, the case can be committed to the Crown Court for sentence at the end of the trial. There are occasions (e.g. criminal damage) that encourage cases to be dealt with by the magistrates' court (where the damage is less than £5,000, if the defendant elects to be tried in the magistrates' court, the case cannot be committed to the Crown Court for sentence).

2.3 Jurisdiction to Deal with Offences Summarily

Section 2 of the Magistrates' Courts Act 1980 provides that:

> (1) A magistrates' court for a county, a London commission area or the City of London shall have jurisdiction to try all summary offences committed within the county, the London commission area or the City (as the case may be).
> (2) Where a person charged with a summary offence appears or is brought before a magistrates' court in answer to a summons issued under paragraph (b) of section 1(2) above, or under a warrant issued under that paragraph, the court shall have jurisdiction to try the offence.
> (3) A magistrates' court for a county, a London commission area or the City of London shall have jurisdiction as examining justices over any offence committed by a person who appears or is brought before the court, whether or not the offence was committed within the county, the London commission area or the City (as the case may be).
> (4) Subject to sections 18 to 22 . . . and any other enactment (wherever contained) relating to the mode of trial of offences triable either way, a magistrates' court shall have jurisdiction to try summarily an offence triable either way in any case in which under subsection (3) above it would have jurisdiction as examining justices.
> (5) A magistrates' court shall, in exercise of its powers under section 24 . . . (summary trial of young persons) have jurisdiction to try summarily an indictable offence in any case in which under subsection (3) above it would have jurisdiction as examining justices.
> (6) A magistrates' court for any area by which a person is tried for an offence shall have jurisdiction to try him for any summary offence for which he could be tried by a magistrates' court for any other area.
> (7) Nothing in this section shall affect any jurisdiction over offences conferred on a magistrates' court by any enactment not contained in this Act.

Keynote

In other words, s. 2 allows a magistrates' court which already has jurisdiction regarding an offence, to deal with any other summary offence alleged against the defendant.

Note that s. 1 of the 1980 Act provides:

(2) A justice of the peace for an area to which this section applies may issue a summons or warrant under this section—

. . .

(b) if it appears to the justice necessary or expedient, with a view to the better administration of justice, that the person charged should be tried jointly with, or in the same place as, some other person who is charged with an offence, and who is in custody, or is being or is to be proceeded against, within the area . . .

2.3.1 Jurisdiction to Deal with Offences on Boundaries and Journeys

Section 3 of the Magistrates' Courts Act 1980 provides that:

(1) Where an offence has been committed on the boundary between two or more areas to which this section applies, or within 500 yards of such a boundary, or in any harbour, river, arm of the sea or other water lying between two or more such areas, the offence may be treated for the purposes of the preceding provisions of this Act as having been committed in any of those areas.

(2) An offence begun in one area to which this section applies and completed in another may be treated for the purposes of the preceding provisions of this Act as having been wholly committed in either.

(3) Where an offence has been committed on any person, or on or in respect of any property, in or on a vehicle or vessel engaged on any journey or voyage through two or more areas to which this section applies, the offence may be treated for the purposes of the preceding provisions of this Act as having been committed in any one of those areas; and where the side or any part of a road or any water along which the vehicle or vessel passed in the course of the journey or voyage forms the boundary between two or more areas to which this section applies, the offence may be treated for the purposes of the preceding provisions of this Act as having been committed in any of those areas.

(4) The areas to which this section applies are any county, any London commission area and the City of London.

Keynote

Normally an offence takes place where it is completed but, where the special circumstances relating to boundaries and journeys apply, s. 3 extends the jurisdiction.

The 500 yards distance should be measured in a straight line (or as the crow flies).

Other useful points concerning s. 3 include:

- The offence of taking excessive hackney carriage/taxi fares is committed where the taking occurred in the jurisdiction, although the journey may have begun in another jurisdiction.

- A letter posted in one jurisdiction for the purpose of obtaining money by false pretences (**see Crime, chapter 13**), and delivered in another jurisdiction may be prosecuted in either.

- The mere unlawful use of a vehicle such as contravening an operators' licence (**see Road Traffic, chapter 13**) is not 'an offence . . . committed . . . on or in respect of any property in or on a vehicle . . .' for the purposes of s. 3(3) above. Section 3(3) applies to offences in respect of property (such as theft or damage, **see Crime, chapters 12 and 14**) in or on a vehicle.

2.4 | **Offences Committed by Juveniles**

Generally offences committed by juveniles are dealt with in the youth court, which is part of the magistrates' court. A juvenile is any person under the age of 18. Apart from homicide (**see Crime, chapter 5**), no other charge against such a person can be heard anywhere other than at a youth court. The general principle is that juveniles should be tried in the youth court and as a result they are not given the option of electing trial by jury. The public do not have access to youth courts and there is also a restriction on what the press can publicise about cases involving juveniles. It is for this reason that many news stories carry a section which says that the writer or broadcaster has been unable to identify the defendant (or others) for 'legal reasons'. (For the situation regarding anonymity of victims of sexual offences, **see Crime, chapter 10**.)

However, a juvenile will have his/her case dealt with at the magistrates' court where he/she is:

- jointly charge with an adult;

- mistakenly taken by the court to be aged 18 or over;

- charged with aiding and abetting an adult to commit a crime (or vice versa);

- charged with a crime which arises out of circumstances which are the same as, or connected with those that resulted in a charge against an adult.

If the adult is committed to the Crown Court then it is for the magistrates to decide whether the juvenile should similarly be committed, or whether the case should be dealt with in the youth court.

Keynote

The position was clarified in *R* v *Uxbridge Youth Court, ex parte H, The Times*, 7 April 1998. H was 17 when arrested and charged. By the time of his first appearance at the youth court he had turned 18. It was held, construing s. 29 of the Children and Young Persons Act 1963, that proceedings are begun when the defendant first appears before the justices and so the youth court did not have jurisdiction under s. 29. Furthermore, the youth court did not have jurisdiction to remit H to the adult magistrates' court for sentence.

Note that s. 47 of the Crime and Disorder Act 1998 addresses this point enabling the youth court to deal with a defendant who attains the age of 18 after charge and to remit him/her to the magistrates' court for sentence.

2.5 | **Limitation on Proceedings**

In the law of England and Wales the general rule is that there is no restriction on the time which may elapse between the commission of an offence and the commencement of a prosecution for it. However, there are a number of statutory provisions prohibiting proceedings once a certain time has elapsed. The relevant provisions are outlined below.

2.5.1 | Summary Offences

Section 127 of the Magistrates' Courts Act 1980 provides that:

> *(1)   Except as otherwise expressly provided by any enactment and subject to subsection (2) below, a magistrates' court shall not try an information or hear a complaint unless the information was laid, or the complaint made, within 6 months from the time when the offence was committed, or the matter of complaint arose.*

Keynote

Examples of offences which provide otherwise are the summary offences under s. 143 of the Road Traffic Act 1988 (uninsured use of a motor vehicle) and s. 8 of the Vehicles (Excise) Act 1971 (using and keeping a vehicle without an excise licence), where proceedings can be instituted up to and including three years after the commission of the offence (for both offences, **see Road Traffic, chapters 6 and 12**).

2.5.2 | Indictable Offences

Section 127 of the Magistrates' Courts Act 1980 provides that:

> *(2)   Nothing in—*
> *(a)   subsection (1) above; or*
> *(b)   subject to subsection (4) below, any other enactment (however framed or worded) which, as regards any offence to which it applies, would but for this section impose a time-limit on the power of a magistrates' court to try an information summarily or impose a limitation on the time for taking summary proceedings,*
> *shall apply in relation to any indictable offence.*
> *(3)   Without prejudice to the generality of paragraph (b) of subsection (2) above, that paragraph includes enactments which impose a time-limit that applies only in certain circumstances (for example, where the proceedings are not instituted by or with the consent of the Director of Public Prosecutions or some other specified authority).*
> *(4)   Where, as regards any indictable offence, there is imposed by any enactment (however framed or worded, and whether falling within subsection (2)(b) above or not) a limitation on the time for taking proceedings on indictment for that offence no summary proceedings for that offence shall be taken after the latest time for taking proceedings on indictment.*

There are two further statutory provisions in relation to time-limits. These are:

- The Sexual Offences Act 1956, sch. 2, para. 10, which provides that prosecutions for unlawful sexual intercourse with a girl under 16 contrary to s. 6 of the 1956 Act must be commenced within 12 months.

- The Sexual Offences Act 1967, s. 7 which provides that prosecutions for gross indecency between men and buggery where no assault is involved and the 'victim' is 16 or over must be commenced within 12 months.

(For both offences, **see Crime, chapter 10.**)

In the case of an offence triable either way, where there is no time-limit for taking proceedings on indictment, there is no time-limit for summary proceedings. Where there is a time-limit on indictment, summary proceedings cannot be taken once the time-limit bars proceedings on indictment.

The definition of 'indictable offence' under s. 64(1)(a) of the Criminal Law Act 1977 includes offences triable either way. Section 127 excludes purely indictable offences and offences triable either way from the operation of s. 127(1) of the Magistrates' Courts Act 1980 (which prohibits summary trial where the information is not laid within six months of the offence being committed). Consequently, an offence triable either way such as theft, contrary to ss. 1 to 7 of the Theft Act 1968 (**see Crime, chapter 12**) can still be tried summarily after the six-month limitation has expired.

The day on which the offence etc. arose is not to be included when determining the time-limit.

The time runs from the *commission of the offence*, not from the date of its discovery. A 'month' means a calendar month and a month ends at midnight on the day of the next month which has the same number as the day on which the offence was committed. For example, X commits a driving licence offence at 10 am on 24 September; the information should be laid before midnight on 24 March the following year, i.e. within six months.

It should be noted that there is one further statutory provision in relation to time-limits. The Trade Descriptions Act 1968, s. 19(1) provides that prosecution for any indictable offence under the 1968 Act must be commenced within three years of the offence or one year from its discovery, whichever is the earlier.

2.6 Appeals

2.6.1 Introduction

A defendant has a right of appeal from the magistrates' court, whether by way of rehearing to the Crown Court or by way of *case stated*, where the magistrates are asked to 'state a case' on a point of law for the Divisional Court of the Queen's Bench to examine and decide whether the magistrates came to the right legal decision (**see para. 2.6.2**).

It is possible for an appeal to go straight from the Divisional Court to the House of Lords where the case is related wholly or mainly on the construction of an enactment or statutory instrument, or where the decision made by the court is one by which the judge is bound by a previous decision to follow.

Appeals from the Crown Court to the Court of Appeal (Criminal Division) normally require leave to be heard unless it is purely an appeal on a point of law. Leave is also required for appeals to the House of Lords.

Whether an appeal to the Court of Appeal will be successful is governed by s. 2 of the Criminal Appeal Act 1968, as amended by the Criminal Appeal Act 1995, which provides that:

> *(1) Subject to the provisions of this Act, the Court of Appeal—*
>   *(a) shall allow an appeal against conviction if they think that the conviction is unsafe; and*
>   *(b) shall dismiss such an appeal in any other case.*

This does not mean that every time a mistake has been made during a trial that a conviction must be overturned. The question is whether the conviction is *unsafe*. If the court take the view that it is, and that there has been a 'miscarriage of justice', then the conviction will not stand. The approach taken by the Court of Appeal is shown in the judgment of *R* v *Cohen* (1909) 2 Cr App R 197, where the court explained:

> There is such a miscarriage of justice not only where the court comes to the conclusion that the verdict of guilty was wrong, but also when it is of opinion that the mistake of fact or omission on the part of the judge may reasonably be considered to have brought about that verdict, and when, on the whole facts and with a correct direction, the jury might fairly and reasonably have found the appellant not guilty. Then there has been not only a miscarriage of justice but a substantial one, because the appellant has lost the chance which was fairly open to him of being acquitted. . . . If, however, the court in such a case comes to the conclusion that, on the whole of the facts and with a correct direction, the only reasonable and proper verdict would be one of guilty, there is no miscarriage of justice, or at all events no substantial miscarriage of justice . . .

The effect of this approach is that, on occasions, even if it concludes that certain evidence was wrongly admitted or that a judge failed to do something relevant to the defendant's trial, the Court of Appeal may still refuse to overturn the conviction.

Where an appellant wishes the Court of Appeal to receive fresh evidence under s. 23 of the Criminal Appeal Act 1968 and the circumstances give rise to the need for a lengthy or complex explanation of why the evidence was not admitted at the original trial, an affidavit or signed statement from the appellant or his/her solicitor, setting out the grounds relied on, should be supplied to the court (*R* v *T, The Times*, 30 June 1998).

2.6.2 The Appeals Process

Cases can be appealed for a number of reasons:

* questions of fact
* questions of law
* mixed questions of fact and law
* level of sentence.

Questions of Fact

This is an appeal on the basis that the facts do not support the decision that has been reached. These appeals are unlikely to succeed as an appellate court will not change a decision of fact unless it feels that no reasonable tribunal could have reached the decision made by the trial court. This approach, where the court will ask itself whether, on the facts presented, any other tribunal could reasonably come to the conclusion that the trial court did, follows the *Wednesbury* principles (**see para. 2.6.4**).

As magistrates are the judges of questions of *fact* in any summary trial (**see para. 1.4**). their interpretation of what happened may be affected by local conditions and different magistrates' courts may arrive at different decisions on the same facts. Take an example of a person in a street shouting the word 'scab'. A magistrates' court in South Yorkshire may be ready to accept that the word 'scab' is in fact 'insulting' for the purposes of public order legislation (**see General Police Duties, chapter 4**), while a magistrates' court in Suffolk may not. As the decisions of magistrates' courts are not binding on each other and as the decision as to what is 'insulting' is a question of fact, there is little likelihood of a successful appeal against such a decision; there is also little likelihood of that decision being followed by other courts.

Keynote

The Crown Court is not bound by the findings of fact by the magistrates' court and so where the defendant appeals against sentence to the Crown Court, the Crown Court may determine the appeal on a different factual basis to that accepted by the magistrates. Where the Crown Court is minded to reflect the view taken by the magistrates, and that view was favourable to the defendant, the Crown Court should warn the defendant that this is so and give him/her the opportunity to challenge the factual basis the Crown Court wishes to adopt (*Bussey* v *Chief Constable of Suffolk, The Independent*, 8 June 1998).

Questions of Law

Unlike questions of fact (which are decided by the jury) questions of law are determined by the trial judge. Of course, in a magistrates' court, the magistrate(s) decides on both questions and therefore, to understand an appeal proceeding from a magistrates' court, it is first necessary to understand whether that appeal is based on a question of fact or law. An appeal on a question of law is one where a party to the proceedings wishes a higher court to give a ruling on the *interpretation* or *application* of the law, for instance, what 'recklessness' means in relation to criminal damage (**see Crime, chapter 1**) or, in the example above i.e., the word 'scab', whether 'insulting' behaviour is covered by the Public Order Act 1986.

Having considered the question of law, the higher court will then give a judgment on the point. This will either allow the original court hearing the case to continue with it or, in some circumstances, allow the appeal court to decide the outcome of the case.

Mixed Questions of Fact and Law

As the heading suggests, this is where a party to the proceedings appeals on an issue which requires the appeal court to consider both a question of fact and a point of law. This often involves the court being asked to make a finding, first on the facts and then to interpret them in relation to the law. This allows parties to take a case to the appeal court on occasions where, if it were just a question of fact, an appeal would not be allowed.

The 'scab' example above might be broken down as follows:

- whether the word 'scab' can be insulting — question of *fact*;

- whether the word 'scab' was in fact used by a defendant on a certain date — question of *fact*;

- whether 'insulting' behaviour is covered by the Public Order Act 1986 — question of *law*;

- whether, simply by shouting 'scab' in an empty street, a defendant commits the entire offence under s. 4 of the Public Order Act 1986 — question *of fact and law*.

Level of Sentence

The courts will also hear appeals on the level of sentence given to a convicted person.

Where an offender gives information, enabling serious criminal activity to be stopped and serious criminals to be brought to book, after he/she has been sentenced, the Court of Appeal will not normally take account of the information. However, if the offender expresses willingness to help prior to sentence but the value of help thereafter given greatly exceeds the help anticipated by the sentence, the Court of Appeal can adjust the sentence to reflect the value of the help given after sentence (*R* v *A (Informer: Reduction of Sentence)*, *The Times*, 1 May 1998).

2.6.3   Appeal by Prosecution

Strictly speaking there is no 'appeal' process by the prosecution. However, the Attorney-General may refer certain cases from the Crown Court to the Court of Appeal for a review of the sentence passed on the offender. Sections 35 and 36 of the Criminal Justice Act 1988 set out the grounds for this review process. The only cases which can be referred by the Attorney-General are:

- offences which are triable only on indictment;

- offences which are triable either way and which have been specified in a statutory instrument.

The offences specified by statutory instrument at the time of writing are:

- indecent assault;

- cruelty to a child under 16 years;

- attempts to commit or incite either of the above two offences.

(See Reviews of Sentencing Order 1994 (SI 1994 No. 119).)

The procedure also includes some serious fraud cases (Reviews of Sentencing Order 1995 (SI 1995 No. 10)).

In each case, leave of the Court of Appeal is required before a referral and the Attorney-General must consider that the offender's sentence was unduly lenient (this would include occasions where the judge failed to impose a sentence as required by the Crime (Sentences) Act 1997).

2.6.4   Judicial Review

Judicial review is a method of challenging decisions made by administrative bodies and office holders such as the police service. Cases can range from policy decisions made by the organisation — such as the decision not to prosecute someone — to decisions made by individual supervisors (e.g. the cautioning of a juvenile). The circumstances under which a matter can go before the High Court for judicial review are quite limited. Generally, applications for judicial review can only proceed if there is no other method by which to appeal the decision. An application for judicial review must be made as soon as reasonably practicable and generally within three months of the decision. In reviewing the decision the court can look at whether the administrative body or individual was acting within the law when making that decision; it will also consider whether the decision was a reasonable one.

Whether a decision was made within the law will be determined by a number of features surrounding the decision-making process. These would include:

- Whether the organisation or individual actually had the authority or power to make the decision.

- What procedure was followed and whether that procedure observed the requirements of 'natural justice'.

- Whether the decision-maker exercised his/her own discretion or whether he/she delegated or fettered that discretion in a way which was not permitted in law.

This is one reason why the documentation and recording of any significant decision-making procedure is important.

In reviewing whether or not a decision is 'reasonable' the court will consider whether the decision is one that any reasonable person in the position of the decision-maker could have made, applying the *Wednesbury* principles (from the case of *Associated Provincial Picture Houses Ltd* v *Wednesbury Corporation* [1948] 1 KB 223). In reviewing the reasonableness of a decision, the court is not asking whether *it* would have made that decision itself; it is asking whether the decision was lawfully and reasonably made in the circumstances. Therefore it would be possible for conflicting decisions made under similar circumstances to be upheld provided both were lawful and reasonable. If the court considers that a decision is unreasonable or unlawful it can make a declaration to that effect. The court can also make an order for mandamus instructing the administrative body to perform a function that it is required to perform (i.e., a chief officer must consider each case involving officers convicted of drink-driving on its merits and not have a blanket policy requiring them to resign). The court may also make an order of certiorari where the court quashes the earlier decision (e.g., a caution given to a juvenile where there was insufficient evidence to obtain a conviction). The court can also make an order of prohibition where it can order the administrative body *not* to perform an act which the court has found to be unlawful or outside that body's power.

The key points to remember are that applications for judicial review are made to the High Court, they will only be heard if there are no other avenues of appeal available and that the application has been made as soon as reasonably practicable.

2.7 Rules of Construction

2.7.1 Interpretation of Statutes

Statutes are to be construed according to the intentions of Parliament. Such intentions can only be assumed from the words used in the Act, except where there is imprecision or ambiguity.

Where imprecision or ambiguity exists the following rules are applied, which are derived from common law sources, to assist in interpretation:

- The 'ordinary meaning' of words is to be used, read in the context of the statute in which they appear.

- The interpretation should suppress the 'mischief' being dealt with by the legislation. (For example, in the Criminal Damage Act 1971, any interpretation issue should be decided in such a way as to prevent criminal damage and provide a punishment for criminal damage.

- The interpretation should not lead to unreasonable, inconvenient, absurd or inconsistent results.

2.7.2 | *Ejusdem Generis* **Rule**

Ejusdem generis means of the same kind or nature.

Numerous Acts of Parliament provide lists of specifically named things or places etc. followed by a generalisation, e.g. 'all signals, warning sign posts, direction posts, signs or other devices'. Where such lists are shown in an Act, the 'generalisation' will be construed by the courts in the light of the words which appear alongside it. This rule of construction is known as the *ejusdem* (pronounced 'use-dem') *generis* rule. In the example above, the expression 'other devices' will be interpreted as being in the same class as those other words ('signals, warning posts' etc.) which appear alongside it; the expression could not be construed as meaning *any* 'other device', say, a breathalyser machine, even though a literal interpretation of 'other devices' might.

2.7.3 | *De Minimis* **Rule**

A further rule of construction commonly used by the courts is the *de minimis* rule. This rule (fully named *de minimis non curat lex* — 'the law is not concerned with trifling matters') means that courts will not deal with trivial infringements of the law. An example of the *de minimis* rule might be where a motorist displays a valid 'pay-and-display' parking ticket clearly in the window of their car; although the requirements on the ticket may say that it must be affixed to the *windshield*. It is likely that an attempt to enforce a penalty against the motorist would fail under the *de minimis* rule (it would probably also fail the test of construction looking at the 'mischief' intended to be addressed by the parking regulations, **see para. 2.7.1**). Some offences of 'absolute' liability, however, may be prosecuted for even the most minor infringement (**see Crime, chapter 1**).

2.7.4 | **The Interpretation Act 1978**

The Interpretation Act 1978 deals with particular words which are in common usage.

'Month' means calendar month. 'Week' can mean a calendar week beginning on a Sunday and ending on the following Saturday or any period of seven days. The onus is on the court to interpret the word according to the appropriate statute.

'Day' can mean between sunrise and sunset as well as from midnight to midnight. The length of time between sunrise and the next sunset is a question of fact and obviously varies according to locality.

Masculine includes feminine and vice versa, and singular includes plural and vice versa.

Service by post is deemed effective at the time the letter would be delivered in the ordinary course of the post, unless the contrary is proved.

2.8 Magistrates' Courts

Magistrates' courts consist of justices of the peace, the majority of whom are unpaid lay men and women. A minority of justices are paid and are known as stipendiaries. These stipendiary magistrates are either qualified barristers or solicitors of at least seven years' standing.

The law relating to justices and magistrates' courts is contained principally in the following legislation:

- Justices of the Peace Act 1997 which deals with appointment, removal etc. of justices and the organisation of magistrates' courts.

- Magistrates' Courts Act 1980 which deals with the jurisdiction and powers of the courts.

- Magistrates' Courts Rules 1981 (SI 1981 No. 552) which deals with practice and procedure.

2.8.1 Justices of the Peace

Justices of the peace are appointed to act for a particular county, and are then assigned to the bench for one of the petty sessions areas into which the county is divided. A justice would normally sit only in the magistrates' court for his/her petty sessions area.

Normally two or more justices comprise a magistrates' court and a minimum of two is required for the bulk of the criminal jurisdiction of the court.

However, s. 49(1) of the Crime and Disorder Act 1998 was introduced to enhance the ability of magistrates' courts to manage business more expeditiously and provides for the following powers of the court to be exercised by a single (lay) justice of the peace:

- to extend, impose or vary bail conditions;

- to mark an information as withdrawn;

- to dismiss a case where the prosecution offer no evidence;

- to order defence costs to be paid out of central funds;

- to request a pre-sentence report following a guilty plea and indicate the seriousness of the offence;

- to request a medical report and remand an accused in custody or on bail;

- to remit an offender to another court for sentence;

- to appoint an earlier appearance time for a person granted police bail;

- to extend, with the accused's consent, a custody or overall time limit;

- to grant representation under legal aid for a case triable on indictment for proceedings in the Crown Court;

- to order the production of an accused's driving licence following conviction;

- to prohibit the publication of matters disclosed or exempted from disclosure in court;

- to give, vary or revoke directions for the conduct of a trial in relation to:

  - the timetable for proceedings
  - the attendance of the parties
  - the service of documents
  - the manner in which evidence is to be given;

- to give, vary or revoke orders for the separate or joint trials in the case of two or more accused or two or more informations.

Justices are appointed by the Lord Chancellor 'on behalf and in the name of Her Majesty' (Justices of the Peace Act 1997, s. 5(1)), following a recommendation from the local advisory committees which are located in each county. They are not required to possess any legal or other qualification though they are obliged to attend a course of basic instruction within 12 months of appointment.

Justices are not paid a salary for their work but s. 10 of the Justices of the Peace Act 1997 does provide for them to receive travel and subsistence allowance and compensation for loss of earnings, etc.

2.8.2 Justices' Clerks

The duties of a justices' clerk consist of: sitting in court with the justices during the conduct of proceedings; advising the justices (whether in court or out of court) on matters of law, practice and procedure; organising the administration of the petty sessional division's work; processing legal aid applications; collecting fines; and preparing summonses for issue by the justices (or issuing summonses himself/herself). It is not necessary for the clerk himself/herself to be in the court as the duties can be delegated to an assistant.

The list of powers of a single justice contained in **para. 2.8.1** above may also be done by a justices' clerk (Crime and Disorder Act 1998, s. 49(2)(a)) with the exception of the following:

- to extend, impose or vary bail conditions without the consent of the prosecutor and accused;

- to give an indication of the seriousness of an offence for the purposes of a pre-sentence report;

- to remand an accused in custody for a medical report or, without the consent of the prosecutor and accused, remand an accused on bail for those purposes on conditions other than those (if any) previously imposed;

- to prohibit the publication of matters disclosed or exempted from disclosure in court;

- to give, vary or revoke orders for the separate or joint trials in the case of two or more accused or two or more informations, without the consent of the parties

(s. 49(3)).

A justices' clerk must be a barrister or solicitor of at least five years' standing, or a barrister or solicitor who has served for not less than five years as assistant to a justices' clerk. They are appointed by the magistrates' courts committee for the county and the Lord Chancellor's approval is required.

The powers under s. 49 of the Crime and Disorder Act 1998 for both a single justice and a justices' clerk are part of the new case management mechanisms designed to speed up the criminal justice system.

Some of the functions exercisable by a justices' clerk may also be exercised by a person appointed by the magistrates' court to assist the clerk (s. 45(2) of the Justices of the Peace Act 1997). Such assistants would normally be senior members of the clerk's staff but there is no necessity for them to have any legal qualifications.

2.8.3   Stipendiary Magistrates

As mentioned in **para. 2.8** above, stipendiary magistrates are both paid and legally qualified. Stipendiaries are also appointed by Her Majesty on the Lord Chancellor's recommendation.

The number of stipendiaries is limited by the Justices of the Peace Act 1997. The number must not exceed 50 in the non-metropolitan areas and 60 in the metropolitan areas. One of the metropolitan stipendiaries is designated by the Lord Chancellor as the chief metropolitan stipendiary magistrate.

2.9   Youth Courts

The procedures and composition of youth courts are contained in the Children and Young Persons Act 1933. Youth courts are required to sit as often as may be required in order to exercise the jurisdiction conferred on them by the 1933 Act and any other legislation (s. 47(1) of the 1933 Act).

2.9.1   Youth Court Panel

Schedule 2, para. 3 of the Children and Young Persons Act 1933 requires every petty sessions area to form a youth court panel. Such panels consist of justices specially qualified for dealing with juvenile cases. Such qualification is obtained by training which is additional to a justice's ordinary training. It is only these justices who are allowed to sit in the youth court (r. 11 of the Youth Courts (Constitution) Rules 1954 (SI 1954 No. 1711)). No more than three justices can sit in the court (r. 12(1)) and wherever possible one shall be a man and one a woman (r. 12(1) and (2)). A stipendiary magistrate may sit alone (r. 2).

2.9.2 | **Restrictions on Persons Present**

Restrictions are placed on those persons who may be present during proceedings in the youth court and this is contained in s. 47(2) of the 1933 Act which provides:

> (2) *No person shall be present at any sitting of a youth court except—*
> (a) *members and officers of the court;*
> (b) *parties to the case before the court, their solicitors and counsel, and witnesses and other persons directly concerned in that case;*
> (c) *bona fide representatives of newspapers or news agencies;*
> (d) *such other persons as the court may specially authorise to be present.*

Keynote

Although the press are allowed to attend proceedings they are not permitted to report the name, address or any other detail which may lead to the identity of the juvenile concerned (s. 49(1)). There are a number of exceptions to this rule. These include where the youth court consider it necessary to avoid injustice to the juvenile or where it is necessary to secure his/her apprehension to either appear at court or be returned to custody (s. 49(5)).

The restrictions on the press identifying the juvenile defendant also apply to other juveniles who may have been concerned in the case, i.e. witnesses in the proceedings (s. 49(4)).

2.9.3 | **Attendance of Parent or Guardian**

The youth court has the power to order the juvenile's parent or guardian to attend the proceedings (s. 34A of the 1933 Act). This power equally applies to the attendance of the parent or guardian in the adult magistrates' court and Crown Court.

2.10 | **The Crown Court**

The Crown Court is part of the Supreme Court and was created by the Courts Act 1971. It derives its jurisdiction from s. 1 of the Supreme Court Act 1981 which provides that:

> (1) *The Supreme Court of England and Wales shall consist of the Court of Appeal, the High Court of Justice and the Crown Court, each having such jurisdiction as is conferred on it by or under this or any other Act.*

The Crown Court is a single court though it sits in many locations across England and Wales. The court has exclusive jurisdiction over trials on indictment and will normally hear cases which involve offences committed within its geographical area but there are no territorial restrictions on the cases it can hear. Section 46 of the Supreme Court Act 1981 provides that:

> (2) *The jurisdiction of the Crown Court with respect to proceedings on indictment shall include jurisdiction of the Crown Court with respect to proceedings on indictment for offences wherever committed, and in particular proceedings on indictment for offences within the jurisdiction of the Admiralty of England.*

The locations in which the Crown Court sits are classified according to:

- geographical position; and
- status.

In relation to 'geographical position', every Crown Court location belongs to one of six 'circuits':

- Midlands and Oxford
- North-Eastern
- Northern
- Wales and Chester
- Western
- South-Eastern.

A High Court judge (known as the 'presiding judge') presides over each of these six 'circuits' and has responsibility for the administration and distribution of work.

In relation to 'status', locations are either first, second or third tier. High Court judges regularly sit at first-tier locations where the more serious cases would normally be heard.

2.10.1 | **Judges**

Section 8 of the Supreme Court Act 1981 provides that:

> *(1)   The jurisdiction of the Crown Court shall be exercisable by—*
> *(a)   any judge of the High Court; or*
> *(b)   any circuit judge or recorder; or*
> *(c)   subject to and in accordance with the provisions of sections 74 and 75(2), a judge of the High Court, circuit judge or recorder sitting with not more than four justices of the peace, and any such persons when exercising the jurisdiction of the Crown Court shall be judges of the Crown Court.*

All proceedings in the Crown Court must be heard and disposed of by a single judge except where a justice is permitted to sit with such a judge (s. 73(1) of the 1981 Act).

2.10.2 | **Modes of Address**

The following guidelines relate to the address of judges in open court. Other conventions may apply when meeting a judge in chambers.

High Court judges should be addressed as 'My Lord' or 'My Lady'.

Circuit judges, recorders and deputy circuit judges should be addressed as 'Your Honour'. Exceptions to this are:

- a judge is sitting at the Central Criminal Court
- any circuit judge who holds the office of honorary Recorder of Liverpool or honorary Recorder of Manchester

who should be addressed as 'My Lord' or 'My Lady' (*Practice Direction (Judges: Modes of Address)* [1982] 1 WLR 101).

2.11 | Tribunals and Inquiries

2.11.1 | Tribunals

Tribunals are alternative mechanisms to the courts which provide remedies for decision making in the public sector and grievances in both central and local government.

There are 78 tribunals in England and Wales which are supervised by the courts and directly supervised by the Council on Tribunals which was created by the Tribunals and Inquiries Act 1958 (now 1992). Tribunals cover a wide area of subject matter: those that deal with the issues of the ordinary citizen (e.g. benefits, education of children, fair rents); those that perform a licensing role (e.g. Civil Aviation Authority); and those that deal with a variety of other functions.

The role of the Council of Tribunals is to:

- to keep under review the constitution and working of tribunals specified in sch. 1 to the 1992 Act and from time to time report on their constitution and working;

- to consider and report in matters referred to the Council under the 1992 Act with respect to tribunals other than ordinary courts of law, whether or not specified in sch. 1 to the Act; and

- to consider and report on these matters, or matters the Council may consider to be of special importance, with respect to administrative procedures which involve or may involve the holding of a statutory inquiry by or on behalf of a Minister

   (s. 1(1) of the Tribunals and Inquiries Act 1992).

This role extends to the Police Appeals Tribunal (as to which, **see General Police Duties, chapter 1**).

Tribunals are subject to the supervisory jurisdiction of the High Court under the application for judicial review procedure (**see para. 2.6.4**). They must act within their powers and are under a duty to act fairly.

2.11.2 | Inquiries

The use of statutory inquiries has grown considerably during the past few decades and are an essential government tool in dealing with large scale public controversy. There are numerous examples of the areas which such inquiries cover, e.g. building nuclear power stations, new airport terminals and extending motorways.

Non-statutory inquiries may also be established by the government to investigate an issue considered to be of public importance. The criminal justice system and particularly the police have recent experience of such non-statutory inquiries, e.g. Lord Justice Scarman's inquiry into the inner city riots of the early 1980s, to the more recent Stephen Lawrence Inquiry by Sir William Macpherson of Cluny (1999, Cm 4262).

In conducting its investigation, the inquiry may be given powers equivalent to the High Court to summon witnesses, send for documents and administer oaths. Inquiries tend to be inquisitorial and they have been formed to apportion blame.

With a view to protecting the position of persons required to give evidence at inquiries a Royal Commission on Tribunals of Inquiry, chaired by Lord Justice Salmon, was set up in 1966. The subsequent report of the Royal Commission contained six cardinal recommendations:

- Before any person becomes involved in an inquiry, the tribunal must be satisfied that there are circumstances which affect him/her and which the tribunal proposes to investigate.

- Before any person who is involved in an inquiry is called as a witness he/she should be informed of any allegations which are made against him/her and the substance of the evidence in support of them.

- Any person called to give evidence should be given an adequate opportunity of preparing his/her case and being assisted by legal advisers. His/her legal expenses should be met out of public funds.

- Any person called should have the opportunity of being examined by his/her own solicitor or counsel and of stating his/her case in public at the inquiry.

- Any material witnesses he/she wishes called at the inquiry should, if reasonably practicable, be heard.

- A witness should have the opportunity of testing, by cross-examination conducted by his/her own solicitor or counsel, any evidence which may affect him/her.

Keynote

Albeit the six cardinal principles of the Salmon Report are used as the template for inquiries, they are not seen as binding *per se*. In the Matrix Churchill Inquiry, conducted by Sir Richard Scott, it was considered that although the safeguards provided by the principles were designed to protect the witness, they also introduced an 'adversarial' element into the proceedings — the right to call and cross-examine witnesses.

In the Stephen Lawrence Inquiry, Sir William Macpherson stated that although the inquiry was alert to Salmon's six cardinal principles, they accorded with Sir Richard Scott's declared 'golden rule' — *'that there should be procedural flexibility, with procedures to achieve fairness tailored to suit the circumstances of each inquiry'*.

2.12 The European Court of Human Rights

This court was established by the European Convention for the Protection of Human Rights and Fundamental Freedoms. It is located in Strasbourg and judges sitting at the court are representative of those countries who have adopted the Convention as part of their domestic legislation. As the name implies, this court deals with matters related to human rights referred to it from any of its signatories.

Section 18 of the Human Rights Act 1998 provides for the holder of a judicial office in the United Kingdom to become a judge of the European Court of Human Rights. Such a judge is not required to perform the duties of his/her UK judicial office whilst a judge of the European Court.

CHAPTER THREE

PARTIES TO CRIMINAL CASES

3.1   Introduction

In addition to the police and the defendant(s), there may be a number of other 'parties' to a criminal case. There may also be a number of individuals or organisations who become involved in the case before it gets to court. This chapter sets out the various roles and functions of those individuals and pubic bodies.

3.2   Attorney-General

The Attorney-General is a member of the government and is responsible to Parliament for the discharge of his/her duties. However, he/she can only be required to account for a decision after a prosecution has reached its conclusion. Although a member of the government, he/she is obliged, by constitutional convention, to exercise an independent discretion when performing non-political functions.

The main functions of the Attorney-General with regard to criminal proceedings are as follows:

* He/she appoints the Director of Public Prosecutions, who discharges his/her functions 'under the superintendence of the Attorney-General' (ss. 2 and 3(1) of the Prosecution of Offences Act 1985, **see para. 3.3**).

* He/she may institute and conduct the prosecution of offences of exceptional gravity or complexity, especially those concerned with the security of the State and/or relationships with other countries.

* He/she may also take over the conduct of a privately-commenced prosecution or require the Director of Public Prosecutions to do so.

* Certain offences may only be prosecuted by or with the consent of the Attorney-General.

- To issue guidelines on aspects of prosecution practice which are meant to be observed by prosecutors in general and not just the Director of Public Prosecutions or the Crown Prosecution Service.

- At any time after the bill of indictment against an accused has been signed and before judgment, the Attorney-General may enter a *nolle prosequi*, which terminates the prosecution.

Either the prosecution or defence may apply informally to the Attorney-General for entry of a *nolle prosequi*. The usual purpose of this power being exercised is that the defendant is physically or mentally unfit to be produced in court and his/her incapacity is likely to be permanent.

There may be other exceptional situations in which a *nolle prosequi* is the best method to halt proceedings. In *R* v *Beresford* (1952) 36 Cr App R 1, a coroner's jury found the cause of a cyclist's death in a collision with B's car to have been manslaughter by B, and B was accordingly committed for trial. However, B had already been convicted of, and fined for dangerous driving arising out of the same incident. The trial judge directed that the matter be referred to the Attorney-General and he entered a *nolle prosequi*.

Since the Law Officers Act 1997, the functions of the Attorney-General may be executed by the Solicitor-General and vice versa in many cases.

3.3   Director of Public Prosecutions

The Director of Public Prosecutions (DPP), a position created in 1879, is a barrister or solicitor of at least ten years' standing. The Director is appointed by the Attorney-General under whose superintendence he/she discharges his/her functions.

The Director's duties are contained in s. 3(2)(a) to (g) of the Prosecution of Offences Act 1985, namely:

- To 'take over the conduct of all criminal proceedings . . . instituted on behalf of a police force (whether by a member of that force or any other person)'. 'Police force', in this context, covers any of the forces maintained by police authorities under the Police Act 1996, plus any other body of constables specified by an order made by the Secretary of State. Those specified include the City of London Police, Metropolitan Police, British Transport Police, Ministry of Defence Police, the Royal Parks Constabulary and numerous harbour police forces.

- To institute and have the conduct of criminal proceedings in any case where it appears appropriate to do so, either on account of the importance or difficulty of the case, or for any other reason.

- To 'take over the conduct of all binding-over proceedings instituted on behalf of a police force'.

- To take over the conduct of all proceedings begun by a summons issued under s. 3 of the Obscene Publications Act 1959 (forfeiture of obscene articles).

- To advise police forces, as appropriate, on all matters relating to criminal offences.

- To appear for the prosecution when directed by the court to do so on:

  - appeals from the High Court to the House of Lords in criminal cases;
  - appeals from the Crown Court to the Court of Appeal (Criminal Division) and thence to the House of Lords; and
  - appeals to the Crown Court against the exercise by a magistrates' court of its powers under s. 12 of the Contempt of Court Act 1981 to deal with offences of contempt of court.

- To discharge such other functions as may from time to time be assigned to him/her by the Attorney-General.

In addition to the above, the 1985 Act also imposes further duties on the Director:

- to make an annual report to the Attorney-General, which the latter is required to lay before Parliament (s. 9);

- to issue a code for the guidance of Crown Prosecutors in the performance of various aspects of their duties (s. 10, **see appendix 1**).

Finally, the Director has one other duty, which is to give or refuse his/her consent to a prosecution in those cases where statute provides that the prosecutor may not proceed without it. Examples where such consent is required include:

- offences of theft or criminal damage where the property in question belongs to the defendant's spouse (Theft Act 1968, s. 30(4));

- offences of assisting offenders and wasting police time (Criminal Law Act 1967, ss. 4(4) and 5(3));

- homosexual offences where either party was under the age of 21 (Sexual Offences Act 1967, s. 8);

- aiding and abetting suicide (Suicide Act 1961, s. 2);

- riot (Public Order Act 1986, s. 7);

- offences under the Prevention of Terrorism (Temporary Provisions) Act 1989, ss. 13A, 13B, 16A, 16B and 16 and sch. 6A;

- offences under the War Crimes Act 1991.

The consent of the Director to a prosecution may be given on his/her behalf by a Crown Prosecutor (s. 1(7) of the Prosecution of Offences Act 1985).

Where an offence requires the consent of the Director before proceedings can be instituted, this does not prevent the arrest of a suspect for the offence in question or his/her initial remand (whether in custody or on bail).

3.4 | **Crown Prosecution Service**

The Prosecution of Offences Act 1985 created the Crown Prosecution Service of which the Director of Public Prosecutions is the head. The Service performs the task required of the Director under s. 3(2)(a) of the 1985 Act to 'take over the conduct of all criminal proceedings . . . instituted on behalf of a police force'.

The Director is responsible for dividing the country into areas and appointing a Chief Crown Prosecutor for each area (s. 1(4)).

The Service is not instructed by the police but takes over prosecutions commenced by the police, providing an independent judgment in deciding any legal questions which arise.

Every Crown Prosecutor has all the powers of the Director as to the institution and conduct of proceedings (s. 1(6)).

Section 10 of the 1985 Act requires the Director to issue a Code for Crown Prosecutors giving guidance on the general principles to be applied by them in:

- determining whether proceedings for an offence should be instituted or (if already instituted) discontinued;

- determining what charges should be preferred; and

- considering what representations should be made by them to a magistrates' court about the mode of trial suitable for a particular case.

The Code issued by the Director, and which may be changed from time to time, is annexed to the annual report which the Director is required to provide to the Attorney-General, and is reproduced in **appendix 1**.

Section 53 of the Crime and Disorder Act 1998 introduced a provision for the Director to designate 'lay staff', under the direction and supervision of Crown Prosecutors, to undertake certain prosecution functions. These functions are provided by s. 7A of the 1985 Act, which states:

> (1)   The Director may designate, for the purposes of this section, members of the staff of the Crown Prosecution Service who are not Crown Prosecutors.
> (2)   subject to such exceptions (if any) as may be specified in the designation, a person so designated shall have such of the following as may be so specified, namely—
>   (a)   the powers and rights of audience of a Crown Prosecutor in relation to—
>   (i)   applications for, or relating to, bail in criminal proceedings;
>   (ii)   the conduct of criminal proceedings in magistrates' courts other than trials;
>   (b)   the powers of such a Prosecutor in relation to the conduct of criminal proceedings not falling within paragraph (a)(ii) above.
> (3)   A person so designated shall exercise any such powers subject to instructions given to him by the Director.

Keynote

Limitations are placed on the powers of 'lay staff'. They do not extend, even for bail applications, to any proceedings for an offence triable only on indictment, which includes, offences such as murder, manslaughter, wounding with intent, robbery and rape, or an either way offence, such as unlawful wounding, theft and indecent assault:

- for which the accused has elected to be tried by a jury;

- which a magistrates' court has decided is more suitable to be so tried; or

- in respect of which a notice of transfer has been given under s. 4 of the Criminal Justice Act 1987 or s. 53 of the Criminal Justice Act 1991

(s. 7A(6)).

The use of 'lay staff' to undertake specified prosecution functions is designed to speed up the criminal justice process.

3.4.1   **Proposals for Reform**

The Crown Prosecution Service is currently undergoing significant changes in the way it is structured and delivers its service in line with the recommendations of the Narey Report (Review of Delay in the Criminal Justice System: A Report (Home Office, 1997)) and an independent review chaired by the Rt. Hon. Sir Iain Glidewell (The Review of the Crown Prosecution Service: A Report (Cm 3960, 1998)).

A number of the recommendations from these reports have been introduced by the Crime and Disorder Act 1998. The Service is currently restructuring itself whereby police administrative support units will, in the future, have Service staff working with them so that the preparation of cases for court can be a shared police/CPS undertaking. Within this relationship it is intended that the independence of the prosecutor and investigator would be retained.

The changes to the Service are again intended to speed up the criminal justice system and with their presence in police administrative support units it is proposed that cases such as simple guilty pleas can be dealt with expeditiously.

3.5   **Serious Fraud Office**

The only other government department, apart from the Crown Prosecution Service, which exists principally to prosecute crime is the Serious Fraud Office. It was set up by the Criminal Justice Act 1987 and is headed by a Director, who is appointed and superintended by the Attorney-General (s. 1(2) of the 1987 Act).

The Director may appoint such staff as he/she considers necessary for the discharge of his/her functions. Those functions are to 'investigate any suspected offence which appears to [the Director] on reasonable grounds to involve serious or complex fraud', and to initiate and conduct (or take over and then conduct) any criminal proceedings relating to such fraud (s. 1(3) and (5)).

The Serious Fraud Office and Crown Prosecution Service resemble each other in many ways. However, the two organisations differ in that:

- The Serious Fraud Office is only concerned with very serious fraud.

- Section 2 of the Criminal Justice Act 1987 gives the Director of the Serious Fraud Office wide investigatory powers. So, whereas the Serious Fraud Office both *investigates* and *initiates* proceedings, by contrast the Crown Prosecution Service have no investigatory role but merely initiate or take over the conduct of proceedings.

- The Serious Fraud Office comprises, not only lawyers, but also accountants and fraud investigators. Some of the staff are seconded to the Office from police fraud squads and branches of government, e.g. the Department of Trade and Industry.

3.6   Other Prosecuting Bodies

Several governmental departments and quasi-government organisations initiate and conduct prosecutions as one aspect of performing the major functions for which they exist. Such departments include:

- the Department of Trade and Industry for some business frauds and violations of the Companies Acts;

- the Data Protection Registrar for failure to comply with applicable legislative requirements;

- the Department of Social Security for fraudulent benefit claims;

- the Inland Revenue for tax evasion;

- Customs and Excise for evading import duties, unlawful importation of drugs, and VAT frauds;

- local authorities for violations of food and hygiene and other health regulations.

CHAPTER FOUR

SUMMONSES AND WARRANTS

4.1   Introduction

In order to secure the attendance of parties to criminal and civil cases, it is important that courts and tribunals have the relevant powers to bring people — and evidence — before them. Many of those powers are exercised through the issuing of summonses and warrants.

Before examining in detail aspects of summonses and warrants, it is useful to identify the meaning of the terms summons, information and complaint.

4.1.1   Information

Generally, an information means a written or verbal allegation made to a magistrate (known as laying an information) that a person has committed an offence or is suspected of having committed such an offence. This has to be done before a summons or warrant can be issued.

4.1.2   Summons

A summons means a written order issued by a magistrate or a magistrates' clerk, on behalf of the magistrate. It orders the person named therein to appear at a named court at a given time and date to answer an allegation of an offence which is set out in the summons or, in the case of a witness summons, to give evidence and/or produce exhibits.

4.1.3   Complaint

A complaint is a verbal allegation made before a magistrate to the effect that a person has committed a breach of the law not being a criminal offence (such as breach of the peace, resulting in a common law binding-over to keep the peace). Acts of Parliament sometimes enact that proceedings are to be taken by way of complaint (e.g., under s. 2 of the Dogs Act 1871 where proceedings instituted by 'information' are invalid).

4.2 The Process

The appearance of a defendant before a magistrates' court is secured by:

- his/her arrest without warrant, followed by his/her being charged with an offence at a police station and being bailed to attend at court on a specified day to answer the charge; or

- as above except, instead of being bailed, the person is brought before the court in police custody; or

- the laying of an information by the prosecutor before a magistrate (or a magistrates' clerk) resulting in the issue of a summons requiring the accused to attend at court on a specified day to answer the allegation in the information; or

- as above except that the magistrate issues a warrant for the defendant to be arrested and brought before the court. Alternatively, the warrant may be backed for bail where the defendant is arrested and then released on bail to attend court on a specified day.

For the law relating to powers and procedures for arrest, entry, search and seizure (with and without warrant), **see General Police Duties, chapter 2**; for the law relating to questioning, detention, charge and bail, **see chapters 5 and 15**.

4.3 Laying an Information

Rule 4(2) of the Magistrates' Courts Rules 1981 (SI 1981 No. 552) provides that an information (i.e. an allegation that a person has committed an offence), may be laid orally or in writing. It may be laid either by the prosecutor in person, or by counsel or a solicitor on his/her behalf, or by any other authorised person (r. 4(1)).

Under the Magistrates' Courts Act 1980, s. 1(1), on an information being laid before him/her, a magistrate may issue either:

- a summons requiring the person named in the information to appear before a magistrates' court to answer thereto; or

- a warrant to arrest that person and bring him/her before a magistrates' court.

An information should provide the following details:

- the name of the informant and his/her address;
- brief particulars of the offence suspected; and
- the law which has been contravened.

A written information is laid when it is received in the office of the clerk of the justices (*R* v *Manchester Stipendiary Magistrate, ex parte Hill* [1983] 1 AC 328). An oral information is laid by the informant going before a magistrate or clerk to make his/her allegation. The information need not be given on oath (r. 4(2) of the Magistrates' Courts Rules 1981) for the issue of a summons. However, in order to obtain the issue of a warrant for arrest, an information must be in writing, and substantiated on oath (s. 1(3) of the Magistrates' Courts Act 1980).

The information must be laid by a named, actual person and must disclose the identity of that person. In *Rubin* v *DPP* [1990] 2 QB 80 it was held that a police force was *not* a named, actual person. Some police forces now have a policy of laying all informations in the name of the Chief Constable or other senior officer.

4.4   Issuing a Summons

Under s. 1(2) of the Magistrates' Courts Act 1980, a justice before whom an information has been laid has jurisdiction to issue a summons requiring the person named in the information to attend court to answer the charge if:

- the offence was committed or is suspected to have been committed within the justice's area; or

- it appears to the justice that it is necessary or expedient for the better administration of justice that the accused should be tried jointly with or in the same place as another person who is charged with an offence and is either in custody in the area or is being proceeded against within the area; or

- the accused resides or is (or is believed to reside or be) within the area; or

- a magistrates' court for the area, by virtue of a statutory provision, has jurisdiction to try the offence alleged; or

- the offence was committed outside England and Wales and (if the offence is summary) a magistrates' court for the area would have jurisdiction to try the offence were the accused before it.

The decision to issue the summons is judicial, not merely administrative (*R* v *Gateshead Justices, ex parte Tesco Stores Ltd* [1981] QB 470). Consequently, the justice or clerk must be satisfied that:

- the information alleges an offence known to the law;

- it was laid within any time-limit applicable to commencing a prosecution for the offence in question;

- any consent necessary for the bringing of the prosecution has been obtained; and

- there is jurisdiction to issue a summons having regard to the provisions of s. 1(2) of the 1980 Act.

Where the above criteria are met it is normal that a summons would be issued. It would only be in exceptional circumstances where the justice or clerk made use of their residual discretion to refuse a summons. Such refusal applies in applications which appear frivolous or vexatious or to be an abuse of the process of the court. For example, in *R* v *Bros* (1901) 66 JP 54, a summons was not issued against a Jewish baker for Sunday trading in a predominantly Jewish area. In *R* v *Clerk to the Medway Justices, ex parte DHSS* (1986) 150 JP 401, the clerk refused to issue a summons because of the failure of the prosecutor to lay an information within a reasonable time. Four months had been allowed to elapse between the interview of the suspect and the laying of the information.

4.5   Service of the Summons

Rule 98(1) of the Magistrates' Courts Rules 1981, requires that a summons must be signed by the justice or clerk issuing it or (in the case of a summons issued by a justice) must state his/her name and be authenticated by the clerk's signature. It is now common practice for the necessary signature to be affixed by means of a rubber stamp.

Under r. 98(2), a summons should state:

- the substance of the information which has been laid against the person summoned; and
- the time and place at which he/she is required to appear to answer the charge.

One summons may be issued in relation to several informations against a person but it is usual for a separate summons to be issued for each information (r. 98(3)).

Under r. 99(1) of the 1981 Rules, a summons may be served on a person by:

- personal delivery; or
- leaving it with another person at his/her last known, or usual place of abode; or
- posting it to the aforementioned place of abode.

Only in relation to the service of a summons by personal delivery will it be 'treated as proved' by the court for the purpose of proceeding with the case in the defendant's absence. This rule further qualifies 'treated as proved' in relation to the other two methods of service above. Where the offence alleged is summary and the summons was either left as required or sent by registered letter or recorded delivery to the person's last known or usual place of abode, it is then not necessary to prove that it came to his/her knowledge. (See also **para. 4.6** in relation to the procedure in the event of non-appearance of the defendant.)

A summons for service on a corporation may be undertaken by delivering it at, or sending it by post to its registered office. Where there is no registered office within the UK, it should be delivered or sent to the corporation's place of trade or business (r. 99(3) and s. 436 of the Companies Act 1948).

References to a person's 'last known or usual place of abode' are construed as including any address which he/she gives for the purposes of service (r. 99(8)). This is of particular relevance to the procedure for the conditional power of arrest under s. 25 of the Police and Criminal Evidence Act 1984 (**see General Police Duties, chapter 2**).

Generally, the service of a summons on a member of the armed forces is effected by it being served on the commanding officer in the case of army and RAF personnel, and the commanding officer of a ship or other establishment in the case of Royal Navy or Royal Marines personnel, as well as on the individual concerned.

The Criminal Law Act 1977 deals with the service of summonses issued throughout the United Kingdom. Section 39 of the 1977 Act provides:

> *(1)   A summons requiring a person charged with an offence to appear before a court in England and Wales may, in such manner as may be prescribed by rules of court, be served on him in Scotland or Northern Ireland.*

(2)   A summons requiring a person charged with an offence to appear before a court in Northern Ireland may, in such a manner as may be prescribed by rules of court, be served on him in England, Wales or Scotland.

(3)   Citation of a person charged with a crime or offence to appear before a court in Scotland may be effected in any part of the United Kingdom in like manner as may be done in Scotland, and for this purpose the persons authorised to effect such citation shall include, in England and Wales and Northern Ireland, constables and prison officers serving in those parts of the United Kingdom.

Keynote

There are occasions where the prosecutor may wish to delay the issue of a summons when laying an information, for example, where the defendant is known to be out of the country. However, an information should be laid with the intention of having the consequent summons served as soon as reasonably possible. Where a prosecutor has not decided to proceed and an information is laid for the purpose of ensuring the prosecution should not be out of time, this amounts to an abuse of the process of the court and the magistrates should stay the proceedings if ultimately he/she does decide to proceed (*R* v *Brentford Justices, ex parte Wong* [1981] QB 445).

4.5.1   Service Elsewhere in the UK

The Scottish term for a summons is a 'citation'. A 'summons' is said to be 'served' in England or Wales and a 'citation' is said to be 'effected' in Scotland.

Postal service of summonses issued in England and Wales is permitted throughout the United Kingdom, although postal service of a summons is not acceptable to courts in Northern Ireland. Therefore, all service of Northern Ireland summonses in England and Wales must be served in person. The service of a Scottish citation in England and Wales by post is permitted.

4.6   Issue of Warrants

There are several different types of warrants which may be issued by justices, some of which are detailed below. For search warrants, **see General Police Duties, chapter 2**.

4.6.1   Warrant to Arrest an Offender

Section 1(1)(b) of the Magistrates' Court Act 1980 provides that, whenever a justice before whom an information is laid has power to issue a summons, he/she may alternatively issue a warrant for the arrest of the person named in the information, save that:

- the information must be in writing and substantiated on oath (s. 1(3)); and
- either the offence alleged must be indictable or punishable with imprisonment, or the accused's address must be insufficiently established for a summons to be served (s. 1(4)).

Warrants for arrest under s. 1 of the 1980 Act are not commonly issued as many offences will carry a power of arrest without warrant.

Unlike the issue of a summons (**see para. 4.4**), the justices' clerk is not allowed to issue a warrant; the information has to be on oath and made to a justice.

4.6.2 Warrant to Arrest a Witness

Section 97 of the Magistrates' Courts Act 1980 provides that, where a magistrate is satisfied that a person who could give material evidence would not voluntarily attend court, then a warrant may be issued. This course of action would only be used where the magistrate considers a summons would not be effective.

A similar power exists for witness warrants for the High Court and the Crown Court.

4.6.3 Warrant to Arrest in Default

This warrant is issued where a person defaults in payment of a fine or other sum and is a type of commitment warrant.

4.6.4 Warrant to Commit to Prison

This is a warrant of arrest directing that the person be taken to a specified place. On arrest the constable should take the person to the place specified and obtain a receipt. This is one of the very rare occasions where a person need not be taken to a police station after arrest.

4.6.5 Warrant to Distrain Property

This warrant is issued in an effect to collect money. It allows certain goods to be seized and sold as prescribed by the Magistrates' Court Rules 1981.

4.7 Execution of Warrants

By virtue of s. 125 of the Magistrates' Courts Act 1980 (as amended), the following warrants do not need to be in the possession of the constable at the time of their being executed:

- warrants to arrest a person in connection with 'an offence';

- warrants under the Army Act 1955, Air Force Act 1955, Naval Discipline Act 1957 or Reserve Forces Act 1980 (desertion etc.);

- warrants for insufficiency of distress (under ss. 102 or 104 of the General Rate Act 1967);

- warrants for the protection of a party to a marriage or of a child of the family (under s. 18 of the Domestic Proceedings and Magistrates' Courts Act 1978); and

- warrants relating to the non-appearance of a defendant, warrants of commitment, warrants of distress and warrants to arrest a witness (under ss. 55, 76, 93 and 97 of the Magistrates' Courts Act 1980).

But in such cases the warrant must, on the demand of the person concerned, be shown to him/her as soon as practicable.

A warrant issued for the arrest of a fine defaulter to bring him/her before the court for an inquiry into his/her means, is *not* one issued 'to arrest a person in connection with an offence'. Therefore, when executing such a warrant, a constable must have it in his/her possession (*R* v *Peacock* (1989) 153 JP 199).

'Possession' has been held to include a warrant which was in a police car approximately 60 yards away from the scene of the arrest (*R* v *Purdy* [1974] 3 All ER 465). In *De Costa Small* v *Kirkpatrick* [1979] Crim LR 41, it was held that a warrant for a civil matter was not in the officer's possession when it was at a police station half a mile away.

In order to execute a warrant of arrest issued in connection with, or arising out of criminal proceedings, or a warrant of commitment issued under s. 76 of the Magistrates' Courts Act 1980, a constable may enter and search any premises when he/she has reasonable grounds for believing the person sought is on the premises.

The search may only be to the extent required and is restricted to the parts of the premises where the constable reasonably believes the person may be. Reasonable force may be used when necessary.

These powers are derived from ss. 17(1)(a) and 117 of the Police and Criminal Evidence Act 1984 and the Codes of Practice (**see appendices 5 to 7**). For the law regulating powers of entry, search and seizure, **see General Police Duties, chapter 2**.

For court orders in relation to harassment and domestic violence, **see General Police Duties, chapter 3**.

4.7.1 Execution of Warrants throughout the UK

Section 38 of the Criminal Law Act 1977 provides:

> (1)   A warrant issued in Scotland or Northern Ireland for the arrest of a person charged with an offence may be executed in England or Wales by a constable acting within his police area; and subsection (3) of section 125 of the Magistrates' Courts Act 1980 (execution without possession of the warrant) shall apply to the execution in England or Wales of any such warrant.
> (2)   A warrant issued in England, Wales or Northern Ireland for the arrest of a person charged with an offence may be executed in Scotland by any constable appointed for a police area in like manner as any such warrant issued in Scotland.
> (3)   A warrant issued in England, Wales or Scotland for the arrest of a person charged with an offence may be executed in Northern Ireland by any member of the Royal Ulster Constabulary or the Royal Ulster Constabulary Reserve; and subsections (4) and (5) of section 159 of the Magistrates' Courts (Northern Ireland) Act 1964 (execution without possession of the warrant and execution on Sunday) shall apply to the execution in Northern Ireland of any such warrant.
> (4)   A warrant may be executed by virtue of this section whether or not it has been endorsed under section 12, 14 or 15 of the Indictable Offences Act 1848 or under section 27, 28 or 29 of the Petty Sessions (Ireland) Act 1851.

Keynote

Section 38A of the 1977 Act provides for Scottish warrants of extract conviction (the Scottish equivalent of a warrant of commitment) to be executed in a similar manner to warrants of arrest for offences except that the former must be in the possession of the constable when executed although they need not be endorsed. Once executed the defaulter may be lodged at a prison in England as though the warrant had been issued in England, as a commitment warrant for non-payment of fine.

Section 38B similarly provides for cross-border execution of such warrants between England and Wales and Northern Ireland. The requirements as to possession of the warrant and the lodging in a prison in England are identical.

CHAPTER FIVE

BAIL

5.1   Introduction

Although the Bail Act 1976 is the source of legislation in relation to all aspects of bail, more recent legislation, i.e. the Police and Criminal Evidence Act 1984, the Criminal Justice and Public Order Act 1994 and the Crime and Disorder Act 1998, have all made important amendments to the original 1976 Act.

The meaning of 'bail in criminal proceedings' is contained in s. 1 of the Bail Act 1976 which provides that:

> (1)   In this Act 'bail in criminal proceedings' means—
> (a)   bail grantable in or in connection with proceedings for an offence to a person who is accused or convicted of the offence, or
> (b)   bail grantable in connection with an offence to a person who is under arrest for the offence or for whose arrest for the offence a warrant (endorsed for bail) is being issued.
> (2)   In this Act 'bail' means bail grantable under the law (including common law) for the time being in force.
> (3)   Except as provided by section 13(3) of this Act, this section does not apply to bail in or in connection with proceedings outside England and Wales.
> . . .
> (5)   This section applies—
> (a)   whether the offence was committed in England or Wales or elsewhere, and
> (b)   whether it is an offence under the law of England and Wales, or of any other country or territory.
> (6)   Bail in criminal proceedings shall be granted (and in particular shall be granted unconditionally or conditionally), in accordance with this Act.

Keynote

Within s. 1(5) it provides that bail can be granted immaterial of whether the offence was committed in 'England or Wales or elsewhere', and immaterial as to which country's law the offence relates to.

5.2   Bail Without Charge

Where one of the following conditions apply then the custody officer must release a detained person either unconditionally or on bail:

- there is insufficient evidence to charge and the officer is not willing to authorise detention for questioning, etc. (s. 37(1) and (2) of the Police and Criminal Evidence Act 1984);

- the officer conducting the review concludes the detention without charge can no longer be justified (s. 40(8) of the 1984 Act);

- at the end of 24 hours' detention without charge unless the detained person is suspected of a serious arrestable offence and continued detention up to 36 hours is authorised by a superintendent (s. 41(7) of the 1984 Act).

In relation to s. 41(7) above, where continued detention is authorised for up to 36 hours, the detained person must be released with or without bail at or before the expiry of this time. Alternatively, an application can be made to a magistrates' court for a warrant of further detention (s. 42(10) of the 1984 Act).

5.3   Bail After Charge

Where a person is charged at the police station (otherwise than on a warrant backed for bail), the custody officer must make a decision:

- to keep the person in custody until he/she can be brought before a magistrates' court, or to release the person; and

- to release the person either unconditionally or on bail

    (s. 38(1) of the 1984 Act).

Keynote

This is a review of the person's detention and therefore the person or his/her legal representative should be given an opportunity to make representations to the custody officer. The review should be conducted with regard to PACE Code of Practice, Code C, paras 15.1 to 15.6 (**see appendix 5**). Where the detained person is a Juvenile an opportunity to make representations should also be given to the 'appropriate adult'.

Where the decision is made to release a person who has been charged, it would be usual for the person to be released on bail being required to attend at the magistrates' court on a specified day.

With the exception of the circumstances set out below in s. 25 of the Criminal Justice and Public Order Act 1994, a person charged with an offence will be given bail unless certain conditions (contained in s. 38 of the 1984 Act) exist allowing the custody officer to refuse bail.

5.4   Bail Restrictions

The decision to deny any unconvicted person bail is a significant one, both personally and constitutionally. Every person has a general right not to be subject to unnecessarily onerous bail conditions, a right which has existed since the Magna Carta in the thirteenth century.

Section 25 of the Criminal Justice and Public Order Act 1994 provides that:

> *(1)   A person who in any proceedings has been charged with or convicted of an offence to which this section applies in circumstances to which it applies shall be granted bail in those proceedings only if the court or, as the case may be, the constable considering the grant of bail is satisfied that there are exceptional circumstances which justify it.*
> *(2)   This section applies, subject to subsection (3) below, to the following offences, that is to say—*
> > *(a)   murder;*
> > *(b)   attempted murder;*
> > *(c)   manslaughter;*
> > *(d)   rape; or*
> > *(e)   attempted rape.*
> *(3)   This section applies to a person charged with or convicted of any such offence only if he has been previously convicted by or before a court in any part of the United Kingdom of any such offence or of culpable homicide and, in the case of a previous conviction of manslaughter or of culpable homicide, if he was then sentenced to imprisonment or, if he was then a child or young person, to long-term detention under any of the relevant enactments.*
> *(4)   This section applies whether or not an appeal is pending against conviction or sentence.*
> *(5)   In this section—*
> *'conviction' includes—*
> > *(a)   a finding that a person is not guilty by reason of insanity;*
> > *(b)   a finding under section 4A(3) of the Criminal Procedure (Insanity) Act 1964 (cases of unfitness to plead) that a person did the act or made the omission charged against him; and*
> > *(c)   a conviction of an offence for which an order is made placing the offender on probation or discharging him absolutely or conditionally;*
> *and 'convicted' shall be construed accordingly; and*
> *'the relevant enactments' means—*
> > *(a)   as respects England and Wales, section 53(2) of the Children and Young Persons Act 1933;*
> > *(b)   as respects Scotland, sections 205(1) to (3) and 208 of the Criminal Procedure (Scotland) Act 1995;*
> > *(c)   as respects Northern Ireland, section 73(2) of the Children and Young Persons Act (Northern Ireland) 1968.*

Keynote

Section 25(1) was amended by s. 56 of the Crime and Disorder Act 1998. The previous wording of the section gave no right to bail where the prescribed offences applied. This was considered to be in contravention of Article 5 of the European Convention on Human Rights (no person to be deprived of his/her liberty except in specified circumstances, etc.). The absolute ban on bail has been replaced by a strong rebuttable presumption against the grant of bail. It seem unlikely that a custody officer would ever be satisfied as to the 'exceptional circumstances' and consequently bail would rarely be granted in such cases.

In all other cases the custody officer must consider the issue of bail and s. 38(1) of the 1984 Act sets out the occasions where bail can be refused (**see para. 5.5 below**). Where bail is refused the custody officer must inform the detained person of the reasons why and make an entry as to these reasons in the custody record (s. 38(3) and (4)).

In accordance with PACE Code C, para. 1.8, if one of the following conditions apply to the detained person he/she must be informed of the decision to refuse bail as soon as practicable:

- the detained person is incapable of understanding what is said;

- the detained person is too violent, or likely to become violent; or

- the detained person is in need of medical attention.

In reaching a decision as to whether a person should be refused bail the custody officer should consider whether the same objective can be achieved by imposing conditions to the bail, that is, for the person to appear at an appointed place at an appointed time. If conditions attached to a person's bail are likely to achieve the same objective as keeping the person in detention, bail must be given.

In *Gizzonio* v *Chief Constable of Derbyshire*, *The Times*, 29 April 1998, Gizzonio had been remanded in custody in respect of certain charges which had not ultimately been pursued. Damages (for the wrongful exercise of lawful authority) were sought on the basis that the police had wrongly opposed the grant of bail. It was held that the decision regarding bail is part of the process of investigation of crime with a view to prosecution and so the police enjoyed immunity in that respect.

5.5   Imprisonable and Non-imprisonable Offences

The decision to grant bail can be divided into two groups:

- those offences that are imprisonable; and

- those offences that do not carry a sentence of imprisonment.

5.5.1   Imprisonable Offences

Section 38(1) of the Police and Criminal Evidence Act 1984 provides that a custody officer need not grant bail to an unconvicted accused who is charged with an *imprisonable* offence if one or more of the following grounds applies.

Name and Address cannot be Ascertained

If the custody officer has reasonable grounds for doubting whether the accused's name and address is correct, these doubts would have to be recorded, along with the decision to refuse bail, on the custody record. If the person refuses to give his/her name, this does not automatically satisfy the requirements of s. 38. The actual wording of the section is that the name *or* address *cannot be ascertained* or that which is given is doubted.

Risk of Absconding

If the custody officer has reasonable grounds for believing that the detained person will fail to appear at court if bailed, there are certain factors which the custody officer should consider when taking a decision to refuse bail under this section. These are:

- the nature and seriousness of the offence;

- the character, antecedents, associations and community ties of the accused;

BAIL

- his/her 'record' for having answered bail in the past;

- the strength of the evidence against him/her.

Further Offences

This exception will apply where the custody officer has reasonable grounds for believing that the detained person will commit other offence(s) if bailed.

Interference with Administration of Justice

This applies where the custody officer has reasonable grounds for believing that detention is necessary to prevent the detained person from interfering with the administration of justice or with the investigation of offences or a particular offence.

Own Protection

There is a further exception where the custody officer has reasonable grounds for believing that detention is necessary for the person's own protection or to prevent the person causing injury or loss or damage to property.

Juvenile: Welfare

If the detained person is a juvenile and the custody officer has reasonable grounds for believing that detention is necessary for his/her own welfare then bail need not be granted. This has a wider meaning than just 'protection' and could apply to juveniles who, if released, might be homeless or become involved in prostitution or vagrancy.

5.5.2   **Non-imprisonable Offences**

Section 38(1) of the Police and Criminal Evidence Act 1984 provides that a custody officer need not grant bail to an unconvicted person who is charged with a *non-imprisonable* offence if one or more of the following grounds applies.

Name and Address cannot be Ascertained

As for imprisonable offences above (**see para. 5.5.1**).

Physical Injury to Another

The custody officer has reasonable grounds for believing that detention is necessary to prevent the detained person causing physical injury to any other person. This differs from the imprisonable offence where bail can be refused for the detained person's own protection.

Prevent Loss or Damage to Property

The custody officer has reasonable grounds for believing that detention is necessary to prevent the detained person causing loss or damage to property.

45

Juvenile: Welfare

As for imprisonable offences above (**see para. 5.5.1**).

A custody officer must record the reasons for imposing or varying bail conditions and indicating details of the relevant risk as set out above. Guidance to courts when approaching the decision to grant bail was given in *R* v *Mansfield Justices, ex parte Sharkey* [1985] QB 613. In that case it was held that any relevant risk (e.g. of absconding etc.) must be a 'real' risk, not just a fanciful one.

5.6 Bail Conditions

The Criminal Justice and Public Order Act 1994 allows the police to impose conditions on bail given to people charged with an offence. These conditions are the same as those which the courts can impose under the Bail Act 1976 with certain modifications outlined below.

5.6.1 General Provisions

The general provisions as to bail are contained in s. 3 of the Bail Act 1976, which provides:

(1) A person granted bail in criminal proceedings shall be under a duty to surrender to custody, and that duty is enforceable in accordance with section 6 of this Act.

(2) No recognisance for his surrender to custody shall be taken from him.

(3) Except as provided by this section—

(a) no security for his surrender to custody shall be taken from him,

(b) he shall not be required to provide a surety or sureties for his surrender to custody, and

(c) no other requirement shall be imposed on him as a condition of bail.

(4) He may be required, before release on bail, to provide a surety or sureties to secure his surrender to custody.

(5) He may be required, before release on bail, to give security for his surrender to custody. The security may be given by him or on his behalf.

(6) He may be required to comply, before release on bail or later, with such requirements as appear to the court to be necessary to secure that—

(a) he surrenders to custody,

(b) he does not commit an offence while on bail,

(c) he does not interfere with witnesses or otherwise obstruct the course of justice whether in relation to himself or any other person,

(d) he makes himself available for the purpose of enabling inquiries or a report to be made to assist the court in dealing with him for the offence,

(e) before the time appointed for him to surrender to custody, he attends an interview with an authorised advocate or authorised litigator, as defined by section 119(1) of the Courts and Legal Services Act 1990;

and, in any Act, 'the normal powers to impose conditions of bail' means the powers to impose conditions under paragraph (a), (b) or (c) above.

(6ZA) Where he is required under subsection (6) above to reside in a bail hostel or probation hostel, he may also be required to comply with the rules of the hostel.

(6A) In the case of a person accused of murder the court granting bail shall, unless it considers that satisfactory reports on his mental condition have already been obtained, impose as conditions of bail—

(a) a requirement that the accused shall undergo examination by two medical practitioners for the purpose of enabling such reports to be prepared; and

(b) a requirement that he shall for that purpose attend such an institution or place as the court directs and comply with any other directions which may be given to him for that purpose by either of those practitioners.

(6B)   Of the medical practitioners referred to in subsection (6A) above at least one shall be a practitioner approved for the purposes of section 12 of the Mental Health Act 1983.

(7)   If a parent or guardian of a child or young person consents to be surety for the child or young person for the purposes of this subsection, the parent or guardian may be required to secure that the child or young person complies with any requirement imposed on him by virtue of subsection (6) or (6A) above but—

(a)   no requirement shall be imposed on the parent or the guardian of a young person by virtue of this subsection where it appears that the young person will attain the age of 17 before the time to be appointed for him to surrender to custody; and

(b)   the parent or guardian shall not be required to secure compliance with any requirement to which his consent does not extend and shall not, in respect of those requirements to which his consent does extend, be bound in a sum greater than £50.

(8)   Where a court has granted bail in criminal proceedings that court or, where that court has committed a person on bail to the Crown Court for trial or to be sentenced or otherwise dealt with, that court or the Crown Court may on application—

(a)   by or on behalf of the person to whom bail was granted, or

(b)   by the prosecutor or a constable,

vary the conditions of bail or impose conditions in respect of bail which has been granted unconditionally.

(8A)   Where a notice of transfer is given under a relevant transfer provision, subsection (8) above shall have effect in relation to a person in relation to whose case the notice is given as if he had been committed on bail to the Crown Court for trial.

(8B)   Subsection (8) above applies where a court has sent a person on bail to the Crown Court for trial under section 51 of the Crime and Disorder Act 1998 as it applies where a court has committed a person on bail to the Crown Court for trial. [This subsection is inserted by the Crime and Disorder Act 1998, sch. 8 and is in force from 4 January 1999 only in certain pilot areas where s. 51 of the 1998 Act is in force.]

(9)   This section is subject to subsection (2) of section 30 of the Magistrates' Courts Act 1980 (conditions of bail on remand for medical examination).

(10)   This section is subject, in its application to bail granted by a constable, to section 3A of this Act.

(10)   In subsection (8A) above 'relevant transfer provision' means—

(a)   section 4 of the Criminal Justice Act 1987, or

(b)   section 53 of the Criminal Justice Act 1991.

Keynote

Section 3(6)(e) was added by s. 54(2) of the Crime and Disorder Act 1998 which provides a court granting bail with a further condition not available to the police. This condition, for the accused to attend an interview with an authorised advocate, was introduced to limit the occasions where an accused attended a first hearing and an adjournment was required for such legal advice to be obtained. This condition does not affect the right of an accused to represent himself/herself in court.

5.6.2   Police Bail

Section 3A of the Bail Act 1976 applies to bail granted specifically by a custody officer thereby amending s. 3 of the Act:

(1)   Section 3 of this Act applies, in relation to bail granted by a custody officer under part IV of the Police and Criminal Evidence Act 1984 in cases where the normal powers to impose conditions of bail are available to him, subject to the following modifications.

(2)   Subsection (6) does not authorise the imposition of a requirement to reside in a bail hostel or any requirement under paragraph (d) or (e).

(3)   Subsection (6ZA), (6A) and (6B) shall be omitted.

(4)   For subsection (8), substitute the following—

'(8)   Where a custody officer has granted bail in criminal proceedings he or another custody officer serving at the same police station may, at the request of the person to whom it was granted, vary the conditions of bail and in doing so he may impose conditions or more onerous conditions.'.

(5) Where a constable grants bail to a person no conditions shall be imposed under subsections (4), (5), (6) or (7) of section 3 of this Act unless it appears to the constable that it is necessary to do so for the purpose of preventing that person from—

(a) failing to surrender to custody, or

(b) committing an offence while on bail, or

(c) interfering with witnesses or otherwise obstructing the course of justice, whether in relation to himself or any other person.

(6) Subsection (5) above also applies on any request to a custody officer under subsection (8) of section 3 of this Act to vary the conditions of bail.

Keynote

The modifications to s. 3, in relation to bail granted by custody officers, are:

- no authority to bail to a bail hostel or probation hostel (s. 3(6ZA));

- no authority to bail for court reports (s. 3(6)(d));

- no authority to bail for medical reports (s. 3(6A)).

5.6.3 Bail Conditions

Section 3A(5) of the Bail Act 1976 provides for the occasions when a custody officer can consider imposing bail conditions. These are where it appears to be necessary to prevent the person from:

- failing to surrender to custody; or

- committing an offence while on bail; or

- interfering with witnesses or otherwise obstructing the course of justice, whether in relation to himself/herself or any other person.

Where the custody officer decides to grant bail and considers one or more of the requirements in s. 3A(5)(a) to (c) apply, one or more of the following conditions can be imposed:

- the accused is to live and sleep at a specified address;

- the accused is to notify any changes of address;

- the accused is to report periodically (daily, weekly or at other intervals) to his/her local police station;

- the accused is restricted from entering a certain area or building or to go within a specified distance of a specified address;

- the accused is not to contact (whether directly or indirectly) the victim of the alleged offence and/or any other probable prosecution witness;

- the accused is to surrender his/her passport;

- the accused's movements are restricted by an imposed curfew between set times (i.e. when it is thought the accused might commit offences or come into contact with witnesses);

- the accused is required to provide a surety or security.

Where conditions are imposed, an accused may make application to the same custody officer or another custody officer serving at the same police station to have the conditions varied or removed. When such an application is received the matter should be considered on its merits at that time. The custody officer can vary the conditions, including making them more onerous, if this can be justified, or leave them the same (s. 5A(2)).

The custody officer either imposing or varying the conditions of bail imposed 'shall include a note of those reasons in the custody record and shall give a copy of that note to the person in relation to whom the decision was taken' (s. 5A(4)).

The application for varying conditions can also be made to a magistrates' court (s. 5A(2)).

5.6.4   Surety and Sureties

Section 3(4) of the Bail Act 1976 provides that before a person is granted bail he/she may be required to provide one or more sureties to secure his/her surrender to custody. A custody officer is entitled (as a court) to require such sureties.

The question of whether or not sureties are necessary is at the discretion of the custody officer (or court) but this condition can only be applied where it is believed the accused may abscond, commit further offences, interfere with witnesses, etc., (sch. 1, part I). It should be noted that sureties have no responsibilities (liability) in relation to an accused committing further offences or interfering with witnesses etc. whilst on bail.

The suitability of sureties is provided by s. 8 of the 1976 Act and provides for the following considerations as to a surety's suitability:

- financial resources

- character and previous convictions

- relationship to the accused

The decision as to the suitability of individual sureties is a matter for the custody officer.

The normal consequence for a surety if the accused does not answer bail is that the surety is required to forfeit the entire sum in which he/she stood surety. The power to forfeit recognisances is a matter for the court and is contained in s. 120(1) to (3) of the Magistrates' Courts Act 1980 and rr. 21 and 21A of the Crown Court Rules 1982.

It is not necessary to prove that the surety had any involvement in the accused's non-appearance (*R* v *Warwick Crown Court, ex parte Smalley* [1987] 1 WLR 237). However, where a surety has taken all reasonable steps to ensure the appearance of an accused it was held that the recognisance ought not to be forfeited (*R* v *York Crown Court, ex parte Coleman* (1987) 86 Cr App R 151). Section 7(3)(c) of the Bail Act 1976 provides for a surety to notify a constable *in writing* that the accused is unlikely to surrender to custody and that for that reason the surety wishes to be relieved of his/her obligations as a surety. Such an action may well be determined to be 'reasonable steps'.

5.6.5 Security

Section 3(5) of the Bail Act 1976 provides that, before a person is granted bail, he/she may be required to give security for his/her surrender to custody. As with sureties, a custody officer is entitled (as a court) to require such security, as far as s. 3(6)(a) to (c) (surrender to custody, not commit an offence on bail, interfere with witnesses, etc.) applies. The security required may be a sum of money or other valuable item and may be given either by the accused or someone on his/her behalf

As with sureties, where an accused absconds this would result in forfeiture of the security. This would not be the case if there appears reasonable cause for the (accused's) failure to surrender to custody (s. 5(7) to (9) of the 1976 Act).

5.7 Appointment of Court Date

In its aim to speed up the criminal justice process, the Crime and Disorder Act 1998, s. 46 has introduced an amendment to s. 47 of the Police and Criminal Evidence Act 1984. Previously, where a custody officer released an arrested person on bail, this section did not provide him/her with any statutory requirements or guidance as to the time by which that person must appear before a magistrates' court.

The amended s. 47 now provides:

> *(3A) Where a custody officer grants bail to a person subject to a duty to appear before a magistrates' court, he shall appoint for the appearance—*
> *(a) a date which is not later than the first sitting of the court after the person is charged with the offence; or*
> *(b) where he is informed by the clerk to the justices for the relevant petty sessions area that the appearance cannot be accommodated until a later date, that later date.*

Keynote

The main reason for the introduction of the amendment is to enable simple 'guilty plea' cases to be dealt with, wherever possible, at the next court hearing.

5.8 Juveniles Refused Bail

Under s. 38(6) of the Police and Criminal Evidence Act 1984, where a juvenile has been refused bail, the custody officer must try and make arrangements for the detained juvenile to be taken into the care of a local authority in order that he/she can be detained pending appearance in court.

Two exceptions are provided:

- where the custody officer certifies that it is impracticable to do so, or

- in the case of a juvenile of at least 12 years of age, where no secure accommodation is available and there is a risk to the public of serious harm from that juvenile which cannot be adequately protected by placing the juvenile in other local authority accommodation.

The certificate signed by the custody officer must be produced when the juvenile first appears at court (s. 38(7)).

PACE Code C, Note 16B makes it clear that the availability of secure accommodation is only a factor in relation to a juvenile aged 12 or over, when the local authority accommodation would not be adequate to protect the public from serious harm from the juvenile.

The obligation to transfer a juvenile to local authority accommodation applies equally to a juvenile charged during the daytime as it does to a juvenile to be held overnight, subject to a requirement to bring the juvenile before a court in accordance with s. 46 of the 1984 Act (see below).

5.9   Treatment of People Refused Bail

The custody officer must continue to comply with the PACE Codes of Practice in relation to the treatment of the person while detained pending his/her appearance at court or any latter decision to give bail. Even though a decision to refuse bail may have been taken properly at the time, the circumstances may change and bail may become appropriate. It may be that bail has been refused because of the fear that the person may interfere with a witness. If that witness then informs the police that he/she is going to stay with friends abroad, it may be sufficient to protect the witness by granting bail on the condition that the accused surrenders his/her passport.

Section 40 of the 1984 Act requires that a person who has been refused bail must have his/her detention reviewed by the custody officer *within nine hours of the last decision to refuse bail*. This can only be delayed if the custody officer is not available to carry out the review and then it must be carried out as soon as practicable. Any reason for the delay must be recorded in the custody record along with the decision. If detention can no longer be justified, the person should be bailed with or without conditions as appropriate.

A person charged with an offence and refused bail must be brought before a magistrates' court in accordance with s. 46 of the 1984 Act. Section 46 provides that:

> (1)   Where a person—
>   (a)   is charged with an offence; and
>   (b)   after being charged—
>   (i)   is kept in police detention; or
>   (ii)   is detained by a local authority in pursuance of arrangements made under section 38(6)
> above,
> he shall be brought before a magistrates' court in accordance with the provisions of this section.
>   (2)   If he is to be brought before a magistrates' court for the petty sessions area in which the police station at which he was charged is situated, he shall be brought before such a court as soon as is practicable and in any event not later than the first sitting after he is charged with the offence.
>   (3)   If no magistrates' court for that area is due to sit either on the day on which he is charged or on the next day, the custody officer for the police station at which he was charged shall inform the clerk to the justices for the area that there is a person in the area to whom subsection (2) above applies.
>   (4)   If the person charged is to be brought before a magistrates' court for a petty sessions area other than that in which the police station at which he was charged is situated, he shall be removed to that area as soon as is practicable and brought before such a court as soon as is practicable after his arrival in the area and in any event not later than the first sitting of a magistrates' court for that area after his arrival in the area.

(5)   If no magistrates' court for that area is due to sit either on the day on which he arrives in the area or on the next day—

(a)   he shall be taken to a police station in the area; and

(b)   the custody officer at that station shall inform the clerk to the justices for the area that there is a person in the area to whom subsection (4) applies.

(6)   Subject to subsection (8) below, where a clerk to the justices for a petty sessions area has been informed—

(a)   under subsection (3) above that there is a person in the area to whom subsection (2) above applies; or

(b)   under subsection (5) above that there is a person in the area to whom subsection (4) above applies,

the clerk shall arrange for a magistrates' court to sit not later than the day next following the relevant day.

(7)   In this section 'the relevant day'—

(a)   in relation to a person who is to be brought before a magistrates' court for the petty sessions area in which the police station at which he was charged is situated, means the day on which he was charged; and

(b)   in relation to a person who is to be brought before a magistrates' court for any other petty sessions area, means the day on which he arrives in the area.

(8)   Where the day next following the relevant day is Christmas Day, Good Friday or a Sunday, the duty of the clerk under subsection (6) above is a duty to arrange for a magistrates' court to sit not later than the first day after the relevant day which is not one of those days.

(9)   Nothing in this section requires a person who is in hospital to be brought before a court if he is not well enough.

Keynote

The person must be brought before the next available court (it is for the clerk of the court to decide when the next available court is sitting (*R v Avon Magistrates, ex parte Broome* [1988] Crim LR 618)). If no court is sitting on the next day after charging, (other than Sundays, Christmas Day or Good Friday), the custody officer must inform the clerk of the court. If the court in which the person is to appear is in another area, the person must be taken to the area as soon as practicable and then be taken to that court at the next available sitting. Section 46(9) provides an exception to this requirement if the person is in hospital and is not fit to appear.

The detained person need not be granted bail if the custody officer is satisfied that there are 'substantial grounds' for believing that the defendant, if released on bail (whether subject to conditions or not) would:

- fail to surrender to custody; or
- commit an offence while on bail; or
- interfere with witnesses or otherwise obstruct the course of justice, whether in relation to himself/herself or any other person.

The detained person may also be refused bail for his/her own protection. Where the accused is a juvenile, bail may also be refused if he/she should be kept in custody for his/her own welfare.

5.10   Offence of Absconding

Section 6 of the Bail Act 1976 Act creates an offence of absconding and provides that:

(1)   If a person who has been released on bail in criminal proceedings fails without reasonable cause to surrender to custody he shall be guilty of an offence.

BAIL

(2) If a person who—
   (a) has been released on bail in criminal proceedings, and
   (b) having reasonable cause therefor, has failed to surrender to custody,
fails to surrender to custody at the appointed place as soon after the appointed time as is reasonably practicable he shall be guilty of an offence.

Keynote

The burden of proof in relation to showing ' reasonable cause' (s. 6(1)) is a matter for the accused (s. 6(3)).

A person who has 'reasonable cause' still commits the offence if he/she falls to surrender 'as soon after the appointed time as is reasonably practicable'. In *Laidlaw* v *Atkinson*, *The Times*, 2 August 1986, it was held that being mistaken about the day on which one should have appeared was not a reasonable excuse.

Section 6(4) also provides that:

A failure to give to a person granted bail in criminal proceedings a copy of the record of the decision shall not constitute reasonable cause for that person's failure to surrender to custody.

5.10.1 Failure to Comply with Bail

There are occasions where a person who has been bailed to return to a police station at a later date or to appear at court may be arrested without warrant. These occasions are dealt with by s. 46A of the Police and Criminal Evidence Act 1984 and s. 7 of the Bail Act 1976.

Section 46A of the Police and Criminal Evidence Act 1984 provides that:

(1) A constable may arrest without a warrant any person who, having been released on bail under this Part of this Act subject to a duty to attend at a police station, fails to attend at that police station at the time appointed for him to do so.
(2) A person who is arrested under this section shall be taken to the police station appointed as the place at which he is to surrender to custody as soon as practicable after the arrest.
(3) For the purposes of—
   (a) section 30 above (subject to the obligation in subsection (2) above), and
   (b) section 31 above,
an arrest under this section shall be treated as an arrest for an offence.

Keynote

The offence for which the person is arrested under subsection (1) above is the offence for which he/she was originally arrested (s. 34(7) of the 1984 Act). This power of arrest only applies where the person *has* failed to attend the police station at the appointed time; it does not extend to situations where there is a 'reasonable suspicion' that the person has failed to attend.

5.10.2 Failure to Appear at Court (or Expected Not to Appear)

Section 7 of the Bail Act 1976 provides that:

(1) If a person who has been released on bail in criminal proceedings and is under a duty to surrender into the custody of a court fails to surrender to custody at the time appointed for him to do so the court may issue a warrant for his arrest.

53

(2) If a person who has been released on bail in criminal proceedings absents himself from the court at any time after he has surrendered into the custody of the court and before the court is ready to begin or to resume the hearing of the proceedings, the court may issue a warrant for his arrest but no warrant shall be issued under this subsection where that person is absent in accordance with leave given to him by or on behalf of the court.

(3) A person who has been released on bail in criminal proceedings and is under a duty to surrender into the custody of a court may be arrested without warrant by a constable—

(a) if the constable has reasonable grounds for believing that that person is not likely to surrender to custody;

(b) if the constable has reasonable grounds for believing that that person is likely to break any of the conditions of his bail or has reasonable grounds for suspecting that that person has broken any of those conditions; or

(c) in a case where that person was released on bail with one or more surety or sureties, if a surety notifies a constable in writing that that person is unlikely to surrender to custody and that for that reason the surety wishes to be relieved of his obligations as a surety.

Keynote

Section 7 therefore provides a power of arrest without warrant if the constable:

- has reasonable grounds for believing that the person is not likely to surrender to custody;

- has reasonable grounds for believing that the person is likely to break, or reasonable grounds for suspecting that the person has broken, any conditions of bail; or

- is notified by a surety in writing that the person is unlikely to surrender to custody and for that reason the surety wishes to be relieved of his/her obligations as a surety.

Where a person is arrested under s. 7 he/she shall be brought before a magistrate in the petty sessions area where he/she was arrested as soon as practicable and in any event within 24 hours (s. 7(4)(a)).

Where a person is arrested within 24 hours of the time appointed for him/her to surrender to custody he/she must be brought before the court at which he/she was to have so surrendered (s. 7(4)(b)). In reckoning the 24 hour period no account is to be taken of Christmas Day, Good Friday or any Sunday (s. 7(4)).

In dealing with a person brought before the court under subsection (4), if the magistrate is of the opinion that the person is not likely to surrender to custody or has broken or is likely to break any bail conditions he/she may:

- remand or commit the person to custody

- grant bail subject to the same or different conditions.

Where the justice is not of such an opinion, he/she shall grant bail with the same conditions (if any) as were originally imposed (s. 7(5)).

Where the person being dealt with is a child or young person and the justice does not grant bail, he/she should remand such person to the care of the local authority (s. 7(6)).

5.11   Courts and Bail

Where a person is accused of an offence and appears before a magistrates' court or Crown Court and applies to the court for bail there is a presumption (under s. 4(1) of the Bail Act 1976) in favour of granting bail:

A person to whom this section applies shall be granted bail except as provided in schedule 1 to this Act.

(**See para. 5.12 below** for sch. 1.)

In addition to a person appearing before the court in connection with proceedings for an offence, s. 4(1) also applies to adjournments for reports before sentencing and persons being dealt with for an alleged breach of a requirement in a probation, community service, combination or curfew order.

With the exception of s. 4(2) (adjournment for report of a convicted person), s. 4(1) does not apply where a person has been convicted and is seeking bail pending an appeal or has been committed to the Crown Court for sentence. In such cases the granting or refusal of bail is at the discretion of the court. If bail were to be granted by the court it would be subject to s. 1(1) of the Bail Act 1976, 'bail in criminal proceedings'.

5.11.1   Bail by Magistrates' Courts

A magistrates' court may remand an accused person in custody or on bail (ss. 5(1), 10(1) and 18(4) of the Magistrates' Courts Act 1980). In exercising their powers of remand or bail the magistrates must do so in accordance with the Bail Act 1976 (s. 128(1) of the 1980 Act). These provisions relate to the magistrates' jurisdiction to adjourn and remand a case. Such jurisdiction applies when the court is:

- inquiring into an offence as examining justices;

- trying an information summarily; or

- determining mode of trial for an offence triable either way.

5.11.2   Bail by the Crown Court

The Supreme Court Act 1981, s. 81(1)(a) to (g), lists the persons to whom the Crown Court may grant bail. Section 81(1) provides:

(1)   The Crown Court may grant bail to any person—
(a)   who has been committed in custody for appearance before the Crown Court or in relation to whose case a notice of transfer has been given under section 4 of the Criminal Justice Act 1987 or who has been sent in custody to the Crown Court for trial under section 51 of the Crime and Disorder Act 1998; or
(b)   who is in custody pursuant to a sentence imposed by a magistrates' court, and who has appealed to the Crown Court against his conviction or sentence; or
(c)   who is in the custody of the Crown Court pending the disposal of his case by that court; or
(d)   who, after the decision of his case by the Crown Court, has applied to that court for the statement of a case for the High Court on that decision; or
(e)   who has applied to the High Court for an order of certiorari to remove proceedings in the Crown Court in his case into the High Court, or has applied to the High Court for leave to make such an application; or
(f)   to whom the Crown Court has granted a certificate under section 1(2) or 11(1A) of the Criminal Appeal Act 1968 or under subsection (1B) below; or

(g)   who has been remanded in custody by a magistrates' court on adjourning a case under—

(i)   section 5 (adjournment of inquiry into offence);

(ii)   section 10 (adjournment of trial);

(iii) section 18 (initial procedure on information against adult for offence triable either way);

or

(iv)   section 30 (remand for medical examination),

of the Magistrates' Courts Act 1980;

and the time during which a person is released on bail under any provision of this subsection shall not count as part of any term of imprisonment or detention or detention under his sentence.

Keynote

Subsection (1)(g) relates to an accused who is remanded in custody by the magistrates' court and makes an application for bail to the Crown Court. The reference to ss. 5, 10 and 18 or 30 of the Magistrates' Courts Act 1980 relates to adjournments before inquiring into an offence as examining justices and adjournments for medical reports respectively. The magistrates' court is required to provide a certificate to the Crown Court that, before refusing bail, it heard full argument.

Section 25 of the Criminal Justice and Public Order Act 1994 (occasions where bail cannot be granted) relates to all the powers of the Crown Court to grant bail (**see para. 5.4 above**).

5.11.3   Bail by the High Court

The High Court has jurisdiction to grant bail to the following people in the following circumstances:

- people refused bail by the magistrates' court (s. 22(1) of the Criminal Justice Act 1967);

- people who have applied to the Crown Court to state a case for opinion or seeking an order to quash that court's decision (s. 37(1)(b) of the Criminal Justice Act 1948);

- people convicted or sentenced by the magistrates' court and seeking an order to quash that decision (s. 37(1)(d) of the 1948 Act).

Keynote

This process is generally referred to as applying for bail to 'judge in chambers' and in practice would require the investigating officer to appear before a single High Court judge.

As with the Crown Court, s. 25 of the Criminal Justice and Public Order Act 1994 (occasions where bail cannot be granted) applies to bail by the High Court (**see para. 5.4 above**).

5.11.4   Bail by Court of Appeal

The Court of Appeal may grant bail to a person who has served notice of appeal or notice of application for leave to appeal against conviction and sentence in the Crown Court (s. 19 of the Criminal Appeal Act 1968). People appealing from the Court of Appeal to the House of Lords can also be granted bail (s. 36 of the 1968 Act).

The provisions of s. 25 of the Criminal Justice and Public Order Act 1994 apply equally to the Court of Appeal (**see para. 5.4 above**).

5.12 Courts Refusing Bail

The considerations of the court in relation to granting bail are similar to those of the custody officer (**see para. 5.5 above**) and can be divided into the same two groups namely:

- those offences that are imprisonable; and

- those offences that do not carry a sentence of imprisonment.

5.12.1 Imprisonable Offences

The Bail Act 1976 (sch. 1, part I, paras 2 to 5) lists the five grounds where a court need not grant bail to an unconvicted accused charged with an imprisonable offence:

2. The defendant need not be granted bail if the court is satisfied that there are substantial grounds for believing that the defendant, if released on bail (whether subject to conditions or not) would
(a) fail to surrender to custody, or
(b) commit an offence while on bail, or
(c) interfere with witnesses or otherwise obstruct the course of justice, whether in relation to himself or any other person.

2A. The defendant need not be granted bail if—
(a) the offence is an indictable offence or an offence triable either way; and
(b) it appears to the court that he was on bail in criminal proceedings on the date of the offence.

3. The defendant need not be granted bail if the court is satisfied that the defendant should be kept in custody for his own protection or, if he is a child or young person, for his own welfare.

4. The defendant need not be granted bail if he is in custody in pursuance of the sentence of a court or of any authority acting under any of the Services Acts.

5. The defendant need not be granted bail where the court is satisfied that it has not been practicable to obtain sufficient information for the purpose of taking the decisions required by this part of this schedule for want of time since the institution of the proceedings against him.

Keynote

In para. 3, where the defendant is being kept in custody for his/her own protection, or where the defendant is a child or young person (under the age of 17 (s. 2(2)), the detention is 'for his/her own welfare'.

There are two further grounds where the court need not grant bail:

- where the defendant has been arrested for absconding or breaking conditions of bail (sch. 1, part I, para. 6);

- where the court wishes further inquiries or a report to be made and is satisfied that the only practical way of achieving this is to remand the defendant in custody (sch. 1, part I, para. 7).

5.12.2 Non-Imprisonable Offences

The Bail Act 1976 (sch. 1, part II, paras 2 to 4) lists the four grounds where a court need not grant bail to an unconvicted accused charged with an imprisonable offence:

> 2. The defendant need not be granted bail if
>   (a)   it appears to the court that, having been previously granted bail in criminal proceedings, he has failed to surrender to custody in accordance with his obligations under the grant of bail and
>   (b)   the court believes, in view of that failure, that the defendant, if released on bail (whether subject to conditions or not) would fail to surrender to custody.
>
> 3.   The defendant need not be granted bail if the court is satisfied that the defendant should be kept in custody for his own protection or, if he is a child or young person, for his own welfare.
>
> 4.   The defendant need not be granted bail if he is in custody in pursuance of the sentence of a court or of any authority acting under any of the Services Acts.

Keynote

There is one further ground (the same as for imprisonable offences) where the court need not grant bail. That is:

* where the defendant has been arrested for absconding or breaking conditions of bail (sch. 1, part II, para. 5).

5.13 Detention of Adults and Juveniles

Where an accused is aged 21 or over and a court refuses bail, that person is detained in prison (or other remand centre) until the next hearing.

In relation to an accused aged 17 to 20 inclusive, who is remanded or committed for trial or sentence in custody, the court must commit him/her to the remand centre where one is available (s. 27(1) of the Criminal Justice Act 1948).

In relation to an accused under 17 years old, where a court remands them or commits them for trial or sentence without bail, that person must be remanded to local authority accommodation unless the criteria laid down in s. 23(5) of the Children and Young Persons Act 1969 are satisfied (s. 23(1)).

Section 23(5) provides

> (5)   This subsection applies to a young person who has attained the age of fifteen, but only if—
>   (a)   he is charged with or has been convicted of a violent or sexual offence, or an offence punishable in the case of an adult with imprisonment for a term of fourteen years or more; or
>   (b)   he has a recent history of absconding while remanded to local authority accommodation, and is charged with or has been convicted of an imprisonable offence alleged or found to have been committed while he was so remanded,
> and (in either case) the court is of opinion that only remanding him to a remand centre or prison would be adequate to protect the public from serious harm from him.

Keynote

When s. 97 of the Crime and Disorder Act 1998 comes into effect, s. 23 will be amended so that it applies to 12 to 16 year olds in categories to be determined by the Home Secretary.

In *R* v *Croydon Crown Court, ex parte G, The Times,* 3 May 1995, 'serious harm' was held to be assessed by reference to the nature of the offences charged and the surrounding circumstances.

Section 23A of the Children and Young Persons Act 1969 provides the police with a power of arrest where a constable has reasonable grounds for suspecting that a person is breaking his/her conditions (i.e. remanded or committed to local authority accommodation). Where the arrested person cannot be brought before the court, before which he/she was to have appeared, within 24 hours then he/she must 'be brought as soon as practicable and in any event within 24 hours after his arrest before a justice of the peace for the petty sessions area in which he was arrested' (s. 23A(2)).

5.14   Remands in Police Custody

As outlined in para. 5.13 above, where a person is remanded in custody it normally means detention in prison or a remand centre. However, s. 128 of the Magistrates' Courts Act 1980 provides that a magistrates' court may remand a person to police custody:

- for a period not exceeding three days (24 hours for persons under 17) (s. 128(7));

- for the purpose of inquiries into offences (other than the offence for which he/she appears before the court) (s. 128(8)(a));

- as soon as the need ceases he/she must be brought back before the magistrates (s. 128(8)(b));

- the conditions of detention and periodic review apply as if the person was arrested without warrant on suspicion of having committed an offence (s. 128(8)(c) and (d)).

This option is colloquially referred to as a 'three day lie down'.

CHAPTER SIX

COURT PROCEDURE AND WITNESSES

6.1 Introduction

Once the various parties to a case have been brought to court, the trial or hearing can proceed. This chapter addresses the way in which those proceedings will be conducted and the relevant requirements made of the parties concerned.

6.2 Conduct of a Prosecution

A summary trial, where there is a 'guilty plea', starts with the prosecution stating the facts of the case. The defence then put any mitigation to the court before sentence.

A 'not guilty' plea allows the prosecution to call its evidence, and before doing so address the court. In something resembling a forensic tennis match, the defendant can then address the court and call evidence, a process which is followed by rebuttal evidence, confined to unexpected matters raised by the defence, being called by the prosecution. At the end of the evidence for the defence (and the rebuttal evidence, if any), the defendant may address the court if he/she has not already done so.

Either party may, with the court's leave, address the court a second time, but if afforded to one party, the opportunity must not be denied the other party. Where both parties address the court twice, the prosecution goes first on the second occasion.

In the event of the non-appearance of the defendant, where he/she has not answered to bail, the court can issue a warrant for his/her arrest under s. 7 of the Bail Act 1976 (**see chapter 5**) or s. 1 of the Magistrates' Courts Act 1980 (**see chapter 4**).

Section 11 of the Magistrates' Courts Act 1980 provides that:

> *(1)   Subject to the provisions of this Act, where at the time and place appointed for the trial or adjourned trial of an information the prosecutor appears but the accused does not, the court may proceed in his absence.*

(2)   Where a summons has been issued, the court shall not begin to try the information in the absence of the accused unless either it is proved to the satisfaction of the court, on oath or in such other manner as may be prescribed, that the summons was served on the accused within what appears to the court to be a reasonable time before the trial or adjourned trial or the accused has appeared on a previous occasion to answer the information.

Section 13 provides that:

(1)   Subject to the provisions of this section, where the court, instead of proceeding in the absence of the accused, adjourns or further adjourns the trial, the court may, if the information has been substantiated on oath, issue a warrant for his arrest.

(2)   Where a summons has been issued, the court shall not issue a warrant under this section unless the condition in subsection (2A) below or that in subsection (2B) below is fulfilled.

(2A)   The condition in this subsection is that it is proved to the satisfaction of the court, on oath or in such other manner as may be prescribed, that the summons was served on the accused within what appears to the court to be a reasonable time before the trial or adjourned trial.

(2B)   The condition in this subsection is that—

(a)   the adjournment now being made is a second or subsequent adjournment of the trial,

(b)   the accused was present on the last (or only) occasion when the trial was adjourned, and

(c)   on that occasion the court determined the time for the hearing at which the adjournment is now being made.

Keynote

'A reasonable time before the trial' should be judged by the justices but it has been held that a summons to appear the following day was in order.

6.3   'Statement of Facts' Procedure

This procedure relates to the service of the appropriate summons on the defendant together with a 'statement of facts' and a prescribed form of explanation enabling the defendant to plead guilty and put forward any mitigation in his/her absence. The magistrates' clerk informs the prosecution of any written guilty plea.

Where service is proved and a guilty plea is sent, the 'statement of facts' and any mitigation is read out in court. Only the 'statement of facts' as served on the defendant may be read to the court. No further facts or evidence can be given.

This procedure can be used for summary offences for which the accused cannot be sentenced to imprisonment exceeding three months.

6.4   Pre-trial Reviews

Pre-trial reviews are provided for by s. 49 of the Crime and Disorder Act 1998 and can be conducted by a single justice or a justices' clerk (**see paras 2.8.1 and 2.8.2**). Their purpose is to provide better management of cases through the courts in that they provide opportunities for:

- the prosecution to amend charges;

- the defence to enter different pleas;

COURT PROCEDURE AND WITNESSES

- the issues in contention to be identified;

- clarifying which witnesses need to attend;

- estimating the amount of time the court will require to hear the case.

Pre-trial reviews have been in use by a number of courts and s. 49 has essentially endorsed these as best practice.

6.5   Early Administrative Hearings

Section 50 of the Crime and Disorder Act 1998 provides that:

(1)   Where a person ('the accused') has been charged with an offence at a police station, the magistrates' court before whom he appears or is brought for the first time in relation to the charge may, unless the accused falls to be dealt with under section 51 below, consist of a single justice.
(2)   At a hearing conducted by a single justice under this section—
(a)   the accused shall be asked whether he wishes to receive legal aid; and
(b)   if he indicates that he does, his eligibility for it shall be determined; and
(c)   if it is determined that he is eligible for it, the necessary arrangements or grant shall be made for him to obtain it.
(3)   At such a hearing the single justice—
(a)   may exercise, subject to subsection (2) above, such of his powers as a single justice as he thinks fit; and
(b)   on adjourning the hearing, may remand the accused in custody or on bail.

Keynote

The purpose of this hearing is for the accused to obtain legal aid and consult a legal adviser. The accused will be remanded to a pre-trial review or to a mode of trial hearing, as appropriate. Early administrative hearings are designed for an accused thought likely to contest the charge(s). Those accused charged with straightforward summary or either way offences are expected to appear before the magistrates' court the next day for sentencing or for committal for sentence.

6.6   Open Court

It has long been established that criminal trials should take place in open court and be freely reported.

Section 4 of the Magistrates' Courts Act 1980 provides that:

(2)   Examining justices shall sit in open court except where any enactment contains an express provision to the contrary and except where it appears to them as respects the whole or any part of committal proceedings that the ends of justice would not be served by their sitting in open court.

Section 121 of the Magistrates' Courts Act 1980 provides that:

(4)   Subject to the provisions of any enactment to the contrary, where a magistrates' court is required by this section to sit in a petty-sessional or occasional court-house, it shall sit in open court.

Keynote

In *Attorney-General* v *Leveller Magazine Ltd* [1979] AC 440 three aspects of the principle of open justice were reported, namely:

- the courts should be open to the public;
- evidence communicated to the court should be communicated publicly; and
- the media should not be impeded from reporting what has taken place publicly in court.

6.7 Sitting in Camera: Common Law

The following instances are contained within the common law, whereby the public may be excluded from court proceedings.

6.7.1 Possibility of Disorder

In *Scott* v *Scott* [1913] AC 417, it was held that:

> . . . the court may be closed or cleared if such a precaution is necessary for the administration of justice. Tumult or disorder, or the just apprehension of it, would certainly justify the exclusion of all from whom such interruption is expected, and, if discrimination is impracticable, the exclusion of the public in general.

6.7.2 Witnesses who Refuse to Testify Publicly

Scott v *Scott* also held that:

> If the evidence to be given is of such a character that it would be impracticable to force an unwilling witness to give it in public, the case may come within the exception to the principle that . . . a public hearing must be insisted on in accordance with the rules which govern the general procedure in English courts of justice.

This *dictum* (speech) needs to be treated with a degree of caution as to its general applicability. The case in question was one relating to proceedings within the divorce court. It might also be appropriate for a witness, to overcome his/her fears, to write down his/her name and address for the eyes of the court only. It may also be more appropriate to deal with a reluctant witness by the threat of contempt proceedings than by depriving the public of their access to the courts.

6.7.3 Effect of Public Hearing on Possible Future Prosecutions

There is limited case law in relation to this particular area. Lord Scarman in *Attorney-General* v *Leveller Magazine Ltd* [1979] AC 440 stated that a court might sit in private, 'if the factor of national safety appears to endanger the due administration of justice, e.g. by deterring the Crown from prosecuting in cases where it should do so'.

A decision to sit *in camera* is not justified solely on the grounds that a witness would find it embarrassing to testify publicly. In *R* v *Malvern Justices, ex parte Evans* [1988] QB 540 it was held to be inappropriate to spare the defendant the ordeal of giving evidence of 'the embarrassing and intimate details' of her personal life.

6.8 *Voir Dire:* Trial within a Trial

In order for a judge to hear applications on matters of law or procedure in the absence of the trial jury, there is a process called a *voir dire*. Colloquially, this is referred to as 'a trial within a trial' and it simply involves the jury being sent out while counsel make their submissions; the court otherwise remains 'open' to the public.

6.9 Statutory Provisions

6.9.1 Official Secrets

Section 8 of the Official Secrets Act 1920 provides that:

> *(4) In addition and without prejudice to any powers which a court may possess to order the exclusion of the public from any proceedings if, in the course of proceedings before a court against any person for an offence under [the Official Secrets Act 1911] or this Act or the proceedings on appeal, or in the course of the trial of a person for [any offence under the Official Secrets Act 1911] or this Act, application is made by the prosecution, on the ground that the publication of any evidence to be given or of any statement to be made in the course of the proceedings would be prejudicial to the national safety, that all or any portion of the public shall be excluded during any part of the hearing, the court may make an order to that effect, but the passing of sentence shall in any case take place in public.*

Keynote

Where the prosecutor intends to apply for the public to be excluded from some or all of the hearing, he/she must serve notice of application seven days before the trial. This application is heard, usually *in camera*, at the beginning of the trial at which time the accused is present but the jury has not been sworn. The trial is then adjourned for 24 hours in order that an appeal may be heard (Crown Court Rules 1982 (SI 1982 No. 1109), r. 24A).

6.9.2 Children

Sections 36 and 37 of the Children and Young Persons Act 1933 provide that:

> *36. No child (other than an infant in arms) shall be permitted to be present in court during the trial of any other person charged with an offence, or during any proceedings preliminary thereto, except during such time as his presence is required as a witness or otherwise for the purposes of justice; and any child present in court when under this section he is not permitted to be so shall be ordered to be removed.*

> *37.—(1) Where, in any proceedings in relation to an offence against, or any conduct contrary to, decency or morality, a person who, in the opinion of the court is a child or young person, is called as a witness, the court may direct that all or any persons, not being members or officers of the court or parties to the case, their counsel or solicitors, or persons otherwise directly concerned with the case, be excluded from the court during the taking of the evidence of that witness:*
> *Provided that nothing in this section shall authorise the exclusion of bona fide representatives of a newspaper or news agency.*
> *(2) The powers conferred on a court by this section shall be in addition and without prejudice to any other powers of the court to hear proceedings in camera.*

Keynote

'Child' for the purpose of s. 36 means a person under the age of 14 and 'young person' is any person under 18.

There are other provisions which allow for the giving of evidence anonymously or remotely by CCTV link or video (**see paras 6.11.4 and 6.11.5**).

6.10 Adjournments and Remands

6.10.1 Adjournments

The power to adjourn is contained in ss. 5, 10 and 18 of the Magistrates' Courts Act 1980 which provides that:

5.—(1) A magistrates' court may, before beginning to inquire into an offence as examining justices, or at any time during the inquiry, adjourn the hearing, and if it does so shall remand the accused.

(2) The court shall when adjourning fix the time and place at which the hearing is to be resumed; and the time fixed shall be that at which the accused is required to appear or be brought before the court in pursuance of the remand [or would be brought before the court were it not for his agreeing to further remands being in his absence].

10.—(1) A magistrates' court may at any time, whether before or after beginning to try an information, adjourn the trial, and may do so, notwithstanding anything in this Act, when composed of a single justice.

(2) The court may when adjourning either fix the time and place at which the trial is to be resumed, or, unless it remands the accused, leave the time and place to be determined later by the court. . . .

[(3) Adjournments after summary conviction.]

(4) On adjourning the trial of an information the court may remand the accused and, where the accused has attained the age of 18 years, shall do so if the offence is triable either way and—

(a) on the occasion on which the accused first appeared, or was brought, before the court to answer to the information he was in custody or, having been released on bail, surrendered to the custody of the court; or

(b) the accused has been remanded at any time in the course of proceedings on the information; and, where the court remands the accused, the time fixed for the resumption of the trial shall be that at which he is required to appear or be brought before the court in pursuance of the remand [or would be brought before the court were it not for his agreeing to further remands being in his absence].

18.—(1) Sections 19 to 23 below shall have effect where a person who has attained the age of 18 years appears or is brought before a magistrates' court on an information charging him with an offence triable either way and—

(a) he indicates under section 17A above that (if the offence were to proceed to trial) he would plead not guilty, or

(b) his representative indicates under section 17B above that (if the offence were to proceed to trial) he would plead not guilty.

. . .

(4) A magistrates' court proceeding under sections 19 to 23 below may adjourn the proceedings at any time, and on doing so on any occasion when the accused is present may remand the accused, and shall remand him if—

(a) on the occasion on which he first appeared, or was brought, before the court to answer to the information he was in custody or, having been released on bail, surrendered to the custody of the court; or

(b) he has been remanded at any time in the course of proceedings on the information; and where the court remands the accused, the time fixed for the resumption of the proceedings shall be that at which he is required to appear or be brought before the court in pursuance of the remand [or would be brought before the court were it not for his agreeing to further remands being in his absence].

Keynote

'Remands' can be either committing the defendant to custody or remanding him/her on bail in accordance with the provisions of the Bail Act 1976 (**see chapter 5**).

References in ss. 10 and 18 to the trial of an 'information' or a defendant appearing in answer to an information extend to cases where the proceedings are brought by way of a police charge. The charge sheet prepared at the police station is conventionally treated as the equivalent of an information laid before a magistrate.

6.10.2   Remands

Section 128 of the Magistrates' Courts Act 1980 provides that:

> (6)   Subject to the provisions of sections 128A and 129 . . ., a magistrates' court shall not remand a person for a period exceeding eight clear days, except that—
>
> (a)   if the court remands him on bail, it may remand him for a longer period if he and the other party consent;
>
> (b)   where the court adjourns a trial under section 10(3) or 30 . . ., the court may remand him for the period of the adjournment;
>
> (c)   where a person is charged with an offence triable either way, then, if it falls to the court to try the case summarily but the court is not at the time so constituted, and sitting in such a place, as will enable it to proceed with the trial, the courts may remand him until the next occasion on which it will be practicable for the court to be so constituted, and to sit in such a place, as aforesaid, notwithstanding that the remand is for a period exceeding eight clear days.
>
> (7)   A magistrates' court having power to remand a person in custody may, if the remand is for a period not exceeding three clear days, commit him to detention at a police station.
>
> (8)   Where a person is committed to detention at a police station under subsection (7) above—
>
> (a)   he shall not be kept in such detention unless there is a need for him to be so detained for the purposes of inquiries into other offences;
>
> (b)   if kept in such detention, he shall be brought back before the magistrates' court which committed him as soon as the need ceases;
>
> (c)   he shall be treated as a person in police detention to whom the duties under section 39 of the Police and Criminal Evidence Act 1984 (responsibilities in relation to person detained) relate;
>
> (d)   his detention shall be subject to periodic review at the times set out in section 40 of that Act (review of police detention).

Keynote

The provisions of s. 129 of the 1980 Act allow a court to further remand a defendant where he/she is unable to appear because of illness or injury.

'Eight clear days' means, for example, from Monday (when the court remanded the defendant) to Wednesday of the following week (when he/she appears before court again).

Sections 10(3) and 30 of the 1980 Act (as mentioned in s. 128(6)(b) above), allow the court to remand for not more than four weeks at a time for a medical report or other enquiries after conviction. The period is reduced to three weeks if the defendant is kept in custody.

A remand in detention under s. 128(7) and (8) may only be made for the purpose of allowing enquiries to be made into other offences for which the person has not been charged. If, for example, the person is eliminated from the enquiry, he/she must then be taken back to the magistrates' court even though the permitted period of detention has not expired.

Section 128A provides that a magistrates' court may remand a defendant in custody for longer than eight days in certain circumstances, but only in a specified area or in proceedings of a specified description. This section will not have any practical effect until an appropriate order is made.

6.11 Witnesses

At the heart of a trial will be the testimony provided by witnesses. A witness is a person called by a party in court proceedings with a view to proving a particular matter material to the case. This section examines the key issues in relation to witnesses:

- who can be called to give evidence;
- when a witness can be forced to give evidence;
- exceptions to the competence and compellability rules;
- hostile witnesses.

6.11.1 Competence and Compellability

In looking at witnesses, it is crucial to consider two related questions:

- Whether there are any restrictions to a witness being called to provide testimony. This question is frequently one of whether a witness is *competent*.

- Whether a witness may be compelled or made to provide testimony. This is a question of whether a witness is *compellable*.

Competence in its simplest interpretation is whether in law a witness is allowed to be a witness. For a witness to be compellable two aspects must be considered:

- the witness must be competent; *and*
- the law requires the witness to give evidence even if the witness would rather not do so.

Failure of a Witness to Attend Court

Should a witness who is compelled to attend court fail to do so, he/she may be found to be in contempt of court and may be punished accordingly. Whilst someone can be physically made to attend court, a witness may refuse to give evidence or to answer some question asked of them. Where a witness is compellable but acts in this way, he/she may also be dealt with for contempt of court. The court has a range of powers to deal with contempt of court and these include imprisonment.

General Rule of Competence and Compellability

There is a general rule in English law as to who is competent and compellable. This rule states that: 'All people are competent and all competent witnesses are compellable.'

Exceptions to the Rule of Competence and Compellability

There are a number of exceptions to the general rule and these relate to:

- the accused

- spouses
- children
- those of defective intelligence
- other special groups.

The Accused

Evidence on behalf of the prosecution
At common law the accused is not competent to give evidence on behalf of the prosecution. Thus, an accused person cannot give evidence against a co-accused at the same time. Should the prosecution wish to use the testimony of an accused against a co-accused he/she must first cease to be accused. This can occur in a number of ways, namely:

- where the accused is first acquitted of all matters against him/her;
- where the accused pleads guilty to the matters against him/her;
- if a successful application is made for separate trials;
- if no evidence is offered against him/her (referred to as entering a *nolle prosequi* a promise not to prosecute).

Example

A and B are jointly charged with the offence of indecent assault on a child. B cannot give evidence against A where they are tried together at the same time. Should the prosecution wish B to give evidence against A, he/she would first have to cease to be an accused person in the proceedings. This can be achieved by any of the methods described above (e.g. an application may be made to the trial judge for separate trials). If this were granted, B would then be able to give evidence against A.

Evidence on behalf of the defence
The Criminal Evidence Act 1898 sets out the position of whether an accused person is competent and compellable for the defence. Section 1 of the 1898 Act provides that:

> *Every person charged with an offence shall be a competent witness for the defence at every stage of the proceedings, whether the person so charged is charged solely or jointly with any other person. Provided as follows:*
>   *(a) A person so charged shall not be called as a witness in pursuance of this Act except upon his own application . . .*

Keynote

An accused person is competent as a witness should he/she choose to be. Once an accused decides to be a witness and provides evidence, he/she is treated as any other witness. In these circumstances the accused will be open to cross-examination by both the prosecution and any co-accused. Thus while an accused cannot give evidence as a witness against a co-accused on behalf of the prosecution, once he/she has given evidence on behalf of the *defence*, he/she may provide testimony against a co-accused. Moreover, the prosecution may cross-examine the accused about the co-accused.

Spouses

The position as to whether a spouse is competent and compellable is laid down by s. 80 of the Police and Criminal Evidence Act 1984. This provides that:

(1)   *In any proceedings the wife or husband of the accused shall be competent to give evidence—*
  (a)   *subject to subsection (4) below, for the prosecution; and*
  (b)   *on behalf of the accused or any person jointly charged with the accused.*
(2)   *In any proceedings the wife or husband of the accused shall, subject to subsection (4) below, be compellable to give evidence on behalf of the accused.*
(3)   *In any proceedings the wife or husband of the accused shall, subject to subsection (4) below, be compellable to give evidence for the prosecution or on behalf of any person jointly charged with the accused if and only if—*
  (a)   *the offence charged involves an assault on, or injury or a threat of injury to, the wife or husband of the accused or a person who at the material time is under the age of sixteen; or*
  (b)   *the offence charged is a sexual offence alleged to have been committed in respect of a person who was at the material time under that age;*
  (c)   *the offence charged consists of attempting or conspiring to commit, or of aiding, abetting, counselling, procuring or inciting the commission of, an offence falling within paragraph (a) or (b) above.*
(4)   *Where a husband and wife are jointly charged with an offence neither spouse shall at the trial be competent or compellable by virtue of subsection (1)(a), (2) or (3) above to give evidence in respect of that offence unless that spouse is not, or is no longer, liable to be convicted of that offence at the trial as a result of pleading guilty or for any other reason.*

Keynote

A spouse (other than when the husband and wife are jointly charged) is competent to give evidence on behalf of the *prosecution*.

A spouse is only compellable to give evidence on behalf of the *prosecution* (unless jointly charged) when:

- the offence charged involves an assault on, or injury or a threat of injury to, the wife or husband of the accused; or

- the offence charged involves an assault on, or injury or a threat of injury to, a person who at the material time is under the age of 16; or

- the offence charged is a sexual offence alleged to have been committed in respect of a person who was at the material time under 16; or

- in the case of aiding, abetting, counselling, procuring or inciting the commission of any of the above offences.

A spouse is competent and compellable to give evidence on behalf of the *accused*, unless jointly charged.

A spouse is competent to give evidence on behalf of any *co-accused*.

Children

The position of children to act as witnesses in criminal proceedings is set out in s. 33A of the Criminal Justice Act 1988 which provides that:

(1)   *A child's evidence in criminal proceedings shall be given unsworn.*
(2)   *A deposition of a child's unsworn evidence may be taken for the purpose of criminal proceedings as if that evidence has been given on oath.*
(2A)   *A child's evidence shall be received unless it appears to the court that the child is incapable of giving intelligible testimony.*
(3)   *In this section 'child' means a person under fourteen years of age.*

Keynote

This statutory provision requires that the evidence of any child under 14 years of age shall be given unsworn. The issue of whether a child is competent is set out in s. 33A(2A) (as inserted by the Criminal Justice and Public Order Act 1994).

There is no fixed age at which a child is incompetent to give evidence. It is for the court to decide whether an individual child is capable of giving 'intelligible testimony'.

Clearly, children will develop at differing ages and have different levels of understanding. The Court of Appeal in the case of *R* v *Hampshire* [1995] 2 All ER 1019 provides guidance in cases where the judge feels it is necessary to conduct an investigation of a child's competence. It was held that:

- the investigation should be dealt with at the earliest possible point;

- competence is based on the judge's perception of the child's understanding demonstrated through ordinary conversation (rather than examination and cross-examination);

- where an application is made to use video evidence, the judge's pre-trial view of the recording should normally allow him/her to decide competence, although this does not prevent further investigation;

- the investigation should be conducted in the presence of the accused but not the jury.

There is no longer a need for the court to establish whether a child understands the difference between telling the truth and telling a lie (*G* v *DPP* [1997] 2 All ER 755).

Issues of Age

The time when a person is deemed to have reached a particular age is covered by s. 9(1) of the Family Law Reform Act 1969.

The time at which a person attains a particular age expressed in years shall be the commencement of the relevant anniversary of the date of his/her birth.

Under s. 150 of the Magistrates' Courts Act 1980 provides that:

> *(4) Where the age of any person at any time is material for the purposes of any provision of this Act regulating the powers of a magistrates' court, his age at the material time shall be deemed to be or to have been that which appears to the court after considering any available evidence to be or to have been his age at that time.*

Keynote

Similar provisions appear in the following Acts:

- s. 1(6) of the Criminal Justice Act 1982 (for the purposes of sentencing young offenders (young offenders institution));

- s. 99 of the Children and Young Persons Act 1933 (parent or guardian assisting in the conduct of the defence);

- s. 28(5) of the Sexual Offences Act 1956 (causing or encouraging prostitution of, intercourse with, or indecent assault on, a girl under 16).

A birth certificate is usually accepted as evidence of age. A statement from a person present at the birth may be useful in difficult cases. If a certificate of birth is produced to prove age, evidence must also be provided to positively identify the person as the person named in the certificate (*R* v *Rogers* (1914) 10 Cr App R 276).

In *R* v *Viazani* (1867) 31 JP 260, it was held that where the statement of an accused as to his/her age is in conflict with his/her appearance the statement of the accused may be disregarded.

People with Defective Intellect

At common law, a person suffering from a defective intellect could be competent as a witness providing he/she understands the nature of the oath. This position was set out in *R* v *Hill* (1851) 2 Den CC 254, although it is contended that the courts will now view this decision with a different emphasis. Following a corresponding decision in *R* v *Hayes* [1977] 1 WLR 234 (which dealt with children's evidence), the courts are likely to take the view that the ability to understand the need to tell the truth was more important than an understanding of the religious meaning attached to the oath. Where such a person gives evidence it is for the jury to determine how much weight to attach to the testimony. Clearly, there is no inherent reason why a person suffering from a mental condition will not make a reliable witness.

Other Groups

In addition to the main exceptions outlined above, other people and groups may be incompetent or not compellable as witnesses. These situations are likely to be less frequent than the earlier exceptions:

- The Sovereign and Heads of State are competent but not compellable.

- Diplomats and consular officers may have total or partial immunity from being compelled.

- Restrictions also apply in respect of bankers and judges.

6.11.2 Hostile Witnesses

A party calling a witness, whether it be the defence or prosecution, would ordinarily do so in the expectation that the witness will be providing testimony that supports a point being advanced by that party. A witness may, however, provide unfavourable testimony to the side calling him/her (i.e. by not proving the matter intended or by proving the opposite). It is a general rule that a party calling a witness does not impeach the credit of his/her witness by asking leading questions or by general evidence of bad character.

However, should a witness not give his/her evidence fairly and show no regard for the truth as against the party calling him/her, the judge may deem that witness to be a hostile witness. In this instance, the party calling the witness may contradict him/her with other evidence or, with the leave of the judge, prove that on another occasion he/she made a statement inconsistent with the present testimony.

It is important to distinguish between an unfavourable witness and one who is hostile. Simply because a witness does not provide testimony to prove a matter does not make them hostile. A hostile witness goes beyond this.

Example

Consider the situation where the defence calls witness A to provide evidence of a particular issue, e.g. that A saw a particular car at a particular place. However, in giving testimony A, in good faith or as a result of an earlier misunderstanding, believes he was mistaken. In this instance A is an unfavourable witness. If, however, A in fact decides to lie and say he did not in fact see the car when he really did then A may be deemed by the judge to be a hostile witness.

6.11.3   Live Television Link

Witnesses will ordinarily give their evidence from the witness box. Statute, however, provides for a witnesses, in specified circumstances, to give their testimony through a live television link. Section 32(1) of the Criminal Justice Act 1988 sets out the circumstances where such a link can be used. A television link may only be used for certain witnesses, in specified proceedings and in relation to proscribed offences.

Witnesses to which s. 32 applies are people (other than the accused) who are either:

- outside the United Kingdom; or
- children.

A live television link may be used in trials on indictment, appeals to the Court of Appeal, proceedings in youth courts and appeals to the Crown Court arising from such proceedings.

Section 32 applies to the following offences:

- assault on, or injury or threat of injury to, a person;

- cruelty to a person under 16 under s. 1 of the Children and Young Persons Act 1933;

- offences under the Sexual Offences Act 1956, the Indecency with Children Act 1960, the Sexual Offences Act 1967, s. 54 of the Criminal Law Act 1977 or the Protection of Children Act 1978;

- attempting or conspiring to commit, or of aiding, abetting, counselling, procuring or inciting the commission of an offence to which s. 32 applies.

Before a television link can to be used, the above criteria must be met and the court then may give leave for witnesses to give their evidence in this way.

In addition, s. 57 of the Crime and Disorder Act 1998 provides for the use of live television links at preliminary court hearings where an accused is being detained in custody in prison or any other institution. The purpose of this provision is to reduce both delays in proceedings and the number of escapees from custody during transportation to and from courts.

Section 57 provides that:

> *(1) In any proceedings for an offence, a court may, after hearing representations from the parties, direct that the accused shall be treated as being present in the court for any particular hearing before the start of the trial if, during that hearing—*
> *(a) he is held in custody in a prison or other institution; and*
> *(b) whether by means of a live television link or otherwise, he is able to see and hear the court and to be seen and heard by it.*
> *(2) A court shall not give a direction under subsection (1) above unless—*
> *(a) it has been notified by the Secretary of State that facilities are available for enabling persons held in custody in the institution in which the accused is or is to be so held to see and hear the court and to be seen and heard by it; and*
> *(b) the notice has not been withdrawn.*
> *(3) If in a case where it has power to do so a magistrates' court decides not to give a direction under subsection (1) above, it shall give its reasons for not doing so.*
> *(4) In this section 'the start of the trial' has the meaning given by subsection (11A) or (11B) of section 22 of the 1985 Act.*

Keynote

For the purposes of s. 57 no consent is required from either the accused or his/her legal adviser; it is a matter for the discretion of the court.

The phrase 'start of trial' (s. 57(4)) means:

- for cases being tried summarily, at the point where the prosecution start to present their evidence or when a guilty plea is accepted;

- for cases being tried on indictment, when a jury is sworn to consider the issue of guilt or fitness to plead, or, before a jury is sworn, at the time a plea of guilty is accepted by the court.

6.11.4 Pre-recorded Video Evidence

In addition to the provision of a live television link under s. 32, s. 32A of the Criminal Justice Act 1988 enables video testimony to be used as evidence. Section 32A provides that in trials on indictment and in proceedings in youth courts, for any offence to which s. 32 applies, and in appeals from such proceedings, a pre-recorded video of an interview between an adult and a child, who is not the accused or one of them, may with the leave of the court, be given in evidence and stand as the child's evidence in chief.

A child is defined as a person who is under 14 years at the time of the recording in category 1 cases (offences of violence or cruelty) and under 17 years at the time of the recording in category 2 offences (sexual offences).

This provision is frequently used in child abuse investigations but applies to the full range of offences stated in s. 32. Providing the provisions of this section are met, instead of obtaining a statement from the child victim or witnesses, a video interview is conducted. This will ordinarily be done by a police officer and social worker who will follow the guidance for undertaking such interviews contained in the Memorandum of

Good Practice. If the court accepts the video it will be used as the child's 'evidence in chief'. Once the video is shown to the court, the child will be cross-examined in the normal way. This cross-examination may be conducted through a television link with the agreement of the court. The effect of these provisions is to reduce the trauma of a child having to recount his/her testimony in court. In *R v Sharman* [1998] 1 Cr App R 406 evidence recorded on video from a child aged 13 at the time of the interview was shown to the jury. The child, who had turned 14 by the time of the trial, was then cross-examined via a live television link. No oath or affirmation was administered and it was held that the 'live' questioning was inadmissible. A re-trial was ordered.

6.11.5   Refreshing Memory

Witnesses are frequently called upon to provide testimony where a considerable time has elapsed between the actual events and their appearance in court. In some instances, this time gap can involve a number of years. For police officers, who will be dealing with many such incidents, the problem is compounded. In addition, it would be unrealistic to expect a witness to provide accurate and reliable evidence without allowing them to refresh their memory by looking at some note or document recording the event.

A witness may refresh his/her memory by referring to a document that they made or verified providing certain criteria are met. Those criteria are:

- that the document was made or verified at the time of the incident, or shortly after, while the circumstances were fresh in the witness's mind;

- that the document is produced in court for inspection;

- where a witness has no recollection of the events, and is giving evidence as to the accuracy of the contents of the document, that the original document is used.

A witness may also refresh his/her memory from his/her own statement outside the court and before giving evidence. Where a witness refreshes his/her memory in this way the document may be inspected by the court.

In the case where a statement was made to the police some time after the event, it is quite reasonable for any witness, whether for the prosecution or defence, to refresh his/her memory by being allowed access to their statement. The giving of evidence is about reliability and not a test of memory (*R v Richardson* [1971] 2 QB 484; and *Lau Pak Ngarn v R* [1966] Crim LR 443).

There is no duty on either the defence or prosecution to inform the other party that the witness has refreshed his/her memory by reading a statement or other document. It should be assumed that the opponent's witnesses have seen their statements (*Worley v Bentley* [1976] 2 All ER 449; *R v Westwell* [1976] 2 All ER 812).

In *Owen v Edwards* (1983) 77 Cr App R 191, a police officer had refreshed his memory from his notebook outside the court, but had not used it in the witness box. It was held that the accused was entitled to examine the contents of the notebook and cross-examine the officer upon the relevant matters contained in it.

R v Skinner (1994) 99 Cr App R 212 determined that, in refreshing their memory, witnesses should not discuss their evidence with other witnesses. It would also not be proper to discuss or acquaint a witness with the contents of a document made by another witness, so as to refresh his/her memory before he/she gives evidence. In *R v Arif, The Times*, 17 June 1993, it was stated that, in criminal trials, pre-trial discussions of evidence between potential witnesses, the rehearsal of evidence and the coaching of witnesses are to be strongly discouraged because of the risk of abuse.

It was held in *R v Bass* [1953] 1 All ER 1064, that two witnesses who have acted together can refresh their memories from notes made in collaboration. A record should be made that the notes were made in collaboration. This is particularly significant for police officers who often witness events while in the company of other officers. The judgment stated:

> The officers' notes were almost identical. They were not made at the time of the interview. One officer made his notes after the appellant had been charged, and the other officer made his an hour later. . . . This court has observed that police officers nearly always deny that they have collaborated in the making of notes, and we cannot help wondering why they are the only class of society who do not collaborate in such a matter. It seems to us that nothing could be more natural or proper when two persons have been present at an interview with a third person than that they should afterwards make sure that they have a correct version of what was said. Collaboration would appear to be a better explanation of almost identical notes than the possession of a superhuman memory.

In *R v Cheng* [1976] Crim LR 379, it was held that a copy or extract of the original notes etc., can be used in court to refresh the witness's memory if once the witness's memory has been refreshed he/she can swear positively to the facts. Comments may be made regarding the use of a copy.

6.11.6 Evidence of Oral Statement made Through an Interpreter

It is inadmissible for a police officer to give evidence of a conversation held through the use of an interpreter. The only valid witness would be the interpreter (*R v Attard* (1958) 43 Cr App R 90).

6.11.7 Interference with Witnesses

The interference with witnesses or potential witnesses is included in the common law offence of perverting the course of public justice (as to which, **see Crime, chapter 15**).

6.11.8 Witnesses in Fear of Testifying

Section 23 of the Criminal Justice Act 1988 allows a witness statement to be read out where the witness 'does not give oral evidence through fear'. There have been a number of decided cases in relation to s. 23, particularly in attempting to define the term 'through fear'. In *R v Acton Justices, ex part McMullen* (1990) 92 Cr App R 98, it was suggested that the fear induced in the witness should be as a direct result of the crime itself or of something said or done afterwards in relation to the offence. However, in *R v Martin* [1996] Crim LR 589 it was held that there should be no restrictions on the manner in which the witness was put in fear. In *Martin*, the witness was put in fear by the appearance of a silent stranger at his door.

Whatever meaning is given to 'through fear', however, the maker's fear must be established by evidence to the appropriate standard of proof and such evidence must itself be admissible. Also, evidence which satisfies the conditions of admissibility under the 1988 Act may nevertheless fail to be excluded under s. 25 or 26 of the Act, under which provision the court is directed to consider where the interests of justice lie with regard to the admission of the offence.

In order to satisfy the requirements of s. 23, it is necessary for the court to hear oral evidence as to the fear. 'Fear' cannot be provided by a written statement made by a witness (*R* v *Belmarsh Magistrates' Court, ex parte Gilligan* [1998] 1 Cr App R 14 and *R* v *Radak, The Times*, 7 October 1998).

6.12 Examination-in-Chief

The party who calls a witness (prosecution or defence) is entitled to examine the witness by asking questions with a view to providing evidence which is favourable to that party's case. This is known as 'examination-in-chief'.

All witnesses are examined in chief with one exception; where the prosecution determine not to examine its witness in chief but allow the witness to be cross-examined by the defence. This is common in the case of police officers whose evidence-in-chief will be identical. Consequently, one police officer can give the evidence-in-chief but other officers involved may be required for cross-examination by the defence.

Cross-examination and re-examination are discussed in more detail below (**see paras 6.13 and 6.14**).

6.12.1 Leading Questions

The general rule is that leading questions, i.e. those which suggest the desired answer, may not be asked of a witness. However, it is quite common practice for a party to lead a witness through certain parts of his/her evidence which are not in dispute.

There are two forms of leading questions; those which indicate to a witness the answer required and those which assume something to be true when it has not been established.

The first form is where a question puts words into the witness's mouth. For example, if evidence is given that A assaulted B and the question for the court is whether the defendant did in fact assault B, a prosecution witness should not be asked 'Did you see the defendant assault B?', but should be asked 'Did you see anyone assault B? If so, who was it?'

6.12.2 Exceptions to the Leading Questions Rule

Where leading questions are asked of a witness, these do not nullify proceedings but the judge will stop a party asking questions in the prohibited form. Evidence obtained from leading questions is not *inadmissible* but may affect the *weight* placed on it by the judge or jury.

Leading questions are admissible in the following circumstances:

• To refresh a witness's memory (**see para. 6.11.5**).

• Where the witness is deemed 'hostile' (**see para. 6.11.2**).

- For identification purposes (**see chapter 16**).

- Usually in matters accepted as being uncontroversial.

- In cross-examination.

6.13   Cross-examination

Cross-examination is the process by which one party may ask questions of the other party's witnesses. This examination is usually focused on either undermining their evidence or supporting that of the party's own witnesses.

Cross-examination, like any other form of questioning, is subject to the rules of evidence. The answers elicited from the witness must be directly relevant to an issue in the case, or indirectly so, concerning evidence of collateral issues. A collateral issue is one which is only relevant to the credibility of the witness. In *Attorney-General* v *Hitchcock* (1847) 1 Exch 91, the court determined the general rule preventing a party from calling evidence on collateral issues. However, there are five exceptions to this general rule. These relate to where a witness:

- is biased;
- has previous convictions;
- has a reputation for untruthfulness;
- is unreliable because of some physical or mental disability or illness;
- has made a statement inconsistent with what he/she has said in the witness box.

The rules in relation to cross-examination do not prevent a party from asking the other party's witnesses about any matter which, if accepted by the witness, will undermine the witness's evidence.

Where a party decides not to cross-examine an opponent's witness, this is held to be an *acceptance* of the witness's evidence-in-chief. Consequently, it is not open to the party that failed to cross-examine to criticise, in a closing speech, the unchallenged evidence of the witness (*R* v *Bircham* [1972] Crim LR 430).

In *R* v *Bingham*, *The Times*, 15 March 1999, it was held that a defendant who goes into the witness box and is sworn thereby exposes himself/herself to cross-examination by the prosecution and any co-accused, even if he/she does not give any evidence-in-chief The prosecution is entitled to cross-examine the defendant even where no questions have been put to him/her by the defence counsel and adverse inferences can be drawn if the defendant does not answer those questions (**see chapter 11**).

6.13.1   Cross-examination in Rape Cases

At common law, evidence of voluntary acts of sexual intercourse between the accused and the complainant, if relevant, are admissible on the issue of consent on a charge of rape (*R* v *Riley* (1887) 18 QBD 481).

Cases dealing with the complainant's sexual experiences with people other than the accused however are subject to statute. Section 2 of the Sexual Offences (Amendment) Act 1976 provides that:

(1)   If at a trial any person is for the time being charged with a rape offence to which he pleads not guilty, then, except with the leave of the judge, no evidence and no question in cross-examination shall be adduced or asked at the trial, by or on behalf of any defendant at the trial, about any sexual experience of a complainant with a person other than that defendant.

(2)   The judge shall not give leave in pursuance of the preceding subsection for any evidence or question except on an application made to him in the absence of the jury by or on behalf of a defendant; and on such an application the judge shall give leave if and only if he is satisfied that it would be unfair to that defendant to refuse to allow the evidence to be adduced or the question to be asked.

Keynote

Under s. 7(2) of the 1976 Act, 'rape' includes rape, attempted rape, incitement to rape, and aiding and abetting or counselling or procuring rape or attempted rape. By the Criminal Justice and Public Order Act 1994, sch. 10, para. 35, the provision also applies to male victims (**see Crime, chapter 10**).

The purpose of s. 2 is to prevent the complainant's evidence from being attacked by general accusations of promiscuity. The provision does not limit the right to cross-examine the witness about his/her sexual experience with the accused. Additionally, there is no effect on examining the complainant on evidence which he/she has given 'in chief' (**see para. 6.12**) concerning his/her sexual experience.

In *R* v *Viola* [1982] 3 All ER 73, the phrase 'sexual experience' within s. 2 was interpreted as meaning more than just sexual activity and may include conversations in which the complainant indicates a willingness for such an activity. It was held that where the complainant's sexual habits or experience are relevant to an issue in the case, the judge should give leave for him/her to be asked about them. The credibility of a witness would not be undermined in considering his/her sexual habits. This case repeated the decision in *R* v *Mills* (1978) 68 Cr App R 327 where the purpose of s. 2 was seen to protect a complainant from irrelevant but distressing cross-examination.

In cases involving sexual offences it may be appropriate for the judge, in the absence of the jury, to elicit the nature of the unrepresented defendant's case and the points where there are issue(s) with the complainant's evidence. The defendant should be allowed to question the complainant but the judge should prevent repetitious questioning, if necessary taking over the questioning of the complainant himself/herself. If the defendant tries to humiliate or intimidate the witness the judge should order the erection of a screen between them (*R* v *Brown*, *The Times*, 7 May 1998).

In *R* v *Holmes* (1871) LR 1 CCR 334 it was held that, where the defence are entitled to cross-examine the complainant in relation to previous sexual relations, they must accept the complainant's answers as final.

Although s. 2 of the 1976 Act does not apply, for example in a case of unlawful sexual intercourse, the court will be mindful that the cross-examination is not abused or extended unnecessarily (*R* v *Funderburk* [1990] 1 WLR 587).

At common law it is permissible to ask the complainant whether she is a prostitute and to call evidence as to this matter if it is denied (*R* v *Holmes* (1891) LR 1 CCR 334 and *R* v *Bashir* [1969] 1 WLR 1303). However, it must be shown that such questioning is relevant and prostitutes may be victims of rape in the same way as anyone else.

For restrictions on the availability of statements and other evidence in sexual offence cases, **see Crime, chapter 10**).

6.14 Re-examination

Following cross-examination, the party calling the witness is entitled to re-examine. The questions put to the witness at this time may only relate to those matters upon which there was a cross-examination. No leading questions are allowed within the re-examination of a witness.

After the defendant has been re-examined it is open to the judge to ask questions to clear up uncertainties, to fill gaps, or to answer queries which might be lurking in the jury's mind. It is not appropriate for the judge to cross-examine the witness (*R* v *Wiggan*, *The Times*, 22 March 1999).

6.15 Further Evidence

It is the general rule that the prosecution must call the whole of their evidence before closing their case (*R* v *Francis* [1991] 1 All ER 225).

However, there are two well established exceptions to the general rule. The first exception is where the prosecution is allowed to call evidence in rebuttal which has arisen *ex improviso* (*R* v *Pilcher* (1974) 60 Cr App R 1). The other exception is where evidence may be called that is a mere formality as distinct from a central issue (*Royal* v *Prescott-Clarke* [1966] 2 All ER 366).

There is a third exception, identified in *R* v *Francis* [1991] 1 All ER 225, which is much wider. The essence of this exception is its flexibility which should only be exercised 'on the rarest of occasions'. The judge did not interpret this discretion but allowed a police inspector to be recalled to provide evidence of a group identification in relation to where particular participants had been standing. This evidence had not been required during the examination-in-chief or cross-examination due to a misunderstanding between counsel.

New evidence may be admitted in appeals for criminal cases as provided by s. 23(1) of the Criminal Appeal Act 1968. Section 23 allows the Court of Appeal, 'if they think it necessary or expedient in the interests of justice' *inter alia* to receive the evidence, if tendered, of any competent but not compellable witness or to order any compellable witness to attend for examination, whether or not that witness was called at the trial. In *R* v *Ahluwalia* [1992] 4 All ER 889, s. 23 was used to admit fresh evidence of the accused's alleged endogenous depression which, if put forward at the trial, may have provided an arguable defence to the charge of murder.

6.16 Presence of Witnesses in Court

It is the general rule for all witnesses not to be present in court until called to give evidence. An exception to the rule relates specifically to expert witnesses who are never excluded from court. The police officer in charge of the case is also allowed to remain in court at least until the start of police evidence. If a witness is in the court, he/she may be required by the judge to withdraw until called to give evidence. If a witness deliberately remains in court after being required to withdraw, the evidence of the witness may not be admitted. However, a judge has no grounds to exclude a witness's testimony solely on the grounds that the witness had been in court before giving evidence (*R* v *Briggs* (1930) 22 Cr App R 68; and *Tomlinson* v *Tomlinson* [1980] 1 WLR 322).

CHAPTER SEVEN

YOUTH JUSTICE

7.1 Introduction

The government, aware of the growth of partnership schemes between agencies to reduce crime and insecurity, have created a framework under the Crime and Disorder Act 1998 in which these partnership schemes can develop.

Sections 6 and 7 of the 1998 Act seek to create this framework, with the responsibility for formulating a strategy for the reduction of crime and disorder resting jointly on local authorities and chief officers of police. The police and councils have equal stakes in this process and both are under a mutual duty to co-operate with every police authority, probation committee and health authority whose area of responsibility coincides with any part of the relevant local government area (s. 5(1)).

The local government areas for which strategies must be formulated are districts, London boroughs, the City of London, the Isle of Wight and the Isles of Scilly, and in Wales counties and county boroughs (s. 5(4)).

The Home Secretary may also prescribe by order other bodies or persons to cooperate or participate in the formulation and implementation of the strategy (s. 5(2) and s. 5(3)). Such other bodies could include youth services, training institutions, schools, the Crown Prosecution Service, Drug Action Teams, Area Criminal Justice Liaison committees, etc.

The Home Office have produced a publication, 'Guidance on Statutory Crime and Disorder Partnerships', which provides detailed guidance on strategies and responsibilities.

It will be important that local crime strategies are consistent with the police authorities annual policing plans.

7.2 Youth Justice Scheme

The importance of the inter-agency approach to youth justice is not new, with joint initiatives for 16 and 17-year-old offenders being encouraged by the Criminal Justice

Act 1991 and Home Office Circular 30/1992. However, the government considered that action was necessary to provide a more consistent approach in dealing with young offenders.

Section 37 of the Crime and Disorder Act 1998 provides the aim of the youth justice scheme:

(1) It shall be the principal aim of the youth justice system to prevent offending by children and young persons.
(2) In addition to any other duty to which they are subject, it shall be the duty of all persons and bodies carrying out functions in relation to the youth justice system to have regard to that aim.

Keynote

The 'persons and bodies' referred to in s. 37(2) will be all those working within the youth justice system. This will include local authorities, health authorities, probation services, voluntary agencies, the police and the courts.

Local authorities will have a duty, acting in co-operation with these persons and bodies, to provide all youth justice services (s. 38(1)). These services will be determined by national standards drawn up by the Youth Justice Board (**see para. 7.5 below**). The duty will be performed in co-operation with every chief officer of police or police authority and every probation committee or health authority (s. 38(2)).

Section 37(1) provides a 'principal aim' and this should not have an effect on other considerations such as: the duty a lawyer owes to his/her client; the duty a Crown Prosecutor has with regard to the Code of Crown Prosecutors (**see appendix 1**); and the means by which re-offending may be dealt with, i.e. the use of a custodial order. The sentencing courts principal aim will be the prevention of re-offending generally by children and young persons.

7.3   Youth Offending Teams

Although multi-agency approaches to crime prevention and crime reduction had already been embraced by the police and local authorities such approaches were diverse and dependent on local arrangements. The provisions of s. 39 of the Crime and Disorder Act 1998 formalises this multi-agency approach with the introduction of youth offending teams. Section 39 provides that:

(1) Subject to subsection (2) below, it shall be the duty of each local authority, acting in co-operation with the persons and bodies mentioned in subsection (3) below, to establish for their area one or more youth offending teams.
(2) Two (or more) local authorities acting together may establish one or more youth offending teams for both (or all) their areas; . . .

The 'persons and bodies' referred to in subsection (1) differ from those found in s. 38(2) and are contained in s. 39(3) which provides:

(3) It shall be the duty of—
(a) every chief officer of police any part of whose police area lies within the local authority's area; and
(b) every probation committee or health authority any part of whose area lies within that area, to co-operate in the discharge by the local authority of their duty under subsection (1) above.

Keynote

Youth offending teams will carry out those functions which are required of the team within the local authority's youth justice plan (**see para. 7.4 below**).

The primary work of the youth offending teams will be quite diverse and is likely to include:

- a 'responsible officer' role in relation to parenting and child safety orders; assessment and intervention work;
- supervision of community sentences;
- an 'appropriate adult' service for police interviews;
- bail information, supervision and support;
- placement of young offenders;
- court work and preparation of reports.

The provisions of both s. 38 (local provision of youth justice services) and s. 39 (youth offending teams) are being piloted in Hammersmith and Fulham, Kensington and Chelsea, and Westminster (jointly); Lewisham; Hampshire, Southampton, Portsmouth and the Isle of Wight (jointly); Devon; Sheffield; St Helens; Wolverhampton; Blackburn and Darwen; and Luton and Bedfordshire (jointly).

7.4 Youth Justice Plans

The purpose of youth justice plans is to prevent re-offending by children and young persons.

A duty to produce these plans is provided by s. 40 of the Crime and Disorder Act 1998 which states:

> (1)   It shall be the duty of each local authority, after consultation with the relevant persons and bodies, to formulate and implement for each year a plan (a 'youth justice plan') setting out—
> (a)   how youth justice services in their area are to be provided and funded; and
> (b)   how the youth offending team or teams established by them (whether alone or jointly with one or more other local authorities) are to be composed and funded, how they are to operate, and what functions they are to carry out.

Keynote

The youth justice plans are a similar provision to those statutory requirements to produce plans already placed upon the police (s. 8 of the Police Act 1996 — annual policing plan), local authorities (Children Act 1989 — children's services plan) and education (s. 9 Education Act 1997 — plan to deal with behaviourally difficult pupils, truants, etc.). These existing plans have different overall objectives there will need to be some coordination and dialogue in the production of youth justice plans.

7.5 Youth Justice Board

Section 41(1) of the Crime and Disorder Act 1998 creates a body corporate known as the Youth Justice Board. The Board consists of 10, 11 or 12 members appointed by the Secretary of State (s. 41(2)) and these members will have extensive experience of the youth justice system (s. 41(4)). Members will be appointed for a fixed period no longer than five years and may be re-appointed provided the total length of service does not exceed ten years (sch. 2, para. 2(5)).

The functions of the Board are provided by s. 41(5) which states:

> *(5)   The Board shall have the following functions, namely—*
>
>   *(a)   to monitor the operation of the youth justice system and the provision of youth justice services;*
>   *(b)   to advise the Secretary of State on the following matters, namely—*
>   *(i)   the operation of that system and the provision of such services;*
>   *(ii)   how the principal aim of that system might most effectively be pursued;*
>   *(iii)   the content of any national standards he may see fit to set with respect to the provision of such services, or the accommodation in which children and young persons are kept in custody; and*
>   *(iv)   the steps that might be taken to prevent offending by children and young persons;*
>   *(c)   to monitor the extent to which that aim is being achieved and any such standards met;*
>   *(d)   for the purposes of paragraphs (a), (b) and (c) above, to obtain information from relevant authorities;*
>   *(e)   to publish information so obtained;*
>   *(f)   to identify, to make known and promote good practice in the following matters, namely—*
>   *(i)   the operation of the youth justice system and the provision of youth justice services;*
>   *(ii)   the prevention of offending by children and young persons; and*
>   *(iii)   working with children and young persons who are or are at risk of becoming offenders.*
>   *(g)   to make grants, with the approval of the Secretary of State, to local authorities or other bodies for them to develop such practice, or to commission research in connection with such practice; and*
>   *(h)   themselves to commission research in connection with such practice.*

Keynote

The Youth Justice Board came into effect on 1 August 1998.

The Board will provide the framework, context and information base within which local authorities and youth offending teams will operate. It will also be responsible for providing advice on the national standards to be used by the youth offending teams and youth justice services.

7.6   Reprimands and Warnings

The system of police cautions is replaced by s. 65 of the Crime and Disorder Act 1998 which introduces a system of reprimands and warnings for young offenders. Although police cautions are considered useful, they are not seen as sufficient without other support structures. The system of cautioning is also believed to be too haphazard; there is no consistency across police forces and repeated and ineffective cautioning has a minimal effect on re-offending.

7.6.1   Reprimand

Section 65(1) and (2) of the 1998 Act provide a constable with a power to reprimand an offender where:

> *(a)   a constable has evidence that a child or young person ('the offender') has committed an offence;*
> *(b)   the constable considers that the evidence is such that, if the offender were prosecuted for the offence, there would be a realistic prospect of his being convicted;*
> *(c)   the offender admits to the constable that he committed the offence;*
> *(d)   the offender has not previously been convicted of an offence; and*
> *(e)   the constable is satisfied that it would not be in the public interest for the offender to be prosecuted.*

Keynote

An offender may only be reprimanded where he/she has not previously been reprimanded or warned (s. 65(2)).

7.6.2   Warning

Section 65(3) of the 1998 Act provides a constable with a power to warn an offender where:

> (a)   the offender has not previously been warned; or
> (b)   where the offender has previously been warned, the offence was committed more than two years after the date of the previous warning and the constable considers the offence to be not so serious as to require a charge to be brought;
> but no person may be warned under paragraph (b) above more than once.

7.6.3   Reprimand and Warning: Police Powers

In relation to the giving of a reprimand or warning s. 65(5) of the 1998 Act provides that a police officer must:

> (a)   give any reprimand or warning at a police station and, where the offender is under the age of 17, in the presence of an appropriate adult; and
> (b)   explain to the offender and, where he is under that age, the appropriate adult in ordinary language—
> (i)   in the case of a reprimand, the effect of subsection 5(a) of section 66 below;
> (ii)   in the case of a warning, the effect of subsections (1), (2), (4) and (5)(b) and (c) of that section, and any guidance issued under subsection (3) of that section.

Keynote

In relation to s. 65(5)(b)(i) above, s. 66(5)(a) provides that a reprimand may be cited in criminal proceedings in the same way as a conviction.

In relation to s. 65(5)(b)(ii) above, explanations of each of the subsections referred to are provided in brackets:

- s. 66(1) (referral to youth offending team);
- s. 66(2) (participation in a rehabilitation programme);
- s. 66(4) (restrictions on a court to impose a conditional discharge);
- s. 66(5)(b) and (c) (citation as a criminal conviction).

Reprimands and warnings have been piloted in specific areas since 30 September 1998 and it is expected they will come into full operation in October 2000.

CHAPTER EIGHT

YOUTH CRIME AND DISORDER

8.1 | **Introduction**

This chapter contains details of the provisions included in the Crime and Disorder Act 1998 designed to address the causes of youth crime. These provisions are contained in Part I of the 1998 Act and relate to:

- parenting orders

- child safety orders

- local child curfew schemes

- removal of truants to designated premises, etc.

Section 16 of the 1998 Act (removal of truants to designated premises, etc.) came into force in December 1998. The provisions relating to parenting orders, child safety orders and local child curfew schemes, are all subject to 18 month pilot studies which commenced in September 1998.

The 18 month pilot studies are taking place in the following nine selected areas: Hammersmith and Fulham, Kensington and Chelsea and Westminster (jointly); Lewisham; Hampshire, Southampton, Portsmouth and the Isle of Wight (jointly); Wolverhampton; Sheffield; Luton and Bedfordshire (jointly); Devon; St Helens; parts of Sunderland.

The main purpose of the pilot studies is to determine appropriate rules of court in relation to parenting and child safety orders.

It is anticipated that these provisions will be dealt with in greater detail in the 2001 edition of this Manual.

8.2 | **Parenting Orders**

These orders are about influencing parental responsibility and control and the importance placed upon this by the government. The orders were introduced to give parents more help and support to change the criminal and/or anti-social behaviour of their children in providing a framework where parents participate in their child's supervision. The strategy here is one of prevention in attempting to dissuade a recurrence of criminality or truancy.

Parenting orders are defined by s. 8 of the Crime and Disorder Act 1998:

> (4)   A parenting order is an order which requires the parent—
>   (a)   to comply, for a period not exceeding twelve months, with such requirements as are specified in the order; and
>   (b)   . . . to attend for a concurrent period not exceeding three months and not more than once in any week, such counselling and guidance sessions as may be specified in directions given by the responsible officer; . . .

In considering the requirements of an order s. 9 of the 1998 Act provides:

> (4)   Requirements specified in, and directions given under, a parenting order shall, as far as practicable, be such as to avoid—
>   (a)   any conflict with the parent's religious beliefs; and
>   (b)   any interference with the times, if any, at which he normally works or attends an educational establishment.

Keynote

For the purpose of the 1998 Act, 'child' is someone under the age of 14 and 'young person' is someone of 14 years or over but under 18 (s. 117).

'Parenting order' should not be confused with 'parental responsibility order' (Children Act 1989) and 'parental order' (Human Embryology and Fertilisation Act 1990) which are available for other purposes.

For the provisions relating to anti-social behaviour orders under the Crime and Disorder Act 1998, **see General Police Duties, chapter 3**.

8.2.1   Counselling and Guidance

Counselling and guidance sessions referred to in s. 8(4)(b) of the 1998 Act are intended to educate parents in how to respond more effectively to the demands of their child. These sessions could include the setting and enforcement of consistent standards of behaviour or a requirement that the child be escorted to school by a responsible adult.

Where a parent has attended counselling and guidance sessions under an earlier parenting order the court may waive this requirement (s. 8(5)).

The requirements provided by s. 8(4)(a) above are not specified but in drafting the legislation certain examples were given. These included a parent escorting their child to school and a child being supervised by a responsible adult during the evenings.

8.2.2   Responsible Officer

The definition of 'responsible officer' is provided in s. 8(8) of the 1998 Act which states:

> In this section and section 9 below 'responsible officer', in relation to a parenting order, means one of the following who is specified in the order, namely—
>   (a)   a probation officer;
>   (b)   a social worker of a local authority social services department; and
>   (c)   a member of a youth offending team

8.2.3 | **The Parenting Order**

Section 8 of the 1998 Act provides that:

> (1) This section applies where, in any court proceedings—
> (a) a child safety order is made in respect of a child;
> (b) an anti-social behaviour order or sex offender order is made in respect of a child or young person;
> (c) a child or young person is convicted of an offence; or
> (d) a person is convicted of an offence under section 443 (failure to comply with a school attendance order) or section 444 (failure to secure regular attendance at a school of registered pupil) of the Education Act 1996.
> (2) Subject to subsection (3) and section 9(1) below, if in the proceedings the court is satisfied that the relevant condition is fulfilled, it may make a parenting order in respect of a person who is a parent or guardian of the child or young person or, as the case may be, the person convicted of the offence under section 443 or 444 ('the parent').

Keynote

An order may be made against:

- One or both biological parents (this could include an order against a father who may not be married to the mother).

- A person who is a guardian.

Guardians are defined as any person who, in the opinion of the court, has for the time being the care of a child or young person (s. 117(1)).

The court will be required to establish whether or not the making of an order is 'desirable' in the circumstances of a particular case. This is seen as an entirely subjective test (except for the requirement in s. 9(1)(a) below), following on from s. 8(2) above which states that the court *may* make an order. Consequently, the court generally retains a discretion not to impose an order.

8.2.4 | **Parenting Order: Statutory Requirement**

Section 9 of the 1998 Act provides:

> (1) Where a person under the age of 16 is convicted of an offence, the court by or before which he is so convicted—
> (a) if it is satisfied that the relevant condition is fulfilled, shall make a parenting order; and
> (b) if it is not so satisfied, shall state in open court that it is not and why not.

Keynote

Section 9(1) provides a statutory requirement in favour of making an order where the relevant condition relates to where a child or young person (under 16) is convicted of an offence (s. 8(1)(c)).

In determining the legislation the government decided to provide a distinction between offenders under 16 and those of 16 and 17. The decision appears to have been made on advice concerning the differences in emotional, intellectual and physical development between juveniles aged 16 and 17 and younger children. It was considered that parents of those under 16 who are subject to criminal proceedings must be involved in preventing a further commission of an offence. For 16 and 17 year olds the court should determine any parental involvement.

8.2.5 | **Procedure**

Apart from considering information about the family circumstances of each case, whatever the age of the child or young person, s. 9(3) of the 1998 Act places the following requirement on the court:

> *(3)   Before making a parenting order, a court shall explain to the parent in ordinary language—*
> *(a)   the effect of the order and of the requirements proposed to be included in it;*
> *(b)   the consequences which may follow (under subsection (7) below) if he fails to comply with any of those requirements; and*
> *(c)   that the court has power (under subsection (5) below) to review the order on the application either of the parent or of the responsible officer.*

Keynote

The parent or responsible officer can apply for the discharge or variation of an order and the court can agree to cancel, add or substitute any of its provisions. This can only be done by the court making the original order.

8.2.6 | **Breach of a Parenting Order**

Section 9(7) of the 1998 Act provides:

> *If while a parenting order is in force the parent without reasonable excuse fails to comply with any requirement included in the order, or specified in directions given by the responsible officer, he shall be liable on summary conviction to a fine not exceeding level 3 on the standard scale.*

Keynote

The section does not specify who would be responsible for instituting proceedings but it is assumed this will be the 'responsible officer' and that the normal processes will be followed whereby the Crown Prosecution Service will make decisions as to a prosecution applying the usual test of public interest.

8.3 | **Child Safety Orders**

These orders have been introduced to help prevent children under 10 from turning to crime. Such orders are concerned with the child's potential offending behaviour and in practice are likely to be used in conjunction with parenting orders under s. 8 of the Crime and Disorder Act 1998.

Section 11 of the 1998 Act provides:

> *(1)   Subject to subsection (2) below, if a magistrates' court, on the application of a local authority, is satisfied that one or more of the conditions specified in subsection (3) below are fulfilled with respect to a child under the age of 10, it may make an order (a 'child safety order') which—*
> *(a)   places the child, for a period (not exceeding the permitted maximum) specified in the order, under the supervision of the responsible officer; and*
> *(b)   requires the child to comply with such requirements as are so specified.*

Keynote

In order to ensure any such proceedings are not viewed as 'criminal', jurisdiction for making the order rests with the magistrates' family proceedings court.

The section provides evidence of the government's determination to deliver crime prevention through a partnership approach. A local authority with social services responsibilities must make the application for such an order. However, it would probably be the police who first become aware of the misconduct which triggers such an application.

8.3.1 | **Child Safety Order: Conditions**

The court must be satisfied that one or more of four conditions are fulfilled before making an order. These are provided by s. 11(3) of the 1998 Act:

> (a)   that the child has committed an act which, if he had been aged 10 or over, would have constituted an offence;
> (b)   that a child safety order is necessary for the purpose of preventing the commission by the child of such an act as is mentioned in paragraph (a) above;
> (c)   that the child has contravened a ban imposed by a curfew notice; and
> (d)   that the child has acted in a manner that caused or was likely to cause harassment, alarm or distress to one or more persons not of the same household as himself.

Keynote

The civil standard of evidence (the 'balance of probabilities') is the standard of proof in determining whether a condition is fulfilled. There is no minimum age for an order. The permitted maximum period of supervision of such an order is three months. If the court is satisfied that the circumstances of the case are exceptional it can extend the order up to a maximum of 12 months (s. 11(4)).

8.3.2 | **Breach of Child Safety Order**

Section 12(6) of the 1998 Act provides:

> (6)   Where a child safety order is in force and it is proved to the satisfaction of the court which made it or another magistrates' court acting for the same petty sessions area, on the application of the responsible officer, that the child has failed to comply with any requirement included in the order, the court—
> (a)   may discharge the order and make in respect of him a care order under subsection 1(a) of section 31 of the 1989 Act; or
> (b)   may make an order varying the order—
>   (i)   by cancelling any provision included in it; or
>   (ii)   by inserting in it (either in addition to or in substitution for any of its provisions) any provision that could have been included in the order if the court had then had power to make it and were exercising the power.

Keynote

'Section 31 of the 1989 Act' relates to the Children Act 1989. The provisions in this subsection provides a new route into care. Although the section does not provide the court with the power to make a supervision order in response to a breach, there is nothing to stop an application being made for such an order by a local authority or other authorised person in the ordinary way.

8.4 | **Child Curfew Schemes**

The government has introduced these schemes to tackle the problem of unsupervised young children (under 10) committing crime, anti-social activities and causing real harm and misery to local communities. Again this is part of the wider community safety strategy with the onus being placed on local councils to make use of local child curfews as a response to identified problems.

Section 14 of the Crime and Disorder Act 1998 provides:

> *(1)   A local authority may make a scheme (a 'local child curfew scheme') for enabling the authority—*
>
> > *(a)   subject to and in accordance with the provisions of the scheme; and*
> >
> > *(b)   if, after such consultation as is required by the scheme, the authority considers it necessary*
>
> *to do so for the purpose of maintaining order,*
>
> *to give a notice imposing, for a specified period (not exceeding 90 days), a ban to which subsection (2) below applies.*
>
> *(2)   This subsection applies to a ban on children of specified ages (under 10) being in a public place within a specified area—*
>
> > *(a)   during specified hours (between 9 pm and 6 am); and*
> >
> > *(b)   otherwise than under the effective control of a parent or a responsible person aged 18 or over.*

Keynote

The authority is required to consult with every chief constable whose force area covers any part of the authority's area. There is also the requirement for the authority to consult such persons or other bodies as the authority considers appropriate (s. 14(3)).

The authority does not need the *consent* of the chief constable, though without this it would be difficult for the curfew conditions to be enforced.

The extent of the authority's obligation to consult with other persons or bodies is totally discretionary. However, should it not consult with appropriate community groups the Home Secretary may not confirm the scheme (see below).

The Home Secretary is required to confirm the introduction of any scheme and may fix the date when it is to come into operation (s. 14(5)). It is envisaged that most schemes would come into force one month after confirmation.

'Public place' for the purpose of the section has the same meaning as in Part II of the Public Order Act 1986 (s. 14(8)) (**see General Police Duties, chapter 4**).

8.4.1   **Contravention of Curfew Notices**

Section 15 of the 1998 Act provides:

> *(1)   Subsections (2) and (3) below apply where a constable has reasonable cause to believe that a child is in contravention of a ban imposed by a curfew notice.*
>
> *(2)   The constable shall, as soon as practicable, inform the local authority for the area that the child has contravened the ban.*
>
> *(3)   The constable may remove the child to the child's place of residence unless he has reasonable cause to believe that the child would, if removed to that place, be likely to suffer significant harm.*

Keynote

This provision does not give the constable a power to use force. However, in applying common law principles, a constable may use reasonable force in exercising a lawful power (**see General Police Duties, chapter 2**).

Section 15(3) does not state what a constable should do with a child if he/she does not remove the child to its home. However, it would seem appropriate to use the power under s. 46 of the Children Act 1989 in removing the child to suitable accommodation, i.e. a police station or care of social services (**see Crime, chapter 11**).

Where a constable has informed the local authority about a contravention of the curfew notice s. 15(4) places a duty on the local authority to enquire into the circumstances of the child and to initiate the investigation within 48 hours of receiving such notification.

8.5   Removal of Truants to Designated Premises, etc.

Truancy from school has been viewed as a significant problem for some time and research has shown that there is a close association between truancy and crime. Although a number of local initiatives between the police and schools have existed for some time the provisions now provide the police with a means of dealing with truants.

Section 16 provides:

> (1)   This section applies where a local authority—
> (a)   designates premises in a police area ('designated premises') as premises to which children and young persons of compulsory school age may be removed under this section; and
> (b)   notifies the chief officer of police for that area of the designation.
> (2)   A police officer of or above the rank of superintendent may direct that the powers conferred on a constable by subsection (3) below—
> (a)   shall be exercisable as respects any area falling within the police area and specified in the direction; and
> (b)   shall be so exercisable during a period specified;
> and references in that subsection to a specified area and a specified period shall be construed accordingly.

Keynote

'Designated premises' are not defined in the 1998 Act and are a matter for the local authority. In drafting the legislation it was considered that in many cases children would ultimately be removed to their own schools.

8.5.1   Police Powers

Section 16(3) provides the police powers in relation to dealing with truants:

> (3)   If a constable has reasonable cause to believe that a child or young person found by him in a public place in a specified area during a specified period—
> (a)   is of compulsory school age; and
> (b)   is absent from school without lawful authority,
> the constable may remove the child or young person to designated premises, or to the school from which he is so absent.

Keynote

Again 'public place' has the same meaning as in Part II of the Public Order Act 1986.

'Without lawful authority' is qualified by subsection (4) in that lawful authority will be that which falls within s. 444 of the Education Act 1996 — leave, sickness, unavoidable cause or day set apart for religious observation.

The power of a constable to remove a child or young person to 'designated premises' is not an arrest in the traditional sense of detention and statutory powers relating to arrests will not apply. However, the duty to explain the reason for a persons 'seizure' may well apply in such cases (as to which, **see General Police Duties, chapter 2**).

As with the powers conferred in relation to curfew notices (**see para. 8.4 above**), it appears probable that the common law rule entitling a constable to use reasonable force would apply. However, legal commentators are not convinced this is the case as the use of force could be seen as having a damaging effect on relations between the police and young persons and the possibility of criminal or civil action against individual officers.

The requirement for the officer to have 'reasonable cause to believe' that the person meets the criteria at (a) and (b) is more stringent than mere suspicion (**see General Police Duties, chapter 2**).

CHAPTER NINE

SENTENCING

9.1 | **Introduction**

This chapter is intended to provide an overview of the powers of the courts in relation to sentencing offenders. It deals with custodial sentences of adults and young offenders, non-custodial sentences, including community sentences.

9.2 | **Custody of Adults**

9.2.1 | **Custodial Sentence**

A court's power to impose a custodial sentence on an offender is provided by s. 1 of the Criminal Justice Act 1991 which states:

> *(1) This section applies where a person is convicted of an offence punishable with a custodial sentence other than one fixed by law or falling to be imposed under section 2(2), 3(2), or 4(2) of the Crime (Sentences) Act 1997.*
> *(2) Subject to subsection (3) below, the court shall not pass a custodial sentence on the offender unless it is of the opinion—*
> *(a) that the offence, or the combination of the offence and one or more offences associated with it, was so serious that only such a sentence can be justified for the offence; or*
> *(b) where the offence is a violent or sexual offence, that only such a sentence would be adequate to protect the public from serious harm from him.*
> *(3) Nothing in subsection (2) above shall prevent the court from passing a custodial sentence on the offender if he fails to express his willingness to comply with—*
> *(a) a requirement which is proposed by the court to be included in a probation order or supervision order and which requires an expression of such willingness; or*
> *(b) a requirement which is proposed by the court to be included in a drug treatment and testing order or an order under section 61(6) of the Crime and Disorder Act 1998.*

Keynote

Where a court imposes a custodial sentence, it is required to state in open court that it is of the opinion that either or both of the requirements of s. 1(2) apply and why it is of that opinion. In any case the court is required to explain to the offender, in open court and ordinary language, why it is passing a custodial sentence (s. 1(4)).

In relation to a magistrates' court, this explanation needs to be specified in the commitment warrant and be entered on the court register (s. 1(5)).

Generally, before imposing a custodial sentence a court would obtain a 'pre-sentence report' in order to ascertain if the grounds outlined in s. 1(2) are met (s. 3(1)).

'Custodial sentence' for a person over 21 means a sentence of imprisonment and includes a discretionary life sentence and a suspended sentence.

'Custodial sentence' for a person under 21 means a sentence of detention in a young offender institution, detention during Her Majesty's pleasure (s. 53(2) of the Children and Young Persons Act 1933), sentence of custody for life (s. 8(2) of the Criminal Justice Act 1982), a secure training order and, a detention and training order (**see below**).

Pre-sentence Report

A 'pre-sentence report' is a written report to assist the court and is prepared by one of the following: probation officer; social worker; member of a youth offending team for persons under 18 (s. 3(5)).

Such a report may not be required by the court if it considers, in the circumstances of the case, that such a report is unnecessary (s. 3(2) of the 1991 Act).

Seriousness of the Offence

In determining whether an offence 'was so serious that only such a sentence can be justified for the offence' (s. 1(2)(a)), guidance is provided by a number of decided cases, the most recent of which being *R* v *Howells* [1998] Crim LR 836. It was argued in this case that laying down prescriptive rules as to what constituted 'serious' was both 'dangerous and wrong'.

However, a number of issues were discussed as to what factors might be considered in determining whether an offence was serious. These included:

* deliberate and premeditated actions as opposed to spontaneous and unpremeditated;

* where personal injury or mental trauma were inflicted as opposed to solely financial loss;

* the offender's previous convictions and response to previous sentences;

* whether the offence was committed while the defendant was on bail.

In borderline cases, it was considered appropriate for the court to take into account the:

* early admission of the offence;

* genuine remorse shown by the offender;

* youth and immaturity of the offender;

* good character of the offender;

- offender's family responsibilities;

- physical or mental disability of the offender;

- offender not previously having served a custodial sentence.

Seriousness of the Offence: Racially Aggravated Offence

In gauging issues relevant to the seriousness of the offence a further factor was introduced by s. 82 of the Crime and Disorder Act 1998. This section states:

> *(1)   This section applies where a court is considering the seriousness of an offence other than one under sections 29 to 32 above.*
> *(2)   If the offence was racially aggravated, the court—*
> *(a)   shall treat that fact as an aggravating factor (that is to say, a factor that increases the seriousness of the offence); and*
> *(b)   shall state in open court that the offence was so aggravated.*
> *(3)   Section 28 above applies for the purposes of this section as it applies for the purposes of sections 29 to 32 above.*

Keynote

Sections 29 to 32 relate to: racially-aggravated assaults; racially-aggravated criminal damage; racially-aggravated public order offences; racially-aggravated harassment etc., respectively, all of which are addressed in the other Manuals in this series.

Violent or Sexual Nature

In determining whether an offence 'is of a violent or sexual nature, that only such a sentence would be adequate to protect the public from serious harm' (s. 1(2)(b)), guidance is provided by s. 31 of the Criminal Justice Act 1991.

Under s. 31(1) 'violent offence' means:

> *an offence which leads, or is intended or likely to lead, to a person's death or to physical injury to a person, and includes an offence which is required to be charged as arson . . .*

Under s. 31(1) 'sexual offence' means:

> *(a)   an offence under the Sexual Offences Act 1956, other than an offence under section 30 [living on immoral earnings], 31 [woman exercising control over a prostitute] or 33 to 36 [keeping brothels and related offences] of that Act;*
> *(b)   an offence under section 128 of the Mental Health Act 1959 [sexual intercourse with patients];*
> *(c)   an offence under the Indecency with Children Act 1960;*
> *(d)   an offence under section 9 of the Theft Act 1968 of burglary with intent to commit rape;*
> *(e)   an offence under section 54 of the Criminal Law Act 1977 [incitement to have sexual intercourse with granddaughter, daughter, sister, under 16];*
> *(f)   an offence under the Protection of Children Act 1978;*
> *(g)   an offence under section 1 of the Criminal Law Act 1977 of conspiracy to commit any of the offences in paragraphs (a) to (f) above;*
> *(h)   an offence under section 1 of the Criminal Attempts Act 1981 of attempting to commit any of those offences;*
> *(i)   an offence of inciting another to commit any of those offences.*

Keynote

For a full discussion of these offences, **see Crime, chapter 10**).

9.2.2 | **Maximum Sentences**

Maximum custodial sentences are reserved for the gravest examples of the offence for which a person has been convicted (*R* v *Carroll* (1995) 16 Cr App R (S) 488). In *R* v *Ambler* (1975) CSP (A1-4C01) it was directed that those responsible for sentencing, in determining the gravity of an offence, should consider the particular case 'within the broad bands of that type'.

9.2.3 | **Reduction for Guilty Plea**

It is a well established principle that the length of a prison sentence is normally reduced in light of the offender entering a plea of guilty (*R* v *Greene* (1993) 14 Cr App R (S) 682). The extent of the reduction appears to vary between one-fifth and one-third of the maximum sentence.

Section 48 of the Criminal Justice and Public Order Act 1994 makes specific provision for reducing sentences for guilty pleas. It requires the court to take into account when the plea of guilty was indicated, and the circumstances in which the plea was made. If the court then passes a less severe sentence than would normally have been the case, it must state in open court that it has done so.

This 'reduction' of sentence can equally apply to the level of a fine, or reducing the duration of a community sentence (Magistrates' Association Guidelines (1997)).

9.2.4 | **Life Sentences**

Life sentences can be categorised into three specific types: mandatory, automatic and discretionary.

Mandatory Life Sentences

Mandatory life sentences are those where an offender, aged 21 or over, is convicted of murder and must be sentenced to imprisonment for life (s. 1(1) of the Murder (Abolition of Death Penalty) Act 1965). Since the sentence is mandatory, there is no right of appeal (s. 9 of the Criminal Appeal Act 1968).

Section 1(2) of the 1965 Act empowers the court to, 'declare the period which it recommends to the Secretary of State as the minimum period which in its view should elapse' before the offender is released on licence. Similarly, with the life sentence, there is no right of appeal against the recommendation (*R* v *Leaney* [1996] 1 Cr App R (S) 30).

Automatic Life Sentences

Section 2 of the Crime (Sentences) Act 1997 requires the Crown Court to impose a life sentence on an offender who is convicted of a serious offence where the offender is aged 18 or over and has already been convicted of another serious offence.

The offences which qualify as 'serious offences' for the purposes of s. 2 include:

• attempted murder, conspiracy to murder or incitement to murder;

- soliciting murder;

- manslaughter;

- wounding or causing grievous bodily harm with intent;

- rape or attempted rape;

- sexual intercourse with a girl under 13;

- an offence under the following sections of the Firearms Act 1968: s. 16 (possession with intent to endanger life), s. 17 (use to resist arrest), s. 18 (carrying to commit indictable offence or resist arrest);

- robbery where the offender had in his/her possession a firearm or imitation firearm.

For a full discussion of these offences, **see Crime and General Police Duties**.

Where s. 2 above applies, it is only in exceptional circumstances that the court may decide not to impose a life sentence. In so doing the court must state in open court what these exceptional circumstances are (s. 2(3)).

In *R* v *Kelly*, *The Times*, 29 December 1998, it was held that for circumstances to be exceptional they need not be unique, unprecedented or very rare, but could not be cases that were regularly, routinely or normally encountered.

Discretionary Life Sentences

A court may only pass a discretionary life sentence in respect to an offence for which life imprisonment is provided as the maximum penalty. The statutory criteria outlined in s. 2 of the Crime (Sentences) Act 1997 above apply to these sentences, in that they can only be imposed in cases involving a violent or sexual offence (*R* v *Robinson* [1997] 2 Cr App R (S) 35).

In relation to the use of discretionary life sentences the Court of Appeal has provided principles whereby such sentences should only be imposed in exceptional circumstances. In *R* v *Wilkinson* (1983) 5 Cr App R (S) 105 it was stated that, with few exceptions, these sentences would only be used for offenders whose mental state was such that they are a danger to the 'life or limb of members of the public'. Obviously, this is where the provisions of the Mental Health Act 1983 cannot be used to deal with the offender.

9.2.5 **Suspended Sentences**

The power for a court to impose a suspended sentence is provided by s. 22 of the Powers of Criminal Courts Act 1973, which states.

(1) Subject to subsection (2) below, a court which passes a sentence of imprisonment for a term of not more than two years for an offence may order that the sentence shall not take effect unless, during a period specified in the order, being not less than one year or more than two years from the date of the order, the offender commits in Great Britain another offence punishable with imprisonment and thereafter a court having power to do so orders under section 23 of this Act that the original sentence shall take effect; and in this Part of this Act 'operational period', in relation to a suspended sentence, means the period so specified.

(2) A court shall not deal with an offender by means of a suspended sentence unless it is of the opinion—

    (a) that the case is one in which a sentence of imprisonment would have been appropriate even without the power to suspend the sentence; and

    (b) that the exercise of that power can be justified by the exceptional circumstances of the case.

(2A) A court which passes a suspended sentence on any person for an offence shall consider whether the circumstances of the case are such as to warrant in addition the imposition of a fine or the making of a compensation order.

Keynote

Section 23 of the 1973 Act provides a court with powers to deal with an offender convicted of an offence punishable with imprisonment during the period of the suspended sentence. The court may deal with the offender in one of four ways:

- order that the suspended sentence take effect with the original term unaltered;

- order that the suspended sentence take effect with a lesser term;

- vary the original order by extending the period expiring not later than two years;

- make an order with respect to the suspended sentence.

The longest sentence which can be imposed is two years, therefore, if consecutive sentences are imposed totalling more than two years, a suspended sentence cannot be used (*R v Coleman* [1969] 2 QB 468).

Suspended Sentence Supervision Orders

Section 26 of the Powers of Criminal Courts 1973 provides that:

(1) Where a court passes on an offender a suspended sentence for a term of more than six months for a single offence, the court may make a suspended sentence supervision order (in this Act referred to as 'a supervision order') placing the offender under the supervision of a supervising officer for a period specified in the order, being a period not exceeding the operational period of the suspended sentence.

. . .

(4) An offender in respect of whom a supervision order is in force shall keep in touch with the supervising officer in accordance with such instructions as he may from time to time be given by that officer and shall notify him of any change of address.

Keynote

Where an offender, without reasonable cause, fails to comply with the requirements of a supervision order, he/she may be fined up to £1,000 (s. 27 of the 1973 Act). There is no power for the court to activate the suspended sentence.

9.2.6 Sentencing Guidelines

Section 80 of the Crime and Disorder Act 1998 enables the Court of Appeal to provide guidance in relation to the principles courts should apply in determining sentences for particular categories of offences. The purpose of these guidelines is not to remove the element of judicial discretion open to a court but to provide greater consistency in passing sentences appropriate to the level of seriousness of the offence.

100

In framing or revising guidelines, the court is obliged to have regard to various matters. Section 80(3) provides that the court must have regard to:

> (a) *the need to promote consistency in sentencing;*
> (b) *the sentences imposed by courts in England and Wales for offences of the relevant category;*
> (c) *the cost of different sentences and their relative effectiveness in preventing re-offending;*
> (d) *the need to promote public confidence in the criminal justice system; and*
> (e) *the views communicated to the Court . . . by the Sentencing Advisory Panel.*

Keynote

The guidelines are intended to provide criteria for assessing:

- the seriousness of the offence;
- the weight to be given to previous convictions; and
- the failure of the accused to respond to previous sentences (s. 80(4)).

Sentencing Advisory Panel

Where the Court of Appeal decides to frame or revise any guidelines as outlined above, it must notify the Panel (s. 81(1)). The Panel must propose guidelines if directed to do so by the Home Secretary (s. 81(3)).

The composition of the Sentencing Advisory Panel is determined by the Lord Chancellor and consists of about 12 people usually appointed for a five year period. There is no restriction as to whom the Lord Chancellor may appoint but it may include:

- sentencers, (including a magistrate)

- people with experience of the prison service

- people with experience of the probation service

- people with academic experience

- people with research experience

- people who are independent of the criminal justice system.

The Lord Chancellor has the power to provide remuneration for Panel members (s. 81(5)).

9.2.7 Fines

The imposition of a fine is the most commonly encountered penalty in criminal courts and amounts to an order that the offender shall pay a sum of money to the State.

The principles for the fixing of fines for both the Crown Court and magistrates' courts are contained in s. 18 of the Criminal Justice Act 1991 which provides that:

> (1) *Before fixing the amount of any fine to be imposed on an offender who is an individual, a court shall inquire into his financial circumstances.*
> (2) *The amount of any fine fixed by a court shall be such as, in the opinion of the court, reflects the seriousness of the offence.*

(3) In fixing the amount of any fine to be imposed on an offender (whether an individual or other person), a court shall take into account the circumstances of the case including, among other things, the financial circumstances of the offender so far as they are known, or appear to the court.

(4) Where—

(a) an offender has been convicted in his absence in pursuance of section 11 or 12 of the Magistrates' Courts Act 1980 (non-appearance of accused),

(b) an offender—

(i) has failed to comply with an order under section 20(1) below; or

(ii) has otherwise failed to cooperate with the court in its inquiry into his financial circumstances, or

(c) the parent or guardian of an offender who is a child or young person—

(i) has failed to comply with an order under section 20(1B) below; or

(ii) has otherwise failed to cooperate with the court in its inquiry into his financial circumstances,

and the court considers that it has insufficient information to make a proper determination of the financial circumstances of the offender, it may make such determination as it thinks fit.

(5) Subsection (3) above applies whether taking into account the financial circumstances of the offender has the effect of increasing or reducing the amount of the fine.

Keynote

There is no statutory limit to the amount of fine which may be imposed by the Crown Court either on an adult or juvenile convicted on indictment.

A magistrates' court following conviction for an offence triable either way, which is listed in sch. 1 of the Magistrates' Courts Act 1980, may fine the offender an amount not exceeding £5,000.

The standard scale of maximum fines for summary offences (s. 37(2) of the Criminal Justice Act 1982) is:

Level on the scale	Amount of fines
1	£200
2	£500
3	£1,000
4	£2,500
5	£5,000

In relation to juveniles, where a person under 18 is being dealt with by the magistrates' court for an offence when the court could normally impose a fine in excess of £1,000, the fine imposed cannot exceed £1,000. For an offender under 14 where the fine would have exceeded £250 the court can only impose a fine not exceeding £250 (s. 36 of the 1980 Act).

A juvenile's parent or guardian may be ordered to pay the fine, costs or compensation order imposed upon a Juvenile if the court considers it appropriate (s. 55 of the Children and Young Persons Act 1933).

9.2.8 Release of Short-term Prisoners on Licence and Subject to Home Curfew

The Crime and Disorder Act 1998 has introduced new provisions for the early release of short-term prisoners on licence and subject to a curfew condition.

Release of Short-term Prisoners on Licence

Section 34A of the Criminal Justice Act 1991 (introduced by s. 99 of the Crime and Disorder Act 1998), provides the Secretary of State with the power to release a prisoner on licence where the prisoner has served the requisite period for the term of his/her sentence. It is aimed at short-term prisoners, over 18 years of age and applies to prisoners serving sentences of three months or more but not more than four years.

Certain categories of prisoners will not be eligible for release under this section.

Release of Short-term Prisoners Subject to Home Curfew

The introduction of home detention curfews is provided by s. 37A of the Criminal Justice Act 1991 (introduced by s. 100(1) of the Crime and Disorder Act 1998).

The home detention curfew will be set up for a prisoner to complete their sentence and will run for a minimum period of 14 days and a maximum period of 60 days. The prisoner is required to agree to the curfew conditions. The governor at the relevant prison will determine the details of the curfew. This will normally be from 7 pm to 7 am and may be varied. The minimum period of curfew is nine hours but there is no maximum. HM Prison Service Parole Unit is responsible for the management and monitoring of home detention curfews. The curfew equipment will be operated and monitored by an approved private contractor. The contractor will install a home monitoring unit at the approved address and fit the prisoner with the personal identification device at this address on the day of release. Although there is no involvement in the release process, the police will be notified of all prisoners subject to home detention curfew 14 days prior to release. The police may request information from the monitoring contractor as to the offender's compliance, or otherwise, with the curfew, including any short-term 'unexplained' absences. Such requests for information would be authorised by an officer of the rank of superintendent or above. Electronic monitoring contractors are obliged to provide such information within 24 hours of the request being made. Home detention curfews came into effect on 28 January 1999.

Breaches of Curfew

The breach of a curfew condition is provided by s. 38A of the 1991 Act (introduced by s. 100(2) of the Crime and Disorder Act 1998), which states:

> *(1)   If it appears to the Secretary of State, as regards a person released on licence under section 34A(3) above—*
>   *(a)   that he has failed to comply with the curfew condition*
>   *(b)   that his whereabouts can no longer be electronically monitored at the place for the time being specified in that condition or*
>   *(c)   that it is necessary to do so in order to protect the public from serious harm from him,*
> *the Secretary of State may, if the curfew condition is still in force, revoke the licence and recall the person to prison.*

Keynote

The reporting of any breaches of a home detention curfew is the responsibility of the independent contractor. Minor infringements will be dealt with by way of a warning but two warnings will constitute a failure to comply with the curfew conditions. Any reports of a breach are made to HM Prison Service Parole Unit. This Unit may make a decision to revoke or vary the curfew order. The relevant prison governor may also make variations to the order.

There is no power to arrest any person solely found breaching his/her curfew and local policy should be followed.

On the revocation of a person's licence following a breach of curfew conditions that person, 'shall be liable to be detained in pursuance of his sentence and, if at large, shall be deemed to be unlawfully at large.' (s. 38A(5)).

Police Arrests

The guidance provided to police forces in relation to persons who are subject of a home detention curfew is as follows:

Where arrested:

- custody officer to notify the monitoring contractor immediately of:

  - details of the prisoner
  - details of the offence
  - whether the prisoner is to be bailed or retained in custody
  - whether the prisoner continues to wear the electronic tag;

- custody officer to notify the monitoring contractor when the prisoner is released.

Where charged:

- custody officer to immediately inform HM Prison Service Parole Unit

- custody officer to inform contractor *if* the prisoner is to be returned to prison to remove and collect the monitoring unit.

Where a person is charged with an offence whilst subject to a home detention curfew the Code of Practice in relation to detention following charge continues to apply.

Where a prisoner has been charged with an offence, the decision to revoke the prisoner's licence is a matter for HM Prison Service Parole Unit and not the police.

Police Requests for Revocation

Where the police consider that a prisoner subject to a home detention curfew represents a serious risk to the public they may make a request for it to be revoked. Any such request should be authorised by an officer of the rank of superintendent or above and made to HM Prison Service Parole Unit at the Home Office.

'Serious risk' means:

- Offenders convicted of a sexual or violent offence: death or serious injury (physical or psychological) occasioned by further offences committed by the offender. Sexual and violent offences are considered the same in that a prisoner convicted of an offence of violence may be recalled following concerns about offences of a sexual nature.

- Offenders convicted of a non-sexual or violent offence: death or serious injury, etc. The offence which may cause that risk need not be the same as the original offence.

- It is only necessary to demonstrate that the prisoner has acted in such a way as to give *reasonable cause for belief* that recall is necessary to protect the public.

9.2.9 | Absolute and Conditional Discharge

Section 1A of the Powers of Criminal Courts Act 1973 provides the court with the power to grant absolute and conditional discharges. This section states:

> *(1) Where a court by or before which a person is convicted of an offence (not being an offence the sentence for which is fixed by law or falls to be imposed under section 2(2) or 3(2) of the Crime (Sentences) Act 1997) is of opinion, having regard to the circumstances including the nature of the offence and the character of the offender, that it is inexpedient to inflict punishment, the court may make an order either—*
> *(a) discharging him absolutely; or*
> *(b) if the court thinks fit, discharging him subject to the condition that he commits no offence during such period, not exceeding three years from the date of the order, as may be specified in the order.*
> *(1A) Subsection 1(b) above has effect subject to section 66(4) of the Crime and Disorder Act 1998 (effect of reprimands and warnings).*
> *(2) An order discharging a person subject to such a condition is in this Act referred to as 'an order for conditional discharge', and the period specified in any such order as 'the period of conditional discharge'.*
> *(3) Before making an order for conditional discharge the court shall explain to the offender in ordinary language that if he commits another offence during the period of conditional discharge he will be liable to be sentenced for the original offence.*
> *(4) Where, under the following provisions of this part of this Act, a person conditionally discharged under this section is sentenced for the offence in respect of which the order for conditional discharge was made, that order shall cease to have effect.*

Keynote

Absolute Discharge

An absolute discharge may be used in all criminal courts granted irrespective of the age of the offender. Such a power is normally used to reflect the trivial nature of the offence, the circumstances in which the offender came to be before the court or special factors concerning the offender himself/herself.

The only occasions where the power to grant an absolute discharge may not be used are in murder cases or where s. 2 or 3 of the Crime (Sentences) Act 1997 applies whatever the offence committed (**see para. 9.2.4 above**).

Conditional Discharge

As with absolute discharge, a conditional discharge may be used in all criminal courts and granted irrespective of the age of the offender. The only 'condition' is that the offender does not commit any further offences during the period of the discharge fixed by the court. This period must not exceed three years.

Section 1B(1) of the 1973 Act provides that a conditional discharge can be breached only by the conviction of the offender of a further offence committed during the period of the discharge. Where a person is in breach of a conditional discharge the court may sentence the offender for the original offence (s. 1B(6)).

If the Crown Court is dealing with a breach where the conditional discharge was granted in a magistrates' court, it can only deal with the offence subject to the lower courts sentencing powers (s. 1B(7)). If the breach is being dealt with in a magistrates' court and the conditional discharge was originally imposed in another magistrates' court, the consent of the original court is required (s. 1B(8)).

In addition to the exceptions already identified for an absolute discharge (murder and s. 2 or 3 of the Crime (Sentences) Act 1997), a conditional discharge cannot be used in the following cases:

- Breach of an anti-social behaviour order (s. 1(11) of the Crime and Disorder Act 1998), where the offender has been, without reasonable excuse, doing anything prohibited by the order. (**See General Police Duties, chapter 3.**)

- Breach of a sex offender order (s. 2(9) of the 1998 Act), where the offender has been, without reasonable excuse, doing anything prohibited by the order. (**See Crime, chapter 10.**)

- Other than in exceptional circumstances, where an offender is convicted of an offence within two years of receiving a warning from a police officer (ss. 65 and 66 of the 1998 Act). (**See chapter 7.**)

9.2.10 | **Binding Over to Keep the Peace**

The power of the magistrates' court to bind over to keep the peace or be of good behaviour is provided by:

- s. 115 of the Magistrates' Courts Act 1980 (in relation to a complaint);

- common law powers (of the court's own motion);

- various statutes but particularly the Justices of the Peace Act 1361.

An order under s. 115 can only be made following a full hearing of the complaint. However, where the court binds over of its own motion it may do so in any of the following circumstances:

- before the end of the proceedings

- where the case is withdrawn by the prosecution

- where the prosecution offer no evidence

- where the case is adjourned

- where the defendant is acquitted

- where the justice believes there may be a breach of the peace in the future

- where the person's behaviour was against public morality

(*Hughes* v *Holley* [1987] Crim LR 253)

SENTENCING

In *Veater* v *Glennon* [1981] 1 WLR 567 it was held that these wide powers were available to the court as a 'measure of preventive justice'.

Powers of Magistrates' Court, Crown Court and Court of Appeal

Section 1 of the Justices of the Peace Act 1968 extends the powers to bind over to be of good behaviour and states:

> *(7) It is hereby declared that any court of record having a criminal jurisdiction has, as ancillary to that jurisdiction, the power to bind over to be of good behaviour, a person who or whose case is before the court, by requiring him to enter into his own recognisances or to find sureties or both, and committing him to prison if he does not comply.*

Keynote

This power relates to 'any court of record' which includes magistrates' courts, the Crown Court and the Court of Appeal (Criminal Division).

This power does not limit itself to the defendant but includes 'a person who . . . is before the court'. It can therefore relate to the following:

- a defendant who is acquitted (*R* v *Inner London Crown Court, ex parte Benjamin* (1986) 85 Cr App R 267);

- a defendant whose prosecution has not been proceeded with (*R* v *Lincoln Crown Court, ex parte Jude* [1998] 1 WLR 24);

- a person who is a witness before the court (*Sheldon* v *Bromfield Justices* [1964] 2 QB 573);

- a person who is a complainant (*R* v *Wilkins* [1907] 2 KB 380).

The general rule as to who may be subject of a binding over appears to be that the person must have given evidence before the court (*R* v *Swindon Crown Court, ex parte Pawitter Singh* [1984] 1 WLR 449; *R* v *Kingston-upon-Thames Crown Court, ex parte Guarino* [1986] Crim LR 325).

Where a court is considering binding over a person other than a person charged with an offence, that person must be given an opportunity to make representations to the court. (*R* v *Hendon Justices, ex parte Gorchein* [1973] 1 WLR 1502). There is no set period that a binding over order may run, it is at the discretion of the court. In binding a person over to be of good behaviour, the court may require that person to enter into a recognisance. Again, there is no set figure but the court is expected to be reasonable and, where appropriate, undertake a means enquiry (*R* v *Lincoln Crown Court, ex parte Jude* [1998] 1 WLR 24).

Refusal and Failure to be Bound Over

The following apply to cases of refusal or failure to enter into a recognisance:

- People aged 21 or over, in a magistrates' court, can be sentenced to a term of imprisonment for up to six months or until they agree to comply (s. 115(3) of the Magistrates' Courts Act 1980).

- People aged 18 to 20 inclusive, can be committed to prison for contempt of court (s. 9 of the Criminal Justice Act 1982).

- People under the age of 18 may be ordered to attend at an attendance centre but there is no power of detention (s. 17(1)(a) of the Criminal Justice Act 1982).

In relation to persons aged 18 to 20 inclusive, a sentence of detention under s. 9 of the 1982 Act is not a 'custodial sentence' for the purposes of part I of the Criminal Justice Act 1991.

Failure to Comply

Where a person fails to comply with the conditions of an order the court may forfeit the whole or part of the recognisance in its discretion. The court cannot impose a term of imprisonment (*R* v *Finch* (1962) 47 Cr App R 58, *R* v *Gilbert* (1974) CSP D10–3A01).

Binding Over of Parent or Guardian

Where a court is satisfied that it is desirable in the interests of preventing the commission by a person under the age of 16 of further offences, it is *obliged* to bind over the parent or guardian (s. 58(1) of the Criminal Justice Act 1991).

In common with a parenting order (**see chapter 8**) where the court is not so satisfied, it should state in open court that it is not and give reasons for that view.

Where the court does bind over it is empowered to order the parent or guardian to:

- enter into a recognisance not exceeding £1,000

- take proper care of the offender

- exercise proper control over him/her

  (s. 58(2) of the 1991 Act).

The recognisance can be imposed for three years or until the offender is aged 18 years, whichever is the shorter.

The parent or guardian is required to consent to the recognisance but if the court consider such a refusal is unreasonable it can impose a fine, not exceeding £1,000, on the parent or guardian.

The requirements under s. 58(1) and (2) apply to both the magistrates' court and the Crown Court.

9.3 Custody of Young Offenders

This section of the chapter examines custodial sentences as they apply to young offenders, that is those under the age of 21.

9.3.1 Young Offenders Institution

The powers of the court in relation to the detention of young offenders under the age of 21, but not less than 15, is provided by s. 1A of the Criminal Justice Act 1982, which states:

> *(1)   Subject to section 8 below and to section 53 of the Children and Young Persons Act 1933, where—*
> *(a)   an offender under 21 but not less than 15 years of age is convicted of an offence which is punishable with imprisonment in the case of a person aged 21 or over; and*
> *(b)   the court is of the opinion that either or both of paragraphs (a) and (b) of subsection (2) of section 1 of the Criminal Justice Act 1991 apply or the case falls within subsection (3) of that section,*
> *the sentence that the court is to pass is a sentence of detention in a young offender institution.*

Keynote

The court is required to comply with those procedures applicable to custodial sentences for adults, namely, 'pre-sentence reports' and 'seriousness of offence' (**see para. 9.2.1 above**).

The new detention and training orders (**see para. 9.3.4 below**) when introduced, will mean that sentences to a young offenders institution will only apply to offenders aged 18, 19 and 20 years. Time spent in custody on remand counts towards this type of sentence (s. 67(5) of the Criminal Justice Act 1967). Section 1A(1) refers to s. 8 of the 1982 Act and s. 53 of the Children and Young Persons Act 1933, which are, sentence of custody for life (**see para. 9.3.2 below**) and detention during Her Majesty's pleasure (**see para. 9.3.3 below**), respectively.

9.3.2 Sentence to Custody for Life

The powers to sentence an offender to custody for life is provided by s. 8 of the Criminal Justice Act 1982, which states:

> *(1)   Where a person under the age of 21 is convicted of murder or any other offence the sentence for which is fixed by law as imprisonment for life, the court shall sentence him to custody for life unless he is liable to be detained under section 53(1) of the Children and Young Persons Act 1933 (detention of persons under 18 convicted of murder).*
> *(2)   Where a person aged 18 years or over but under the age of 21 is convicted of any other offence for which a person aged 21 years or over would be liable to imprisonment for life, the court shall, if it considers that a custodial sentence for life would be appropriate, sentence him to custody for life.*

Keynote

The requirements for the imposition of a life sentence on young offenders is very similar to that described for adults (**see para. 9.2.4 above**), in relation to discretionary life sentence and automatic life sentence. Similarly with adults, it would only be in exceptional circumstances that custody for life would be imposed, i.e. where the offender has a marked degree of mental instability.

9.3.3 Detention during Her Majesty's Pleasure

This is confined to murder cases where s. 53(1) of the Children and Young Persons Act 1933 provides a mandatory sentence of detention during Her Majesty's pleasure for an offender who is under 18 at the time of the offence.

Detention during Her Majesty's pleasure relates to a child or young person of at least 10 but not more than 17 years. A person receiving this sentence will be detained in a place and under such conditions as directed or arranged by the Secretary of State.

9.3.4 Detention and Training Orders

The Crime and Disorder Act 1998, as part of its overall strategy to target young offenders, when brought into force, will introduce a number of changes in sentencing young offenders (ss. 73 to 79 of the 1998 Act). In terms of custodial sentences the main change will be to replace the existing sentence of detention in a young offenders institution for offenders aged 15, 16 and 17, together with the secure training order, a custodial sentence for offenders aged 12, 13 and 14. The replacement will be a new custodial sentence for young offenders known as *the detention and training order*. In addition to this new custodial sentence, the legislation also introduces or amends other sentencing provisions which include: action plan order; reparation order; supervision order; attendance centre order. All these 'sentences' are discussed below. The sentence of detention in a young offenders institution still will be available to offenders aged 18, 19 and 20.

The Court's Powers

The new detention and training order is intended to be used by both the youth courts and the Crown Court in sentencing offenders under 18 who have been convicted of an offence punishable with imprisonment in the case of an adult (s. 73(1) of the 1998 Act).

Section 73(2) of the 1998 Act identifies those occasions where a court will not make a detention and training order:

> (2)   A court shall not make a detention and training order—
> (a)   in the case of an offender under the age of 15 at the time of the conviction, unless it is of the opinion that he is a persistent offender;
> (b)   in the case of an offender under the age of 12 at that time, unless—
> (i)   it is of the opinion that only a custodial sentence would be adequate to protect the public from further offending by him; and
> (ii)   the offence was committed on or after such date as the Secretary of State may by order appoint.

Keynote

The term of a detention and training order is 4, 6, 8, 10, 12, 18 or 24 months (s. 73(5) of the 1998 Act), and it may not exceed the maximum term of imprisonment that the Crown Court could impose in the case of a person aged 21 or over (s. 73(6)).

The court is required to take into account any period for which the offender has been remanded in custody in determining the term of the detention and training order (s. 74(5)). 'Remanded in custody' also includes where the offender has been held in police detention (s. 74(6)) and 'police detention' for the purposes of this subsection comes within the meaning of s. 118(2) of the Police and Criminal Evidence Act 1984 (**see chapter 15**).

These 'orders' will be deemed to be a custodial sentence for the purposes of s. 31 of the Criminal Justice Act 1991. The 1991 Act provides that before passing a custodial sentence the court must justify it by taking account of the seriousness of the offence/ offences (s. 1(2)(a)) and the fact they are violent or sexual offences (s. 1(2)(b)).

Period of Detention and Training

The period of detention and training is served in secure accommodation (s. 75(1)). Such accommodation in s. 75(7) is:

- a secure training centre;

- a young offender institution;

- secure accommodation provided by a local authority;

- accommodation provided for the purpose under s. 82(5) of the 1989 Act (financial support by the Secretary of State); or

- accommodation so authorised by the Secretary of State for the purpose of restricting liberty.

The period of training and detention is one-half of the term of the order (s. 75(2)).

The Secretary of State may order the release of a person subject to a detention and training order in three circumstances:

- in exceptional circumstances on compassionate grounds (s. 75(3));

- for an order of more than eight months but less than 18 before the half-way term of the order (s. 75(4)(a));

- for an order of 18 months or more, one month or two months after that point (s. 75(4)(b)).

Period of Supervision

A person who is subject to a detention and training order is subject to a period of supervision. This begins with the offender's release at the half-way point of the order or otherwise and ends when the term of the order ends. (s. 76(1) of the 1998 Act).

For the purpose of supervision under s. 76(3) the offender is under the supervision of one of the following:

- a probation officer;

- a social worker of a local authority social services department;

- a member of a youth offending team.

Whoever has responsibility for supervision, a notice is required to be served on the offender (on behalf of the Secretary of State), informing him/her of who is responsible for the supervision and any requirements with which the offender needs to comply (s. 76(6)). This notice must be given to the offender before supervision commences (s. 76(7)).

Breaches of Supervision

Where an offender fails to comply with the requirements of their supervision an information can be laid before a justice who may:

- issue a summons for the offender to appear before a youth court;

- issue a warrant for the offender to be arrested and brought before a youth court (s. 77(1) of the 1998 Act).

Where it is proved to the satisfaction of the youth court that an offender has failed to comply with the terms of his/her supervision under s. 77(3) the court may:

- order the offender to be detained in secure accommodation for a period not exceeding the shorter of three months;

- order the offender to be returned to custody for the remainder of the term of the detention and training order, as the court may specify; or

- impose a fine not exceeding level 3 on the standard scale.

Where a person is subject to a detention and training order and commits a further offence(s), punishable with imprisonment in the case of an adult, the court may order the offender to serve a term of detention in secure accommodation. This is in addition to any other disposal (s. 78(2)).

A justice may only issue a warrant if the information is in writing and on oath.

9.4   Community Orders

Community orders are provided by the Criminal Justice Act 1991 and the Crime and Disorder Act 1998 and include:

- community service orders

- probation orders

- combination orders

- curfew orders

- supervision orders

- attendance centre orders

- drug treatment and testing orders

- action plan orders

  (s. 6(4)).

112

Before imposing a community order a court is required to justify its decision in terms of the seriousness of the offence or offences (s. 6(1) of the 1991 Act).

9.4.1 | **Community Service Orders**

The powers of a court to make a community service order is provided by s. 14 of the Powers of Criminal Courts Act 1973, which states:

> *(1) Where a person of or over 16 years of age is convicted of an offence punishable with imprisonment (not being an offence the sentence for which is fixed by law or falls to be imposed under section 2(2), 3(2) or 4(2) of the Crime (Sentences) Act 1997), the court by or before which he is convicted may, instead of dealing with him in any other way (but subject to subsection (2) below) make an order (in this Act referred to as 'a community service order') requiring him to perform unpaid work in accordance with the subsequent provisions of this Act.*

Keynote

A community service order may only be made for an offender whose minimum age is 16.

Before it makes a community service order the court is required to explain to the offender, in ordinary language: the purpose and effect of the order; the consequences of failure to comply with the order; the court's power to review the order on application from the offender or probation officer (s. 14(5)).

Requirements

Under the 1973 Act the following requirements *may* be included in a community service order:

- to keep in touch with the relevant officer as required (s. 15(1)(a));

- to notify the relevant officer of any change of address (s. 15(1)(a));

- to perform the number of hours required doing such work at such times as instructed (s. 15(1)(b)).

Under s. 14(1A) the number of hours which a person may be required to work will be in the aggregate:

- not less than 40; and

- not more than 240.

The work required is to be completed during the period of 12 months from the date the order was made (s. 15(2) of the 1973 Act).

The court can only make an order if it is satisfied that the offender is a suitable person to perform work under such an order (s. 14(2)).

An offender may be sentenced to consecutive community service orders by the same or another court but the total number of hours ordered must not exceed 240 (*R* v *Evans* [1977] 1 WLR 27).

'Relevant officer' means a probation officer or social worker of a local authority social services department (s. 14(2)).

Breach of Community Service Orders

Where an offender fails to comply with the requirements of a community service order an information can be laid before a justice who may:

- issue a summons for the offender to appear before a youth court

- issue a warrant for the offender to be arrested and brought before a youth court (sch. 2, para. 2 of the Criminal Justice Act 1991).

Where it is proved to the satisfaction of the youth court that an offender has failed, without reasonable excuse, to comply with the terms of the order the court may:

- impose a fine not exceeding £1,000

- make a community service order

- deal with him/her for the offence in respect of which the order was made (sch. 2, para. 3 of the 1991 Act).

9.4.2 Probation Orders

The powers of a court to make a probation order is provided by s. 2 of the Powers of Criminal Courts Act 1973, which states:

> *(1) Where a court by or before which a person of or over the age of sixteen years is convicted of an offence (not being an offence for which the sentence is fixed by law or falls to be imposed under section 2(2) or 3(2) of the Crime (Sentences) Act 1997) is of the opinion that the supervision of the offender [by a probation officer] is desirable in the interests of—*
> *(a) securing the rehabilitation of the offender; or*
> *(b) protecting the public from harm from him or preventing the commission by him of further offences,*
> *the court may make a probation order, that is to say, an order requiring him to be under the supervision of a probation officer for a period specified in the order of not less than six months nor more than three years.*
> *(2) A probation order shall specify the petty sessions area in which the offender resides or will reside and the offender shall, subject to paragraph 12 of schedule 2 to the Criminal Justice Act 1991 (offenders who change their residence), be required to be under the supervision of (a) a probation officer appointed for or assigned to that area or (b) where the offender is under the age of 18 years, a member of a youth offending team as established by the local authority within whose area it appears to the court that the offender resides or will reside.*

Keynote

Before it makes a probation order the court is required to explain to the offender, in ordinary language: the effect of the order; the consequences of failure to comply with the order; the court's power to review the order on application from the offender or probation officer (s. 2(3) of the 1973 Act).

In s. 2(2) above and the reference to 'youth offending team', this was introduced by the Crime and Disorder Act 1998 and such teams are subject to an 18 month pilot scheme commencing in September 1998 (**see chapter** 7).

Requirements

Under the 1973 Act the following requirements *may* be included in a probation order, i.e. a requirement to:

- keep in touch with the probation officer as required (s. 2(6) of the 1973 Act);

- notify the probation officer of any change of address (s. 2(6));

- reside in an approved hostel or other institution (sch. 1A, para. 1);

- present himself/herself to a person or persons at a place or places so specified, and to participate or refrain from participating in activities specified in the order (sch. 1A, para. 2);

- attend at a probation centre (sch. 1A, para. 3)

- obtain treatment for drug or alcohol dependency (sch. 1A, para. 6(1));

- and any requirements considered desirable to:

  - secure the offender's rehabilitation
  - protect the public from harm
  - prevent the commission of further offences (s. 3 (1)).

A condition cannot include preventing the offender leaving the country and not returning (*R* v *McCartan* [1958] 1 WLR 933) or a condition that would 'introduce a custodial or other element' (*Rogers* v *Cullen* [1982] 1 WLR 729).

Breach of a Probation Order

The provisions as to the breach of a probation order are identical to those for a community service order (**see para. 9.4.1 above**).

9.4.3 ## Combination Orders

The powers of a court to make a combination order is provided by s. 11 of the Criminal Justice Act 1991, which states:

> *(1)   Where a court by or before which a person of or over the age of sixteen years is convicted of an offence punishable with imprisonment (not being an offence for which the sentence is fixed by law or falls to be imposed under section 2(2) or 3(2) of the Crime (Sentences) Act 1997) is of the opinion mentioned in subsection (2) below, the court may make a combination order, that is to say, an order requiring him both—*
> *(a)   to be under [the] supervision [of a probation officer] for a period specified in the order, being not less than twelve months nor more than three years; and*
> *(b)   to perform unpaid work for a number of hours so specified, being in the aggregate not less than 40 nor more than 100.*

Keynote

A combination order is made where it is desirable in the interest of:

- securing the rehabilitation of the offender; or

- protecting the public from harm or preventing the commission of further offences

  (s. 11(2)).

9.4.4 | **Curfew Orders**

The powers of a court to make a curfew order is provided by s. 12 of the Criminal Justice Act 1991, which provides:

> *(1)   Where a person is convicted of an offence (not being an offence for which the sentence is fixed by law or falls to be imposed under section 2(2) or 3(2) of the Crime (Sentences) Act 1997), the court by or before which he is convicted may make a curfew order, that is to say, an order requiring him to remain, for periods specified in the order, at a place so specified.*
>
> *(2)   A curfew order may specify different places or different periods for different days, but shall not specify—*
>
> > *(a)   periods which fall outside the period of six months beginning with the day on which it is made; or*
> >
> > *(b)   periods which amount to less than 2 hours or more than 12 hours in any one day.*

Keynote

Where the offender is under the age of 16, the six months period referred to in subsection (2)(a) above should read three months (s. 12(2A)).

Arrangements for monitoring an offender's whereabouts need to be available for the court to make a curfew order. Such availability is notified by the Secretary of State s. 12(4A)).

A curfew order may include requirements for securing electronic monitoring of an offender's whereabouts where such arrangements are available (s. 13 of the 1991 Act).

9.4.5 | **Supervision Orders**

The powers of a court to make a supervision order is provided by the Children and Young Persons Act 1969.

Such orders can only be made in respect of a child or young person found guilty of an offence, in criminal proceedings, in a youth court or Crown Court (s.7(7)).

A supervision order lasts for three years or such shorter period as specified (s. 17(a)) and places the offender under the supervision of a probation officer or social worker of a local authority (s. 11).

A child means a person aged 10 to 13 inclusive and a young person means a person aged 14 to 17 inclusive.

An adult magistrates' court cannot make a supervision order (s. 7(8)).

Requirements

Under the 1969 Act the following requirements *may* be included in a supervision order, i.e. a requirement to:

- reside with an individual named in the order (s. 12(1));

- live at a place or places so specified (s. 12(2)(a));

- present himself/herself to a person or persons, at a place or places, on a day or days so specified (s. 12(2)(b));

- participate in activities so specified (s. 12(2)(c));

- impose a 'night restriction' requirement (s. 12A(3)(b));

- reside in local authority accommodation for a specified period (s. 12AA(1));

- comply with arrangements for his/her education (s. 12C(1));

- require the offender to be subject to medical treatment (s. 1B(1)).

The 'night restriction' condition means, 'to remain for specified periods between 6 pm and 6 am' at a specified place or places (s. 12A(3)(b)). The specified period cannot exceed 10 hours on any one night (s. 12A(9)).

Breach of Supervision Orders

Where it is proved to the satisfaction of the youth court that an offender has failed to comply with certain requirements of the order the court may:

- impose a fine not exceeding £1,000

- make a curfew order

- make an attendance centre order

  (s. 15(3)(a) of the 1969 Act).

The 'certain requirements' relate to all those requirements discussed above with the exception of the condition to require attendance for medical treatment under s. 12B of the 1969 Act.

9.4.6 ## Attendance Centre Orders

The powers of a court to make an attendance centre order is provided by s. 17 of the Criminal Justice Act 1982, which provides:

(1)   Where a person under 21 years of age is convicted by or before a court of an offence punishable with imprisonment (not being an offence the sentence for which is fixed by law or fails to be imposed under section 2(2), 3(2) or 4(2) of the Crime (Sentences) Act 1997, or where a court—
(a)   would have power, but for section 1 above, to commit a person under 21 years of age to prison in default of payment of any sum of money or for failing to do or abstain from doing anything required to be done or left undone; or
(b)   has power to deal with a person under 21 years of age under part II of schedule 2 to the Criminal Justice Act 1991 for failure to comply with any of the requirements of a probation order, the court may, if it has been notified by the Secretary of State that an attendance centre is available for the reception of persons of his description, order him to attend at such a centre, to be specified in the order, for such number of hours as may be so specified; or
(bb)   has power to deal with a person under 16 years of age under that part of that schedule for failure to comply with any of the requirements of a curfew order; or
(c)   has power to commit to prison for default in payment of any sum of money a person who is under 25 but is not less than 21 years of age.

117

Keynote

The aggregate number of hours for attendance is dependent on the age of the offender as follows:

- Under 14 — not less than 12 hours, except where the court determines that 12 hours would be excessive (s. 17(4));

- Under 16 — must not exceed 24 hours where the court considers 12 hours inadequate;

- Under 21 — must not exceed 36 hours but not less than 16 (s. 17(5)).

An attendance centre order can also be imposed by the youth court or Crown Court for the breach of a supervision order (ss. 15(3)(a) and 16A(1) of the Children and Young Persons Act 1969).

Breach of Attendance Centre Orders

Where an offender fails, without reasonable excuse, to comply with the requirements of an attendance centre order, an information can be laid before a justice who may:

- impose a fine not exceeding £1,000

- revoke the order

- deal with the offender for the offence in respect of which the order was made

(s.19 of the 1982 Act).

In dealing with the breach a justice may impose a fine without revoking the order.

Where an attendance centre order is revoked the offender must be dealt with in accordance with his/her age at the time the order was made (*R* v *Wyre Magistrates' Court, ex parte Boardman* (1987) 9 Cr App R (S) 214).

9.4.7 **Drug Treatment and Testing Orders**

The powers of a court to make a drug treatment and testing order is provided by s. 61 of the Crime and Disorder Act 1998, which provides:

> *(1)   This section applies where a person aged 16 or over is convicted of an offence other than one for which the sentence—*
> *(a)   is fixed by law; or*
> *(b)   falls to be imposed under section 2(2), 3(2) or 4(2) of the 1997 Act.*
> *(2)   Subject to the provisions of this section, the court by or before which the offender is convicted may make an order (a 'drug treatment and testing order') which—*
> *(a)   has effect for a period specified in the order of not less than six months nor more than three years ('the treatment and testing period'); and*
> *(b)   includes the requirements and provisions mentioned in section 62 below.*
> *(3)   A court shall not make a drug treatment and testing order unless it has been notified by the Secretary of State that arrangements for implementing such orders are available in the area proposed to be specified in the order and the notice has not been withdrawn.*
> *(4)   A drug treatment and testing order shall be a community order for the purposes of Part I of the 1991 Act and the provisions of that Part, which include provisions with respect to restrictions on*

imposing, and procedural requirements for, community sentences (sections 6 and 7), shall apply accordingly.

    (5)   The court shall not make a drug treatment and testing order in respect of the offender unless it is satisfied—

        (a)   that he is dependent on or has a propensity to misuse drugs and

        (b)   that his dependency or propensity is such as requires and may be susceptible to treatment.

Keynote

Although treatment for drug and alcohol dependency may be provided as a condition within a probation order, the new section has both introduced a testing requirement without any causal link between drugs and the offence.

Section 61(6) provides:

    (6)   For the purpose of ascertaining for the purposes of subsection (5) above whether the offender has any drug in his body, the court may by order require him to provide samples of such description as it may specify but the court shall not make such an order unless the offender expresses his willingness to comply with its requirements.

Keynote

Before making a requirement under s. 61(6) the offender must state a willingness to comply. If not, the order cannot be imposed.

Requirements

Under the 1998 Act the following requirements *may* be included in a drug treatment and testing order, i.e. a requirement:

- that the offender submit to treatment (s. 62(1));

- to provide such treatment as a resident in an institution or place specified (s. 62(2)(a));

- to provide such treatment as a non-resident in an institution or place and at such intervals specified (s. 62(2)(b));

- that the offender provide samples of such description as determined by the treatment provider (s. 62(4));

- specifying for each month the minimum number of occasions where samples are to be provided (s. 62(5));

- specifying in the order the petty sessions area in which the offender resides or will reside (s. 62(6));

- that the offender be under the supervision of a probation officer (s. 62(7)(a));

- that the offender keep in touch with probation officer as specified (s. 62(7)(b));

- that the offender communicate to the probation officer the results of the tests carried out on the samples (s. 62(7)(c)).

119

Supervision by the probation officer should be for the purpose of reporting to the court on the offender's progress, and reporting to the court any failure to comply with the requirements of the order (s. 62(8)).

The offender's progress is periodically reviewed by the court at intervals of not less than one month (s. 63(1)). Initially the offender is required to attend these hearings though if progress is satisfactory subsequent reviews can be carried out without a full review hearing. If progress becomes unsatisfactory, further review hearings in court should be convened (s. 63(8) to (10)).

Breach of Drug Treatment and Testing Order

The provisions to the breach of a drug treatment and testing order are identical to those for a community service order (**see para. 9.4.1 above**).

9.4.8 Action Plan Orders

Action plan orders are new powers provided to the court by the Crime and Disorder Act 1998. These are intended to be, 'a short intensive programme of community intervention combining punishment, rehabilitation and reparation to change offending behaviour and prevent further crime' (Government White Paper: *No More Excuses*, 1997 (Cm 3809)).

Section 69 of the Crime and Disorder Act 1998 provides:

> *(1) This section applies where a child or young person is convicted of an offence other than one for which the sentence is fixed by law.*
> *(2) Subject to the provisions of this section and section 70 below, the court by or before which the offender is convicted may, if it is of the opinion that it is desirable to do so in the interests of securing his rehabilitation, or of preventing the commission by him of further offences, make an order (an 'action plan order') which—*
> *(a) requires the offender, for a period of three months beginning with the date of the order, to comply with an action plan, that is to say, a series of requirements with respect to his actions and whereabouts during that period;*
> *(b) places the offender under the supervision for that period of the responsible officer; and*
> *(c) requires the offender to comply with any directions given by that officer with a view to the implementation of that plan.*
> *(3) The court shall not make an action plan order unless it has been notified by the Secretary of State that arrangements for implementing such orders are available in the area proposed to be named in the order and the notice has not been withdrawn.*
> *(4) The court shall not make an action plan order in respect of the offender if—*
> *(a) he is already the subject of such an order; or*
> *(b) the court proposes to pass on him a custodial sentence or a sentence under section 53(1) of the 1933 Act, or to make in respect of him a probation order, a community service order, a combination order, a supervision order or an attendance centre order.*
> *(5) Requirements included in an action plan order, or directions given by a responsible officer, may require the offender to do all or any of the following things, namely—*
> *(a) to participate in activities specified in the requirements or directions at a time or times so specified;*
> *(b) to present himself to a person or persons specified in the requirements or directions at a place or places and at a time or times so specified;*
> *(c) to attend at an attendance centre specified in the requirements or directions for a number of hours so specified;*
> *(d) to stay away from a place or places specified in the requirements or directions;*
> *(e) to comply with any arrangements for his education specified in the requirements or directions;*

(f)   to make reparation specified in the requirements or directions to a person or persons so specified or to the community at large; and

(g)   to attend any hearing fixed by the court under section 70(3) below.

Keynote

Action plan orders are only available for offenders aged between 10 and 17 years inclusive.

In imposing an action plan order the court is required to justify making the order in terms of the seriousness of the offence or offences as provided by s. 6(4) of the Criminal Justice Act 1991.

As with the supervision element of detention and training orders, the 'responsible person' for action plan orders is:

- a probation officer

- a social worker of a local authority social services department

- a member of a youth offending team

  (s. 69(10) of the 1998 Act).

Action plan orders are being piloted in a number of courts for a period of 18 months which began in October 1998.

Requirements

Under s. 69(5) of the 1998 Act the following requirements *may* be included in an action plan order or given by a responsible officer to require the offender:

- to participate in activities at a specified time or times;

- to present himself/herself at a place or places at a specified time or times;

- to attend an attendance centre for a specified number of hours;

- to stay away from a specified place or places;

- to comply with any arrangement for his/her education;

- to make reparation to a specified person or persons or to the community at large;

- to attend court within 21 days of the order to consider its effectiveness.

The requirement to attend an attendance centre (s. 69(5)(c)) only applies if the offence committed would be punishable with imprisonment in the case of a person aged 21 or over (s. 69(7)).

In relation to reparation (s. 69(5)(f)) above, s. 69(8) provides:

(8)   A person shall not be specified in requirements or directions under subsection (5)(f) above unless—

(a)   he is identified by the court or, as the case may be, the responsible officer as a victim of the offence or a person otherwise affected by it; and

(b)   he consents to the reparation being made.

Keynote

The court can normally make an action plan order without the requirement to obtain a pre-sentence report. However, under s. 70(1) of the 1998 Act the court is required to consider a written report from a 'responsible person' which would indicate:

- the requirements proposed to be included in the order;

- the benefits to the offender of these proposals;

- the attitude of a parent or guardian to the proposals;

- information about family circumstances and likely effect of the order (this only applies to offenders under 16 years).

An action plan order cannot be imposed where the offender receives a custodial sentence (s. 69(4)). However, it can be combined with a drug treatment and testing order (**see para. 9.4.7**) and a curfew order (**see para. 9.4.4**). Reparation orders and action plan orders cannot be combined (s. 67(4)).

Discharge, Breach and Revocation

Either a 'responsible person' or the offender can make application to the court for the action plan order to be discharged or varied. If it appears appropriate, 'the court may make an order discharging the reparation order or action plan order or varying it: by cancelling any provision included in it; or by inserting in it any provision that could have been included in the order if the court had then had power to make it and were exercising the power (sch. 5, para. 2 of the 1998 Act).

Where such an application for discharge is dismissed there can be no further application without the consent of the court (sch. 5, para. 2).

Where it is proved to the satisfaction of the appropriate court that an offender has failed to comply with any requirement included in the order, the court may:

- impose a fine not exceeding £1,000; or

- make an attendance centre order; or

- make a curfew order.

If the youth court made the original order it can deal with the offender for the original offence(s). If the order was made by the Crown Court, the court may commit the offender in custody or release them on bail pending their appearance before the court (sch. 5, para. 3).

A summons or warrant may be issued for the purpose of securing the attendance of an offender before the court. Where a warrant is executed and the offender cannot be brought immediately before the appropriate court he/she can be held in detention in a place of safety for a period not exceeding 72 hours from the time of the arrest (sch. 5, para. 4).

9.4.9 Reparation Orders

Reparation orders have also been introduced by the Crime and Disorder Act 1998. Youth courts or Crown Courts have the power to impose a reparation order on an offender aged under 18 who is convicted of any offence. The legislation requires the court to consider imposing a reparation order where it does not impose a compensation order (**see para. 9.5**).

Section 67 of the 1998 Act provides that:

(1)   This section applies where a child or young person is convicted of an offence other than one for which the sentence is fixed by law.
(2)   Subject to the provisions of this section and section 68 below, the court by or before which the offender is convicted may make an order (a 'reparation order') which requires the offender to make reparation specified in the order:
(a)   to a person or persons so specified; or
(b)   to the community at large;
and any person so specified must be a person identified by the court as a victim of the offence or a person otherwise affected by it.

Keynote

Reparation orders are being piloted in a number of courts for a period of 18 months which began in October 1998.

Requirements

The requirements in relation to reparation orders are provided by s. 67(5) to (8) which states:

(5)   A reparation order shall not require the offender—
(a)   to work for more than 24 hours in aggregate; or
(b)   to make reparation to any person without the consent of that person.
(6)   Subject to subsection (5) above, requirements specified in a reparation order shall be such as in the opinion of the court are commensurate with seriousness of the offence, or the combination of the offence and one or more offences associated with it.
(7)   Requirements so specified shall, as far as practicable, be such as to avoid—
(a)   any conflict with the offender's religious beliefs or with the requirements of any community order to which he may be subject; and
(b)   any interference with the times, if any, at which the offender normally works or attends school or any other educational establishment.
(8)   Any reparation required by a reparation order—
(a)   shall be made under the supervision of the responsible officer; and
(b)   shall be made within a period of three months from the date of the making of the order.

Under s. 67(4), a court cannot make a reparation order where it passes one of the following:

• a custodial sentence;

- a community service order;

- a combination order;

- a supervision order which includes requirements under ss. 12 to 12C of the Children and Young Persons Act 1969;

- an action plan order.

The meaning of 'responsible officer' (s. 67(8)(a)) is the same as for action plan orders (**see para. 9.4.8 above**).

Although the court can impose a reparation order without obtaining a pre-sentence report, before making such an order it must obtain and consider a report from a 'responsible person'. This report includes the type of work suitable for the offender and the attitude of the victim(s) (s. 68(1)).

Drug treatment and testing orders (in the case of a person 16 or 17), probation orders, curfew orders or attendance centre orders could be combined with a reparation order.

Discharge, Breach and Revocation

The discharge, breach and revocation of reparation orders is the same as that for action plan orders (**see para 9.4.8 above**).

9.5   Compensation Orders

The powers of a court to make compensation orders is provided by ss. 35 to 38 of the Powers of Criminal Court Act 1973. Section 35 of the 1973 Act provides:

> *(1)   Subject to the provisions of this part of this Act and to section 40 of the Magistrates' Courts Act 1980 (which imposes a monetary limit on the powers of a magistrates' court under this section), a court by or before which a person is convicted of an offence, instead of or in addition to dealing with him in any other way, may, on application or otherwise, make an order (in this Act referred to as a 'compensation order') requiring him to pay compensation for any personal injury, loss or damage resulting from that offence or any other offence which is taken into consideration by the court in determining sentence or to make payments for funeral expenses or bereavement in respect of a death resulting from any such offence, other than a death due to an accident arising out of the presence of a motor vehicle on a road; and a court shall give reasons, on passing sentence, if it does not make such an order in a case where this section empowers it to do so.*
> *(1A)   Compensation under subsection (1) above shall be of such an amount as the court considers appropriate, having regard to any evidence and to any representations that are made by or on behalf of the accused or the prosecutor.*

Keynote

There is no restriction on the Crown Court to the amount of compensation it may order though it must take into account the offender's means. The maximum sum that the magistrates' court may order by way of compensation for any offence is £5,000 (Magistrates' Courts Act 1980, s. 40(1)).

Compensation orders may also be made to compensate for distress and anxiety (*Bond* v *Chief Constable of Kent* [1983] 1 WLR 40, and *R* v *Godfrey* (1994) 15 Cr App R (S) 536).

Compensation is the loss to the victim rather than the benefit to the offender and where there has been no damage or loss no compensation order can be made (*R* v *Hier* (1976) 62 Cr App R 233 and *R* v *Tyce* (1994) 15 Cr App R (S) 415).

In relation to compensation orders where a child or young person is convicted of an offence, the order is normally made against the parent or guardian (s. 55 of the Children and Young Persons Act 1969).

CHAPTER TEN

PRIVILEGE AND PUBLIC POLICY

10.1 Introduction

This chapter deals with another exception to the general principle that evidence which is relevant to the issues in legal proceedings should be admitted. There are occasions where the courts will allow a person or body of people to refuse to disclose information or documents (and, sometimes, prevent others disclosing such evidence), *even though the evidence in question is reliable and clearly relevant to the issues in a particular case.*

This chapter looks at two main categories of such occasions:

- **Privilege** — where a person has a specific *right* in respect of non-disclosure. This includes legal professional privilege.

- **Public policy** — where there is no specific right in respect of non-disclosure but it is nevertheless accepted that public policy justifies the non-disclosure of certain evidence.

10.2 Privilege

10.2.1 Privilege against Self-incrimination

This privilege may be claimed generally by any person in any proceedings (civil or criminal). Any person, when called upon to answer questions or disclose documents, may refuse to do so on the grounds that they may incriminate themselves. This was recognised in *Blunt* v *Park Lane Hotel* [1942] 2 KB 253 where it was said that:

> The rule is that no-one is bound to answer any question if the answer thereto would, in the opinion of the judge, have a tendency to expose [him/her] to any criminal charge, penalty or forfeiture which the judge regards as reasonably likely to be preferred or sued for.

This privilege has been developed by the courts and means that a witness may refuse to answer questions in court and refuse to produce documents if this would have a tendency to incriminate him/her or lead to a criminal charge. While this principle is still seen as another fundamental right (alongside the right to silence), there are many exceptions which are set out below. It is also important to see what use can be made of such testimony. The right to claim this privilege *is for the witness himself/herself*; it does not include the right to claim the privilege in order to protect others, even the accused's spouse. If the courts demand that a person comply with an order to disclose certain evidence, he/she may substitute a different protection in place of the privilege, provided the alternative gives sufficient protection to the witness (as when the prosecuting authorities unequivocally agree not to make use of the information — *AT & T Istel* v *Tully* [1992] 3 WLR 344).

Protection may be refused if the evidence against the witness is already so strong that, if proceedings are to be taken, they will be taken whether or not the witness responds to the demand.

10.2.2 Exceptions to the Rule against Self-incrimination

The exceptions to the rule against self-incrimination include:

- s. 31 of the Theft Act 1968
- s. 9 of the Criminal Damage Act 1971
- s. 98 of the Children Act 1989
- s. 2 of the Criminal Justice Act 1987
- s. 1(e) of the Criminal Evidence Act 1898.

Section 31 of the Theft Act 1968

Section 31 of the Theft Act 1968 provides that:

(1) A person shall not be excused, by reason that to do so may incriminate that person or the wife or husband of that person of an offence under this Act—

(a) from answering any question put to that person in proceedings for the recovery or administration of any property, for the execution of any trust or for an account of any property or dealings with property; or

(b) from complying with any order made in any such proceedings;

but no statement or admission made by a person in answering a question put or complying with an order made as aforesaid shall, in proceedings for an offence under this Act, be admissible in evidence against that person or (unless they married after the making of the statement of admission) against the wife or husband of that person.

(2) Notwithstanding any enactment to the contrary, where property has been stolen or obtained by fraud or other wrongful means, the title to that or any other property shall not be affected by reason only of the conviction of the offender.

Keynote

Section 31 simply requires questions to be answered and orders to be complied with in proceedings for the recovery or administration of any property or dealing with property. Where such answers may incriminate the witness or his/her spouse and leave them liable to a charge for an offence under the Theft Act 1968, the answers may not be used in proceedings for any such offence.

In *Renworth* v *Stephansen* [1996] 3 All ER 244 it was held that the fact that the witness might incriminate himself/herself in respect of a non-Theft Act offence (as well as a Theft Act offence) will not necessarily preclude the application of s. 31.

Even though compliance may expose the witness or his/her spouse to a charge for an offence under the Theft Act 1968, the answers may not be used in proceedings for any such offence but might be useful in pointing towards areas where evidence might be found linking the witness to the offence.

For Theft Act offences, **see Crime, chapter 12**.

Section 9 of the Criminal Damage Act 1971

Section 9 of the Criminal Damage Act 1971 provides that:

> *A person shall not be excused, by reason that to do so may incriminate that person or the wife or husband of that person of an offence under this Act—*
>
> *(a) from answering any question put to that person in proceedings for the recovery or administration of any property, for the execution of any trust or for an account of any property or dealings with property; or*
>
> *(b) from complying with any order made in any such proceedings;*
>
> *but no statement or admission made by a person in answering a question put or complying with an order made as aforesaid shall, in proceedings for an offence under this Act, be admissible in evidence against that person or (unless they married after the making of the statement or admission) against the wife or husband of that person.*

Keynote

This provision is virtually identical to s. 31 of the Theft Act 1968 except the offences relate to those under the Criminal Damage Act 1971.

Wife or husband for the purpose of this section includes: where a man and woman have acquired the reputation of being man and wife by cohabitation, a valid marriage between them will generally be presumed.

For Criminal Damage Act offences, **see Crime, chapter 14**.

Section 98 of the Children Act 1989

Section 98 of the Children Act 1989 provides that:

> *(1) In any proceedings in which a court is hearing an application for an order under Part IV or V [relating to the care, supervision and protection of children], no person shall be excused from—*
>
> *(a) giving evidence on any matter; or*
>
> *(b) answering any question put to him in the course of his giving evidence,*
>
> *on the ground that doing so might incriminate him or his spouse of an offence.*
>
> *(2) A statement or admission made in such proceedings shall not be admissible in evidence against the person making it or his spouse in proceedings for an offence other than perjury.*

Keynote

A statement or admission made in such proceedings shall not be admissible in evidence against the person making it or his/her spouse in proceedings for an offence other than perjury. Case law is unclear as to the definition of a statement or admission and it is uncertain whether it would include an oral admission made by a parent to a guardian after the proceedings have started. An oral statement to a social worker carrying out the local authority's duties of investigation in a child protection case may be so construed and such information should be forwarded to the Crown Prosecution Service for advice.

Section 2 of the Criminal Justice Act 1987

This section gives the Serious Fraud Office powers to require people in some circumstances to produce documents and answer any questions relevant to an investigation being conducted by that office (a notable example being the case against the family of Robert Maxwell in the mid-1990s).

Section 1 of the Criminal Evidence Act 1898

Section 1 of the Criminal Evidence Act 1898 provides that:

> *Every person charged with an offence shall be a competent witness for the defence at every stage of the proceedings, whether the person so charged is charged solely or jointly with any other person. Provided as follows:*
>
> *(a) A person so charged shall not be called as a witness in pursuance of this Act except upon his own application;*
>
> . . .
>
> *(e) A person charged and being a witness in pursuance of this Act may be asked any question in cross-examination notwithstanding that it would tend to criminate him as to the offence charged;*
>
> *(f) A person charged and called as a witness in pursuance of this Act shall not be asked, and if asked shall not be required to answer, any question tending to show that he has committed or been convicted of or been charged with any offence other than that wherewith he is then charged, or is of bad character, unless—*
>
> *(i) the proof that he has committed or been convicted of such other offence is admissible evidence to show that he is guilty of the offence wherewith he is then charged; or*
>
> *(ii) he has personally or by his advocate asked questions of the witnesses for the prosecution with a view to establish his own good character, or has given evidence of his good character, or the nature or conduct of the defence is such as to involve imputations on the character of the prosecutor or the witnesses for the prosecution or the deceased victim of the alleged crime; or*
>
> *(iii) he has given evidence against any other person charged in the same proceedings.*
>
> *(g) Every person called as a witness in pursuance of this Act shall, unless otherwise ordered by the court, give his evidence from the witness box or other place from which the other witnesses give their evidence.*

Keynote

Section 1 means that, should a defendant decide to give evidence from the witness box, he/she may be cross-examined about matters which might incriminate him/her.

Section 1(f) allows for this cross-examination to include questions which tend to show that the defendant has committed, or been convicted of, or been charged with, any offence other than that for which he/she is charged *or* that he/she is of bad character.

Section 1(e) removes the privilege against self-incrimination which the accused would otherwise enjoy in respect of the offence with which the defendant is charged if he/she gives evidence.

The approach to s. 1(e) and (f) were explained in *Jones* v *DPP* [1962] AC 635:

> Proviso (e) permits questions to be asked. The corollary is that they must be answered. Proviso (f) does not say that certain questions may be asked: it says that certain questions may not be asked. This means that even if the questions are relevant and have to do with the issue before the court they cannot be asked unless covered by the permitting provisions of proviso (f).

Without s. 1 the prosecution would be very limited in the questions it could ask of a defendant in contradicting his/her assertions. It is for this reason that many defendants choose not to give evidence from the witness box during their trial. Section 35 of the Criminal Justice and Public Order Act 1994 (inferences from an accused's silence during trial) has also had a major influence in this area (**see chapter 11**).

10.3 Legal Professional Privilege

At common law, no privilege attaches to communications made in confidence except communications:

- between a client and a legal adviser made *for the purpose of the obtaining and giving of legal advice*; and

- between a client or his/her legal adviser and third parties, *the dominant purpose of which was preparation for contemplated or pending litigation.*

10.3.1 Extent of the Privilege

The privilege which applies to communications between client and legal adviser is considered by the courts to be of great importance. If legal professional privilege applies to a piece of evidence, this overrides all other considerations. This view was highlighted in *R v Derby Magistrates' Court, ex parte B* [1996] AC 487 where the appellant was acquitted of murder. His step-father was subsequently charged with the murder and, at his committal proceedings, the appellant was called as a prosecution witness. Counsel for the defence sought to cross-examine the appellant on certain factual instructions that he had given to his solicitors when he had been charged with the offence. The appellant declined to waive his privilege.

The issue was whether a witness summons could properly be issued to compel production by a prosecution witness in committal proceedings of proofs of evidence and attendance notes giving factual instructions to his solicitor in earlier criminal proceedings, arising out of the same event in which he had been acquitted. Lord Taylor of Gosforth CJ stated:

> The principle . . . is that a man must be able to consult his lawyer in confidence, since otherwise he might hold back half the truth. The client must be sure that what he tells his lawyer in confidence will never be revealed without his consent. Legal professional privilege is thus much more than an ordinary rule of evidence, limited in its application to the facts of a particular case. It is a fundamental condition on which the administration of justice as a whole rests. . . . But it is not for the sake of the applicant alone that the privilege must be upheld. It is in the wider interests of all those hereafter who might otherwise be deterred from telling the whole truth to their solicitors.

10.3.2 Scope of Privilege

As discussed above, a client *may*, and his/her legal adviser *must* (subject to the client's waiver), refuse to give oral evidence or to produce documents relating to:

- communications between the client and his/her legal adviser made for the purpose of enabling the client to obtain or the adviser to give legal advice about any matter, whether or not litigation was contemplated at the time;

- communications between the client or his/her legal adviser and third parties, the sole or dominant purpose of which was to enable the legal adviser to advise or act in relation to litigation that was pending or in the contemplation of the client.

A legal adviser, for the purposes of legal professional privilege, includes:

- a solicitor; or
- a barrister;
- employed advisers; and
- overseas advisers.

In the case of communications with third parties, the privilege can be claimed in respect of a document brought into existence before deciding to instruct a solicitor, provided that litigation was reasonably in prospect and the document was prepared for the sole or dominant purpose of enabling the solicitor to advise whether a claim should be made or resisted.

A document that is not privileged in the hands of the client does not become privileged if given into the custody of a lawyer for the purposes of obtaining legal advice (or if sent by the lawyer to a third party in connection with pending or contemplated litigation). If the item could be seized from a suspect it would not become privileged just because it has been sent to his/her lawyer.

10.3.3 Exceptions to Legal Privilege

An exception to the principle of legal professional privilege are communications in furtherance of crime or fraud. This would apply where a client asks to a legal adviser for advice in the commission of a crime or fraud. Where the legal adviser is ignorant of the purpose for which his/her advice is sought, the communication between the two is not privileged.

The exception can be relied upon only if there is *prima facie* evidence that it was the client's intention to obtain advice in furtherance of his/her criminal or fraudulent purpose.

10.3.4 Items Subject to Legal Privilege

This principle of legal professional privilege is set out in s. 10 of the Police and Criminal Evidence Act 1984. Section 10 is intended to reflect the common law and provides that:

> (1) Subject to subsection (2) below, in this Act 'items subject to legal privilege' means—
> (a) communications between a professional legal adviser and his client or any person representing his client made in connection with the giving of legal advice to the client;
> (b) communications between a professional legal adviser and his client or any person representing his client or between such an adviser or his client or any such representative and any other person made in connection with or in contemplation of legal proceedings and for the purposes of such proceedings; and
> (c) items enclosed with or referred to in such communications and made—
> (i) in connection with the giving of legal advice; or
> (ii) in connection with or in contemplation of legal proceedings and for the purposes of such proceedings,
> when they are in the possession of a person who is entitled to possession of them.
> (2) Items held with the intention of furthering a criminal purpose are not items subject to legal privilege.

Keynote

For the law governing the search for, and seizure of 'privileged' material, **see General Police Duties, chapter 2.**

10.3.5   By-passing the Privilege and Waiver of Privilege

Often there will be facts which are subject to legal professional privilege which would be useful to the prosecution case. While the rule of privilege is absolute, the facts can still be put to the courts in certain cases, namely:

- by-passing the privilege; and
- waiving the privilege.

By-passing the Privilege

Legal professional privilege prevents facts being proved in a particular way (i.e. through the client or through the lawyer or certain third parties). However, if enquiries reveal *other sources* by which the same fact(s) can be proved, the privilege is not breached. This could be achieved by obtaining a copy of the communication or by making use of documents legally coming in to the hands of police even if by accident.

Waiving the Privilege

The privilege is that of the client and he/she can waive it. However, he/she must take care to mark clearly the *extent* of any waiver otherwise communications which relate to the same subject matter may be taken to have been waived by implication.

Privilege is not taken to be waived where communications are disclosed for a limited purpose (e.g. to assist the police with enquiries).

In *R* v *Bowden* (1999) 149 NLJ 249, the Court of Appeal considered the waiver of legal professional privilege. It was held that, if in the course of questioning by the police, a suspect went beyond saying that he declined to answer on legal advice and explained the basis on which he had been so advised, legal professional privilege would be waived. Such waiver would similarly apply if a solicitor, acting as the authorised representative, gave such an explanation.

If a defendant gave evidence at his/her trial of the grounds on which the advice to make no comment was given, this would be construed as the defendant voluntarily withdrawing his/her protection to confidential information between client and legal adviser. Again, the same waiver would apply to the solicitor required to give evidence. Such waiver of legal privilege would enable questioning directed to the nature of the advice and the factual premises on which it was based.

10.4   Exclusion on Grounds of Public Policy

This is an area of disclosure and needs to be read in conjunction with the Criminal Procedure and Investigations Act 1996 (**see chapter 14**).

Generally, it is in the public interest that all relevant information should be made available to the court. However, it is also important on occasions to withhold material, the disclosure of which would harm the nation or the proper functioning of the public service. At times the needs of justice conflict with the needs of public policy and the courts have to balance these competing needs in deciding whether relevant information should be disclosed.

When public policy is claimed as a reason for not disclosing evidence in a trial, the process is known as claiming *public interest immunity*.

10.4.1   Public Interest Immunity

Public interest immunity may be raised by:

- The relevant minister or the Attorney-General (or Solicitor-General) intervening in a case.

- The party seeking to withhold the evidence either on his/her own initiative or at the request of the relevant government minister or department.

- The judge in the case.

10.4.2   Effect of Immunity

Where the claim is successful:

- A person entitled to claim privilege may refuse to answer the question(s) put or disclose the document sought.

- The facts may be proved by other evidence, if available.

- No adverse inferences may be drawn against a party or witness claiming privilege.

If a person entitled to claim privilege fails to do so or waives his/her privilege, no other person may object. The privilege *is that of the witness* (**see para. 10.2.1**). The trial judge is under a continuous duty, in the light of the way in which the trial develops, to keep his/her initial decision under review.

10.4.3   How Immunity is Claimed

This was set out in *R* v *Ward* [1993] 1 WLR 619.

> If, in a criminal case, the prosecution wish to claim public interest immunity for documents helpful to the defence, the prosecution are in law obliged to give notice to the defence of the asserted right to withhold the documents so that, if necessary, the court can be asked to rule on the legitimacy of the prosecution's claim. If the prosecution, in an exceptional case, are not prepared to have the issue determined by a court, the prosecution must be abandoned.

In *R* v *Keane* [1994] 1 WLR 746, Lord Taylor CJ held that it is for the prosecution to put before the court only those documents which it regards as material but wishes to withhold. However, if, in an exceptional case, the prosecution are in doubt about the materiality of some documents or information, the court may be asked to rule on that issue.

In assessing the interests of justice, the court must ask whether a document to which the immunity relates is *material* (i.e. relevant) to the proceedings. Its materiality will depend on the purpose for which it is sought to be deployed. If the disputed material may prove the defendant's innocence or avoid a miscarriage of justice, then the balance comes down resoundingly in favour of disclosing it.

Evidence which may be affected by a claim of public interest immunity might be a specific piece of evidence (such as an internal memorandum) which falls under one of the recognised heads (**see para. 10.4.4**); alternatively, it may fall within a *class* of documents which are generally protected (such as communications between government ministers and advisers — see below).

10.4.4   Types of Public Interest Immunity

The types of material under the heads of public interest immunity which are recognised by the courts are:

- national security and diplomatic relations;
- the proper functioning of the public service;
- police communications;
- informers and information for the detection of crime;
- judges and jurors;
- sources of information contained in publications.

National Security and Diplomatic Relations

A claim here will normally be successful where a ministerial certificate is presented to the court. In *Balfour* v *Foreign and Commonwealth Office* [1994] 1 WLR 681 it was held that, once there is an actual or potential risk to national security demonstrated by an appropriate ministerial certificate, the court should not exercise its right to inspect the material in question.

The Proper Functioning of Public Service

Public interest immunity may be claimed for correspondence and communications between ministers and high-level government officials, regarding the formulation of government policy.

Such communications were involved in the case against the directors of Matrix-Churchill, the company at the heart of the allegations that a 'supergun' had been sold and exported to Iraq.

Police Communications

Public interest immunity also attaches to police communications relating to the investigation of crime, such as:

- Documents or information upon the strength of which search warrants have been obtained.

- Reports sent by the police to the Director of Public Prosecutions.

- Police complaints and disciplinary files (see *Halford* v *Sharples* [1992] 1 WLR 736). (There is no immunity, however, for written complaints against the police prompting investigations under Part IX of the Police and Criminal Evidence Act 1984, **see General Police Duties, chapter 1.**)

- Working papers and reports prepared by investigating officers involved in complaints against police (production will be ordered where the public interest in disclosure of the contents outweighs the public interest in preserving confidentiality).

Public interest immunity does not attach to statements made during the course of a police grievance procedure, initiated by an officer, alleging either racial or sexual discrimination (*Commissioner of Police of the Metropolis* v *Locker* [1993] 3 All ER 584). For the law relating to equality of opportunity and discrimination, **see General Police Duties, chapter 12**.

There is no 'class' immunity (**see para. 10.4.3**) for statements obtained for the purposes of investigations concerning complaints against police. However, immunity may be claimed in the case of a particular document by reason of its contents (*R* v *Chief Constable of the West Midlands Police, ex parte Wiley* [1995] 1 AC 274).

Informers and Information for the Detection of Crime

The courts recognise that the police require information in order to detect crimes and that often, disclosure of this information would be detrimental to the efficiency of police investigations. The courts have recognised two sources of information in this area:

- informants;
- observation points.

Informants

This is a very important area relating to every day police work and the management of crime. This source was recognised by the courts in *R* v *Hennessey* (1978) 68 Cr App R 419 where Lawton LJ held that:

> The courts appreciate the need to protect the identity of informers, not only for their own safety but to ensure that the supply of information about criminal activities does not dry up.

Although the courts recognise the importance in protecting informants, they have held that this needs to be balanced with occasions where it is necessary to establish the innocence of the accused.

In *Marks* v *Beyfus* (1890) 25 QBD 494 Lord Esher MR said that:

> . . . if upon the trial of a prisoner the judge should be of opinion that the disclosure of the name of the informant is necessary or right in order to show the prisoner's innocence, then one public policy is in conflict with another public policy, and that which says that an innocent man is not to be condemned when his innocence can be proved is the policy that must prevail.

Again, the antiquity of this case, like any other, does not mean it is of limited applicability in today's climate; rather it *gains* in its authority as it stands the test of time (**see chapter 1**).

The fact that information has come from an informant should be recorded and the Crown Prosecution Service consulted on the matter of disclosure. The Service can apply to the courts for guidance on disclosure (**see chapter 14**).

Observation points

The principles for informants also apply to observation points used by police. These principles are intended to protect the identity of those people who have allowed their premises to be used for police surveillance, and the identity of their premises. If the accused submits that disclosure of the identification of the premises is necessary in order to show his/her innocence it is for the prosecution to show why the information should not be provided to the defence (**see chapter 14**).

In *R* v *Johnson* [1988] 1 WLR 1377, Watkins LJ gave the following guidance as to the minimum matters that should be dealt with when using such methods of detecting crime:

> (a)   The police officer in charge of the observations to be conducted, no one of lower rank than a sergeant should usually be acceptable for this purpose, must be able to testify that beforehand he visited all observation places to be used and ascertained the attitude of occupiers of premises, not only to the use to be made of them, but to the possible disclosure thereafter of the use made and facts which could lead to the identification of the premises thereafter and of the occupiers. He may of course in addition inform the court of difficulties, if any, usually encountered in the particular locality of obtaining assistance from the public.
> (b)   A police officer of no lower rank than a chief inspector must be able to testify that immediately prior to the trial he visited the places used for observations, the results of which it is proposed to give in evidence, and ascertained whether the occupiers are the same as when the observations took place and whether they are or are not, what the attitude of those occupiers is to the possible disclosure of the use previously made of the premises and of facts which could lead at the trial to identification of premises and occupiers.

The guidelines in *Johnson* do not require a threat of violence before protection can be afforded to the occupier of an observation post; it suffices if the occupier is in fear of harassment (*Blake* v *DPP* (1993) 97 Cr App R 169).

A Code of Practice in relation to surveillance methods will come into operation in October 1999 (**see General Police Duties, chapter 1**).

For the effect of privilege and the *Johnson* ruling on disclosure, **see chapter 14**.

Judges and Jurors

A judge cannot be compelled to give evidence of matters of which he/she became aware *as a result of the performance of his/her judicial functions*. However, the judge remains 'competent' to give evidence and, if a situation arises where his/her evidence is vital, the judge should be able to be relied on not to allow his/her non-compellability to stand in the way of giving evidence. Of course, if a judge's evidence is entirely unrelated to his/her judicial office (e.g. if he/she were to witness someone breaking into a neighbour's house), then the normal rules regarding compellability and competence will generally apply.

A jury's verdict cannot be impeached by the testimony of a juror as to what happened in the jury room. Unlike some other countries — notably the USA — it is a contempt of court to question a juror about the deliberations within the jury room, even after the trial.

Sources of Information Contained in Publications

Section 10 of the Contempt of Court Act 1981 provides that:

> *No court may require a person to disclose, nor is any person guilty of contempt of court for refusing to disclose, the source of information contained in a publication for which he is responsible, unless it*

be established to the satisfaction of the court that disclosure is necessary in the interests of justice or national security or for the prevention of disorder or crime.

Keynote

Section 10 applies to information which has been communicated and received for the purposes of publication, even if it is not 'contained in a publication', because the purpose underlying the statutory protection of sources of information is as much applicable before as after publication.

Disclosure will be ordered if it is shown to be necessary, either for the prevention of crime generally, or for the prevention of a particular and identifiable future crime.

PART TWO

THE LAW OF EVIDENCE

CHAPTER ELEVEN

EVIDENCE

11.1   Introduction

Evidence can be described as information that may be presented to a court so that it may decide on the probability of some facts asserted before it, that is information by which facts in issue tend to be proved or disproved. There are several types of evidence by which facts are open to proof — or disproof — and these are discussed later in the chapter.

11.2   Weight and Admissibility of Evidence

The two questions that need to be applied to any evidence are:

*   admissibility; and
*   weight.

The question of admissibility, to be decided by the judge in all cases, is whether the evidence is relevant to a fact in issue. All evidence of facts in issue and all evidence which is sufficiently relevant to prove (or disprove) facts in issue are potentially admissible.

The admissibility of evidence is very important to the outcome of any trial as it is from this that a person's guilt is decided. When collecting evidence in a case it should always be a consideration whether the evidence being collected is the best available (**although see para. 11.8**) and whether it will be admissible.

Once it is established that the evidence is admissible, it is put before the court to determine what weight it will attach to the evidence; that is, how much effect does it have on proving or disproving the case.

11.2.1   Evidence Gathering

The word evidence must not be confused with information. In relation to preparing an offence file, the investigation of the offence will result in the collection of information.

What is and what is not evidence can be decided at a later stage with the help of the Crown Prosecution Service. The importance of this distinction is that rules of evidence should not restrict the initial collection of information, otherwise a fact vital to the outcome of the case may be disregarded as irrelevant and/or inadmissible.

11.2.2 Reasons for Excluding Admissible Evidence

Even though evidence may be admissible in criminal cases, at common law, the trial judge has a general discretion to exclude legally admissible evidence tendered by the prosecution. This can be seen in *R* v *Sang* [1980] AC 402, where it was held that:

- A trial judge, as part of his/her duty to ensure that an accused receives a fair trial, always has a discretion to exclude evidence tendered by the prosecution if in his/her opinion its prejudicial effect outweighs its probative value.

- Other than in cases of admissions and confessions and generally with regard to evidence obtained from the accused after the commission of the offence, the judge has no discretion to exclude relevant admissible evidence on the ground that this was obtained by improper or unfair means.

Evidence may also be excluded for the following reasons:

- the incompetence of the witness;
- it relates to previous convictions, the character or disposition of the accused;
- it falls under hearsay;
- it is non-expert opinion evidence;
- it is privileged information;
- it is withheld as a matter of public policy.

There is also a power to exclude evidence under ss. 76 and 78 of the Police and Criminal Evidence Act 1984 (**see chapter 13**).

11.3 Facts in Issue

In a criminal case, facts in issue are those facts which must be proved by the prosecution in order to establish the defendant's guilt, or those facts which are the essential elements of a defence.

Such facts will include:

- the identity of the defendant;
- the *actus reus* (**see Crime, chapter 2**);
- any necessary knowledge or intent (**see Crime, chapter 1**).

The relevant criminal conduct (*actus reus*) and state of mind (*mens rea*) will always be facts in issue, and it is therefore essential that these features are understood, both as general concepts and also in relation to the particular offence being investigated.

11.4 Burden of Proof

The facts in issue fall into two distinct categories:

- the facts that the *prosecution* bear the burden of proving or disproving in order to establish the defendant's guilt;

- the facts which, in exceptional circumstances, the *defence* need to prove to show that the defendant is not guilty.

11.4.1 Duty of the Prosecution

'Throughout the web of the English criminal law one golden thread is always to be seen; that is the duty of the prosecution to prove the prisoner's guilt.' This famous passage is taken from the House of Lords' decision in *Woolmington* v *DPP* [1935] AC 462. The underlying principle was perhaps best explained by Geoffrey Lawrence QC in an address to the jury in a murder trial:

> The possibility of guilt is not enough, suspicion is not enough, probability is not enough, likelihood is not. A criminal matter is not a question of balancing probabilities and deciding in favour of probability.

> If the accusation is not proved beyond reasonable doubt against the man accused in the dock, then by the law he is entitled to be acquitted, because that is the way our rules work. It is no concession to give him the benefit of the doubt. He is entitled by law to a verdict of not guilty.

(See Brian Harris, *The Literature of the Law*, Blackstone Press Ltd.)

Therefore the duty to prove guilt is always on the prosecution. The standard of proof *is beyond all reasonable doubt*.

Where the defendant enters a plea of not guilty to the charge, the onus is on the prosecution to prove the whole of their case. This includes 'the identity of the accused, the nature of the act and the existence of any necessary knowledge or intent' (*R* v *Sims* [1946] KB 531).

Generally the onus is on the prosecution in the first instance to establish particular facts to prove the accused's guilt beyond all reasonable doubt. However, once a prima facie case is made out, the defence has to establish particular facts in order to rebut the prosecution evidence. Here there is a shift of the onus to establish particular facts.

11.4.2 Duty on the Defence

The standard of proof for the defence is less rigorous than for the prosecution when establishing guilt (beyond all reasonable doubt). The defence will succeed if the court or jury are satisfied that the defence evidence is more probably true than false. This standard of proof is referred to as *the balance of probabilities*.

Generally the prosecution bear the duty of proving or disproving certain facts and, if they fail to do so, the defence need say nothing; the prosecution fails and the defendant is acquitted.

In a number of cases, however, the particular statute may impose a burden on the defence to prove certain facts. This evidential burden can be seen in many cases, e.g. the law relating to the carrying of weapons. Once the prosecution have proved (beyond a reasonable doubt) that a defendant was carrying an offensive weapon, the burden then shifts to the defence to prove (on the balance of probabilities) that he/she had lawful authority or reasonable excuse (**see General Police Duties, chapter 6**).

11.5 Formal Admissions

Where a fact is accepted by the defence, there is a process by which this can be formally admitted under the Criminal Justice Act 1967, s. 10. In such formal admissions the fact ceases to be an issue.

The Criminal Justice Act 1967, s. 10 provides that:

(1) Subject to the provisions of this section, any fact of which oral evidence may be given in any criminal proceedings may be admitted for the purpose of those proceedings by or on behalf of the prosecutor or defendant, and the admission by any party of any such fact under this section shall as against that party be conclusive evidence in those proceedings of the fact admitted.

(2) An admission under this section—

(a) may be made before or at the proceedings;

(b) if made otherwise than in court, shall be in writing;

(c) if made in writing by an individual, shall purport to be signed by the person making it and, if so made by a body corporate, shall purport to be signed by a director or manager, or the secretary or clerk, or some other similar officer of the body corporate;

(d) if made on behalf of a defendant who is an individual, shall be made by his counsel or solicitor;

(e) if made at any stage before the trial by a defendant who is an individual, must be approved by his counsel or solicitor (whether at the time it was made or subsequently) before or at the proceedings in question.

(3) An admission under this section for the purpose of proceedings relating to any matter shall be treated as an admission for the purpose of any subsequent criminal proceedings relating to that matter (including any appeal or retrial).

(4) An admission under this section may with the leave of the court be withdrawn in the proceedings for the purpose of which it is made or any subsequent criminal proceedings relating to the same matter.

Keynote

Where the accused enters a not guilty plea at a plea directions hearing, both the prosecution and defence are expected to inform the court of facts which are to be admitted and which are then accepted in written form in accordance with s. 10(2)(b) of the 1967 Act (see *Practice Direction (Crown Court: Plea and Directions Hearings)* [1995] 1 WLR 1318, para. 10(f)).

Formal admission may be made by counsel or a solicitor during court proceedings. In such cases the admission is written down and signed by or on behalf of the party making the admission. This procedure applies for the purpose of summary trial or proceedings before magistrates acting as examining justices (Magistrates' Courts Rules 1981, r. 71).

11.6 Inferences from Silence

At common law, when being questioned about involvement in a criminal offence, a person is under no obligation to answer any of the questions. This is another key feature of the criminal justice system in England and Wales and is the reason behind the cautioning of suspects required by the Police and Criminal Evidence Act 1984 (**see General Police Duties, chapter 2**). However, ss. 34 to 38 of the Criminal Justice and Public Order Act 1994, now contain the substance of the law in relation to the accused's silence.

Sections 34 to 37 permit the court to draw 'such inferences as appear proper' against the accused in the circumstances contained within the sections.

11.6.1   Inferences from Silence when Questioned or Charged

Section 34 of the Criminal Justice and Public Order Act 1994 provides that inferences can be drawn if, when questioned by the police under caution, charged or officially informed that he/she may be prosecuted, the accused fails to mention a fact on which he/she later relies in his defence, and which he/she could reasonably have been expected to mention at the time.

Section 34 provides that:

(1) Where, in any proceedings against a person for an offence, evidence is given that the accused—

(a) at any time before he was charged with the offence, on being questioned under caution by a constable trying to discover whether or by whom the offence had been committed, failed to mention any fact relied on in his defence in those proceedings, or

(b) on being charged with the offence or officially informed that he might be prosecuted for it, failed to mention any such fact,

being a fact which in the circumstances existing at the time the accused could reasonably have been expected to mention when so questioned, charged or informed, as the case may be, subsection (2) below applies.

(2) Where this subsection applies—

(a) a magistrates' court inquiring into the offence as examining justices;

(b) a judge, in deciding whether to grant an application made by the accused under—

(i) section 6 of the Criminal Justice Act 1987 (application for dismissal of charge of serious fraud in respect of which notice of transfer has been given under section 4 of the Act); or

(ii) paragraph 5 of Schedule 6 to the Criminal Justice Act 1991 (application for dismissal of charge of violent or sexual offence involving child in respect of which notice of transfer has been given under section 53 of that Act);

(c) the court, in determining whether there is a case to answer; and

(d) the court or jury, in determining whether the accused is guilty of the offence charged,

may draw such inferences from the failure as appear proper.

(3) Subject to any directions by the court, evidence tending to establish the failure may be given before or after evidence tending to establish the fact which the accused is alleged to have failed to mention.

(4) This section applies in relation to questioning by persons (other than constables) charged with the duty of investigating offences or charging offenders as it applies in relation to questioning by constables; and in subsection (1) above 'officially informed' means informed by a constable or any such person.

(5) This section does not—

(a) prejudice the admissibility in evidence of the silence or other reaction of the accused in the face of anything said in his presence relating to the conduct in respect of which he is charged, in so far as evidence thereof would be admissible apart from this section; or

(b) preclude the drawing of any inference from any such silence or other reaction of the accused which could properly be drawn apart from this section.

(6) This section does not apply in relation to a failure to mention a fact if the failure occurred before the commencement of this section.

Keynote

Where a defendant says that advice was received from his/her solicitor not to answer questions, the accused is entitled to give evidence of the conversation with the solicitor prior to interview to rebut any allegation of post-interview fabrication. The defendant is also entitled to call the solicitor to give evidence of the advice given before interview (*R v Daniel* (1998) 162 JP 578) (**See chapter 10.**)

In *R v Argent* [1997] 2 Cr App R 27 the court stated that personal factors which might be relevant to an assessment of what an individual could reasonably have been expected to mention were age, experience, mental capacity, state of health, sobriety, tiredness and personality.

Section 34 differs from the other 'inference' sections in that the questioning need not occur at a police station and therefore the presence of a legal representative is not required. However, it appears clear that, should the prosecution seek to draw any inferences of an accused's silence where such questioning has occurred, the questions would need to be asked of the suspect again once he/she had access to legal advice.

A requirement to caution the person is contained in s. 34(1)(a) to make it clear of the risks connected with a failure to mention facts which later form part of the defence (**see General Police Duties, chapter 2**):

In relation to s. 34, the accused cannot be convicted solely on an inference drawn from a failure or refusal (s. 38(3) of the 1994 Act) (**see para. 11.6.5 below**).

Murray v United Kingdom

A judgment of the European Court of Human Rights in the case of *Murray v United Kingdom* (1996) 22 EHRR 29 has had implications in relation to inferences being drawn from the silence of an accused when denied access to legal advice. The European Court held that this constituted a breach Article 6(1), in conjunction with Article 6(3) of the European Convention on Human Rights (the requirement for a fair trial). The government intends to amend the law in the forthcoming Youth Justice and Criminal Evidence Bill to ensure that domestic law is fully compatible with UK obligations under the European Convention.

This case has led to new arrangements for use by police officers and prosecutors of evidence obtained from a suspect during the course of an interview in which legal advice was sought but delayed by the police.

Guidance has been provided by the government (Home Office Circular 53/1998). This requires that where access to legal advice has been delayed in accordance with Annex B of PACE Code C (**see appendix 4**), the procedures for conducting the interview at the police station should be as follows:

- the interviewing officer should conduct any interview with the suspect at the police station in accordance with PACE Code C, para. 11.2A;

- the interviewing officer should make a written note of those questions which the suspect has failed or refused to answer;

- once the suspect has had the opportunity of access to legal advice, the interviewing officer should put these questions to the suspect again; and ask the suspect whether he/she wishes to say/add anything further.

11.6.2 Inferences from Silence at Trial

Section 35 of the Criminal Justice and Public Order Act 1994 provides that inferences can be drawn from an accused's failure to give evidence or refusal to answer any question, without good cause, where the person has been sworn. Section 35 provides that:

> (1) At the trial of any person who has attained the age of fourteen years for an offence, subsections (2) and (3) below apply unless—
> (a)   the accused's guilt is not in issue; or
> (b)   it appears to the court that the physical or mental condition of the accused makes it undesirable for him to give evidence;
> but subsection (2) below does not apply if, at the conclusion of the evidence for the prosecution, his legal representative informs the court that the accused will give evidence or, where he is unrepresented, the court ascertains from him that he will give evidence.
> (2) Where this subsection applies, the court shall, at the conclusion of the evidence for the prosecution, satisfy itself (in the case of proceedings on indictment, in the presence of the jury) that the accused is aware that the stage has been reached at which evidence can be given for the defence and that he can, if he wishes, give evidence and that, if he chooses not to give evidence, or having been sworn, without good cause refuses to answer any question, it will be permissible for the court or jury to draw such inferences as appear proper from his failure to give evidence or his refusal, without good cause, to answer any question.
> (3) Where this subsection applies, the court or jury, in determining whether the accused is guilty of the offence charged, may draw such inferences as appear proper from the failure of the accused to give evidence or his refusal, without good cause, to answer any question.
> (4)   This section does not render the accused compellable to give evidence on his own behalf, and he shall accordingly not be guilty of contempt of court by reason of a failure to do so.
> (5) For the purposes of this section a person who, having been sworn, refuses to answer any question shall be taken to do so without good cause unless—
> (a)   he is entitled to refuse to answer the question by virtue of any enactment, whenever passed or made, or on the ground of privilege; or
> (b)   the court in the exercise of its general discretion excuses him from answering it.
> (6)   Where the age of any person is material for the purposes of subsection (1) above, his age shall for those purposes be taken to be that which appears to the court to be his age.
> (7)   This section applies—
> (a)   in relation to proceedings on indictment for an offence, only if the person charged with the offence is arraigned on or after the commencement of this section;
> (b)   in relation to proceedings in a magistrates' court, only if the time when the court begins to receive evidence in the proceedings falls after the commencement of this section.

Keynote

Section 35 only applies to a person who has attained the age of 14 years; this is not contained in the other 'inference' sections. This also applies to those whose 'physical or mental condition make it undesirable' for them to give evidence. However, there are rare cases where this may not apply.

In *R* v *Friend* [1997] 1 WLR 1433, the accused was aged 15 with a mental age of nine and an IQ of 63. It was held that the accused's mental condition did not make it 'undesirable' for him to give evidence and it was right that inferences be drawn under s. 35(3).

As with s. 34, in relation to s. 35 the accused cannot be convicted solely on an inference drawn from a failure or refusal (s. 38(3)) (**see para. 11.6.5 below**).

11.6.3 Inferences from Silence: Failure to Account for Objects, Substances and Marks

Section 36 of the Criminal Justice and Public Order Act 1994 provides that inferences can be drawn from an accused's failure to give evidence or refusal to answer any question about any object, substance or mark which may be attributable to the accused in the commission of an offence.

Section 36 provides that:

> (1) Where—
> (a) a person is arrested by a constable, and there is—
> (i) on his person; or
> (ii) in or on his clothing or footwear; or
> (iii) otherwise in his possession; or
> (iv) in any place in which he is at the time of his arrest,
> any object, substance or mark, or there is any mark on any such object; and
> (b) that or another constable investigating the case reasonably believes that the presence of the object, substance or mark may be attributable to the participation of the person arrested in the commission of an offence specified by the constable; and
> (c) the constable informs the person arrested that he so believes, and requests him to account for the presence of the object, substance or mark; and
> (d) the person fails or refuses to do so,
> then if, in any proceedings against the person for the offence so specified, evidence of those matters is given, subsection (2) below applies.
> (2) Where this subsection applies—
> (a) a magistrates' court inquiring into the offence as examining justices;
> (b) a judge, in deciding whether to grant an application made by the accused under—
> (i) section 6 of the Criminal Justice Act 1987 (application for dismissal of charge of serious fraud in respect of which notice of transfer has been given under section 4 of that Act); or
> (ii) paragraph 5 of Schedule 6 to the Criminal Justice Act 1991 (application for dismissal of charge of violent or sexual offence involving child in respect of which notice of transfer has been given under section 53 of that Act);
> (c) the court, in determining whether there is a case to answer; and
> (d) the court or jury, in determining whether the accused is guilty of the offence charged,
> may draw such inferences from the failure or refusal as appear proper.
> (3) Subsections (1) and (2) above apply to the condition of clothing or footwear as they apply to a substance or mark thereon.
> (4) Subsections 1 and 2 above do not apply unless the accused was told in ordinary language by the constable when making the request mentioned in subsection (1)(c) above what the effect of this section would be if he failed or refused to comply with the request.
> (5) This section applies in relation to officers of customs and excise as it applies in relation to constables.
> (6) This section does not preclude the drawing of any inference from a failure or refusal of the accused to account for the presence of an object, substance or mark or from the condition of clothing or footwear which could properly be drawn apart from this section.
> (7) This section does not apply in relation to a failure or refusal which occurred before the commencement of this section.

Keynote

Similarly with s. 37 below, an inference may only be drawn where four conditions are satisfied:

- the accused has been arrested;

- a constable reasonably believes that the object, substance or mark (or the presence of the accused (s. 37)) may be attributable to the accused's participation in a crime (s. 36 (an offence 'specified by the constable') or s. 37 (the offence for which he/she was arrested);

- the constable informs the accused of his/her belief and requests an explanation;

- the constable tells the suspect (in ordinary language) the effect of a failure or refusal to comply with the request.

It is considered that the request for information under both s. 36 and s. 37 are a form of questioning and should be undertaken during the interview at the police station. The request for such information prior to this would be an exception to the rule.

The interviewing officer is required to give the accused a 'special warning' for an inference to be drawn from a suspect's failure or refusal to answer a question about one of these matters or to answer it satisfactorily. This 'special warning' is provided by PACE Code C, para. 10.5B, which states that the interviewing officer must first tell the suspect *in ordinary language*:

- what offence is being investigated;

- what fact the suspect is being asked to account for;

- that the interviewing officer believes this fact may be due to the suspect's taking part in the commission of the offence in question;

- that a court may draw a proper inference if the suspect fails or refuses to account for the fact about which he/she is being questioned;

- that a record is being made of the interview and that it may be given in evidence at any subsequent trial.

As with the preceding two sections, in relation to s. 36 the accused cannot be convicted solely on an inference drawn from a failure or refusal (s. 38(3)) (**see para. 11.6.5 below**).

11.6.4 Inferences from Silence: Failure to Account for Presence

Section 37 of the Criminal Justice and Public Order Act 1994 provides that inferences can be drawn from an accused's failure to give evidence or refusal to answer any question about his/her presence at a place or time when the offence for which he/she was arrested was committed.

Section 37 provides that:

> *(1)   Where—*
> *(a)   a person arrested by a constable was found by him at a place at or about the time the offence for which he was arrested is alleged to have been committed; and*
> *(b)   that or another constable investigating the offence reasonably believes that the presence of the person at that place and at that time may be attributable to his participation in the commission of the offence; and*
> *(c)   the constable informs the person that he so believes, and requests him to account for that presence; and*
> *(d)   the person fails or refuses to do so,*
> *then if, in any proceedings against the person for the offence, evidence of those matters is given, subsection (2) below applies.*
> *(2)   Where this subsection applies—*

(a) a magistrates' court inquiring into the offence as examining justices;

(b) a judge, in deciding whether to grant an application made by the accused under—

(i) section 6 of the Criminal Justice Act 1987 (application for dismissal of charge of serious fraud in respect of which notice of transfer has been given under section 4 of that Act); or

(ii) paragraph 5 of Schedule 6 to the Criminal Justice Act 1991 (application for dismissal of charge of violent or sexual offence involving child in respect of which notice of transfer has been given under section 53 of that Act);

(c) the court, in determining whether there is a case to answer; and

(d) the court or jury, in determining whether the accused is guilty of the offence charged,

may draw such inferences from the failure or refusal as appear proper.

(3) Subsections (1) and (2) do not apply unless the accused was told in ordinary language by the constable when making the request mentioned in subsection (1)(c) above what the effect of this section would be if he failed or refused to comply with the request.

(4) This section applies in relation to officers of customs and excise as it applies in relation to constables.

(5) This section does not preclude the drawing of any inference from a failure or refusal of the accused to account for his presence at a place which could properly be drawn apart from this section.

(6) This section does not apply in relation to a failure or refusal which occurred before the commencement of this section.

Keynote

Section 37 appears somewhat restrictive in that it is only concerned with the suspect's location at the time of arrest and applies only when he/she was found at the location of the crime at or about the relevant time.

PACE Code C, para. 10.5B also applies to s. 37 in relation to the 'special warning' required to be given by the interviewing officer.

Unlike s. 36, here the officer that sees the person at or near the scene of the alleged offence must be the arresting officer.

As with ss. 35 and 36, in relation to s. 37 the accused cannot be convicted solely on an inference drawn from a failure or refusal (s. 38(3)) (**see para. 11.6.5 below**).

11.6.5 Inferences from Silence: No Conviction on Silence Alone

Section 38 of the Criminal Justice and Public Order Act 1994 applies to all of the four provisions relating to inferences from silence (ss. 34, 35, 36 and 37) and provides that an inference cannot be the sole basis for a finding of a case to answer, issue or dismissal of a notice to transfer, or for a finding of guilt. Nothing in s. 38 prejudices the courts general powers to exclude evidence (**see chapter 13**).

11.7 Relevant Facts

The cardinal rule of the law of evidence is that, subject to the exclusionary rules, all evidence which is sufficiently relevant to the facts in issue is admissible, and all evidence which is irrelevant or insufficiently relevant to the facts in issue should be excluded.

In *DPP* v *Kilbourne* [1973] AC 729, Lord Simon of Glaisdale stated that: '. . . relevant . . . evidence is evidence which makes the matter which requires proof more or less probable'.

Evidence of the *facts in issue* (**see para. 11.3**) might include a statement that the witness saw the accused hit the victim over the head with a bottle. This is directly relevant to the charge of assault. Other *relevant facts*, on the other hand, might require the court to put together pieces of evidence in order to come to the conclusion that some other relevant incidents occurred. For instance, that the witness saw the accused walk past the victim, heard a scream, looked round to see blood coming from a cut on the victim's head and the accused running away. In these circumstances, the witness does not actually see the assault but there may be sufficient evidence from that witness for the court to draw the conclusion that the accused assaulted the victim.

11.8 The Best Evidence Rule

This rule of evidence covers the best evidence that the nature of the case will allow. The rule was propounded in 1745 and generally required that only the people having immediate personal knowledge of a fact in issue (**see para. 11.3**) could give evidence as to that fact. With the social and technological changes since the rule was introduced has come a gradual erosion, leaving us with a much less strict interpretation.

Nevertheless, for the purpose of evidence gathering, the general principle to produce evidence from the best practicable source still holds good.

Besides a general requirement to produce the best evidence for a court, the rule's main application now relates to documentary evidence. This is usually defined as primary (meaning the original document) and secondary (meaning a copy of the original). Therefore the original of a private document must be produced unless its absence can be explained.

The best evidence rule was invoked in *R* v *Stevenson, Hulse and Whitney* [1971] Crim LR 95, to declare a tape recording inadmissible on the grounds that it was likely that the tape recording was not the original.

11.9 Sources of Evidence

Evidence can be categorised into the following groups:

- original (primary) evidence
- real evidence
- secondary evidence
- documentary evidence
- hearsay evidence
- circumstantial evidence
- presumptions
- evidence of character
- opinion
- corroboration
- judicial notice.

Each of these categories is considered in detail below.

11.9.1 Original (Primary) Evidence

This is where a witness gives evidence to the court directly from the witness box. The evidence is presented to the court *as evidence of the truth of what he/she states* (contrast this with the exceptions to hearsay; **see para. 11.9.5**). Here the witness is giving direct testimony about a fact of which he/she has personal or first-hand knowledge and therefore can be challenged on the truth of that fact in cross-examination (**see chapter 6**).

11.9.2   Real Evidence

Real evidence usually takes the form of a material object for inspection by the court. This evidence is to prove, either that the material object in question exists, or to enable the court to draw an inference from its own observation as to the object's value and physical condition (an example would be pornographic material to determine whether it is 'obscene'). Such material objects, referred to as exhibits, produced to the court would normally be accompanied by written testimony and identified by a witness. This testimony usually includes an explanation of the connection between the exhibit and the facts in issue or the relevance to an issue.

Little if any weight can attach to real evidence in the absence of accompanying testimony identifying the object and connecting it with the facts in issue. So, in the example of the assault (**see para. 11.7**) simply producing a bottle without an accompanying statement identifying it as the one actually used would prove nothing.

There is no rule of law that an object must be produced, or its non-production excused, before oral evidence may be given about it. For example, it is not necessary for the police to produce the very breath test device used by them on a particular occasion (see *Castle* v *Cross* [1984] 1 WLR 1372). However, the weight of the oral evidence may be adversely affected by the non-production of the object in question (*Armory* v *Delamirie* (1722) 1 Str 505).

In addition to material objects, behaviour, appearance and demeanour may be regarded as real evidence. Examples would be:

- Behaviour (e.g. a person's misconduct in a court of law for the purposes of contempt of court).

- Appearance (e.g. a person's physical appearance in relation to evidence of identification or on the question of the existence or causation of personal injuries).

- Demeanour (e.g. a person's attitude may be relevant to the weight to be attached to his/her evidence, or whether he/she is to be treated as a hostile witness (**see para. 6.10.3**).

The court has the responsibility to preserve and retain exhibits until the conclusion of the trial. It is usual for the court to entrust the exhibits to the police or Crown Prosecution Service and this places a duty on them to:

- take all proper care to preserve the exhibits safe from loss or danger;

- co-operate with the defence in order to allow them reasonable access to the exhibits for the purpose of inspection and examination; and

- produce the exhibits at the trial (*Lambeth Metropolitan Stipendiary Magistrate, ex parte McComb* [1983] QB 551). (**See chapter 14** for the general rules on disclosure.)

11.9.3 Secondary Evidence

Secondary evidence is evidence of an inferior kind, e.g. a copy of a document or a copy of such a copy. Such evidence can be admissible, e.g. in *Butler* v *Board of Trade* [1971] Ch 680 where a copy of a letter from the plaintiff's solicitor to the plaintiff had been accidentally included in papers handed over to the Official Receiver. It was held that, although the original letter was privileged, a copy was admissible in the criminal proceedings. (See also *Calcraft* v *Guest* [1898] 1 QB 759.)

Secondary documentary evidence is admissible by way of exception in the following cases (although the list is not exhaustive):

- Where the other party fails to produce a document at court after being served with a notice to do so.

- Where a stranger to the case lawfully refuses to produce a document, e.g. where he/she could claim privilege.

- Where a document has been lost and after due search cannot be found or has been destroyed.

- Where the production of the original document is impossible, such as, writing on a wall or where the law requires the document to remain where it is for reasons of security.

- Where a public document is concerned, on the grounds that its production would be illegal or inconvenient.

Nowadays the court is not confined to the best evidence but can admit all relevant evidence (*Kajala* v *Noble* (1982) 75 Cr App R 149).

11.9.4 Documentary Evidence

Documentary evidence consists of documents produced for inspection by the court, either as items of real evidence or as hearsay or original evidence. Here the word 'document' includes maps, plans, graphs, drawings, photographs, discs, tapes, video tapes and films. This would include CCTV recordings and tapes from police control rooms. The contents of a document may be admissible *as evidence of their truth* or *for some other purpose*. Documents produced to the court are usually accompanied by some testimony and identified by a witness.

Evidence by Certificate of Plan or Drawing

Section 41 of the Criminal Justice Act 1948 provides that:

> *(1)   In any criminal proceedings, a certificate purporting to be signed by a constable, or by a person have the prescribed qualifications, and certifying that a plan or drawing exhibited thereto is a plan or drawing made by him of the place or object specified in the certificate, and that the plan or drawing is correctly drawn to a scale so specified, shall be evidence of the relative position of the things shown on the plan or drawing.*
>
> . . .
>
> *(4)   Nothing in this section shall be deemed to make a certificate admissible as evidence in proceedings for an offence except in a case where and to the extent to which oral evidence to the like effect would have been admissible in those proceedings.*

(5) Nothing in this section shall be deemed to make a certificate admissible as evidence in proceedings for any offence unless a copy thereof has, not less than seven days before the hearing or trial, been served in the prescribed manner on the person charged with the offence; or if that person, not later than three days before the hearing or trial or within such further time as the court may in special circumstances allow, serves notice in the prescribed form and manner on the prosecutor requiring the attendance at the trial of the person who signed the certificate.

(6) In this section the expression prescribed means prescribed by rules made by the Secretary of State.

Keynote

Police officers are quite often required to produce plans or drawings, the most common example of this being the road layout and positions of vehicles following a road traffic accident.

Prescribed qualification as mentioned in s. 41(1) refers to registered architects, chartered surveyors, civil engineers, municipal engineers and members of the Land Agents Society.

Where a witness makes a statement to the police and video footage of the events subsequently becomes available, it is acceptable for the witness to be permitted to see the video and to be allowed to correct or modify his/her statement in the light of the video evidence (*R v Rebuts*, *The Times*, 2 May 1998).

Admissibility of Written Statements in Summary Proceedings

Section 9 of the Criminal Justice Act 1967 provides that:

(1) In any criminal proceedings, other than [committal proceedings], a written statement by any person shall, if such of the conditions mentioned in the next following subsection as are applicable are satisfied, be admissible as evidence to the like extent as oral evidence to the like effect by that person.

(2) The said conditions are—

(a) the statement purports to be signed by the person who made it;

(b) the statement contains a declaration by the person to the effect that it is true to the best of his knowledge and belief and that he made the statement knowing that, if it were tendered in evidence, he would be liable to prosecution if he wilfully stated in it anything which he knew to be false or did not believe to be true;

(c) before the hearing at which the statement is tendered in evidence, a copy of the statement is served, by or on behalf of the party proposing to tender it, on each of the other parties to the proceedings; and

(d) none of the other parties or their solicitors, within seven days from the service of the copy of the statement, serves a notice on the party so proposing objecting to the statement being tendered in evidence under this section:

Provided that the conditions mentioned in paragraphs (c) and (d) of this subsection shall not apply if the parties agree before or during the hearing that the statement shall be so tendered.

Keynote

The declaration at s. 9(2)(b) need not be separately signed.

Note that s. 9(2)(c) and (d) need not apply if the parties so agree before or during the hearing. In other words, a statement can still be tendered in evidence even though the other parties have not had copies or the seven-day requirement has not been observed.

Section 9 goes on to provide that:

(3)   The following provisions shall also have effect in relation to any written statement tendered in evidence under this section, that is to say—

(a)   if the statement is made by a person under the age of [eighteen], it shall give his age;

(b)   if it is made by a person who cannot read it, it shall be read to him before he signs it and shall be accompanied by a declaration by the person who so read the statement to the effect that it was so read; and

(c)   if it refers to any other document as an exhibit, the copy served on any other party to the proceedings under paragraph (c) of the last foregoing subsection shall be accompanied by a copy of that document or by such information as may be necessary in order to enable the party on whom it is served to inspect that document or a copy thereof.

(4)   Notwithstanding that a written statement made by any person may be admissible as evidence by virtue of this section—

(a)   the party by whom or on whose behalf a copy of the statement was served may call that person to give evidence; and

(b)   the court may, of its own motion or on the application of any party to the proceedings, require that person to attend before the court and give evidence.

(5)   . . .

(6)   So much of any statement as is admitted in evidence by virtue of this section shall, unless the court otherwise directs, be read aloud at the hearing and where the court so directs an account shall be given orally of so much of any statement as is not read aloud.

(7)   Any document or object referred to as an exhibit and identified in a written statement tendered in evidence under this section shall be treated as if it had been produced as an exhibit and identified in court by the maker of the statement.

(8)   A document required by this section to be served on any person may be served by—

(a)   delivering it to him or to his solicitor; or

(b)   by addressing it to him or leaving it at his usual or last known place of abode or place of business or by addressing it to his solicitor and leaving it at his office; or

(c)   by sending it in a registered letter or by recorded delivery service or by first class post addressed to him at his usual or last known place of abode or place of business or addressed to his solicitor at his office; or

(d)   in the case of a body corporate, by delivering it to the secretary or clerk of the body at its registered or principal office or sending it in a registered letter or by the recorded delivery service or by first class post addressed to the secretary or clerk of that body at that office.

Keynote

The provisions of s. 9 of the Criminal Justice Act 1967, had a major impact on both witness's time (particularly the police) and the cost of court cases. The section allows for evidence to be admitted without the necessity of physically calling the witness who gave the statement.

Documentary Records

Section 23 of the Criminal Justice Act 1988 provides that:

(1)   Subject—

(a)   to subsection (4) below;

(b)   to paragraph 1A of Schedule 2 to the Criminal Appeal Act 1968 (evidence given orally at original trial to be given orally at retrial); and

(c)   to section 69 of the Police and Criminal Evidence Act 1984 (evidence from computer records),

a statement made by a person in a document shall be admissible in criminal proceedings as evidence of any fact of which direct oral evidence by him would be admissible if—

(i)   the requirements of one of the paragraphs of subsection (2) below are satisfied; or

(ii)   the requirements of subsection (3) below are satisfied.

(2)   The requirement mentioned in subsection (1)(i) above are—

(a)   that the person who made the statement is dead or by reason of his bodily or mental condition unfit to attend as a witness;

(b)   that—

(i)   the person who made the statement is outside the United Kingdom; and

(ii)   it is not reasonably practicable to secure his attendance; or

(c)   that all reasonable steps have been taken to find the person who made the statement, but that he cannot be found.

(3)   The requirements mentioned in subsection (1)(ii) above are—

(a)   that the statement was made to a police officer or some other person charged with the duty of investigating offences or charging offenders; and

(b)   that the person who made it does not give oral evidence through fear or because he is kept out of the way.

(4)   Subsection (1) above does not render admissible a confession made by an accused person that would not be admissible under section 76 of the Police and Criminal Evidence Act 1984.

Keynote

Subject to s. 23(1)(a) to (c), a statement made by a person in a document shall be admissible if any one of the requirements detailed in s. 23(2) is satisfied, or both of the requirements detailed in s. 23(3) are satisfied.

Business Documents

Section 24 of the Criminal Justice Act 1988 provides that:

(1)   Subject—

(a)   to subsections (3) and (4) below;

(b)   to paragraph 1A of Schedule 2 to the Criminal Appeal Act 1968; and

(c)   to section 69 of the Police and Criminal Evidence Act 1984,

a statement in a document shall be admissible in criminal proceedings as evidence of any fact of which direct oral evidence would be admissible, if the following conditions are satisfied—

(i)   the document was created or received by a person in the course of a trade, business, profession or other occupation, or as the holder of a paid or unpaid office; and

(ii)   the information contained in the document was supplied by a person (whether or not the maker of the statement) who had, or may reasonably be supposed to have had, personal knowledge of the matters dealt with.

(2)   Subsection (1) above applies whether the information contained in the document was supplied directly or indirectly but, if it was supplied indirectly, only if each person through whom it was supplied received it—

(a)   in the course of a trade, business, profession or other occupation; or

(b)   as the holder of a paid or unpaid office.

(3)   Subsection (1) above does not render admissible a confession made by an accused person that would not be admissible under section 76 of the Police and Criminal Evidence Act 1984.

(4)   A statement prepared otherwise than in accordance with section 3 of the Criminal Justice (International Co-operation) Act 1990 below or an order under paragraph 6 of Schedule 13 to this Act or under section 30 or 31 . . . for the purposes—

(a)   of pending or contemplated criminal proceedings; or

(b)   of a criminal investigation,

shall not be admissible by virtue of subsection (1) above unless—

(i)   the requirements of one of the paragraphs of subsection (2) of section 23 above are satisfied; or

(ii)   the requirements of subsection (3) of that section are satisfied; or

(iii)   the person who made the statement cannot reasonably be expected (having regard to the time which has elapsed since he made the statement and all the circumstances) to have any recollection of the matters dealt with in the statement.

Keynote

Subject to the provisions of s. 24(1)(a) to (c), a statement in a document will be admissible if both conditions (i) and (ii) of subsection (1) are satisfied. A statement:

- other than a statement obtained on request outside the United Kingdom (s. 3 of the Criminal Justice (International Co-operation) Act 1990),
- for use in a Service court (sch. 13 of the 1988 Act),
- an expert's report (s. 30), or
- provision of material to help members of a jury to understand complicated issues or technical terms (s. 31),

will only be admissible if one of the requirements of (i) to (iii) of s. 24(4) are satisfied.

Statements in Documents

Section 26 of the Criminal Justice Act 1988 provides that:

Where a statement which is admissible in criminal proceedings by virtue of section 23 or 24 above appears to the court to have been prepared, otherwise than in accordance with section 3 of the Criminal Justice (International Co-operation) Act 1990 below or an order under paragraph 6 of Schedule 13 to this Act or under section 30 or 31 below, for the purposes—
(a)   of pending or contemplated criminal proceedings; or
(b)   of a criminal investigation, the statement shall not be given in evidence in any criminal proceedings without the leave of the court, and the court shall not give leave unless it is of the opinion that the statement ought to be admitted in the interests of justice; and in considering whether its admission would be in the interests of justice, it shall be the duty of the court to have regard—
(i)   to the contents of the statement;
(ii)   to any risk, having regard in particular to whether it is likely to be possible to controvert the statement if the person making it does not attend to give oral evidence in the proceedings, that its admission or exclusion will result in unfairness to the accused or, if there is more than one, to any of them; and
(iii)   to any other circumstances that appear to the court to be relevant.

Keynote

Under s. 27 of the 1988 Act, where a statement contained in a document is admissible as evidence in criminal proceedings, it may be proved by the production of that document, or a copy authenticated to the court's approval.

Notwithstanding the provisions of the Criminal Justice Act 1988, documentary evidence is also admissible under other enactments.

Proof of Public Documents and By-laws

Where necessary the proof of a public document can be made as follows. A certified copy of an entry under the hand of the deputy superintendent registrar of births, deaths and marriages, is admissible evidence provided he/she also certifies the register was in his/her lawful custody (s. 14 of the Evidence Act 1851).

Computer Records

Section 69 of the Police and Criminal Evidence Act 1984 provides that:

(1)   In any proceedings a statement in a document produced by a computer shall not be admissible as evidence of any fact stated therein unless it is shown—
(a)   that there are no reasonable grounds for believing that the statement is inaccurate because of improper use of the computer;
(b)   that at all material times the computer was operating properly, or if not, that any respect in which it was not operating properly or was out of operation was not such as to affect the production of the document or the accuracy of its contents; and

(c)   that any relevant conditions specified in rules of court under subsection (2) below are satisfied.

(2)   Provision may be made by rules of court requiring that in any proceedings where it is desired to give a statement in evidence by virtue of this section such information concerning the statement as may be required by the rules shall be provided in such form and at such time as may be so required.

Keynote

In the case of computer printouts, before the judge can decide whether they are admissible as real or hearsay evidence, appropriate authoritative evidence is required to describe the function and operation of the computer (*R* v *Cochrane* [1993] Crim LR 48). Section 69 also requires anyone who wishes to admit a statement in a document produced by a computer, whether the statement is or is not hearsay, to produce evidence that will establish that it is safe to rely on the document (*R* v *Shephard* [1993] AC 380).

Note the power under s. 20 of the Police and Criminal Evidence Act 1984 to require information from a computer to be printed out or copied when exercising powers of search (**see General Police Duties, chapter 2**).

Provision is made in the 1984 Act for allowing evidence by certificate. Such evidence would identify a document produced by a computer, give details of how it was produced and show that the conditions specified in s. 69(1) have been fulfilled (sch. 3, part II, para. 8).

These requirements are particularly relevant in proving drink/driving offences (**see Road Traffic, chapter 5**).

Section 69 must be satisfied in order for any kind of statement produced by a computer to be admissible in court whether or not the statement is hearsay. The term 'computer' is not defined by the 1984 Act but the courts have held that the word should be given its ordinary meaning. A written certificate signed by a person holding a responsible position in relation to the operation of the computer is normally sufficient proof that the conditions in s. 69 have been satisfied.

Subject to the provisions of the Police and Criminal Evidence Act 1984, information obtained from a computer may be admitted in evidence.

Any statement obtained from a computer must relate to fact and not to opinion in order to be admissible in evidence. A court will have to be satisfied that at the time the document was produced the computer was operating properly and that there had been no improper use of it.

11.9.5   Hearsay Evidence

Simply put, any statement made out of court is hearsay.

It is evidence of something a person does not know for themselves but has been told by another.

In *Subramanium* v *Public Prosecutor* [1956] 1 WLR 965, it was stated that evidence of a statement made to a witness by a person who is not himself called as a witness may or may not be hearsay. It is hearsay and inadmissible when the object of the evidence is to the truth of what is contained in the statement.

The rule against hearsay is that any statement, other than one made by a witness while giving evidence, is inadmissible *as evidence of the facts stated*. Hearsay evidence may, on some limited occasions, be admissible *for other, specific purposes*.

When dealing with hearsay evidence you should consider:

- Is the evidence *admissible*?
- If so, *for what purpose*?
- How much *weight* will it carry?

Example

Kingsley tells Gurinder that Ronald stole a cheque book. If Gurinder tells the court that Ronald stole a cheque book this would constitute hearsay because Gurinder is presenting the statement (that Ronald stole a cheque book) as being evidence of that fact (that Ronald actually *did* steal a cheque book).

If, however, the statement is used in court for some reason other than proving the truth of its contents, then this is not hearsay. For example, if Gurinder were to give evidence that Kingsley spoke to him about Ronald stealing a cheque book and that conversation was relevant to show that Kingsley was with Gurinder at that particular time, then the statement would be admissible for *that purpose only*. It would not be admissible to prove what was actually said.

A good test for deciding whether a statement is hearsay is to ask yourself whether the witness giving the evidence of the statement can be cross-examined as to the truth of its contents (**see chapter 6**). If the witness is unable to support the truth of the *content* of a statement that he/she is making to a court (as opposed to whether it was actually said or not) then it is hearsay.

Exceptions

There are a number of exceptions to the hearsay rule when evidence will be admissible for certain purposes.

Statement by the accused
Statement(s) made by an accused person are admissible as to their factual content provided they are made in compliance with PACE Code of Practice (**see appendix 5**).

Statements made in the presence and hearing of the accused
The rule against hearsay is partly based on the fact that when a statement is made in the accused's absence he/she has no opportunity to deny or question its truth. Therefore statements made in the presence of an accused are an exception to the rule but *only to prove the reaction of the accused*. Therefore, when getting a victim or witness to repeat an allegation in the presence and hearing of a suspect the most important thing to record is the reaction of the suspect. Statements made in the presence and hearing of an accused are *not* admissible as evidence of the truth of what was said.

Dying declarations
These are admissible in trials for murder or manslaughter provided that:

- the declarant was in 'hopeless expectation of death';

EVIDENCE

- the death was the subject of the charge; *and*
- the circumstances of the death were the subject of the declaration (i.e. identifying who or what killed them).

Statements made by deceased
These are generally inadmissible. Exceptions to this general rule include:

- where the deceased was under a duty to make declarations contemporaneously in the course of his/her business (either written or oral), e.g. a verbal statement to an inspector made by a police constable to the effect that he was going to keep observations on a prisoner who later killed him, has been admitted (*R* v *Buckley* (1873) 13 Cox CC 293), and

- declarations against one's own pecuniary interest (*R* v *Rogers* [1995] 1 Cr App R 374).

Entries in public documents
These are exceptions to the hearsay rule provided:

- the statements and entries have been made by the authorised agents of the public in the course of official duties; and

- the facts recorded are of public interest or notoriety, or required to be recorded for the benefit of the public.

This exception is largely superseded by the effects of the Criminal Justice Act 1988 (**see para. 11.9.4**).

Besides the exceptions above, the practical problems of proving such facts by the production of witnesses would be in some cases insurmountable.

Res gestae
These are statements which are so closely associated with an action or state of affairs which is relevant to a fact in issue that they become part of that action or state of affairs. These statements may be admissible as evidence *of the truth of their contents* if they concern contemporaneous actions, physical sensations or state of mind, or they are closely associated with a dramatic event.

These statements fall into four main categories, i.e. statements relating to:

- a specific event;
- the maker's physical state;
- the maker's state of mind;
- the maker's performance of an act.

A specific event This principle can best be explained by use of the case of *R* v *Andrews* [1987] 2 WLR 413. Two men entered M's flat and attacked him with knives and stole some property. Shortly afterwards M, grievously wounded, made his way to the flat below his own to get help. Two police officers arrived within minutes and M told them that O and the defendant had been the assailants. Two months later M died as a result of his injuries. The defendant was jointly charged with O with aggravated burglary and the murder of M.

EVIDENCE

The prosecution sought to have the deceased's statement admitted, not as a dying declaration (**see above**), but *as evidence of the truth of the facts that he had asserted,* namely that he had been attacked by O and the defendant. Ordinarily the rule against hearsay would exclude such a statement from being used for that purpose. The prosecution argued that the statement made by the deceased was *so closely connected with the specific event (the stabbing) that it ought to be admitted in evidence under the res gestae exception.*

The case went to the House of Lords who held that, where the victim of an attack informed a witness of what had occurred, such a statement may be admitted in evidence if the circumstances in which it was made satisfy the trial judge that:

- the event was so unusual or startling or dramatic as to dominate the thoughts of the victim; and

- that very effect on the thoughts of the victim excluded the possibility of their lying or being mistaken; and

- the statement was made at approximately (although not *exactly*) the same time as the event.

Under these conditions evidence of what the victim said would be admissible as to the truth of the facts recounted.

The maker's physical state A statement concerning its maker's physical sensations, made at the time when he/she felt them is admissible to prove that he/she did in fact experienced that sensation.

If, for example, a person states 'my hand hurts' or 'my hand really hurt yesterday', both statements would be admissible by another to show that the person's hand had hurt. Similarly, 'I feel really embarrassed', might be admissible to show that the person felt embarrassed at the time.

Such statements are only admissible to prove that *the sensation* existed; they may not be used to show what *caused* the sensation and must, as with all evidence, be relevant to a fact in issue in the case.

The maker's state of mind Statements concerning the maker's state of mind at the time when he/she made it are admissible to prove what the maker *intended* or *believed* at that time. Such statements *are not admissible as evidence of the truth of the maker's beliefs.*

In *Ratten* v *The Queen* [1972] AC 378 the defendant's wife had been shot dead in her home. The defendant, in his defence to the charge of murder, claimed that the shooting was an accident. He also denied that any telephone call had been made from his house, where only he and his wife and small children were present, before the shooting. In these circumstances evidence of a telephone call made by the wife to an emergency operator was held to be admissible.

In deciding that the telephone call was admissible, Lord Wilberforce said:

> . . . [the operator's statement] can be analysed into the following elements. (1) At about 1.15 pm the number Echuca 1494 rang. I plugged into that number. (2) I opened the speak key and said 'number please'. (3) A female voice answered. (4) The voice was hysterical and sobbed. (5) The voice said 'Get me the police please.'

The factual items numbered (1)–(3) were relevant in order to show that, contrary to the evidence of the appellant, a call was made, by a woman only some 3–5 minutes before the fatal shooting. It not being suggested that there was anybody in the house other than the appellant, his wife and small children, this woman, the caller, could only have been the deceased. Items (4) and (5) were relevant as possibly showing . . . that the deceased woman was at this time in a state of emotion or fear. They were relevant and necessary evidence in order to explain and complete the fact of the call being made. . . .

The longer the time gap between the making of the statement and the performance of the act, the lower the probative value of the statement and the likelihood of its being admissible.

The maker's performance of an act Where an act carried out by a person needs to be proved, the statement of the person undertaking the act is likely to be the best evidence of why that act was completed. In order to amount to an exemption under the *res gestae* rule, the statement must be reasonably contemporaneous with the act; it must also be *related to* the act. For example, a person (X) boarding a plane saying 'I'm leaving the country to avoid being arrested' may be admissible as evidence of the reason why X got on the plane or why X left the country.

An example of this principle in practice is the case of *R* v *McCay* [1990] 1 WLR 645. Here a witness was asked to attend an identification parade to see if he could identify the defendant who was suspected of an attack on another man. The witness, a police inspector, and the appellant's solicitor watched the parade from behind a screen. The witness identified the defendant and said, 'It is number 8'. The defendant was charged with the assault and, at the trial, the witness gave evidence that he had attended the parade, made an identification but that he was unable to recall the number of the person whom he identified. The inspector was then called and gave evidence that the appellant had occupied position number 8 on the parade and that the witness had said 'It is number 8'. The defence argued that what the inspector said should be inadmissible hearsay. It was held that, although the words spoken by the witness at the parade were said in the absence of the appellant, they accompanied the relevant act of identification and therefore were contemporaneous with, and necessary to explain, the act of identification.

11.9.6 Circumstantial Evidence

In contrast to direct evidence which is evidence of facts in issue, circumstantial evidence is evidence of relevant facts *from which the facts in issue may be presumed with more or less certainty.*

An example would be where a bank robbery has occurred and a witness sees the defendant hurriedly climbing into a vehicle near to the bank at the relevant time and carrying bank cash bags. The witness has not actually *seen* the defendant inside the bank committing the offence, but can still provide evidence of relevant facts.

Pollack CB in *R* v *Exall* (1866) 4 F & F 922 described circumstantial evidence as:

> . . . a combination of circumstances, no one of which would raise a reasonable conviction, or more than a mere suspicion; but the whole, taken together, may create a strong conclusion of guilt. . . .

Circumstantial evidence may be admissible if it is relevant to a fact in issue and examples of circumstantial evidence include:

- evidence of facts which supply a motive;

- facts which tend to suggest that a person made plans or preparations relevant to a subsequent action performed;

- evidence of a person's mental or physical capacity to do a particular act;

- evidence of opportunity — or lack of opportunity to act in a certain way;

- evidence of identity, e.g. fingerprints (**see para. 16.5**);

- inferences from silence, e.g. s. 35 of the Criminal Justice and Public Order Act 1994;

- presumptions of fact (**see para. 11.9.7**).

11.9.7 Presumptions

Facts in issue and relevant facts must generally be proved before a court by admissible evidence before they can be accepted by the court as being true. There are occasions, however, when the courts will allow the proof of a fact or number of facts which lead it to presume the existence of a further fact, without any evidence of that fact being given in evidence. That is, from the facts that have been given in evidence, the court will then presume another fact for which no direct evidence has been given. A presumption is normally a conclusion which can be drawn until, where permissible, the contrary is proved.

There are three types of these 'presumptions':

- irrebuttable presumptions of law;
- rebuttable presumptions of law;
- presumptions of fact.

Irrebuttable Presumptions of Law

This is also known as a conclusive presumption. In these cases, where the courts accept the existence of certain basic fact(s) then they must also assume the existence of another fact and the other party to the proceedings cannot produce evidence questioning its existence.

For instance, s. 50 of the Children and Young Persons Act 1933 provides that:

> It shall be conclusively presumed that no child under the age of ten years can be guilty of any offence.

Where the defence produce a birth certificate for the accused showing he/she is only nine then, from that basic fact, the courts *must* presume that the defendant is not guilty of the offence charged. It is an irrebuttable presumption that a child under ten can never be guilty of an offence and matters not what other evidence the prosecution call. Once the birth certificate is accepted as being that of the defendant, the court will find him/her not guilty.

EVIDENCE

Rebuttable Presumptions of Law

In these cases, once one party has satisfied the court of the basic fact from which a presumption about other facts must be made, it is for the other party to prove that the presumed fact does not exist. That is, the other party can *rebut* the presumption but, if he/she is unable to do so, the court will draw the appropriate inference from it.

Where the prosecution have to disprove an assumption they must do so beyond reasonable doubt but the defence only have to show on a balance of probabilities that the fact (the presumption) exists (**see para. 11.4**).

There are a number of rebuttable presumptions but the most likely to apply to criminal cases are 'presumptions of regularity'.

Presumption of regularity
It is presumed that where evidence shows that a person acted in a public or official capacity, in the absence of contrary evidence, that that person was regularly and properly appointed and the act was regularly and properly performed. A typical example is on a charge of assaulting a police officer in the course of his/her duty (**see Crime, chapter 8**). Evidence that the police officer acted in that capacity is sufficient proof of his/her due appointment (*R v Gordon* (1789) 1 Leach 515; and see *Cooper* v *Rowlands* [1971] RTR 291).

There is also a presumption that mechanical and other instruments were in working order at the time of their use. For example, automatic traffic signals are presumed to be in proper working order unless the contrary is proved (*Tingle Jacobs & Co.* v *Kennedy* [1964] 1 WLR 638). However, there must be evidence of usually correct operation, for example, in relation to the admissibility of evidence of the results of a breath test in excess alcohol cases, where the reliability of the testing device is in question (*Cracknell* v *Willis* [1988] AC 450 and *Newton* v *Woods* [1987] RTR 41).

One of the best known rebuttable presumptions of law was *doli incapax* (incapable of crime), the principle that a child over 10 but under 14 could only be guilty of an offence if he/she knew what he/she was doing was 'seriously wrong'. This was abolished by s. 34 of the Crime and Disorder Act 1998, which came into force on 30 September 1998. It will only be for offences committed on or after that date that children aged 10 to 13 will be criminally responsible in the same way as adults.

Presumptions of Fact

The court may, after evidence is given about certain facts, presume (in the absence of sufficient evidence to the contrary), that another fact exists. This differs from rebuttable presumptions of law in that here the court *may* presume the fact exists from other facts presented to the court. With rebuttable presumptions of fact the court *must* presume the fact exists unless it is proved to the contrary. In reality this is just another way of showing that the courts use circumstantial evidence to infer that a fact is true.

Cases where the courts regularly infer the existence of facts from other circumstantial evidence are labelled 'presumptions of fact'. The following are examples of presumptions of fact:

Presumption of intention
Section 8 of the Criminal Justice Act 1967 provides that:

A court or jury in determining whether a person has committed an offence—
(a)   shall not be bound in law to infer that he intended or foresaw a result of his actions by reason only of its being a natural and probable consequence of those actions; but
(b)   shall decide whether he did intend or foresee that result by reference to all the evidence, drawing such inferences from the evidence as appear proper in the circumstances.

(See Crime, chapter 1).

Guilty knowledge in cases of handling and theft
Section 27(3) of the Theft Act 1968 allows for the admissibility of previous misconduct and provides:

(3)   Where a person is being proceeded against for handling stolen goods (but not for any offence other than handling stolen goods), then at any stage of the proceedings, if evidence has been given of his having or arranging to have in his possession the goods the subject of the charge, or of his undertaking or assisting in, or arranging to undertake or assist in, their retention, removal, disposal or realisation, the following evidence shall be admissible for the purpose of proving that he knew or believed the goods to be stolen goods—
(a)   evidence that he has had in his possession, or has undertaken or assisted in the retention, removal, disposal or realisation of, stolen goods from any theft taking place not earlier than 12 months before the offence charged and
(b)   (provided that seven days' notice in writing has been given to him of the intention to prove the conviction) evidence that he has within the five years preceding the date of the offence charged been convicted of theft or of handling stolen goods.

Keynote

This provision applies to all forms of handling (*R* v *Ball* [1983] 1 WLR 801) and can be used where handling is the only offence involved in the proceedings.

The question as to what constitutes recent possession is a matter of fact and degree dependent on the circumstances of each case. This presumption can be rebutted by the person offering a true explanation for the possession (*R* v *Schama* (1914) 84 LJ KB 396, *R* v *Garth* [1949] 1 All ER 773, *R* v *Aves* [1950] 2 All ER 330 and *R* v *Williams* [1962] Crim LR 54).

The term 'recent possession' is not defined and so is a question of fact in each case. In *R* v *Smythe* (1980) 72 Cr App R 8, the Court of Appeal held that property found in the possession of an accused, stolen two or three months earlier during some robberies and burglaries, did not amount to recent possession for the offence of handling stolen goods generally, (**see Crime, chapter 12**).

Presumption of life
Where evidence that a person was alive on a certain date is given to the court, it may be presumed that he/she was still alive on some subsequent date. Of course, where additional evidence is provided showing that the person was in good health and spirits, the chances of such an inference being made will be greater.

11.9.8   Evidence of Character

Character evidence may be admissible, either in relation to some fact in issue, or to the credibility of a witness. Evidence of a person's character may be relevant in three ways:

* the reputation in which the person is held in the community by those that know him/her;

- the disposition of a person to behave in a particular way;
- specific incidents involving the witness, for example, previous convictions.

Evidence of the character of a witness, other than the accused, is admissible provided that it is relevant to a fact in issue or because it may be relevant to the credibility of that witness.

An example of this is the case of *R* v *Edwards* [1991] 1 WLR 207. The evidence against the accused consisted of a witness, who was an accomplice, and of certain police officers, who produced interview notes and spoke about interviews with the accused. At these interviews the accused had made admissions but had refused to sign the interview notes, two of which had been certified by senior officers. The accused denied making the admissions and claimed that the interview was a charade, that the interrogating officers had written down what suited them, that it was unrelated to what he had said and that he had been 'fitted up' with false evidence.

The prosecution had been asked to supply the names of any police officers subject to investigation for fabricating evidence. They failed to provide the details of one of the certifying officers who had recently been disciplined internally in relation to another case. In this case the officer had certified interview notes which, to his knowledge, had been wrongly re-written; resulting in the case against the defendants failing.

The Court of Appeal held that a police officer giving evidence, who had allegedly fabricated an admission, could properly be cross-examined to make the jury aware of the fact that his evidence of an admission in a previous case was demonstrably disbelieved; it would have been relevant and admissible to put to the officers concerned that they had given evidence in the earlier trials involving an issue whether alleged confessions had been fabricated and that the trials had ended as they had; that the cross-examination would have been as to credit alone.

Where the defence adduce evidence alleging misconduct on the part of the prosecution witnesses, it is not open to the Crown to adduce evidence of good character to boost the testimony of these witnesses (*R* v *Hamilton*, *The Independent*, 6 July 1998).

Previous Inconsistent Statements

Where a witness makes a previous inconsistent statement (oral or written) and the inconsistency relates to the witness's standing after cross-examination, by ss. 4 and 5 (s. 5 only applies to written statements) of the Criminal Procedure Act 1865, the witness may be asked about these earlier statements and if he/she denies making them or denies their inconsistency the earlier statement can then become admissible evidence.

Convictions of Witnesses

Section 6 of the Criminal Procedure Act 1865 provides:

> *A witness may be questioned as to whether he has been convicted of any [offence], and upon being so questioned, if he either denies or does not admit the facts, or refuses to answer, it shall be lawful for the cross-examining party to prove such conviction.*

Keynote

Previous convictions may be proved by the production of a certificate of the court of conviction. The certificate must be properly signed by the appropriate officer and deal with the substance and effect of the charge and the conviction recorded, coupled with evidence of the identity of the witness as the person so convicted (see s. 73 of the Police and Criminal Evidence Act 1984).

In *Martin* v *White* [1910] 1 KB 665 it was held that evidence of identity need not be conclusive and only be such that the court can properly draw the inference that it has been established.

The Rehabilitation of Offenders Act 1974 and s. 16 of the Children and Young Persons Act 1963 govern and restrict the use of certain previous convictions. In other words, s. 6 of the 1865 Act must be read as relating to those previous convictions which may properly be put to a witness.

Where an accomplice is giving evidence for the Crown, his/her previous convictions should normally be disclosed by the prosecution to the jury at the outset of a trial unless counsel for the defence indicates otherwise (*R* v *Taylor*, *The Times*, 3 November 1998).

The circumstances in which the *accused* may be asked about his/her previous convictions are provided for in s. 1(e) and (f) of the Criminal Evidence Act 1898 (**see below**).

Character Evidence of the Accused

Character evidence in relation to the accused may be admissible to show:

- good character
- bad character.

Good character
The accused is allowed to call evidence of his/her good character provided that it is confined to evidence of general reputation.

The leading case on the use of the good character of an accused is *R* v *Vye* [1993] 1 WLR 471. Evidence of good character may be relevant to:

- credibility in relation to statements made to the police or others on oath to the court;

- demonstrate to the court that the accused has not done this type of thing before and so may not have done it on this occasion.

Good character in itself cannot amount to a defence.

Bad character
Evidence of the accused's bad character may be admissible either at common law or under statute.

At common law the prosecution may call evidence of the accused's bad character or cross-examine the accused:

- where the evidence is admissible under the similar facts doctrine (**see chapter 12**);
- where the defence adduces evidence of the accused's good character.

EVIDENCE

Under statute, this topic is covered by s. 1 of the Criminal Evidence Act 1898, which allows the prosecution to cross-examine the accused about his/her character but only in limited circumstances.

Section 1 of the Criminal Evidence Act 1898 provides that:

> *(1)* . . .
>
> *(e) A person charged and being a witness in pursuance of this Act may be asked any question in cross-examination notwithstanding that it would tend to criminate him as to the offence charged;*
>
> *(f) A person charged and called as a witness in pursuance of this Act shall not be asked, and if asked shall not be required to answer, any question tending to show that he has committed or been convicted of or been charged with any offence other than that wherewith he is then charged, or is of bad character, unless—*
>
> *(i) the proof that he has committed or been convicted of such other offence is admissible evidence to show that he is guilty of the offence wherewith he is then charged; or*
>
> *(ii) he has personally or by his advocate asked questions of the witnesses for the prosecution with a view to establish his own good character, or has given evidence of his good character, or the nature or conduct of the defence is such as to involve imputations on the character of the prosecutor or the witnesses for the prosecution or the deceased victim of the alleged crime; or*
>
> *(iii) he has given evidence against any other person charged in the same proceedings.*

Keynote

Section 1(e) permits questions which tend *directly* to incriminate the accused, whereas s. 1(f) protects the accused from being asked questions which would tend *indirectly* to incriminate the accused (i.e. questions which refer to his/her misconduct on other occasions or his/her commission of other offences or his/her bad character generally), unless s. 1(f)(i), (ii) or (iii) applies.

This gives the accused a 'shield' against the use by the prosecution of his/her previous bad character which is lost if any of the conditions in s. 1(f) are met. The accused will lose the shield if he/she puts his/her good character in issue either:

- by cross-examination of witnesses; or
- by giving evidence about his/her own good character or by attacking the character of prosecution witnesses.

The shield will not be lost if the accused merely asserts his/her innocence or emphatically denies the allegation. If the accused is of previous good character, attacking prosecution witnesses will be of less detriment.

However, where the accused elects to give evidence and has embarked on doing so, he/she cannot avoid evidence of his/her own character going before the jury simply by refusing to return to the witness box so that he/she cannot be cross-examined. In such circumstances the Crown is entitled to adduce evidence as to his/her bad character (*R v Forbes, The Times*, 5 May 1999).

In *Barley v DPP, The Times*, 30 July 1998, the defendant contended that a memorandum of conviction bearing his name and address did not relate to him. Evidence had to be adduced to disprove the suggestion that some other person had given the defendant's details to the police and court in respect of the earlier offence.

Section 16 of the Children and Young Persons Act 1963 prevents an accused who is over the age of 21 from being asked about any offences that he/she may have committed when under the age of 14.

11.9.9 Opinion

The general rule is that the opinion of a witness is inadmissible. However, where it is admissible it can be divided into two groups:

- non-expert evidence;
- expert evidence.

Non-expert Evidence

The courts have allowed the following non-expert opinion evidence from a witness:

- identification of a person or object;
- the speed of a moving vehicle;
- evidence as to temperature or time;
- the value of an item (provided it does not require specialist knowledge to estimate the price).

Two examples of non-expert evidence that are likely to be given by police officers are provided by the following two cases:

- *R v Davies* [1962] 1 WLR 1111: any competent witness may give evidence that in his/her opinion a person is drunk provided that he/she describes the facts on which his/her opinion is based.

- *R v Hill* (1993) 96 Cr App R 456: police officers could identify substances as prohibited drugs (as to which, **see Crime, chapter 6**).

Expert Evidence

There will be instances in which the issues that the court will need to decide on are beyond its knowledge. In such instances it may be necessary to call on witnesses who, through their own experience or training or both, have the necessary expertise. It is for the judge to decide whether a witness is competent to give expert opinion. The expert witness is only there to assist the court in deciding the facts of the case.

Where more than one expert witness is called and their opinions differ, it will be for the tribunal of fact to decide which evidence they prefer. It must be remembered that expert evidence is not admissible where the issue before the court is one that should fall within the experiences of those deciding the case.

Expert evidence has been held appropriate in the following areas:

- medical issues and science;
- determining mental illness and the effects of a mental condition on mental processes;
- handwriting samples and facial mapping;

Section 81 of the Police and Criminal Evidence Act 1984 provides for regulations to be made requiring pre-trial disclosure. These rules, contained within Crown Court (Advance Notice of Expert Evidence) Rules 1987 (SI 1987 No. 716), require any party intending to produce expert evidence to furnish to the other parties in the proceedings a statement in writing of the expert finding. This allows the other parties to review the statement and, if necessary, call a countering expert witness. (Note that this applies equally to the defence as it does to the prosecution.)

High standards of accuracy and objectivity are required of an expert witness. An expert witness should provide independent assistance to the court by way of objective unbiased opinion in relation to the matters within his/her expertise (*National Justice Compania Naviera* v *Prudential Assurance Co. Ltd* [1993] 2 Lloyd's Rep 68). If a witness provides evidence of an opinion that he/she does not genuinely believe, he/she may commit an offence of perjury (**see Crime, chapter 15**).

11.9.10 Corroboration

The classic definition of corroboration is to be found in *R* v *Baskerville* [1916] 2 KB 658 (per Lord Reid):

> . . . evidence in corroboration must be independent testimony which affects the accused by connecting or tending to connect him with the crime. In other words, it must be evidence which implicates him, that is, which confirms in some material particular not only the evidence that the crime has been committed, but also that the prisoner committed it.

In order to satisfy the full technical meaning of the term corroboration, evidence must be:

- admissible in itself;
- from a source independent of the evidence required to be corroborated; and
- such as to tend to show, by confirmation of some material particular, not only that the offence charged was committed, *but also that it was committed by the accused.*

Although a conviction may be based on the testimony of a single prosecution witness who swears that he/she saw the accused commit the crime, it was recognised by Lord Morris in *DPP* v *Hester* [1973] AC 296 that:

> Any risk of the conviction of an innocent person is lessened if conviction is upon the testimony of more than one acceptable witness.

Where possible, supporting evidence should be collected while offences are being investigated to strengthen the prosecution case (or, where appropriate, to support the case the suspect has put forward).

The corroborating evidence does not have to confirm *all* the evidence already given by the witness requiring corroboration. In *R* v *Hill* (1988) 86 Cr App R 337, Lord Lane said:

> For example, in a rape case where the defendant denies he ever had sexual intercourse with the complainant, it may be possible to prove (1) by medical evidence that she had had sexual intercourse within an hour or so prior to the medical examination, (2) by other independent evidence that the defendant and no other man had been with her during that time, (3) that her underclothing was torn and that she had injuries to her private parts. None of these items of evidence on their own would be sufficient to provide the necessary corroboration, but the judge would be entitled to direct the jury that if they were satisfied so as to feel sure that each of those three items had been proved the combined effect of the three items would be capable of corroborating the girl's evidence.

When Corroboration is Needed

The general rule is that a court's decision can be based on the evidence of one witness but there are some exceptions to the general rule. These are:

- where corroboration is required as a matter of law;
- obligatory care warnings;
- discretionary care warnings;
- in relation to identification evidence.

Corroboration required as a matter of law
A conviction in the following cases can only be successful if the evidence is corroborated. There are three offences that fall into this category:

- treason;
- perjury;
- speeding (corroboration as to the speed the vehicle was travelling).

Obligatory care warnings
There used to be a number of cases that fell into this group but with recent legislation it now only applies to cases involving persons who are mentally handicapped where they have made a confession which was not witnessed by an independent person. This is now covered by s. 77 of the Police and Criminal Evidence Act 1984, which provides that:

> *(1)   Without prejudice to the general duty of the court at a trial on indictment to direct the jury on any matter on which it appears to the court appropriate to do so, where at such a trial—*
> *(a)   the case against the accused depends wholly or substantially on a confession by him;*
> *(b)   and the court is satisfied—*
> *(i)   that he is mentally handicapped; and*
> *(ii)   that the confession was not made in the presence of an independent person,*
> *the court shall warn the jury that there is special need for caution before convicting the accused in reliance on the confession, and shall explain that the need arises because of the circumstances mentioned in paragraphs (a) and (b) above.*
> *(2)   In any case where at the summary trial of a person for an offence it appears to the court that a warning under subsection (1) above would be required if the trial were on indictment, the court shall treat the case as one in which there is a special need for caution before convicting the accused on his confession.*
> *(3)   In this section—*
> *'independent person' does not include a police officer or a person employed for, or engaged on, police purposes;*
> *'mentally handicapped' in relation to a person, means that he is in a state of arrested or incomplete development of mind which includes significant impairment of intelligence and social functioning . . .*

Discretionary care warnings
The rules of evidence in this area have changed considerably in recent years. The current position is summarised by Lord Taylor LCJ in the Court of Appeal case of *R v Makanjuola* [1995] 1 WLR 1348.

Sections 32 and 33 of the Criminal Justice and Public Order Act 1994 abolished the rule requiring a corroboration warning be given in relation to the evidence of accomplices and the evidence of complainants in sexual offences and the requirement for corroboration in certain offences under the Sexual Offences Act 1956 (i.e. ss. 2 to 4, 22 and 23).

EVIDENCE

In *R* v *Isham* (1998) 162 JP 391 it was held that in cases involving sexual offences, where the prosecution adduces evidence of complaints made by the complainant after the alleged assault, the jury must be directed that the evidence of the complaint is only of limited relevance and, since it does not come from a source which is independent of the complainant, does not amount to independent confirmation of the complainant's evidence.

When a judge chooses to give a corroboration warning he/she will normally point out that evidence must satisfy two requirements, namely:

* that the corroborative evidence must be independent of the witness whose evidence requires corroboration; and

* that the corroborative evidence must connect the accused with the commission of the crime by confirming that the crime was committed and that it was committed by the accused.

These requirements for corroboration provide the court with a safeguard against evidence that might be considered to be unreliable. It is often not known at the time of investigating a case whether a witness will be reliable and, where possible, corroboration should be sought to avoid this becoming an issue at court.

Identification evidence
R v *Turnbull* [1976] 3 WLR 445 is the leading case on the admissibility of identification evidence. In this case the Court of Appeal outlined those factors that should be considered when identification evidence is presented to the court and therefore those factors that should be considered by police when investigating offences.

Factors that should be considered include:

* How long did the witness have the accused under observation?

* At what distance and in what light?

* Was the observation impeded in any way (for example by passing traffic or people)?

* Had the witness ever seen the accused before and, if so, how often?

* If only occasionally, had the witness any special reason for remembering the accused?

* How long had elapsed between the original observation and the subsequent identification to the police?

* Was there any material discrepancy between the description of the accused given to the police by the witness when first seen by him/her and his/her actual appearance? (As a matter of course, 'first descriptions' are now provided to an accused.)

Keynote

Within the PEACE model used to train police officers, in relation to the taking of both witness statements and suspect statements, the mnemonic **ADVOKATE** is used as an *aide-memoire*:

A — Amount of time under observation
D — Distance between suspect and witness
V — Visibility at time
O — Any Obstructions
K — Known or seen before
A — Any reason to remember
T — Time lapse since witness saw suspect
E — Error or material discrepancy.

The court noted that recognition of someone known by the witness may be more reliable than identification of a stranger; but even when the witness is purporting to recognise someone whom he/she knows, the jury should be reminded that mistakes in recognition of close relatives and friends are sometimes made.

For an examination of the law relating to identification, **see chapter 16**.

In relation to corroboration of identification evidence, the court made it clear that this is wider than corroboration in the strict legal sense. The court held:

> This may be corroboration in the sense lawyers use that word; but it need not be so if its effect is to make the jury sure that there has been no mistaken identification: for example, X sees the accused snatch a woman's handbag; he gets only a fleeting glance of the thief's face as he runs off but he does see him entering a nearby house. Later he picks out the accused on an identity parade. If there was no more evidence than this, the poor quality of the identification would require the judge to withdraw the case from the jury; but this would not be so if there was evidence that the house into which the accused was alleged by X to have run was his father's.

An example of supporting identification evidence is *R* v *Long* (1973) 57 Cr App R 871. Here the defendant was charged with robbery. He had been identified by three witnesses in different places on different occasions but each had only a momentary opportunity for observation. Immediately after the robbery the accused had left his home and could not be found by the police. When he was later seen by the police he claimed to know who had done the robbery and offered to help to find the robbers. At his trial he put forward an alibi which the jury rejected. The court considered that it was an odd coincidence that the eye-witnesses should have identified a man who had behaved in this way and without some explanation by the defence this was admissible as supporting the identification.

For high treason, perjury and offences of speeding the requirement for corroboration remains.

11.9.11 Judicial Notice

The courts may take judicial notice of various matters that are so well known or clearly established that proof thereof is not required. Judicial notice is another way of saying that a court accepts a fact or facts without formal proof.

Examples of the operation of the exception to the burden of proof include matters which are common knowledge, Acts of Parliament, and custom such as the Home Secretary's approval of certain breath test devices (**see Road Traffic, chapter 5**).

CHAPTER TWELVE

SIMILAR FACT EVIDENCE

12.1   Introduction

This chapter looks at similar fact evidence. This can be a complex area of the law of evidence and the aim of this chapter is to give the reader an understanding of the subject. The chapter also considers what evidence should be collected against a suspect in relation to other matters with similar fact evidence in mind.

As discussed earlier, evidence is admissible if it is relevant to a fact in issue necessary to prove or disprove the case against the accused. Normally such evidence will be directly related to the offence in question, for instance the defendant was seen hitting the victim using a bottle. But what if the victim described the bottle as being a green lager bottle with a German name on it? What relevance would this have if a suspect has been convicted of previous assaults using a green lager bottle from a German brewer or where there are several victims all of whom have been assaulted in the same way? Should this evidence be admissible at the defendant's trial or is there too big a risk that such evidence will be prejudicial to his/her case? Throughout this particular aspect of the law of evidence there is a common theme; balancing the usefulness of the evidence in proving the case in question (its 'probative value') against the possible detrimental effects of that evidence on the defendant.

Thus this chapter is concerned with when evidence of the defendant's previous convictions or conduct on other occasions may be admissible as evidence of his/her guilt.

12.2   The Similar Fact Principle

This principle was recognised as far back as 1894 in *Makin* v *Attorney-General for New South Wales* [1894] AC 57, where Lord Herschell LC said that:

> It is undoubtedly not competent for the prosecution to adduce evidence tending to show that the accused has been guilty of criminal acts other than those covered by the indictment, for the purpose of leading to the conclusion that the accused is a person likely from his criminal conduct or character to have committed the offence for which he is being tried. On the other

hand, the mere fact that the evidence adduced tends to shew the commission of other crimes [or similar actions of the accused] does not render it inadmissible if it be relevant to an issue before the jury, and it may be so relevant if it bears upon the question whether the acts alleged to constitute the crime charged in the indictment were designed or accidental, or to rebut a defence which would otherwise be open to the accused.

This passage sets out the two key propositions surrounding the similar fact doctrine. The first proposition is that evidence which shows that the accused has a *particular disposition* to commit crimes in general, or to commit the kind of crime with which he/she has been charged, is *not* admissible. This is because, although it may appear to be relevant to a case, there is no direct link between the crime committed and the past actions of the accused. Such evidence is excluded, not because it does not support the fact that the accused might have committed the offence, but because of the danger that the jury might attach a disproportionate importance to this evidence compared with other evidence directly concerning the commission of the offence charged.

The second proposition really takes us back to the question of what facts are admissible in court. The answer is those facts which are relevant to prove or disprove the offence(s) charged. Evidence is likely to be admissible if it goes beyond mere evidence of a propensity to commit crime and has a crucial bearing upon the question whether the offence charged was committed by this defendant. In these cases the evidence of previous offences or actions of the accused *may be* admissible because they *connect* the defendant with the offence charged. If so, the evidence that he/she has a disposition to commit that kind of offence or act in a particular way *is* relevant because it makes it more likely that he/she committed the offence charged. Therefore the probative value of that evidence may outweigh any prejudicial effect it might have on the defendant's case.

Example

An example of such a case is the infamous one of *R* v *Smith* (1915) 11 Cr App R 229 where a man was charged with the murder of his wife who was found dead in the bath. There was evidence of two further marriages where his former wives had been found dead in a bath, along with other similarities including the defendant's profiting financially from the death on each occasion. Lord Reading approved the direction given by the trial judge to the jury:

> If you find an accident which benefits a person and you find that the person has been fortunate to have that accident happen to him a number of times, benefiting each time, you draw a very strong, frequently irresistible inference that the occurrence of so many accidents benefiting him is such a coincidence that it cannot have happened unless it was designed.

12.3 Evidence of Similar Facts

As the cases above illustrate, it is a common law rule that evidence which merely shows a similarity to the fact in issue is irrelevant and just because a person has acted in a particular way previously, does not make it probable that he/she so acted on a given occasion. This is one of the reasons why, generally, a person's previous convictions may not be put before a court until the case has been proved (**see chapter 11**).

An exception to this exclusionary rule is when such evidence is positively probative (helpful or evidential) of the offence before the court. Striking similarity is also an exception where other facts are so similar to the act being investigated that it would an affront to common-sense to say that the similarity could be explained by coincidence.

Similar fact evidence is not just evidence of previous crimes; it can include evidence of non-criminal misconduct and evidence of a disposition to behave in a particular way. The categories falling within the doctrine of similar fact evidence could be relevant to any case where the courts feel that the evidence has probative value in deciding an issue before them.

12.4 Admissibility of Similar Fact Evidence

Similar fact evidence is admissible in a number of ways:

- striking similarity;
- non-criminal behaviour;
- probative force without striking similarity;
- multiple offence cases;
- possession of objects by the accused;
- association with an event;
- previous sexual conduct and the 'same transaction' rule;
- use of similar fact evidence by a co-accused.

Each of these is examined in detail below.

12.4.1 Striking Similarity

Here the court will look for something more than some feature which is common place. Offences may be identical without being 'striking', e.g. where the *modus operandi* of a burglary is common to thousands of other offences of burglary. However, if a burglar has used a blow torch to crack the window of a building before entering in the past, that feature may be admissible against him/her if charged with similar burglaries in the future (*R v Mullen* [1992] Crim LR 735). So it may be better to think in terms of similarities which are really peculiarities to the accused. Lord Hailsham gave a very extreme but memorable example in *DPP v Boardman* [1975] AC 421. This example was of a man who commits repeated homosexual offences and whose victims all state that he was attired in 'ceremonial head-dress . . . or other eccentric garb'. If a victim of an offence of gross indecency described the assailant as being dressed in a North American native 'war bonnet', that fact may be so similar to previous offences committed by the defendant that the courts would accept evidence of those earlier offences as 'similar fact' evidence. Whether or not evidence of similar facts will be accepted under this head will depend on the likelihood or otherwise of repetition being attributable to mere coincidence.

In assessing similar fact evidence the question is one of relevance; it does not matter whether similar fact evidence displays its relevance by revealing features of a striking similarity with the offence itself, or simply with its surrounding circumstances.

Probably the best example of such evidence is the case against Rosemarie West. Here, Mrs West was accused of assisting her husband who had been convicted of ten murders before killing himself in prison. In seven of the murders the bodies had been naked, bound and mutilated and had been found under the defendant's house. Evidence from witnesses that the defendant actively engaged in violent sexual assaults with her husband at that address was admitted under the striking similarity rule (*R v West* [1996] 2 Cr App R 374).

Dissimilarities in the evidence, which detract from its probative value, must be taken into account and should be presented to the prosecutor along with the other evidence (**see chapter 14**).

In determining the admissibility of similar fact evidence the question, as always, is whether the probative value outweighs the prejudicial effect the evidence could have on the accused.

12.4.2 Non-criminal Behaviour

Evidence of non-criminal behaviour of the accused is admissible if such behaviour has a sufficient degree of probative force linking that behaviour and the circumstances surrounding the commission of the offence charged.

In *R* v *Barrington* [1981] 1 WLR 419, the accused was charged with indecently assaulting three girls. The prosecution alleged that the girls had been lured to the house of a co-accused as baby-sitters, had been shown pornographic photographs, had been asked to pose for photographs in the nude and had then been indecently assaulted. Evidence was also admitted from three other girls concerning another incident. They had not been indecently assaulted, but they had been lured to the house on the same pretext, had been shown the photographs and had been asked to pose in the nude. The Court of Appeal held that the evidence had been properly admitted on the grounds that, although it included no evidence of the commission of offences, it was logically probative of guilt because it was *inexplicable on the basis of coincidence*. Consequently, while the actions were not part of the offence itself, the evidence went to link all the cases together and would assist the jury in deciding the case.

12.4.3 Probative Force without Striking Similarity

The courts have recognised that there may be occasions where similar fact evidence can be admitted which is not so strikingly similar. These occasions will be rare as the risk of allowing such evidence carries greater risk to the defendant. The type of case where such evidence might be allowed is where there is no dispute about the identity of the accused but the issue for the court bears more on the motive of the accused.

The point was considered in *DPP* v *P* [1991] 2 AC 447 where Lord Mackay LC held that:

> . . . Where the identity of the perpetrator is in issue, and evidence of this kind is important in that connection, obviously something in the nature of . . . a signature or other special feature . . .

The case concerned charges of rape and incest by a father in respect of his two daughters. The evidence included:

- both girls describing a prolonged course of conduct in relation to each;
- force was used in relation to each;
- their father was obsessed with 'keeping his daughters for himself';
- when the elder daughter left home, the younger daughter adopted her role;
- there was evidence that the father had paid for his daughters' abortions.

No issue of identification arose, the question being whether the alleged offences had in fact been committed. The House of Lords held that the 'similar fact' evidence possessed sufficient probative force to justify its admission in evidence. The statements were relevant in that the issue was whether the acts took place at all and not whether it was the particular defendant to whom the victim/witness was referring.

12.4.4 Multiple Offence Cases

Where a defendant faces more than one charge of a similar nature or where evidence of similar allegations is tendered in support of one charge, the evidence of one accuser may be admissible to support the evidence of another. Often this point becomes an issue before a trial starts, when the defence apply to the court to have counts which are of a similar nature tried separately to avoid the overall evidence being heard at one time. This type of evidence has also been used where corroboration was in issue.

The underlying principle here is that the probative value of multiple accusations may depend in part on their similarity, but also on the unlikely probability that the same person would find himself/herself falsely accused on different occasions by different and independent individuals. The making of multiple accusations may be a coincidence in itself, which has to be taken into account in deciding admissibility.

The use of similar fact evidence in this area was considered in *R* v *Sims* [1946] KB 531, where it was observed that the evidence of a number of accusations taken together is much greater than one alone, for:

> whereas the jury might think one man might be telling an untruth, three or four are hardly likely to tell the same untruth unless they were conspiring together.

In cases of multiple complainants/witnesses there is always a chance of collusion and this should be borne in mind when taking witness statements.

12.4.5 Possession of Objects by the Accused

There may be occasions where a suspect is arrested and during subsequent searches articles are found which could be used in the type of offence suspected. Such items may be admitted as similar fact evidence *provided the evidence goes beyond mere criminal disposition*. In the assault case referred to above (**see para. 12.1**), if the bottle used was a distinctive or unusual one, the defendant's previous possession of a similar bottle might be used to identify him/her as the offender.

12.4.6 Association with an Event

Another function which similar fact evidence may be called upon to perform is to show an event involving an accused person in its true light. For instance, it may be relevant in deciding whether an event occurred by accident or innocently or intentionally. It may also be relevant against an alibi, i.e. to show that the accused committed another crime in the vicinity shortly before or after the offence charged. In such cases the evidence may not relate to the actual offence but to the background leading up to the incident.

12.4.7 Previous Sexual Conduct and the 'Same Transaction' Rule

Evidence of sexual or other behaviour which is not the subject of the charge may also be admissible to show the true nature of the relationship between the relevant parties (i.e. the defendant and the victim). In *DPP* v *Boardman* [1975] AC 421, evidence of the accused's previous approaches to a boy with whom he was alleged to have committed buggery was admitted, including evidence of an indecent assault taking place several months before. Similar evidence was given by another complainant of indecent conduct leading over a period of time to incitement to buggery.

There is also a general rule which allows evidence of continuing behaviour to be adduced as part of the 'same transaction', for instance, where a 9-year-old girl gave evidence of indecent assaults, rapes and threats by the defendant, leading up to a final offence of rape which was the subject of the charge against him. The court held that the preliminary behaviour was all part of the 'same transaction' and therefore admissible (*R v Rearden* (1864) 4 F & F 76).

Strictly speaking, the 'same transaction' rule is not part of similar fact evidence and therefore does not require the same safeguards when deciding on its prejudicial effect on the defendant (*R v Bond* [1906] 2 KB 389).

12.4.8 Use of Similar Fact Evidence by Co-accused

A co-accused can also rely on similar fact evidence if it is relevant to an issue before the court. This will normally be to support the accused's defence or damage his/her co-accused's case.

12.5 Discretionary Exclusion of Similar Fact Evidence

It will always be for the judge to decide whether in a particular case similar fact evidence should be admissible. It is for the prosecution, based on the evidence provided by the police, if it feels that the evidence is relevant to the case, to raise the issue of admissibility for the judge to rule on. The discretion to exclude similar fact evidence may be used where its prejudicial effect may be so disproportionate to its probative value (i.e. it will do more harm than good) that it ought not to be admitted (*R v Straffen* [1952] 2 QB 911).

CHAPTER THIRTEEN

EXCLUSION OF ADMISSIBLE EVIDENCE

13.1   Introduction

Under the law, every person is presumed innocent until proven guilty. The duty of the courts is not only to decide on the guilt or innocence of a person, but also to ensure that the person has a fair hearing. When considering the second question, the courts will consider the evidence that the prosecution intend to use in the case and how that evidence was obtained.

In ensuring that a person has a fair trial the court may exclude evidence, *even though the evidence itself is admissible.* The court may exclude any evidence in certain circumstances and has additional powers in relation to evidence obtained by confession. The courts' powers come generally from ss. 76 and 78 of the Police and Criminal Evidence Act 1984, although the courts also have common law powers to exclude evidence. The exclusion of confession evidence is the most common and occupies the bulk of this chapter. However, the exclusion of evidence generally will also be discussed here.

13.2   Confessions

There are three general ways in which you can prove a person's involvement in an offence:

- confessions (or admissions);
- witnesses;
- forensic science.

In many cases where the suspect confesses to the offence, the case is still pleaded not guilty with the defence alleging that the confession is unreliable or that it should be excluded as having been unfairly obtained. The courts are concerned with the reliability of evidence and often regard confessions as the least reliable way to prove a person's involvement in an offence.

A confession, which is defined by s. 82 of the Police and Criminal Evidence Act 1984 (see below), is an out of court statement made by a person and therefore falls into the category of evidence known as 'hearsay' evidence (**see chapter 11**). Hearsay evidence is generally inadmissible for any purpose, although there are some limited categories where it may be admissible for very specific purposes.

Confessions are such an exceptional category and are admissible in evidence as outlined in s. 76(1) of the 1984 Act. However, evidence of confession may be excluded by a court if the manner in which the confession was obtained was, or *appears to have been*, unfair to the defendant.

Section 76 of the Police and Criminal Evidence Act 1984 provides that:

> *(1)   In any proceedings a confession made by an accused person may be given in evidence against him in so far as it is relevant to any matter in issue in the proceedings and is not excluded by the court in pursuance of this section.*

A 'confession' is defined by s. 82 of the 1984 Act, which provides that:

> *(1)   In this Part of this Act—*
> *'confession' includes any statement wholly or partly adverse to the person who made it, whether made to a person in authority or not and whether made in words or otherwise; . . .*

Keynote

A confession, therefore, is a positive action by the person making it. The person must use words or some other method of communication (e.g. nodding his/her head to a question, or a video tape of the suspect taking police to a murder weapon). Therefore confessions do not include silence by a person (although this may be relevant to special warnings, **see chapter 17**).

The confession does not have to be a pure statement of guilt and can include the answers to questions asked in interview which are *adverse to the defendant*. In *R v Sat-Bhambra* (1988) 88 Cr App R 55 the court held that a statement which was not adverse to the person making it *at the time of it being made* is not a 'confession', even if it later became adverse to him/her. Therefore any such statement would be classed as hearsay evidence and would not be admissible.

13.2.1   The Exclusion of Confession Evidence

Section 76(2) of the Police and Criminal Evidence Act 1984 gives the courts a responsibility to exclude confessions where they have been obtained by oppression (s. 76(2)(a)), or where the court considers they are unreliable (s. 76(2)(b)). There is also a general power (under s. 78 of the 1984 Act and at common law) to exclude *any* evidence that the court considers would be unfair to the defence if allowed, which can also be applicable to the exclusion of confessions. These powers are dealt with at **para. 13.3.1**. Here the court is more concerned about the circumstances in which the confession was obtained than the truthfulness of what was said.

Oppression

Section 76 of the Police and Criminal Evidence Act 1984 provides that:

(2)   If, in any proceedings where the prosecution proposes to give in evidence a confession made by an accused person, it is represented to the court that the confession was or may have been obtained—

(a)   by oppression of the person who made it; or

. . .

the court shall not allow the confession to be given in evidence against him except in so far as the prosecution proves to the court beyond reasonable doubt that the confession (notwithstanding that it may be true) was not obtained as aforesaid.

Keynote

A court can exclude a confession where it has been, or may have been, obtained by the oppression of the person making the confession. This means that there must be some link between the oppressive behaviour and the confession. So for instance, if the confession was made *before* the oppressive behaviour, this would not justify exclusion *under this subsection* (it may, however, justify exclusion under the general power of the courts; **see chapter 13**). It does not matter whether the confession is true or not; the issue under s. 76(2)(a) is *how* the person has been treated and whether any mistreatment led, or might have led, the person to make the confession. This issue is of particular importance in the interviewing of suspects (**see chapter 17**). In looking at this the courts seem to take into account the nature of the person being interviewed. It was said in *R* v *Gowan* [1982] Crim LR 821, that hardened criminals must expect vigorous police interrogation.

Section 76(8) gives some guidance as to what oppression means and it includes torture (**see Crime, chapter 9**), inhuman or degrading treatment and the use or threat of violence (whether or not amounting to torture).

In *R* v *Fulling* [1987] QB 426, the Court of Appeal held that oppression is:

[The] exercise of authority or power in a burdensome, harsh or wrongful manner; unjust or cruel treatment of subjects, inferiors etc., the imposition of unreasonable or unjust burdens.

It is suggested by some commentators that oppression involves some kind of impropriety on the part of the police, which might be suggested by a failure to follow the PACE Codes of Practice, although a failure to follow the Codes is not of itself an automatic reason for excluding evidence. Given that the courts have occasionally excluded evidence even where the relevant Code of Practice *has* been followed, the converse does not appear to be true and it is possible that a court might conclude that treatment had been 'oppressive' under all the circumstances even though the Codes of Practice had been followed.

The oppression must have been against the person who makes the confession.

If it is suggested that evidence has been obtained by oppression it will be for the prosecution to show beyond reasonable doubt (**see chapter 11**) that this was not the case. For these reasons (as well as those of professional ethics) it is of great importance to comply with the PACE Codes of Practice. It is also important to keep records of how a case is investigated, together with the reasons for taking decisions during the course of the investigation so that the prosecution can present a case which demonstrates that there was no oppressive or improper conduct in gathering evidence.

EXCLUSION OF ADMISSIBLE EVIDENCE

What is Oppression?

It is a question of fact on each occasion whether a person's treatment was oppressive and whether there was any link between that person's treatment and his/her decision to make the confession. The legislation itself gives little guidance as to what will amount to oppression. For this reason it is necessary to look at the case law. Below are examples where the courts have held that the treatment of a person was 'oppressive':

- Where a person who was on the border of being mentally impaired admitted the offence after denying it over 300 times because of the bullying manner of the questioning (*R* v *Paris* (1993) 97 Cr App R 99). This case does not mean that interviewers cannot go over the same point several times or even suggest to the interviewee that he/she is lying. However, *Paris* does suggest that this should be done in moderation and not to the point where it becomes oppressive.

- Where a person confessed but had been kept in custody longer than the court felt was justified and therefore lawful (*R* v *Davison* [1988] Crim LR 442).

- Where the suspect was wrongly informed that he/she had been recognised when this was not true (*R* v *Heron* (1993), unreported).

- Where there was a failure to have an appropriate adult present (*R* v *Silcott*, *The Times*, 9 December 1991).

- Where the defendant was a choir master and the police had told him that if he did not make a statement they would have to interview all the members of the choir and this could disclose other offences on his part (*R* v *Howden-Simpson* [1991] Crim LR 49).

- Where a police officer told the defendant that her boy friend had been having an affair with another woman for the last three years and that the woman was in custody in the next cell to the defendant. The suspect confessed as she felt she had to get out and to confess was the only way she could obtain her release (*R* v *Fulling* [1987] 2 WLR 923).

There is also an argument that oppressive behaviour may apply in circumstances where a person smokes and is refused access to cigarettes. However, there is no case law on this point.

Unreliability

Section 76 of the Police and Criminal Evidence Act 1984 provides that:

> (2)   If, in any proceedings where the prosecution proposes to give in evidence a confession made by an accused person, it is represented to the court that the confession was or may have been obtained—
>
> . . .
>
> (b)   in consequence of anything said or done which was likely, in the circumstances existing at the time, to render unreliable any confession which might be made by him in consequence thereof, the court shall not allow the confession to be given in evidence against him except in so far as the prosecution proves to the court beyond reasonable doubt that the confession (notwithstanding that it may be true) was not obtained as aforesaid.

Keynote

A court can exclude a confession where it is, has been or may have been obtained in consequence of anything which was likely, in the circumstances that existed at the time, to render it *unreliable*.

When looking at whether a confession is reliable, the court will consider the circumstances as they actually were at the time and not as they were believed to be. For instance, if it was believed that a suspect was in a fit state to be interviewed but it later transpires that he/she was medically unfit, there is likely to be some doubt as to whether a confession made at that time is reliable. (The belief of the officers at the time of acting, however, may be relevant to any disciplinary matters.)

For instance in *R* v *Walker* [1998] Crim LR 211 the court held that the defendant's mental state may be taken into account when considering the surrounding circumstances, regardless of whether it was known to the police. The prosecution bore the burden of proof to show that the confession was *admissible*. The court went further and said that s. 76(2)(b) was not restricted in its application to use by the police of oppression. It was not necessary to show that the confession was unreliable by reference to the old common law test of 'threat or inducement'. A successful submission under s. 76(2)(b) does not require a breach of a Code of Practice.

It is not for the defendant to prove that his/her confession is unreliable; it is for the prosecution to show (beyond reasonable doubt) that the confession is reliable.

In *R* v *Fulling* [1987] QB 426 it was suggested that:

> . . . questioning which by its nature, duration, or other attendant circumstances (including the fact of custody) excites hopes (such as the hope of release) or fears, or so affects the mind of the subject that his will crumbles and he speaks when otherwise he would have stayed silent.

Thus the circumstances of a case can affect the reliability of the accused's statement. It is for this reason that PACE Code of Practice C, para. 11.3, gives guidance as to when a person can be informed about possible consequences of making a confession.

What is Unreliable?

It is a question of fact on each occasion whether the reliability of a person's confession is in question as a result of something said or done. Below are examples where the courts have held that a confession was unreliable:

- Where no caution was given to the suspect, the suspect was not asked if he wanted his solicitor present and was not shown the note of the interview (*R* v *Trussler* [1998] Crim LR 446).

- Where the PACE Codes of Practice were flagrantly breached (*R* v *Delaney* (1988) 88 Cr App R 338).

- Where a suspect who had just vomited was interviewed (any medical condition could affect the reliability of a confession; if in doubt have the person examined by a doctor) (*R* v *McGovern* (1991) 92 Cr App R 228).

- Where the appropriate adult had a low IQ and was unable to assist the detained person (*R* v *Silcott*).

- Where it was suggested to a suspect of a sexual assault that it would be better for them to receive treatment than go to prison (*R* v *Delaney*).

- Where a person had been kept in custody for 14 hours, had been interviewed four times before confessing and had been refused any visits from family (*R* v *Silcott*).

- Where the officers had a 'warm up chat' with the suspect before the interview, and the 'chat' lasted over two hours (*R* v *Trussler*).

- Where an offer of bail is made subject to the suspect admitting the offence or conversely, telling the suspect that he/she will be kept in custody until he/she admits the offence (*R* v *Barry* (1992) 95 Cr App R 384).

- Where psychiatric evidence suggested that the suspect suffered from a severe personality disorder and that her admissions in her interview were unreliable (*R* v *Walker* [1998] Crim LR 211).

13.2.2 Effect of Excluding Confessions

The exclusion of a confession may have implications on the value of other evidence.

Often further evidence is obtained after a person makes a confession. If a court excludes all or any part of a confession, then this may impact on the value of the additional evidence obtained by the prosecution.

While the additional evidence obtained after a confession may be admissible, much of the value of the evidence may be lost because s. 76(5) of the 1984 Act prevents the prosecution from linking the discovery of the additional evidence to any confession which has been excluded.

If the additional evidence cannot be linked to the confession then it might not be possible to link the evidence to the suspect (and the evidence may also be excluded under s. 78 of the 1984 Act or at common law).

Example

For instance, in the case of a murder, if a suspect confesses to the murder and tells the investigators where he/she has hidden the murder weapon, this would be good evidence that the person committed the offence. If the confession is excluded then, although evidence can be given that the weapon found is in fact the murder weapon, it will not be possible to show any connection between the suspect and the weapon and, unless there is some other evidence to link the weapon to the suspect, the case may fail. The reason is that it would not be possible to say that the police went to the location where the weapon was hidden without at least implying that the suspect had indicated that it was there when interviewed. All that can be said is that the weapon was found at the particular location, which could be accessible to any number of people.

Section 76(4) of the Police and Criminal Evidence Act 1984 provides that the exclusion of such additional evidence is not affected by the exclusion of the confession. Even where a confession is excluded, it may still be admissible for other matters such as the fact that the accused speaks in a certain way or writes or expresses himself/herself in a particular fashion. In such a case it would only be that part of the confession which is necessary to prove the point that will be admissible. Once again, this illustrates the point that evidence is often only admissible for a specific purpose.

13.3   Exclusion of Evidence Generally

Although there is no equivalent of the American doctrine of 'due process' whereby any evidence which is not obtained by proper procedures is rendered inadmissible, the courts in England and Wales can exclude any evidence under certain circumstances.

Those circumstances will usually be concerned with the way in which the evidence has been obtained (as with confessions above) or with the potential effect of allowing it to be adduced at trial.

13.3.1   Exclusion of Unfair Evidence

Section 78 of the Police and Criminal Evidence Act 1984 provides that:

> *(1)   In any proceedings the court may refuse to allow evidence on which the prosecution proposes to rely to be given if it appears to the court that, having regard to all the circumstances, including the circumstances in which the evidence was obtained, the admission of the evidence would have such an adverse effect on the fairness of the proceedings that the court ought not to admit it.*
> *(2)   Nothing in this section shall prejudice any rule of law requiring a court to exclude evidence.*
> *(3)   This section shall not apply in the case of proceedings before a magistrates' court inquiring into an offence as examining justices.*

Keynote

Section 78 is wider than s. 76 and applies to *all evidence that the prosecution intend to produce in court.*

When applying s. 78, the courts will look at the fairness of allowing the evidence to be admitted against the defendant.

Once again compliance with the Codes of Practice is vital. In *Batley* v *DPP*, *The Times*, 5 March 1998, the court said that where steps required by the Codes were not observed and where material was entered as evidence, without those checks which formed an important aspect of the case, there was a real risk to the fairness of the proceedings against the defendant.

In *R* v *Samuel* [1988] QB 615 the court stated that it is undesirable to attempt any general guidance as to the way in which a judge's discretion under s. 78 should be exercised. It is a question of fact in each case and, while s. 76 requires links with the treatment of the person spoken to, the only issue under s. 76 is whether it would be unfair to admit the evidence in court. It is therefore difficult to give specific guidance but the following are examples of evidence that has been excluded.

What will be Excluded?

- Evidence of a driver being over the prescribed limit where the officer did not suspect the driver had alcohol in his/her body (**see Road Traffic, chapter 5**).

187

- Some cases of 'entrapment' where the court are not satisfied that the person would have committed such an offence had it not been for the action of the police/customs officers. The court may look to see whether the person was pressurised into committing the offence/providing information or whether by some ruse, the person was given an opportunity of so doing.

- Informing the suspect and his/her solicitor that the suspect's fingerprints had been found on items at the scene of the offence when this was not true.

- Undercover operations where the officers failed to record conversations in accordance with the PACE Codes of Practice.

- Failure by custody officers to inform a detained person of his/her rights.

- Interviewing a suspect without informing him/her of his/her rights.

- Failing to provide the detained person with adequate meals.

- 'Off the record' interviews that were not recorded as required by the PACE Codes of Practice.

- Failing to make a contemporaneous note of a conversation.

- Failing to get an interpreter or appropriate adult.

- Interviewing a person suffering from schizophrenia without an appropriate adult being present (R v *Aspinall*, *The Times*, 4 February 1999).

13.3.2 Exclusion at Common Law

Section 82(1) of the Police and Criminal Evidence Act 1984 retained the courts' common law power to exclude evidence at its discretion (as to which see R v *Sang* [1980] AC 402. For evidence to be excluded at common law the court will not so much concern itself with *how* evidence is obtained, but rather the *effect* that the evidence will have at trial. The court can exclude evidence at common law where the prejudicial effect of the evidence on the defendant greatly outweighs its probative value.

In these cases the courts are looking at the trial process itself, as opposed to the investigation, and therefore this power has less impact on how investigations should be conducted.

CHAPTER FOURTEEN

DISCLOSURE OF EVIDENCE

14.1 Introduction

The rules for disclosure have developed piecemeal through case law, mostly after the acquittal of Judith Ward in 1992. These cases put an increasingly onerous burden on the police and prosecutors to provide the defence with every conceivable document which may have a bearing on a prosecution case.

This position changed with the introduction of the Criminal Procedure and Investigations Act 1996, introduced by the government after a number of successful appeals against conviction. As well as putting the requirements to disclose information to the defence on a statutory footing, the 1996 Act also introduced a new concept in criminal law where the defence have a duty to advise the prosecution of certain matters relating to their case.

The rules of disclosure in civil cases already required detailed disclosure of each side's case and the courts have recognised the importance of this in criminal cases. In *R v Kingston upon Hull Justices, ex parte McCann* (1991) 155 JP 569 the court advised that:

> A prosecutor was under no general obligation to provide witness statements in advance of a summary trial. However, prosecutors would be well advised to inform defendants of the material on which the Crown intend to rely in the interest of fairness. (The court did go on to recognise exceptions unless prosecution witnesses might be at risk of reprisals as, for instance, where the defendant has a history of violence.)

The 1996 Act is still further recognition of the need to disclose material to each side to allow the case to be dealt with fairly.

14.2 The Criminal Procedure and Investigations Act 1996

The Criminal Procedure and Investigations Act 1996 is made up of seven parts. It is the first two parts which are of interest to the police:

- Part I sets out the procedures for disclosure and the effects of failing to comply with the Act; and

- Part II sets out the duties of police officers in relation to the disclosure provisions.

The Act is supported by a Code of Practice (**see appendix 3**).

It is important for police officers to understand Part I in the context of Part II. The case law that has developed through the common law is still relevant when looking at cases starting before the 1996 Act came into force, public interest immunity and a small number of other cases which will be dealt with below. As the 1996 Act is still relatively new, there is little guidance on its interpretation and we shall have to wait for case law to develop.

14.2.1 Aims of the 1996 Act

The aim of the disclosure rules within the Criminal Procedure and Investigations Act 1996 is to make sure that a defendant gets a fair trial and speeds up the whole trial process. This was confirmed by *R* v *Stratford Justices, ex parte Imbert, The Times*, 25 February 1999, where the court said that the legislation was to try to ensure that nothing which might assist the defence was kept from the accused. It places a responsibility on the prosecution to make *primary* disclosure of material to the defence; a responsibility for the defence — under certain conditions — to disclose their case to the prosecution with a further responsibility on the prosecution to make a *secondary* disclosure to the defence. As a 'catch all' the prosecution also have a continuing duty to review the material they have disclosed.

There is a duty placed on the prosecutor to disclose to the defence material which may prove helpful to the defendant's case. This has to be balanced against the risk of disclosing so much material under their duty to disclose that the defence collapses under the sheer volume of paperwork. Alternatively, allowing the defence relentless requests for material which may be of no real value ('fishing expeditions') could lead to situations where a guilty person is acquitted.

While the duty of disclosure is placed on the prosecutor, the police have a responsibility to assist in this process. The Home Secretary's Consultation Document recognised the critical role of the police in an effective and fair disclosure process:

> There will be a heavy reliance on the investigator (the police) to identify material which ought to be disclosed, given the material itself will not necessarily be scrutinised by the prosecutor. . . . The investigator will also need to assist the prosecutor by telling him what he thinks are the issues of the case: the system demands a significant degree of liaison between the prosecutor and the investigator as a case develops and the issues in the case change.

It is therefore vital that police officers understand, not only the statutory requirements made of them, but also the extent of their role within the whole disclosure process.

14.2.2 Jurisdiction of the 1996 Act

In cases dealt with in the Crown Court, and either way offences dealt with in the magistrates' court, the prosecution must provide the defence with copies of the material that will form the prosecution case. For summary offences there is no such obligation, although in practice, statements or a summary of the prosecution case is normally provided in all but traffic cases (s. 1). The Criminal Procedure and Investigations Act 1996 is concerned with the disclosure of material which does not form part of the prosecution case resulting from a criminal investigation (i.e. 'unused material').

A criminal investigation is defined by s. 1(4) of the 1996 Act (**see para. 14.3.1**) and para. 2.1 of the Code of Practice (**see appendix 3**).

In order to satisfy the disclosure requirements police officers should consider recording and retaining material in the early stages of an investigation, including investigations:

- to detect a crime *after* it has been committed and in order to bring a prosecution;

- to discover *whether* a crime has been committed, for instance where a motorist is stopped and then enquiries are made as to whether the car has been stolen;

- that are the result of a belief/information that an offence *might be* committed.

In these cases the investigation may well have started some time before the defendant became a suspect. In such cases all the material from the investigation/operation would have to be considered to see if it was relevant to the defence case. In cases where there is a surveillance operation or observation point, the details of the observation point and the surveillance techniques would not be revealed but it would be necessary to retain material generating from it (**see para. 14.5.3**). For the Code of Practice in relation to surveillance operations, **see General Police Duties, chapter 1**.

14.2.3 Failure to Comply

Compliance with the rules of disclosure, by both the defence and prosecution, is essential if the 1996 Act is to have any real value. First, in cases where the defence are obliged to make disclosure to the prosecution, failure to do so may lead to the court or jury drawing such inferences as appear proper in deciding the guilt or innocence of the accused (s. 11(3)). Should the *prosecution* fail to comply with their obligations then an accused does not have to make a defence disclosure and no such inference can be made. Secondly, failure by the prosecution to comply with the rules could lead to the court staying the proceedings on the grounds that there has been an abuse of process (s. 5(1)(b) and s. 10).

Example

The risk of non-compliance with the rules can be seen in *DPP* v *Chipping* 1999, unreported, where the prosecution failed to disclose that there was a closed circuit television at the site where the offences were alleged to have taken place. The police officers viewed the tape but felt that it had no use and it was taped over. The court held that this information should have been disclosed. The result of this failure to disclose the evidence led to the case being dismissed as an abuse of process.

14.3 Part I of the 1996 Act: Rules of Disclosure

14.3.1 Application of the Disclosure Provisions

Section 1 of the Criminal Procedure and Investigations Act 1996 provides that:

> *(1)   This Part applies where—*
> *(a)   a person is charged with a summary offence in respect of which a court proceeds to summary trial and in respect of which he pleads not guilty,*

(b)   a person who has attained the age of 18 is charged with an offence which is triable either way, in respect of which a court proceeds to summary trial and in respect of which he pleads not guilty, or

(c)   a person under the age of 18 is charged with an indictable offence in respect of which a court proceeds to summary trial and in respect of which he pleads not guilty.

(2)   This Part also applies where—

(a)   a person is charged with an indictable offence and he is committed for trial for the offence concerned,

(b)   a person is charged with an indictable offence and proceedings for the trial of the person on the charge concerned are transferred to the Crown Court by virtue of a notice of transfer given under section 4 of the Criminal Justice Act 1987 (serious or complex fraud),

(c)   a person is charged with an indictable offence and proceedings for the trial of the person on the charge concerned are transferred to the Crown Court by virtue of a notice of transfer served on a magistrates' court under section 53 of the Criminal Justice Act 1991 (certain cases involving children),

(d)   a count charging a person with a summary offence is included in an indictment under the authority of section 40 of the Criminal Justice Act 1988 (common assault etc.), or

(e)   a bill of indictment charging a person with an indictable offence is preferred under the authority of section 2(2)(b) of the Administration of Justice (Miscellaneous Provisions) Act 1933 (bill preferred by direction of Court of Appeal, or by direction or with consent of a judge).

Keynote

In reality this applies to all cases other than those where the defendant pleads guilty at the magistrates' court. These rules only apply where no criminal investigation into the alleged offence took place before 1 April 1997. If an investigation began before 1 April 1997, then it will be necessary to refer to the common law rules.

Some guidance is given by the case of *R v Norfolk Stipendiary Magistrate, ex parte Keable* [1998] Crim LR 510 as to the time an investigation begins. There it was said that the phrase 'criminal investigation' in s. 1(3) of the 1996 Act could be broadly construed to include investigations as to whether a person ought to be charged and was not limited to investigations after charges. The term 'alleged offences' means those offences which have been the subject of a charge, rather than 'suspected' offences. Where an offence is alleged to have occurred after 1 April 1997, the prosecutors duties under Part I of the 1996 Act arise, whatever prior investigations may have taken place into related offences.

Section 1 also defines a criminal investigation:

(4)   For the purposes of this section a criminal investigation is an investigation which police officers or other persons have a duty to conduct with a view to it being ascertained—

(a)   whether a person should be charged with an offence, or

(b)   whether a person charged with an offence is guilty of it.

Keynote

Consequently, this Part of the Act also applies to other people, besides the police, who carry out investigations where they have a duty to ascertain whether criminal offences have been committed (e.g. HM Customs and Excise; Benefits Agency investigators). It does not apply to those whose primary responsibility does not relate to criminal offences (e.g. local authorities). It also includes the situation where an investigation is started before any offence has been committed, for instance where a surveillance operation is being conducted with a view to gathering prosecution evidence. In this case it is only the information obtained and not the surveillance operation that is disclosable.

While there are exceptions to the duty of disclosure, the courts have indicated that in all but the most exceptional cases disclosure ought to be given following a defence request (*R v Stratford Justices, ex parte Imbert, The Times*, 25 February 1999).

14.3.2   Primary Disclosure by Prosecutor

Section 3 of the Criminal Procedure and Investigations Act 1996 provides that:

(1)   The prosecutor must—

(a)   disclose to the accused any prosecution material which has not previously been disclosed to the accused and which in the prosecutor's opinion might undermine the case for the prosecution against the accused, or

(b)   give to the accused a written statement that there is no material of a description mentioned in paragraph (a).

(2)   For the purposes of this section prosecution material is material—

(a)   which is in the prosecutor's possession, and came into his possession in connection with the case for the prosecution against the accused, or

(b)   which, in pursuance of a code operative under Part II, he has inspected in connection with the case for the prosecution against the accused.

(3)   Where material consists of information which has been recorded in any form the prosecutor discloses it for the purposes of this section—

(a)   by securing that a copy is made of it and that the copy is given to the accused, or

(b)   if in the prosecutor's opinion that is not practicable or not desirable, by allowing the accused to inspect it at a reasonable time and a reasonable place or by taking steps to secure that he is allowed to do so;

and a copy may be in such form as the prosecutor thinks fit and need not be in the same form as that in which the information has already been recorded.

. . .

(6)   Material must not be disclosed under this section to the extent that the court, on an application by the prosecutor, concludes it is not in the public interest to disclose it and orders accordingly.

(7)   Material must not be disclosed under this section to the extent that—

(a)   it has been intercepted in obedience to a warrant issued under section 2 of the Interception of Communications Act 1985, or

(b)   it indicates that such a warrant has been issued or that material has been intercepted in obedience to such a warrant.

(8)   The prosecutor must act under this section during the period which, by virtue of section 12, is the relevant period for this section.

Keynote

This section talks about material which 'might undermine the prosecution case against the accused'. The courts are likely to consider this to include material which has an adverse affect on the strength of the prosecution case.

It is up to the prosecutor to decide on the format in which material is disclosed to the accused. If material is to be copied, s. 3(3) leaves the question of whether this should be done by the prosecutor or the police open.

The prosecutor must also provide the defence with a *schedule* of all non-sensitive material (s. 4(2)). This includes all other information in police possession, or material that has been examined by the police other than 'sensitive material' (this is disclosed to the prosecutor separately).

'Sensitive material' is material which is not in the public interest to disclose and material obtained as a result of a warrant under s. 2 of the Interception of Communications Act 1985. Such material must not be disclosed to the accused or his/her representatives (s. 3(6) and (7)).

At this stage the defence is not entitled to inspect items on the schedule that have not been disclosed.

The 1996 Act does not specifically address disclosure during the period between arrest and committal. In most cases prosecution disclosure can wait until after committal without jeopardising the defendant's right to a fair trial. However, the prosecutor must always be alive to the need to make advance disclosure of material that should be disclosed at an earlier stage. Examples include:

- previous convictions of a complainant or a deceased if that information could reasonably be expected to assist the defence when applying for bail;

- material that might enable a defendant to make a pre-committal application to stay the proceedings as an abuse of process;

- material that might enable a defendant to submit that he/she should only be committed for trial on a lesser charge, or perhaps that he/she should not be committed for trial at all;

- depending on what the defendant chooses to reveal about his/her case at this early stage, material that would enable the defendant and his/her legal advisers to make preparations for trial that would be significantly less effective if disclosure were delayed, for example, names of eye witnesses whom the prosecution did not intend to use.

Any disclosure by the prosecution prior to committal would not normally exceed the primary disclosure which, after committal, would be required by s. 3 of the 1996 Act (material which in the prosecutor's opinion might undermine the case for the prosecution (*R v DPP, ex parte Lee, The Times*, 26 April 1999).

14.3.3 Disclosure by the Defence

The duty on the defence to make disclosure only arises *after* the prosecution has made the primary disclosure (s. 5(1)).

This duty falls into two categories:

- compulsory;
- voluntary.

Compulsory Disclosure by Defence (s. 5)

The duty for the defence to make disclosure does not apply to cases being tried summarily.

The duty on the defence, whether the accused is represented or not, is to provide a defence statement to the court and the prosecutor within 14 days of the prosecution making primary disclosure (this can be extended by the courts).

The defence statement should outline the defence case in general terms. In addition, those issues, relevant to the case, which the accused disputes with the prosecution must be set out with reasons. This requirement to give reasons is intended to stop the defence going on a 'fishing expedition' to speculatively look at material in order to find some kind of defence.

Where the defence case involves an alibi, the statement must give details of the alibi, including the name and address of any alibi witness. In cases where there are co-accused, there is no duty to disclose this information to the other defendants, although this could be done voluntarily.

Voluntary Disclosure by Defence (s. 6)

The purpose of s. 6 of the 1996 Act is to allow the defence, in cases where the case is being tried summarily, to obtain further disclosure from the prosecution after the primary disclosure. This is only likely to happen where:

- The defence is not satisfied with the material disclosed at the primary disclosure stage or where they wish to examine items listed in the schedule of non-sensitive material.

- The defence wish to show the strength of their case in order to persuade the prosecution not to proceed.

If the defence decide to make a defence statement they must comply with the same conditions imposed on compulsory defence disclosure.

14.3.4 Secondary Disclosure by Prosecutor (s. 7)

Once a defence statement has been provided (whether compulsorily or voluntarily), the prosecution must disclose any prosecution material that:

- has not already been disclosed; and
- that might be reasonably expected to assist the accused's defence.

It will be a question of fact whether material in police possession might be reasonably expected to assist the defence case. If the court feels that material that was not disclosed would to any reasonable person have been expected to help the defence case, the case may fail.

If there is no additional material to be disclosed then the prosecutor must give a written statement to this effect. It is not the responsibility of the prosecutor or the police to examine material held by third parties which the defence have stated they wish to examine (the defence can request this from the third party or apply for a witness summons). However, there may be occasions where matters disclosed in the defence statement lead investigators to look at material held by third parties as it might impact on the prosecution case. This stage of the disclosure process may require further inquiries prompted by the defence statement. The result of those enquiries may then have to be disclosed because it either undermines the prosecution case or it assists the accused's defence.

14.3.5 Appeal to Court by Defence at Level of Disclosure by Prosecution

If the defence are not satisfied that the prosecution have disclosed all they should have to them they can apply to the court for further disclosure under s. 8 of the 1996 Act. Section 8 provides that:

(1)   This section applies where the accused gives a defence statement under section 5 or 6 and the prosecutor complies with section 7 or purports to comply with it or fails to comply with it.

(2)   If the accused has at any time reasonable cause to believe that—

(a)   there is prosecution material which might be reasonably expected to assist the accused's defence as disclosed by the defence statement given under section 5 or 6, and

(b)   the material has not been disclosed to the accused,

the accused may apply to the court for an order requiring the prosecutor to disclose such material to the accused.

(3)   For the purposes of this section prosecution material is material—

(a)   which is in the prosecutor's possession and came into his possession in connection with the case for the prosecution against the accused,

(b)   which, in pursuance of a code operative under part II, he has inspected in connection with the case for the prosecution against the accused, or

(c)   which falls within subsection (4).

(4)   Material falls within this subsection if in pursuance of a code operative under part II the prosecutor must, if he asks for the material, be given a copy of it or be allowed to inspect it in connection with the case for the prosecution against the accused.

(5)   Material must not be disclosed under this section to the extent that the court, on an application by the prosecutor, concludes it is not in the public interest to disclose it and orders accordingly.

(6)   Material must not be disclosed under this section to the extent that—

(a)   it has been intercepted in obedience to a warrant issued under section 2 of the Interception of Communications Act 1985, or

(b)   it indicates that such a warrant has been issued or that material has been intercepted in obedience to such a warrant.

14.3.6   Continuing Duty of Prosecutor to Disclose (s. 9)

There is duty on the prosecution to continue to review the disclosure of prosecution material right up until the case is completed (acquittal, conviction or discontinuance of the case).

The duty to review is in two stages:

- after primary disclosure the prosecutor must review material not disclosed in terms of whether it might undermine the prosecution case (s. 9); and
- after secondary prosecution disclosure (s. 7).

The review of the material must also be in terms of whether material might be reasonably expected to assist the accused's defence as disclosed by the defence statement. This responsibility is mirrored in the Code of Practice.

14.4   Roles and Responsibilities under the 1996 Act

The Code of Practice (**see appendix 3**) identifies certain roles within the disclosure process:

- prosecutor;
- officer in charge of the case (OIC);
- disclosure officer;
- investigator;
- supervisor of OIC and disclosure officer.

In addition, it is the responsibility of the chief officer of police of each force to put arrangements in place to ensure that the identity of the OIC and disclosure officer is recorded for each criminal investigation (Code of Practice, para. 3.2). Force policy should be followed in recording this information.

The roles described within the 1996 Act are independent of each other but all must be completed for the disclosure provisions to work (para. 3.1). All police officers involved in an investigation are likely to have to comply with the role of investigator.

Although the police roles are independent they may be combined, and the OIC may also be an investigator and, depending on the complexity of the case, may also be the disclosure officer. Whether there is one officer involved in the case or several, each role can be considered separately and must be completed fully in order that the right information can be given to the prosecutor who, ultimately, is responsible for the disclosure of material to the defence. It is important that all officers consult fully in order that the disclosure officer can complete his/her task properly. Each role is considered below as if undertaken by a different person.

14.4.1 Prosecutor

This role is defined by s. 2(3) of the 1996 Act as being 'any person acting as prosecutor, whether an individual or a body'. In other words, the person who will be taking the case to court. On most occasions this will be the Crown Prosecution Service. It would also apply to the Serious Fraud Office or the Data Protection Registrar (**see chapter 3**). In the case of private prosecutions, the prosecutor is obliged to comply with the disclosure provisions of the 1996 Act but does not have to comply with the Codes of Practice. The prosecutor is responsible for ensuring that *primary* disclosure is made to the defence and, where appropriate, *secondary* disclosure. The prosecutor should also be available to advise the OIC, disclosure officer and investigators on matters relating to the relevance of material recorded and retained by police, sensitive material and on any other disclosure issues that might arise.

14.4.2 Officer in Charge of the Case (OIC)

This role may be performed by a person directly involved in the investigation or by a person who has been given the role of overseeing the investigation (Code, paras 3.1 and 3.3). Whoever has this role is both responsible and accountable for the investigation (para. 3.3).

The OIC is responsible for ensuring that proper procedures are in place for the recording of information and that records and materials are retained for the required period (**see para. 14.6**). Paragraph 4.1 of the Code requires that the material is recorded in a durable and retrievable form and that, where possible, the record is made contemporaneously. If not, the record must be made as soon as practicable. Guidance is given in para. 5.4. These requirements to record information should be paramount in the mind of all investigators, as well as the OIC. The need for contemporaneous records is also required under the Police and Criminal Evidence Act 1984 and if not complied with could affect the admissibility of important evidence (see s. 78 of the 1984 Act in **chapter 13**). Note that, under para. 4.3, relevant material to be recorded includes *negative* material. Such material might include the fact that several people at the scene of a crime were spoken to and claimed to have seen nothing, or that they saw several other people at the scene as well. This last point reiterates the position at common law; that police officers have a duty to get to the truth and allow a suspect a fair trial, a duty which includes recording and retaining material which helps the defence.

Having made sure that material is recorded and retained by the investigators in the case, the OIC must make the material available to the disclosure officer (Code, para. 3.3).

Where the function of disclosure officer is carried out by the OIC, there is little problem as the OIC should have a full understanding of the case and the implication of all the material collected, in terms of it being adverse to the case or being of a sensitive nature. In cases where the roles are performed by different people, it is important that the OIC and the disclosure officer consult fully about the material in order that the disclosure officer has as full an understanding of the case as he/she can in order to carry out his/her functions properly (para. 3.1). This must be done in order that the disclosure officer can complete the certification stage (paras 3.1 and 9). These responsibilities can be delegated to other police officers or non-police staff but it remains the responsibility of the OIC to ensure that the tasks are completed (para. 3.3).

As with all people involved in the disclosure process, s. 9 of the 1996 Act places a duty on the OIC to review material in the case. This duty is emphasised by para. 5.3 so that, where the OIC becomes aware that previously examined material which has not been disclosed has since become relevant to the case, he/she must take steps to ensure that the material is retained and inform the prosecutor so that disclosure can be made to the defence. At this stage it will be for the OIC to decide in which format that material should be retained (para. 4.1).

14.4.3   Disclosure Officer

The disclosure officer creates the link between the investigation team and the prosecutor (Crown Prosecution Service) and is therefore very important to the disclosure process. For investigations carried out by the police, there is no restriction on who performs this role. It could be the OIC or, equally, it could be performed by unsworn support staff (Code, paras 2.1 and 3.3). The disclosure officer is responsible for providing information and material to the prosecutor at the primary disclosure stage (para. 7.1) and, where necessary, carrying out any additional work requested by the prosecutor before the primary disclosure is made (paras 7.4 and 14.1).

The disclosure officer is responsible for examining all material retained by the police during the investigation (para. 2.1). The first step is to establish that all material which has been retained in relation to the case has been recorded and made available for examination. The disclosure officer should verify with the OIC that all material has been made available to him/her.

Section 12 of the 1996 Act allows provision for time limits governing when primary disclosure must be made. At the time of writing, no such provisions have been made. Instead disclosure must be made:

- as soon as is reasonably practicable after a not guilty plea in the magistrates' court; and

- in all trials at the Crown Court, once the Crown Court has received the case (which effectively means after it has been committed from the magistrates' court or transferred from that court).

Should the disclosure officer fail to provide information to the prosecutor within a reasonable time or to comply with any requests made by the prosecutor for additional material, this could lead to the defence not having to provide a defence statement or adverse remarks being made in court. At worse it could lead to a stay of proceedings for an abuse of process (s. 10 of the 1996 Act; see s. 5(4)).

DISCLOSURE OF EVIDENCE

Duties of the Disclosure Officer: Primary Disclosure

Where disclosure is required, the first task is to create a schedule of all *non-sensitive material*, which has been retained by the police and which does not form part of the prosecution case, which may be relevant to the investigation (Code, para. 6.3). If in doubt, the prosecutor should be consulted so that they can advise on the relevance of material (para. 6.1). This schedule must be endorsed by the disclosure officer to the effect that, to his/her best ability, it does not contain any sensitive material.

Initially, these schedules only have to be produced where the person is charged with an indictable offence, where the offence is triable either way or where the defendant will be tried summarily and is likely to plead not guilty. If the offence is witnessed by a police officer, or the person has admitted an either way or summary offence, then a schedule is not required unless the person then pleads not guilty. This provision has been added to avoid preparing material which will never be needed. If the person then pleads not guilty the schedule must be prepared as soon as practicable (para. 6.8).

The next step is to create a separate schedule of all sensitive material, which must include the reasons why the disclosure officer believes the material is of a sensitive nature (para. 6.4). Paragraph 6.12 gives examples of the type of material that would be classed as sensitive. If all material has been disclosed and there is no sensitive material, then a statement to that effect-should be included on the main schedule. The schedule(s) should include all material, excluding that which forms part of the prosecution case (para. 6.2).

There may he cases where material is so sensitive that the disclosure officer or other investigators consider that it should not even appear on the schedule (such as where disclosure would be likely to lead directly to the loss of life or directly threaten national security (para. 6.13)). In these cases the prosecutor should be informed of these separately (para. 6.4). It is the responsibility of the investigator who knows the details of the sensitive material to inform the prosecutor.

Once the schedules have been completed, the disclosure officer must decide what material, if any (whether listed on the schedules or not), might undermine the prosecution case. The disclosure officer must draw this information to the attention of the prosecutor and the reasons why he/she believes that the material undermines the prosecution case (para. 7.2). This creates a catch all provision and presumably requires the disclosure officer to make enquires of the other officers in the case to ensure all material is included.

This stage of the process is of particular importance. There will be a great reliance placed on the opinion of the disclosure officer as to what material might undermine the prosecution case. It is only material that falls into this category that the defence can inspect at this stage. Should the defence wish to inspect any other material on the schedule, this can only happen after the defence statement (outlining the defence case and giving reasons why they wish to inspect other items on the schedule) has been received.

It is important that the schedules themselves are completed fully. Guidance is given by paras 6.9 to 6.11 of the Code. The schedule should have each item numbered consecutively with a description of the item in sufficient detail to allow the prosecutor, when examining the schedule to make an informed decision about the importance of the item, and whether it needs to be disclosed to the defence, in addition to the items suggested by the disclosure officer, as undermining the prosecution case. While items should be listed separately, there may be occasions where items are similar or the same, in which case these may be listed together.

The schedules and copies of any material which is considered to undermine the prosecution case should be given to the prosecutor (paras 7.1 to 7.3). The disclosure officer should include an explanation as to why they consider that the material should be disclosed (para. 7.2). As it is unlikely that the prosecutor will have a chance to examine all the material, it is important that the disclosure officer gives clear reasons in his/her report. For the type of material which might undermine the prosecution case, **see para. 14.5.2**.

In addition to the schedules and copies of material which undermine the prosecution case, para. 7.3 requires the disclosure officer to provide a copy of any material, *whether or not they consider it to undermine the prosecution case*, which is:

- a record of the first description of a suspect given to the police by a potential witness, *whether or not the description differs from that of the alleged offender*;

- information provided by an accused person which indicates an explanation for the offence with which he/she has been charged;

- any material casting doubt on the reliability of a confession;

- any material casting doubt on the reliability of a witness.

The disclosure officer must certify that, to the best of his/her knowledge, all material which has been retained by police and made available to them has been revealed to the prosecutor in accordance with the para. 9.1.

While the disclosure officer may not always be able to know if all material has been made available to him/her, he/she should consult with the OIC to verify as far as possible that it has been (para. 3.1).

Often the police may not possess all the material that could become relevant in a case. It may be that this material has been inspected and a decision made that the material is not relevant to the case at this stage, or that it was not necessary to inspect the material. To cover the risk of material being lost, the disclosure officer should inform third parties of the investigation and invite them to retain material. The disclosure officer should inform the prosecutor that third parties may have such material (para. 3.1).

Under para. 8, information provided by the disclosure officer may be accepted by the prosecutor or might be returned with requests for additional information or for amendments to be made to the schedule or items to be disclosed to the defence.

The disclosure officer should comply with any instructions given by the prosecutor and any request for the inspection or copying of material should be met (para. 7.4). If the disclosure officer and OIC consider that material is so sensitive it should not be copied, the disclosure officer should inform the prosecutor and make arrangements for the prosecutor to inspect the material instead (para. 7.4). If copies of materials which are not in writing are requested, the disclosure officer and prosecutor must agree on the format of how it will be provided to the prosecutor (para. 7.5).

Once this stage is complete, the prosecutor is able to make primary disclosure to the defence. It will be the responsibility of the disclosure officer to disclose material to the defence if requested to do so by the prosecutor (para. 10.1).

Duties of the Disclosure Officer: Secondary Disclosure

Once primary disclosure has been made it is likely that the defence will provide a defence statement setting out their case, together with reasons why they wish to inspect additional items on the schedule which have not been disclosed. Under para. 8.2, once the defence statement has been provided, the disclosure officer must:

- review the material which is contained on the schedules; and

- inform the prosecutor of any material which might reasonably be expected to assist the defence as disclosed by the defence statement.

This role will often be performed in conjunction with the prosecutor and, at times, may even be undertaken by the prosecutor. However, the Code of Practice does require the disclosure officer to carry out this function and as such there is a duty to review this material *even if it is also done by the prosecutor.*

After the material has been reviewed, secondary disclosure can be made to the defence. As with the primary disclosure stage, the disclosure officer must certify that, to the best of his/her knowledge, all material which has been retained by the police and made available to them has been revealed to the prosecutor in accordance with para. 9.1. Again, while the disclosure officer may not always be able to know if all material has been made available to him/her, he/she should consult with the OIC to verify as far as possible that it has been (para. 3.1).

Continuing Duty of Disclosure Officer

Once primary disclosure has been made, the disclosure officer has a continuing duty to review material for items that should be disclosed to the defence as undermining the prosecution case. This continuing duty also applies after secondary disclosure in relation to material which might assist the defence case as disclosed in the defence statement (para. 8.3).

Disclosing Material to the Defence

The disclosure officer may also be involved in the actual disclosure of material to the defence which is covered in para. 10 of the Code of Practice. This is material which the prosecutor has agreed that the disclosure officer will disclose to the defence because it falls within the material disclosed:

- at the primary disclosure stage (adverse to prosecution case);
- at the secondary disclosure stage (it assists the defence case); or
- where the court has ordered disclosure after an application by the defence; or
- where, through the continuing duty to review material, it has been disclosed because it has been decided it might undermine the prosecution case or assist the defence case.

The court can also order disclosure of material which the prosecution contend is sensitive. In such cases it may be appropriate to seek guidance on whether to disclose the material or offer no evidence thereby protecting the sensitive material or the source of that material (e.g. where informants or surveillance techniques are involved).

The disclosure officer can make disclosure to the defence by either:

- providing copies of the material; or
- allowing the defence to inspect the material.

Where a request is made for copies, the material must be provided unless it is not practicable or desirable to do so. Examples of such occasions are given in para. 10.3. In cases where the material is not recorded in a written format (for instance an audio or video tape) then the disclosure officer has a discretion whether to provide a copy of the item or transcript of what is contained on the tape. This must be certified as a true copy of the tape (para. 10.4).

14.4.4 Duties of Investigators

The roles of investigator may involve just one officer or several officers. An 'investigation' may be completed in a very short time, e.g. from stopping a car, discovering it was stolen, arresting the suspect, obtaining a victim statement and charging the suspect.

Alternatively, the case may involve a long, protracted enquiry with several officers and numerous suspects, arrests and interviews.

Irrespective of the type of investigation, para. 3.4 requires investigators to pursue all reasonable lines of inquiry, *whether these point towards or away from the suspect.* To ensure that this duty is performed, it may be appropriate for investigators to meet and review the case and co-ordinate the allocated 'actions'.

What amounts to pursuing all reasonable lines of inquiry will be a question of fact in each case. What is reasonable in a case may well depend on such factors as the staff and resources available, the seriousness of the case, the strength of evidence against the suspect and the nature of the line of inquiry to be pursued.

Where an investigator discovers material that is relevant to the case, he/she must record that information or retain the material (para. 4.1). Once again, this duty to record and retain material relevant to the case includes material that would be regarded as negative to the prosecution case (para. 4.3). This does not just mean witness statements and evidence from inquiries but would include arrest notes, custody records, forensic reports, records of interview and all other material the investigator is aware of that might be relevant to the investigation. To this end, para. 5.1 places a duty on the investigator to retain all relevant material. Often, particularly at the early stages of an investigation (sometimes not until the defence statement is provided outlining the defence case), it will not be possible to know whether material is relevant. If in doubt it should be recorded and placed on the schedule of undisclosed material. Throughout the case, investigators and all others involved should continually review the material in the light of the investigation. Any material which becomes relevant and which has not been disclosed should be disclosed and, where it has not been retained, the OIC should be informed in order that he/she can decide what action to take (para. 5.3).

The issue of sensitive material is discussed below (**see para. 14.5.3**). Often it is only the investigator who obtained the evidence who will be fully aware of the sensitive nature of the material. In order to balance the need to protect sensitive material yet give the prosecutor full details of why the material is sensitive, para. 6.14 places the responsibility of informing the prosecutor of details of sensitive material on the investigator. That investigator must take steps to ensure the prosecutor can inspect the material. This does not mean that the disclosure officer or any other officer cannot carry out this function; simply that the investigator must ensure that it is carried out.

Continuing Duty of Investigators

The continuing duty of disclosure imposed by ss. 7 and 9 of the 1996 Act mean that investigators have a corresponding duty to keep under review the revelation of material which meets the test for disclosure. It is therefore important that investigators are aware of which material might undermine the prosecution case and which might assist the defence case. It is also important therefore that investigators are aware of the content of defence statements provided after primary disclosure.

If investigators do not carry out their function properly, this has an impact on all the others involved in the disclosure process and may lead to disclosure on the defence being defective.

14.4.5 Supervisor of OIC and Disclosure Officer

In all cases there must be an OIC and a disclosure officer. If for any reason, either the OIC or the disclosure officer can no longer perform their respective tasks, para. 3.6 places a responsibility on that person's supervisor to assign another person to take over that role.

14.5 Definitions

Paragraph 2.1 of the Code of Practice provides definitions to be used when considering the Code and some additional guidance is provided below.

14.5.1 Relevant Material

The 1996 Act is concerned with the disclosure of material which is obtained during the course of a criminal investigation and which may be relevant to the investigation. Material can be in any form and should be widely interpreted. This applies to any material coming to the knowledge of officers involved in the case at any stage of the investigation or even after a suspect has been charged. This is material which the investigator, OIC or disclosure officer consider has some bearing on any offence being investigated or any people being investigated for those offences or any of the surrounding circumstances.

The material will be *relevant* whether it is beneficial to the prosecution case, weakens the prosecution case or assists the defence case. It is not only material that will become 'evidence' (**see chapter 11**) in the case that should be considered; any information, record or thing which may have a bearing on the case can be material for the purposes of disclosure.

What is relevant to the offence is once again a question of fact and will not include everything. In *DPP* v *Metten* 1999, unreported, it was claimed that the constables who had arrested the defendant had known the identities of potential witnesses to the arrest and these had not been disclosed. The court said that this was not relevant to the case as it did not fall within the definition of an investigation in s. 2(1) in that it concerned the time of arrest not what happened at the time the *offence* was committed.

Paragraph 5.4 gives guidance on items that might be considered to be relevant material in a case (**see appendix 3**).

Relevant material may relate to the credibility of witnesses such as previous convictions, the fact that they have a grudge against the defendant or even the weather conditions for the day if relevant to the issue of identification. It may include information that house to house inquiries were made and that no one witnessed anything.

In cases where officers are in doubt as to whether material should be recorded and retained, the prosecutor should be consulted. If this cannot be done, the material should be retained and recorded. If the material is not in a format that it can be retained (for instance because it was said orally), material should be recorded in a durable and retrievable form (paras 4.1 and 4.2).

14.5.2 Material that Undermines the Prosecution Case

Before the Criminal Procedure and Investigations Act 1996, when disclosure was required the prosecution had to disclose all material that was relevant to the case. Under the 1996 Act, while a schedule of all relevant material must be provided, only material that undermines the prosecution case must be disclosed at the primary disclosure stage. There is only limited case law in this area but it is likely that such material will consist mainly of material which raises question marks over the strength of the prosecution case, the value of evidence given by witnesses and issues relating to identification. If officers feel that the material is not relevant to the prosecution case but may be useful to the defence in cross-examination, it may well come within the category of material which undermines the prosecution case.

Disclosure of previous convictions and other matters that might affect the credibility of a witness may 'undermine the prosecution case' as it may limit the value of the witness's testimony. This factor may not be apparent at the time but may come to light after primary disclosure, such as where it becomes known that the witness has a grudge against the defendant. This is one reason why the 1996 Act requires the decision as to whether material undermines the prosecution case to be continuously monitored throughout the case.

Not only might the credibility of witnesses undermine the prosecution case, but so too might complaints against officers involved the case, together with any occasions where officers have not been believed in court in the past. In these cases, it will be necessary to decide whether this information should be disclosed to the defence and if disclosed, in how much detail. This question is probably best answered by the following extract from advice given to prosecutors by the Director of Public Prosecutions:

> It is, of course, necessary in the first instance for the police to bring such matters to the notice of the prosecutor, but it is submitted that the prosecutor should have a greater element of discretion than with the disclosure of previous convictions. With convictions against prosecution witnesses, disclosure normally follows, whereas in relation to disciplinary findings regard should be had to the nature of the finding and its likely relevance to the matters in issue. Findings which involve some element of dishonesty should invariably be disclosed, while matters such as disobedience to orders, neglect of duty and discreditable conduct will often

have no relevance to the officer's veracity or the guilt or otherwise of a defendant. Certainly, there should be no duty on the prosecution to disclose details of unsubstantiated complaints even though this is a popular type of inquiry from some defence representatives. The imposition of such a duty would only encourage the making of false complaints in the hope that they might be used to discredit an officer in the future.

The prosecutor should be informed if officers involved in a case have discipline matters on their record. This may well appear on the schedule in order that the prosecutor can consider the matter and amend the schedule if necessary. It is suggested that advice should be sought from the prosecutor as to what information is included on the schedule and if disclosure is to be made, advice on what information to be included should also be sought.

Some guidance is given by the case of *R* v *Guney* [1998] 2 Cr App R 242. Here the court said that the defence are not entitled to be informed of every occasion when any officer has given evidence 'unsuccessfully' or whenever allegations are made against him/her. However, in this case the court felt that disclosure should have been made. It will therefore be a question of fact in each case and consultation with the Crown Prosecution Service is advisable if there is any doubt.

It is important to note that the material itself does not have to be admissible in court for it to undermine the prosecution case. This point was made in *R* v *Preston* (1994) 98 Cr App R 405, where it was said that:

> In the first place, the fact that an item of information cannot be put in evidence by a party does not mean that it is worthless. Often, the train of inquiry which leads to the discovery of evidence which is admissible at a trial may include an item which is not admissible, and this may apply, although less frequently, to the defence as well as the prosecution.

Once again, if in doubt advice should be sought from the Crown Prosecution Service.

14.5.3 Sensitive Material

Put simply, this is material which it is not in the public interest to disclose. The disclosure officer has to decide what material, if any, in a case falls into this category. Guidance is given by para. 6.12 of the Code of Practice (**see appendix 3**), which provides a list of examples of such material.

Many of these items are included within the common law principles of public interest immunity discussed in **chapter 10**. The case law in this area will still apply to decisions regarding the disclosure of such material. These groups are not exclusive and the areas most likely to apply will be those concerning the protection of intelligence and intelligence methods. It will almost certainly apply where there is a need to protect the sources of information used in the detection and prevention of crime. What sources of information the courts will protect is a question of fact but may well include material given in confidence, observation points, informants, crime-stopper type telephone hot lines and police communications. As evidence obtained from observation points normally falls into this category of disclosure, it will be important that the correct procedures are followed if the court are going to protect the location used. Guidance is given by the *Johnson* ruling.

The *Johnson* Ruling

In *R* v *Johnson* [1988] 1 WLR 1377, Watkins LJ gave the following guidance as to the *minimum evidential requirements* in this regard:

- The police officer in charge of the observations — not lower than the rank of sergeant — must be able to testify that beforehand he/she visited all observation places to be used and ascertained the attitude of the occupiers of premises, not only as to the use to be made of them, but also as to the possible disclosure of their use and other facts which could lead to the identification of the premises and of the occupiers. The officer may, of course, in addition inform the court of difficulties, if any, usually encountered in the particular locality of obtaining assistance from the public.

- A police officer of no lower rank than a chief inspector must be able to testify that, immediately before the trial, he/she visited the places used for observations and ascertained whether the occupiers are the same as when the observations took place and what the attitude of the current occupiers is as to the possible disclosure of the use made of the premises and of other facts which could lead to the identification of both premises and occupiers.

In *Johnson*, the appellant was convicted of supplying drugs. The only evidence against him was given by police officers, who testified that, while stationed in private premises in a known drug-dealing locality, they had observed him selling drugs. The defence applied to cross-examine the officers on the exact location of the observation posts, in order to test what they could see, having regard to the layout of the street and the objects in it. In the jury's absence the prosecution called evidence as to the difficulty of obtaining assistance from the public, and the desire of the occupiers, who were also occupiers at the time of the offence, that their names and addresses should not be disclosed because they feared for their safety.

The judge ruled that the exact location of the premises need not be revealed. The appeal was dismissed: although the conduct of the defence was to some extent affected by the restraints placed on it, this led to no injustice. The jury were well aware of the restraints, and were most carefully directed about the very special care they had to give to any disadvantage they may have brought to the defence. *Johnson* was applied and approved in *R v Hewitt* (1992) 95 Cr App R 81 (see also *R v Grimes* [1994] Crim LR 213). The guidelines in *Johnson* do not require a threat of violence before protection can be afforded to the occupier of an observation post; it suffices if the occupier is in fear of harassment (*Blake* v *DPP* (1993) 97 Cr App R 169). (For the Code of Practice in relation to surveillance operations, **see General Police Duties, chapter 1**).

This extended the rules established in *R v Rankine* [1986] QB 861 and is based on the protection of the owner or occupier of the premises, and not on the identity of the observation post. Thus, where officers have witnessed the commission of an offence as part of a surveillance operation conducted from an unmarked police vehicle, information relating to the surveillance and the colour, make and model of the vehicle should not be withheld (*R v Brown* (1987) 87 Cr App R 52). Hodgson J said in *Brown*:

> We do not rule out the possibility that with the advent of no doubt sophisticated methods of criminal investigation, there may be cases where the public interest immunity may be successfully invoked in criminal proceedings to justify the exclusion of evidence as to police techniques and methods. But if and when such an argument is to be raised, it must, in the judgment of this court, be done properly.

As an indication of the importance of intelligence, it should be noted that at no stage must disclosure be made of material that has been intercepted in obedience to a warrant issued under s. 2 of the Interception of Communications Act 1985, or which indicates that such a warrant has been issued or that material has been intercepted in obedience to such a warrant (s. 3(7) of the Criminal Procedure and Investigations Act 1996).

14.5.4   Confidentiality

The defence may only use material disclosed to them under the 1996 Act for purposes related to the defence case; any other use will be a contempt of court (for which see *Blackstone's Criminal Practice*, 1999, section B14). Once evidence has been given in open court, however, the material is available for other purposes.

14.6   Retention Periods

Material must be retained in all cases until a decision is taken whether to institute proceedings against a person for an offence. Where a decision is taken to institute proceedings material must then be retained until the case has been dealt with. The Code of Practice under the Criminal Procedure and Investigations Act 1996 gives specific guidance in cases where a person is convicted as to how long material must be retained for (**see appendix 3**). Paragraphs 5.6 to 5.10 set out the retention periods where a person has been convicted. All material which may be relevant must be retained at least until:

- the person is released from custody or discharged from hospital in cases where the court imposes a custodial sentence or hospital order;

- in all other cases, for six months from the date of conviction.

If the person is released from the custodial sentence or discharged from hospital earlier than six months from the date of conviction, the material must be retained for at least six months from the date of conviction. If an appeal is in progress at the end of one of these periods, or an application is being considered by the Criminal Cases Review Commission, the period is extended until:

- the appeal is concluded; or

- the Commission decide not to refer the application to the Court of Appeal; or

- the Court of Appeal determines the appeal resulting from the reference.

In these cases, if material was seized from its owner it may be returned (Code, para. 5.10).

Where material has been seized under the powers provided by the Police and Criminal Evidence Act 1984 (**see General Police Duties, chapter 2**), para. 5.2 confirms that retention of the material should reflect the provisions of s. 22 of the 1984 Act.

PART THREE

POLICE STATION PROCEDURE

CHAPTER FIFTEEN

CUSTODY OFFICER'S DUTIES

15.1   Introduction

The powers to detain people who have been arrested and the manner in which they must be dealt with are primarily contained in the Police and Criminal Evidence Act 1984 and the PACE Codes of Practice whose creation and status come from s. 66 of the Act. The 1984 Act provides directions to police officers in how detained persons should be treated. The main responsibility for detained persons lies with the custody officer, however it is important that *all* officers, including supervisors involved in investigations or those dealing with detained persons are aware of the provisions of the Act and the Codes. Failure to follow the requirements of the law could lead to prosecutions failing because evidence is excluded (**see chapter 13**), civil actions against forces, bad publicity and the possibility of disciplinary action or even criminal proceedings against officers.

The custody officer carries the main responsibility towards prisoners who are brought to the police station. Initially it must be decided whether the person should be detained as a prisoner at the police station. If there are grounds to detain him/her then the detention period must be *for those reasons only*. Once a decision to detain a person has been made, the manner in which he/she must be treated while in detention is set out in the PACE Codes (**see appendices 5 to 7**). These Codes are intended to protect the basic rights of detained people. If these codes are followed it is more likely that evidence obtained while people are in custody will be admissible. The provisions of the 1984 Act give guidance in numerous areas including:

- length of time in detention;
- information about the detained person's arrest;
- searching;
- taking of samples;
- interviewing of suspects;
- identification methods;
- charging; and
- bail.

The PACE Codes set out the minimum standard of treatment that a detained person can expect. These requirements may soon be extended by the incorporation of the Convention on Human Rights and Fundamental Freedoms when the Human Rights Act 1998 comes into force (this is likely to be October 2000). The maximum length of detention is also prescribed by the Act, as are the requirements for charging, bailing and appearances at court.

The following chapter outlines some of the requirements of the legislation and the powers police have in relation to detained people. The chapter is aimed at providing guidance when using the legislation and it is intended to point the reader to the correct sections of the 1984 Act and the PACE Codes of Practice when dealing with detained people and investigations.

15.2   Designated Police Stations

Section 30 of the Police and Criminal Evidence Act 1984 requires that a person who has been arrested must be taken to a police station *as soon as practicable* after arrest. However, not all police stations have charge rooms or facilities for dealing with prisoners, so the 1984 Act requires that prisoners who will be detained (or who are likely to be detained) for more than six hours must go to a 'designated' police station. A designated police station is one that has enough facilities for the purpose of detaining arrested people. Section 35 requires the Chief Officer of Police to designate sufficient police stations to deal with prisoners. It is for the Chief Officer to decide which stations are to be designated stations and these details are then published. Police stations can be designated permanently or for any specified periods provided that they are not designated for part of a day.

15.3   Custody Officers

Custody officers are responsible for the reception and treatment of prisoners brought to the police station.

The role of the custody officer is to act independently of those conducting the investigation, thereby ensuring the welfare and rights of the detained person. This requirement is contained in s. 36(5) of the 1984 Act. PACE Code C, para. 3.4 also supports this point in that it makes it clear that the custody officer must not ask a detained person any questions regarding his/her involvement in any offence. The custody officer should not make any comment which may be seen as placing a value judgement on what the person is alleged to have done, nor should he/she make any other comment which in any way casts doubt on his/her impartiality.

Section 36 requires that one or more custody officers must be appointed for each designated police station. However, in *Vince* v *Chief Constable of Dorset* [1993] 1 WLR 415 it was held that there does not have to be a custody officer available all the time at such a police station. The provision of the facility of a custody officer must be reasonable. Section 36(3) states that a custody officer must be an officer of at least the rank of sergeant. However, s. 36(4) allows constables to perform the functions of a custody officer if a sergeant is not readily available to perform them. The effect of s. 36(3) and (4) is that the practice of allowing constables to perform the role of custody officer where a sergeant (*who has no other role to perform*) is in the police station must therefore be unlawful.

For cases where arrested people are taken to a non-designated police station, s. 36(7) states that an officer of any rank not involved in the investigation should perform the role of custody officer. If no such person is at the station, the arresting officer (or any other officer involved in the investigation) should perform the role. In these cases, an officer of at least the rank of inspector at a designated police station must be informed.

The role of the custody officer is crucial to the effective and fair operation of the criminal justice system. In addition to protecting the rights of detained people the role, if performed properly, should also prevent evidence being declared inadmissible because of a violation of the rules. In order to provide as full a record as possible about the detention of a person, the custody officer is required to open a custody record for each detained person (Code C, para. 2.1) and entries should be recorded *as soon as practicable*. Guidance on the completion of custody records is given in Code C, paras 2.1 to 2.7. Custody officers must become very familiar with this guidance, as they are responsible for the accuracy and completeness of the custody record (para. 2.3). It is important that all entries in the custody record are timed and signed by the maker (Code C, para. 2.6). If a person is requested to sign an entry in accordance with the Codes and refuses, this too should be recorded (Code C, para. 2.7).

It is also recognised that the role of custody officer is very demanding and, on occasions, the time restraints created by the legislation can become unrealistic. For this reason Code C, para. 1.1A states that a custody officer will not be in breach of the Codes if a delay in taking some action was justifiable and steps had been taken to prevent the delay.

However, if that delay was not 'reasonable', it could lead to actions for unlawful detention and false imprisonment and any evidence obtained as a result may be held to be inadmissible (*Roberts* v *Chief Constable of Cheshire Constabulary* [1999] 1 WLR 662).

15.4 Police Detention and the Treatment of Detained Persons

Depriving a person of his/her liberty is a serious step (**see General Police Duties, chapter 2**). The legislation and the PACE Codes of Practice are intended to ensure that where a person's liberty is taken it is for no longer than is necessary. There is a growing trend towards civil action against the police for unlawful detention and false imprisonment, some of which is as a result of a failure to follow the guidelines. There are strict limits on a person's detention period and the best defence to such cases is to ensure that the 1984 Act and its Codes of Practice are followed.

15.4.1 Meaning of Police Detention

Police detention is defined by section 118 of the Police and Criminal Evidence Act 1984 which provides that:

> (2)   *A person is in police detention for the purposes of this Act if—*
> (a)   *he has been taken to a police station after being arrested for an offence or after being arrested under section 14 of the Prevention of Terrorism (Temporary Provisions) Act 1989 or under paragraph 6 of Schedule 5 to that Act by an examining officer who is a constable; or*
> (b)   *he is arrested at a police station after attending voluntarily at the station or accompanying a constable to it,*
> *and is detained there or is detained elsewhere in the charge of a constable, except that a person who is at a court after being charged is not in police detention for those purposes.*

PACE Code of Practice C also provides that:

1.10 . . . Section 15 (reviews and extensions of detention) however applies solely to people in police detention, for example those who have been brought to a police station under arrest for an offence or have been arrested at a police station for an offence after attending there voluntarily. [Those who have been removed to a police station as a place of safety under ss. 135 and 136 of the Mental Health Act 1983 are not in police detention but are subject to the Codes.]

1.11 Persons in police detention include persons taken to a police station after being arrested under section 14 of the Prevention of Terrorism (Temporary Provisions) Act 1989 or under paragraph 6 of schedule 5 to that Act by an examining officer who is a constable.

1.12 This code does not apply to the following groups of people in custody:
   (i) people who have been arrested by officers from a police force in Scotland exercising their powers of detention under section 137(2) of the Criminal Justice and Public Order Act 1994 (cross border powers of arrest etc.) [see General Police Duties, chapter 2]*;*
   (ii) people arrested under section 3(5) of the Asylum and Immigration Appeals Act 1993 for the purpose of having their fingerprints taken;
   (iii) people who have been served a notice advising them of their detention under powers contained in the Immigration Act 1971;
   (iv) convicted or remanded prisoners held in police cells on behalf of the Prison Service under the Imprisonment (Temporary Provisions) Act 1980);
   but the provisions on conditions of detention and treatment in sections 8 and 9 of this code must be considered as the minimum standards of treatment for such detainees.

Keynote

This last two lines of Code C, para. 1.12, above, makes it clear that the way such prisoners are treated should be of no lower standard than that for other detained people. If in doubt as to whether a person falls within the definition of a detained person, it is suggested that he/she should be afforded all the rights and privileges outlined in the Codes of Practice.

15.4.2 Right to Have Someone Informed

Section 56 of the Police and Criminal Evidence Act 1984 provides that a person arrested and held in custody at a police station or other premises may, on request, have one person known to him/her or who is likely to take an interest in his/her welfare, informed at public expense of his/her whereabouts as soon as practicable (Code C, para. 5.1). (If the detainee's first choice cannot be contacted, see Code C, para. 5.1 and Notes 5C and 5D.) This fundamental human right is known as the right not to be held *incommunicado* and guidance on this right is contained in Code C, paras 5.1 to 5.8. If a person transfers to another police station, the same right applies at the next police station (Code C, para. 5.3), even if they have already had someone informed at the previous places of detention.

This right can only be delayed if the offence is a 'serious arrestable offence' (**see General Police Duties, chapter 2**) and an officer of the rank of superintendent or above (whether or not connected to the investigation) authorises the delay (see Code C, Annex B) (**see para. 15.4.4**). Where a person has to be given information under the Code but is not in a fit state to understand it, it is to be given to him/her as soon as practicable but only when he/she is in a fit state to understand it (Code C, para. 1.8). The delay can only be for a maximum of 36 hours (48 hours in cases involving terrorism), and the 36-hour period is calculated from the 'relevant time' (**see para. 15.4.5**). In the case of a juvenile, the power to authorise the delay does not apply to the appropriate adult, but only to any other person the juvenile wishes to have informed (Code C, para. 3.7).

There may be occasions where officers wish to conduct a search under s. 18 of the 1984 Act (**see General Police Duties, chapter 2**) and the detained person has requested to have someone informed. Clearly if such a person is informed before the search is conducted, vital evidence or property may be lost. Often the custody officer has two methods by which he/she can inform the person requested about the detained person's detention; either in person or on the phone. Contacting the person by telephone is likely to be the quickest, however there is no requirement to use the quickest method in order to pass on this information. While there is no case law on this point, Code C, Note 5D, supports the view that, where the s. 18 search is to be conducted relatively quickly after the request is made by the detained person, it would be permissible to inform that person at the time the s. 18 search is conducted. Where the search is not to be conducted straight away, it is suggested that consideration would have to be given to obtaining the authority of a superintendent to delay the notification as outlined in **para. 15.4.4**.

Detained people may also be allowed to speak to a person on the telephone for a reasonable time or send letters. If a person has an interpreter, he/she can do this on the detained person's behalf. This right can be denied or delayed in the case of arrestable and serious arrestable offences by an officer of the rank of inspector or above (Code C, para. 5.6). Where a person is allowed to make a telephone call or send a letter, the procedure in Code C, para. 5.7 should be followed. Should there be any delay in complying with a request by a detained person to have someone informed of his/her detention or to communicate with someone, the detained person should be informed of this and a record kept (s. 56(6) of the 1984 Act). The custody officer also has a discretion to allow visits to the detained person at the police station (Code C, para. 5.4 and Note 5B).

There are also special requirements for juveniles and detained people from other countries.

Juveniles

In the case of juveniles, an appropriate adult must be informed, regardless of whether the juvenile wishes to have someone informed or has requested that some other person other than the appropriate adult be informed.

Code C, para. 3.7 provides:

> *If the person is a juvenile, the custody officer must, if it is practicable, ascertain the identity of a person responsible for his welfare. That person may be his parent or guardian (or, if he is in care, the care authority or voluntary organisation) or any other person who has, for the time being, assumed responsibility for his welfare. That person must be informed as soon as practicable that the juvenile has been arrested, why he has been arrested and where he is detained. This right is in addition to the juvenile's right in section 5 of the code not to be held incommunicado. [See Note 3C]*

Keynote

Where a juvenile is subject to a supervision order reasonable steps must be taken to notify the person supervising him/her (Code C, para. 3.8).

Detained People from Other Countries

Citizens of independent commonwealth countries or foreign nationals may communicate with their High Commission, Embassy or Consulate as soon as practicable (Code C, para. 7.1). If the country is included on the list at Annex F of Code C, the High Commission, Embassy or Consulate must be informed unless the detained person is a political refugee or is seeking political asylum (para. 7.1).

Where a person who is a friend, relative or a person with an interest in the detained person's welfare, makes enquires about that person, the detained person should be asked whether he/she agrees to the person being informed prior to any information being given (Code C, para. 5.5). The information must not be given if a delay has been authorised.

15.4.3 Right to Legal Advice

Section 58 of the Police and Criminal Evidence Act 1984 provides an almost inalienable right for a person arrested and held in custody at a police station or other premises to consult privately with a solicitor free of charge if he/she requests it (or the appropriate adult makes the request (Code C, para. 3.13)). This provision is very similar to that of s. 56 of the Act; the right to have a person informed of the arrest. This right to consult a solicitor is considered to be so important that a detained person must be informed of the right when he/she first arrives at the police station and asked for reasons if he/she declines to exercise this right. Detainees are also reminded of this right at other times, e.g. prior to interview and when detention is being reviewed. In R v *Alladice* (1988) 87 Cr App R 380 the Court of Appeal made it clear that:

> no matter how strongly and however justifiably the police may feel that their investigation and detection of crime is being hindered by the presence of a solicitor . . . they are nevertheless confined to the narrow limits imposed by section 58.

Section 58 provides only two exceptions to this right to legal advice:

- Cases where an officer of the rank of superintendent or above (whether or not connected to the investigation) authorises the exercise of the right to be delayed. This only applies if the offence is a serious arrestable offence (**see General Police Duties, chapter 2**) and Code C Annex B applies.

- Where the person is held under the prevention of terrorism legislation and the conditions in Code C, Annex B apply. Here a uniformed officer may be present.

The delay can only be for a maximum of 36 hours (48 hours in terrorism cases) or until the time the person will first appear at court, which ever is the sooner (**see below**). The 36-hour period is calculated from the 'relevant time' (**see para. 15.4.5**). The authorisation can initially be made orally either in person or by telephone but must be recorded in writing as soon as practicable.

The consultation with a solicitor can be either on the telephone, in person or in writing and it must be in private (Code C, para. 6.1).

Once a person has indicated a wish to have a solicitor, and has not yet been advised by a solicitor, he/she can only be interviewed in limited circumstances as set out in Code

C, para. 6.6, but it is not necessary to delay taking breath, blood or urine samples from a motorist until a solicitor arrives (Code C, Note 3E and **Road Traffic, chapter 5**).

A solicitor for these purposes means a solicitor who holds a current practising certificate, a trainee solicitor, a duty solicitor representative or an accredited representative included on the register of representatives maintained by the Legal Aid Board (Code C, para. 6.12). A non-accredited or probationary representative may also attend and give advice unless an officer of the rank of inspector or above considers that such a visit will hinder the investigation of crime and directs otherwise and once admitted he/she should be treated as any other legal adviser.

In deciding whether to admit a non-accredited or probationary representative, the officer should take into account in particular whether the identity and status of the non-accredited or probationary representative have been satisfactorily established; whether he/she is of suitable character to provide legal advice (a person with a criminal record is unlikely to be suitable unless the conviction was for a minor offence and is not of recent date); and any other matters in any written letter of authorisation provided by the solicitor on whose behalf the person is attending the police station (Code C, para. 6.13). The Law Society has advised solicitors that if a non-accredited or probationary representative is refused admission, a written reason for the decision should be requested. If access is refused or a decision is taken that such a person should not be permitted to remain at an interview, he/she must forthwith notify a solicitor on whose behalf the non-accredited or probationary representative was to have acted or was acting, and give him/her an opportunity to make alternative arrangements. The detained person must also be informed and the custody record noted (Code C, para. 6.14 and Note 6F).

15.4.4 Authority to Delay Rights under ss. 56 or 58 (Code C, Annex B)

An officer of the rank of superintendent or above can only authorise a delay if he/she has reasonable grounds for believing that by exercising the right it will:

- interfere with or cause harm to evidence connected with a serious arrestable offence or interfere with or cause physical injury to other people; or

- alert other people suspected of having committed such an offence but not yet arrested for it; or

- hinder the recovery of property obtained as a result of such an offence.

The delay can also be authorised in cases involving drug offences which are:

- drug trafficking offences (as to which, **see Crime, chapter 6**) and the officer has reasonable grounds for believing that the detained person has benefited from drug trafficking, and that the recovery of the value of that person's proceeds of drug trafficking will be hindered by the exercise of either right; or

- offences to which Part VI of the Criminal Justice Act 1988 (covering confiscation orders) applies and the officer has reasonable grounds for believing that the detained person has benefited from the offence, and that the recovery of the value of the property obtained by that person from or in connection with the offence, or if the pecuniary advantage derived by him/her from or in connection with it, will be hindered by the exercise of the right.

In cases where the person is detained under the Prevention of Terrorism (Temporary Provisions) Act 1989 an officer of the rank of superintendent or above may delay the exercise of either right or both if he/she has reasonable grounds for believing that the exercise of the right:

- will lead to interference with the gathering of information about the commission, preparation or instigation of acts of terrorism; or

- by alerting any person, will make it more difficult to prevent an act of terrorism or to secure the apprehension, prosecution or conviction of any person in connection with the commission, preparation or instigation of an act of terrorism.

If the delay is authorised the detained person must be given the reason for the delay which must correspond to one of the above grounds and an entry record must be made in the custody record.

Once the reason for authorising the delay has ceased, the detained person must be allowed to exercise his/her rights. Once this point has been reached, the detained person must as soon as practicable be asked if he/she wishes to exercise the right (or rights), the custody record must be noted accordingly, and the relevant action taken (Code C, Annex B, para. 4).

The grounds for delaying the right to have someone informed or of access to legal advice are the same. When considering whether to authorise the delay of these rights, Code C, Annex B, Note B5 makes it clear that the authority to delay these rights should be considered separately and if authority to delay the right to notify a person is given it does not automatically mean that the right to legal advice can be delayed.

When considering whether to deny access to a solicitor the fact that he/she might advise the person not to answer any questions or that the solicitor was initially asked to attend the police station by someone else, provided that the person himself/herself then wishes to see the solicitor, is not a reason for delaying access to a solicitor (Code C, Annex B, para. 3). When considering the delay of access to a solicitor the authorising officer must bear in mind that access to a solicitor is 'a fundamental right of a citizen' (*R* v *Samuel* [1988] 2 WLR 920). The authorising officer must actually believe that by allowing access to the solicitor he/she will intentionally or inadvertently alert other suspects. There must also be objective reasons upon which the officer authorising the delay can base his/her beliefs. If the reason for authorising the delay of access to a solicitor is because there are concerns with the particular solicitor who has been requested or is offering his/her services to the detained person the officer should offer the detained person access to a solicitor (who is not the specific solicitor referred to above) on the Duty Solicitor Scheme (Code C, Annex B, Note B4).

15.4.5 Relevant Time

As discussed above, there are limits on how long a person can be detained. The Police and Criminal Evidence Act 1984 and the Codes of Practice talk of the 'relevant time'. This is the time from which the limits of detention are calculated. The relevant time of a person's detention starts in accordance with s. 41(2) to (5) of the 1984 Act. Section 41 provides that:

> (2) The time from which the period of detention of a person is to be calculated (in this Act referred to as 'the relevant time')—
>   (a) in the case of a person to whom this paragraph applies, shall be—
>   (i) the time at which that person arrives at the relevant police station; or

>   *(ii)   the time 24 hours after the time of that person's arrest,*
>   *whichever is the earlier;*
>   *(b)   in the case of a person arrested outside England and Wales, shall be—*
>   *(i)   the time at which that person arrives at the first police station to which he is taken in the police area in England or Wales in which the offence for which he was arrested is being investigated; or*
>   *(ii)   the time 24 hours after the time of that person's entry into England and Wales,*
>   *whichever is the earlier,*
>   *(c)   in the case of a person who—*
>   *(i)   attends voluntarily at a police station; or*
>   *(ii)   accompanies a constable to a police station without having been arrested, and is arrested at the police station, the time of his arrest;*
>   *(d)   in any other case, except where subsection (5) below applies, shall be the time at which the person arrested arrives at the first police station to which he is taken after his arrest.*
>   *(3)   Subsection (2)(a) above applies to a person if—*
>   *(a)   his arrest is sought in one police area in England and Wales;*
>   *(b)   he is arrested in another police area, and*
>   *(c)   he is not questioned in the area in which he is arrested in order to obtain evidence in relation to an offence for which he is arrested;*
>   *and in sub-paragraph (i) of that paragraph 'the relevant police station' means the first police station to which he is taken in the police area in which his arrest was sought.*
>   *(4)   Subsection (2) above shall have effect in relation to a person arrested under section 31 above as if every reference in it to his arrest or his being arrested were a reference to his arrest or his being arrested for the offence for which he was originally arrested.*
>   *(5)   If—*
>   *(a)   a person is in police detention in a police area in England and Wales ('the first area'); and*
>   *(b)   his arrest for an offence is sought in some other police area in England and Wales ('the second area'); and*
>   *(c)   he is taken to the second area for the purposes of investigating that offence, without being questioned in the first area in order to obtain evidence in relation to it,*
>   *the relevant time shall be—*
>   *(i)   the time 24 hours after he leaves the place where he is detained in the first area; or*
>   *(ii)   the time at which he arrives at the first police station to which he is taken in the second area,*
>   *whichever is the earlier.*

Keynote

Note that under s. 41(5), the detainee has, in effect, two detention clocks running. It is important to note that the second clock will start earlier if the detained person is questioned about the offence under investigation in the other police area.

For the provisions of s. 31 relating to people who have been arrested for one offence and if released from the police station would be liable to arrest for some other offence, **see General Police Duties, chapter 2.**

15.4.6   Detention of People under Arrest

People who have been arrested, or voluntarily given themselves up at a police station, will be brought before a custody officer who must decide whether the person should be detained at the police station or released. People who attend police stations voluntarily to assist the police with their investigations are not subject to this procedure; their treatment is dealt with by PACE Code C, paras 3.15 and 16 (**see General Police Duties, chapter 2**).

The arresting officer informs the custody officer of the reasons for arrest. This will include *what* offence the person was arrested for and brief details of the *grounds* for the arrest, e.g.

the arrest is for robbery and the accused was seen to punch the victim in the face and steal his holdall. In the case of a non-arrestable offence, an example might be that the detained person was seen to drive his car through a red light and has refused to give his name and address, thereby making it impossible to serve a summons on him (**see General Police Duties, chapter 2**). As this information must be given to the person on arrest — in most cases — the details given to the custody officer should be fresh in the mind of the arresting officer; they should also accord with the reasons and grounds given to the person on arrest!

Having heard the details of and for the arrest, the custody officer must then decide whether or not there are reasons which justify authorising that person's detention (s. 37 of the Police and Criminal Evidence Act 1984 deals with the procedures to be followed before a person is charged). Some commentators have suggested that it is also the role of the custody officer to establish that the arrest itself was lawful. While this would seem to be sensible and good practice, the custody officer's duty is confined to acting in accordance with the requirements set out in s. 37 of the 1984 Act. These duties do not appear to include considering whether the arrest was lawful unless this is relevant to the main question of whether there is sufficient evidence to charge the suspect. The view is supported by the decision of the Divisional Court in *DPP* v *L and S*, *The Times*, 1 February 1999, where the court held that there was no express or implied requirement imposing a duty on a custody officer to inquire into the legality of an arrest and in that case the custody officer was therefore entitled to assume that it was lawful. A subsequent finding that the arrest was unlawful did not invalidate the decision of the custody officer to hold the person in custody.

Section 37 of the 1984 Act provides that:

> *(1) Where—*
> > *(a) a person is arrested for an offence—*
> > > *(i) without a warrant; or*
> > > *(ii) under a warrant not endorsed for bail, or*
> *the custody officer at each police station where he is detained after his arrest shall determine whether he had before him sufficient evidence to charge that person with the offence for which he was arrested and may detain him at the police station for such period as is necessary to enable him to do so.*
> *(2) If the custody officer determines that he does not have such evidence before him, the person arrested shall be released either on bail or without bail, unless the custody officer has reasonable grounds for believing that his detention without being charged is necessary to secure or preserve evidence relating to an offence for which he is under arrest or to obtain such evidence by questioning him.*
> *(3) If the custody officer has reasonable grounds for so believing, he may authorise the person arrested to be kept in police detention.*
> *(4) Where a custody officer authorises a person who has not been charged to be kept in police detention, he shall, as soon as is practicable, make a written record of the grounds for the detention.*
> *(5) Subject to subsection (6) below, the written record shall be made in the presence of the person arrested who shall at that time be informed by the custody officer of the grounds for his detention.*
> *(6) Subsection (5) above shall not apply where the person arrested is, at the time when the written record is made—*
> > *(a) incapable of understanding what is said to him;*
> > *(b) violent or likely to become violent; or*
> > *(c) in urgent need of medical attention.*

Keynote

If the person is arrested on a warrant (**see General Police Duties, chapter 2**), any directions given by the court in the warrant must be followed. (If the warrant was issued for the arrest of a person who has not yet been charged or summonsed for an offence, he/she should be dealt with as any other person arrested for an offence without warrant unless there are any additional directions on the warrant that must be followed.)

15.4.7   Authorising a Person's Detention

A custody officer can authorise the detention of a person when there is sufficient evidence to charge and, in some circumstances, when there is *not* sufficient evidence to charge the suspect. If there is insufficient evidence to charge, the custody officer must decide if the detention is necessary to secure or preserve evidence relating to an offence for which the person is under arrest or to obtain such evidence by questioning him/her.

Sufficient Evidence to Charge

Here the custody officer is looking at the evidence in order to satisfy himself/herself that no further investigation is needed before the person can be charged. If this is the case, detention may be authorised. In considering whether this position has been reached it is worth considering Code C, para. 16.1 which states that:

> When an officer considers that there is sufficient evidence to prosecute a detained person, and that there is sufficient evidence for a prosecution to succeed, and that the person has said all that he wishes to say about the offence, he shall without delay . . . bring him before the custody officer who shall then be responsible for considering whether or not he should be charged . . .

This paragraph suggests that a charge should not be brought until there is sufficient evidence for a prosecution to succeed.

Where there is sufficient evidence for a prosecution to succeed, under s. 37(7) of the Police and Criminal Evidence Act 1984, the custody officer must charge the person or release him/her without charge, either on bail or without bail. Often the reason for not charging the person will be to allow a decision to be made by the Crown Prosecution Service as to whether to charge the person, caution them or not to proceed with the case. In these circumstances s. 37(8) requires the custody officer to inform the person that a decision to charge has not yet been made.

Under s. 37(9) release can be delayed if the person is not in a fit state to be released (e.g. he/she is drunk), until he/she is fit. Where a person is detained for charge, the custody officer should record the grounds for detention in the custody record in the presence of the detained person if practicable (Code C, para. 3.17). For the situation relating to drunk drivers, **see Road Traffic, chapter 5**.

Insufficient Evidence to Charge

This creates two separate criteria for detention, that is to say, where detention is necessary to:

- secure and preserve evidence relating to an offence for which the person is arrested; and/or

- obtain such evidence by questioning the detained person.

If the custody officer has determined that there is not sufficient evidence to charge the person, the person must be released unless the custody officer has *reasonable grounds* for believing that the person's detention is necessary to preserve or to obtain such evidence by questioning the person. 'Reasonable grounds for believing' requires a greater amount of evidence than 'reasonable cause to suspect' (**see General Police Duties, chapter 2**) and the custody officer must be able to justify any decision not to release a person from detention.

When deciding if detention should be authorised in order to preserve evidence by questioning, the case of *R* v *McGuinness* (1998, unreported) should be considered. There the court held that the words 'sufficient evidence to prosecute' and 'sufficient evidence for a prosecution to succeed', in Code C, para. 16.1, had to involve some consideration of any explanation, or lack of one, from the suspect. While an interview may not be needed in all cases, questioning of detained people before they are charged may be necessary, particularly where intention or dishonesty (**see Crime, chapter 1**) is involved or where there may be a defence (**see Crime, chapter 4**).

The custody officer can detain the person for such period as is necessary in order to make this decision (s. 37(1) of the 1984 Act). Clearly any such period must be 'reasonable' in all the circumstances. For instance, where there are several prisoners waiting to be dealt with it may be reasonable that the last prisoner is not dealt with for 30 minutes because the custody officer is busy with the other prisoners. For the custody officer to be able to make this decision, the arresting officer needs to give sufficient detail about the offence. The account given by the arresting officer should be made in the presence of the arrested person (Code C, para. 3.4) and any comment made by that person in response should be recorded in the custody record (unless the person is violent or it is impractical to do so for some other reason, in which case this fact should also be recorded).

Section 37(4) and (5) of the 1984 Act require the custody officer to make a written record of the grounds of detention and to make that record in the presence of the detained person, informing him/her at the same time of the grounds of his/her detention (unless s. 37(6) applies).

Section 37(6) states:

> (6) *Subsection (5) above shall not apply where the person arrested is, at the time when the written record is made—*
> (a) *incapable of understanding what is said to him;*
> (b) *violent or likely to become violent; or*
> (c) *in urgent need of medical attention.*

15.4.8   Additional Action to be Taken by the Custody Officer

The action to be taken by the custody officer when receiving detained people is set out in Code C, paras 3.1 to 3.5A. For the action relating to special groups, **see para. 15.9**.

Paragraph 3.1 sets out the information the detained person is entitled to. These are *continuing* entitlements and can be requested at any time during the person's detention.

Paragraph 3.2 deals with written notices which must be given to the detained person in relation to his/her rights. (Code C, para. 1.2 requires that a copy of the Codes of Practice must also be readily available to detained persons should they request it.)

Paragraph 3.5 requires the custody officer to establish whether the detained person wishes to have a solicitor at this stage. If he/she declines, the custody officer should ask the person the reason why and, if any reasons are given, these should be recorded in the custody record (Code C, para. 6.5).

15.5   Limits on Detention and Review

Once detention has been authorised this does not mean that a person can be detained indefinitely. Section 34 of the Police and Criminal Evidence Act 1984 requires the custody officer to release a person if he/she becomes aware that the grounds for detention no longer apply and that no other grounds exist for the continuing detention (unless the person appears to be unlawfully at large). If there are additional grounds, these should be recorded in the custody record and the person informed of these additional grounds in the same way as when a person is first detained. For example, this could be for new offences or it could be that it becomes necessary to preserve evidence by questioning the detained person.

It is only the custody officer who can authorise the release of a detained person (s. 34(3)). It is a breach of the PACE Codes of Practice for anyone else to release a detained person without first obtaining the authority of the custody officer. In addition to the requirement to release a person should the grounds for detention no longer exist, there are also maximum time limits for which a person can be detained without charge (**see para. 15.5.1**). Once this limit has been reached, it will be necessary to proceed by summons or by warrant. There are also limits on the time a person can be kept in custody after being charged, refused bail and appearing at court (**see below**).

15.5.1   Time Limits: Without Charge

While a person is in police detention there is a requirement that his/her continuing detention is reviewed. This is dealt with below. There are minimum time requirements for when these reviews must be conducted, with the timing of the first review being calculated from the time detention is authorised. This time can be considered as the 'review time'.

The maximum period that a person can be detained without charge (with the exception of suspected acts of terrorism) is 96 hours. The necessity for the continued detention of the person must be reviewed throughout this time. The period of detention is calculated from the 'relevant time' (**see para. 15.4.5**) which can be calculated from the chart below (**see para. 15.5.3**). (*Do not confuse the relevant time with the time from which reviews are due.*) The relevant time 'clock' will always start before, or at the same time as the review 'clock'. This is because the review clock does not start until detention has been authorised which clearly cannot happen until the person is brought before the custody officer which, as can be seen from the chart below, is at the very latest, the time the prisoner walks into the charge room.

This relevant time period (that is, the maximum period a person can be detained for) relates to the actual time spent in custody and not a 24-hour period in time. This means that every time the person is bailed the clock stops and usually continues from the time that the person returns to custody for the offence(s) for which he/she was bailed. Where a person is taken to hospital, the time spent at hospital (and travelling to and from hospital) does not count towards the detention period (except for any period where the person was questioned).

Where a person has been released and re-arrested for an offence, it is possible that the relevant time will start again. This is covered by s. 47(7) of the 1984 Act:

> *(7)   Where a person who was released on bail subject to a duty to attend at a police station is re-arrested, the provisions of this Part of this Act shall apply to him as they apply to a person arrested for the first time but this subsection does not apply to a person who is arrested under section 46A above or has attended a police station in accordance with the grant of bail (and who accordingly is deemed by section 34(7) above to have been arrested for an offence).*

Keynote

In cases where this subsection applies, the relevant time starts again and a fresh clock starts. This will apply where the person has been re-arrested for the same offence because of some new evidence (except at such time as when he/she is returning on bail at the appointed time) under s. 41(9) or 47(2).

Section 41 provides that:

> *(9)   A person released under subsection (7) above shall not be re-arrested without a warrant for the offence for which he was previously arrested unless new evidence justifying a further arrest has come to light since his release; but this subsection does not prevent an arrest under section 46A below.*

Section 47 provides that:

> *(2)   Nothing in the Bail Act 1976 shall prevent the re-arrest without warrant of a person released on bail subject to a duty to attend at a police station if new evidence justifying a further arrest has come to light since his release.*

Keynote

The issue will be whether there is new evidence and it will be a question of fact as to what the new evidence is. It is suggested that this must be evidence which was not available at the time the person was last in detention or which would not have been available even if all reasonable enquiries had been conducted.

15.5.2   The Three Stages of Detention

After the custody officer has authorised detention but before a person has been charged there are three distinct stages of detention. These are distinguished by the level at which authorisation for continuing detention is required.

The three stages of detention under the 1984 Act are:

* Those authorised by an officer of the rank of inspector or above (s. 41) up to 24 hours. This will be the period first authorised by the custody officer and continued by reviews conducted (usually) by an inspector (**see para. 15.5.3**).

* Those authorised by an officer of the rank of superintendent or above (s. 42) up to 36 hours (**see para. 15.5.4**).

* Those authorised by a magistrates' court (ss. 43 and 44) up to a maximum of 96 hours (**see para. 15.5.5**).

Each of these is examined in detail below.

15.5.3   Detention Authorised by an Inspector

The majority of people detained by the police are detained for less than six hours; most other cases are dealt with within 24 hours. If a person's continued detention is not authorised beyond 24 hours by a superintendent and the person is not charged with an offence, he/she *must* be released (with or without bail) and cannot be re-arrested for the offence unless new evidence comes to light (s. 41(7) and (9) of the 1984 Act). New evidence is not defined by the 1984 Act but is evidence which was not available at the time the person was detained, or which would not have been available if the investigating officers had conducted reasonable enquiries.

Maximum Periods of Detention

Arrest	Relevant time starts	Review clock starts	24 hours from relevant time	24 to 36 hours' detention	36 to 42 hours' detention	42 to 78 hours' detention	up to 96 hours' detention
Arrested locally	24 hours from arrest or arrival at police station whichever earliest.		All offences other than serious arrestable offences.	Only serious arrestable offences.	Only serious arrestable offences.	Only serious arrestable offences.	Only serious arrestable offences
Arrested outside England and Wales	Time first arrives at police station in police area where matter being investigated or 24 hours after first entered England or Wales whichever earliest.	Time custody officer authorises detention.	Release unless s. 41(1) applies.	Detention authorised by superintendent or above (s. 42).	Where delay in applying for warrant of further detention is reasonable (s. 43(5)).	First warrant for further detention issued by magistrates' court (s. 42).	Further warrants of detention issued by magistrates' court (s. 43).
Arrested for offence in other police area and being transferred	24 hours from time he/she leaves police station first detained at or the time first arrives at police station in force area where crime being investigated or first time questioned about the offence whichever is the earliest.	This timing applies where the person was in detention for an offence in the first police area (s. 41(5)).			**See para. 15.5.5.** for the dangers of not applying within the 36-hour period.	Remember the warrant can be applied for at any stage of detention.	
Voluntarily attends police station or accompanies constable to station but not under arrest	Time of arrest.						

225

During this period of detention the custody officer has a responsibility to monitor whether the grounds for detention still exist. An officer of at least the rank of inspector not involved in the investigation (s. 40(1)(b)) must review the person's detention *at least once in the first six hours* and then, after the first review, *within nine hours of that review*. Further reviews must then be conducted *no later than nine hours after the last review* was conducted, until the person is released or charged.

If a detained person is taken to hospital for medical treatment, the time at hospital and the period spent travelling to and from the hospital does not count towards the relevant time unless the person is asked questions for the purpose of obtaining evidence about an offence. Where questioning takes place, this period would count towards the relevant time and therefore the custody officer must be informed of it (s. 41(6)).

The Review

During the first 24 hours before charging, a detained person's detention must be reviewed by an officer of the rank of inspector or above (inspector reviews). This review acts as another safeguard to protect the detained person's right to be detained for only such periods as are necessary to allow for the investigation of an offence. Reviews of police detention are covered by s. 40 of the Police and Criminal Evidence Act 1984.

Section 40(3) sets out the times when reviews must be conducted:

> (3) Subject to subsection (4) . . .—
> (a) the first review shall be not later than six hours after the detention was first authorised;
> (b) the second review shall be not later than nine hours after the first;
> (c) subsequent reviews shall be at intervals of not more than nine hours.

Keynote

These periods are the *maximum* periods that a review can be left; should an inspector wish to review before this time for operational reasons etc., the review could be brought forward. The first review must be made within six hours of the custody officer authorising detention (this, it must be remembered, is not the time from which the relevant time starts, i.e. the time the detainee came into the station, but the time at which the custody officer decided that the person should be detained and not released). Thereafter, each review must be made within nine hours of the last review.

For the situation regarding 'acting' ranks, **see General Police Duties, chapter 2**.

Section 40(4) does allow reviews to be delayed if it is not practicable to carry out the review. Conducting late reviews should be avoided where at all possible (see *Roberts* v *Chief Constable of Cheshire Constabulary* [1999] 1 WLR 662).

In *Roberts* the defendant had his first review conducted 8 hours, 20 minutes after his detention had been authorised. The Court of Appeal held that under s. 40(1)(b) of the 1984 Act a review of his detention should have taken place by an officer of the rank of inspector or above six hours after detention was first authorised. Section 34(1) was mandatory and provided that a person must not be kept in police detention except in accordance with the relevant provisions of the Act. Therefore, the respondent's detention had been unlawful unless some event occurred to have made it lawful.

The Court made it clear that the 1984 Act existed in order to ensure members of the public were not detained except in certain defined circumstances. In the absence of a review, the time spent in detention between 5.25 am, and 7.45 am meant that for that period the defendant's detention was unlawful and amounted to a false imprisonment.

The fact that the review officer is not at the station would not automatically allow the review to be postponed: Code C, Note 15C allows reviews at this stage to be conducted over the telephone if it is the only practical way to conduct the review. If the review is delayed then it must still be conducted as soon as practicable and the reason for the delay must be recorded in the custody record by the review officer. In these circumstances the nine-hour period until the next review is calculated from the latest time the review should have been carried out and not from the time it was actually carried out. For instance, if the review was due at 3.15 pm and was delayed until 4 pm, the next review would have to be conducted no later than 12.15 am and not 1 am. When the review is conducted the review officer does not have to authorise detention for the full nine-hour period; he/she could decide that the case should be reviewed again within a shorter period and the review decision would reflect this.

When reviewing the detention of a person the review officer goes through the same process as the custody officer did when detention was first authorised (s. 40(8)), namely by asking:

- Is there sufficient evidence to charge? If 'yes', charge or release the person with or without bail. If 'no', then:

- Is detention necessary in order to secure or preserve evidence or is it necessary to detain the person in order to obtain such evidence by questioning him/her? If 'yes', authorise continued detention. If 'no', release the person with or without bail.

In cases where it has been decided that a person should be charged but he/she has been detained because he/she is not in a fit state to be charged (s. 37(9)), the review officer must determine whether the person is yet in a fit state. If the detainee is in a fit state, the custody officer should be informed that the person should be charged or released. If the detainee is not in a fit state, detention can be authorised for a further period (s. 40(9)). In such cases, if the person is still unfit, it may be prudent to consider the welfare of the detained person.

During the process of reviewing a person's detention, the review officer must give the detained person (unless he/she is asleep) or any solicitor representing the detained person who is available at the time of the review, an opportunity to make representations about his/her continued detention (s. 40(12)). If the detained person is likely to be asleep at the time the review is to be carried out, the review should be brought forward to allow the detained person to be present at the time of the review (Code C, Note 15A). The review officer must also ensure that the detained person is reminded of his/her right to free legal advice and that this reminder is recorded in the custody record (Code C, para. 15.3). In the case of juveniles, the appropriate adult should also be allowed to make representations and the review officer has the discretion to allow other people having an interest in the welfare of the detained person to make representations (Code C, para. 15.1). These representations may be in writing or oral (s. 40(13)). If made in writing, the document should be retained (Code C, para. 15.5). The review officer can refuse to hear oral representations from the detained person if the review officer considers that the person is unfit to make such representations, either because of his/her condition or behaviour (e.g. drunk or violent) (s. 40(14)). The detained person should be informed of the decision to authorise further detention and any comments made by the detainee should be recorded. However, the review officer must not put any questions to the person about his/her comments (Code C, para. 15.2A). Also, as the role of review officer is intended to be independent of the investigation, he/she should not put any questions to the person about his/her involvement in any offence; this mirrors the instruction to custody officers (Code C, para. 15.2A).

Whatever decision is reached regarding detention, a record should be made of it (Code C, para. 15.6). Invariably this will be in the custody record, but where it is done over the telephone the review officer will need to make an independent record of his/her decision. In all cases an entry should be made in the custody record of the time of the decision, who made the decision and the outcome.

If at any stage an officer of a rank higher than the review officer gives directions which are at variance with a decision made or action taken by the review officer, or which would have been made by the review officer but for the directions by the more senior officer, then s. 40(11) requires the matter to be referred *at once* to an officer of the rank of superintendent or above who is *responsible for the police station*.

15.5.4 Detention Authorised by an Officer of the Rank of Superintendent

Under s. 42(1) of the Police and Criminal Evidence Act 1984, detention can only be authorised beyond 24 hours and up to a maximum of 36 hours from the relevant time if:

* the offence being investigated is a 'serious arrestable offence' (see s. 116 of the 1984 Act and **General Police Duties, chapter 2**); *and*

* it is authorised by an officer of the rank of superintendent or above who is responsible for the station at which the person is detained; *and*

* that that senior officer is satisfied that:

  * there is not sufficient evidence to charge; *and*
  * the investigation is being conducted diligently and expeditiously; *and*
  * that the person's detention is necessary to secure or preserve evidence relating to the offence or to obtain such evidence by questioning that person.

At this stage if the review officer considers that there is sufficient evidence to charge, he/she cannot authorise further detention beyond 24 hours unless the detained person is in custody for another serious arrestable offence for which further detention can be, authorised (*R v Samuel* [1988] QB 615 and Code C, para. 16.1).

The grounds for this continuing detention are the same as those when the custody officer made the initial decision to detain, with the additional requirements that the case has been conducted diligently and expeditiously. To be able to satisfy the senior officer of this, it will be necessary for the custody record to be available for inspection and details of what inquiries have been made and evidence that the investigation has been moving at a pace that will satisfy the senior officer that the inquires should not already have been completed.

The reviewing officer (which here must be an officer of the rank of superintendent or above who is responsible for the station at which the person is detained) can authorise detention up to a maximum of 36 hours from the 'relevant time' of detention. The period can be shorter than this and can then be further reviewed by that officer or any other officer of the rank of superintendent or above who is responsible for the station at which the person is detained to allow the period to be further extended up to the maximum 36-hour period (s. 42(2)).

A review of a person's detention by a superintendent or above must be made within 24 hours of the relevant time and cannot be made before at least two reviews have been carried out by a review officer under s. 40 of the 1984 Act (those normally carried out by an inspector) (s. 42(4)).

For the situation regarding 'acting' ranks, **see General Police Duties, chapter 2**.

Section 42(5) to (8) mirrors the responsibility on the review officer at this stage with those of the review officer during the 'general period' of detention with regard to allowing representations, informing the detained person of the decision to authorise further detention and the need to record the decision. The main difference here is that the review officer must look into how the case is being investigated and whether this is being done diligently and expeditiously. Consequently, the review officer must also consider any representations on these points and these points should also be covered in any record as to whether detention should continue. When considering whether to authorise further detention the review officer must check whether the detained person has exercised his/her right to have someone informed and to consult with a legal representative. If these options have not been taken, s. 42(9) requires the review officer to inform the detained person of these rights and also whether he/she will be allowed to exercise these rights if it is a serious arrestable offence and the right has so far been delayed as per Code C, Annex B. The review officer should record the detainee's decision in the custody record and the grounds for denying the person those rights where appropriate.

If it is proposed to transfer a detained person from one police area to another for the purpose of investigating the offences for which he/she is detained, the review officer may take into consideration the period it will take to get to the other police area when deciding whether detention can go beyond 24 hours (s. 42(3)).

15.5.5   Detention Authorised by a Magistrates' Court

Once the 36-hour-limit has been reached, a person's detention can only continue with the authority of the courts through the issuing of a warrant of further detention. If a person's continued detention is not authorised beyond 36 hours by a court and the person is not charged with an offence, he/she must be released with or without bail and cannot be re-arrested for the offence unless new evidence comes to light.

Warrants of Further Detention

Applications for warrants of further detention are made at the magistrates' court. Initially, the magistrates can issue a warrant for further detention for a period of up to 36 hours. This can be extended by the courts on further applications by police up to a maximum total period of detention of 96 hours. The warrant will specify what period of further detention the court has authorised. If detention of the person is required for any longer period, further applications can be made to the court up to a maximum of 96 hours' detention. The grounds on which the court must decide whether to grant a warrant authorising further detention are the same as those that must be considered by a 'superintendent's review' (**see para. 15.5.4**).

Should it be necessary to apply for a warrant it is important that the time restraints are kept in mind at all times and the application procedure followed closely.

Procedure
The application is made in the magistrates' court and both the detained person and the police must be in attendance (s. 43(1) and (2) of the Police and Criminal Evidence Act 1984). The application is made by laying an information before the court. The officer making the application does so on oath and is subject to cross-examination (**see chapter 6**). Under s. 43(14) the information must set out:

- the nature of the offence;
- the general evidence on which the person was arrested;
- what inquiries have been made;
- what further inquiries are proposed; and
- why it is believed that continuing detention is necessary for the proposed inquiries.

It will be important to be able to demonstrate why the person needs to remain in detention while additional inquiries are made, for instance, that further facts need to be verified before further questioning of the suspect can continue and that this cannot be done effectively if the person is released. The detained person must be provided with a copy of the information before the matter can be heard (s. 43(2)). He/she is also entitled to be legally represented. If the person is not legally represented but then requests legal representation at court, the case must be adjourned to allow representation (s. 43(3)). In cases where the person is not represented it may be prudent to remind the person of his/her right to legal representation prior to the court hearing and to make a record of this in the custody record. Should the detained person choose to be legally represented at court, and thereby try and delay the police investigation, s. 43(3)(b) allows the person to be taken back into police detention during the adjournment.

Timing of the application
If it appears likely that the investigation of the serious arrestable offence requires the person's detention to go beyond 36 hours, then thought must be given as to when to make the application to the magistrates' court. Section 43(5) allows the application to be made before the expiry of the 36-hour period (calculated from the relevant time) or, where it has not been practicable for the court to sit within the 36-hour period, the application can be made within the next six hours. There are dangers in applying outside the 36-hour period in that if the court feels that it would have been reasonable to make the application within the 36-hour period then it must refuse the application for the warrant regardless of the merits of the case (s. 43(7)).

The court may either refuse the application or adjourn the hearing until such time as it specifies up to the end of the 36-hour period of detention (s. 43(8)). If the application is refused, the person must be charged or released with or without bail at the expiry of the current permissible period of detention (s. 43(15)).

The application for the warrant can be made at any time, *even before a superintendent's review has been carried out*. If the application is made within the 36-hour period and it is refused, it does not mean the person must be released straight away. Section 43(16) allows the person to be detained until the end of the current detention period (24 hours or 36 hours). The benefit of an early application has to be set against the risk that, once the court has refused an application, it is not allowed to hear any further applications for a warrant of further detention unless new evidence has come to light since the application was refused (s. 43(17)). Code C, Note 15B gives guidance on when an application should be made to the court. Note 15B provides that:

> *An application for a warrant of further detention or its extension should be made between 10 am and 9 pm, and if possible during normal court hours. It will not be practicable to arrange for a court to sit specially outside the hours of 10 am to 9 pm. If it appears possible that a special sitting may be needed (either at a weekend, Bank/Public Holiday or on a weekday outside normal court hours but between 10 am and 9 pm) then the clerk to the justices should be given notice and informed of this possibility, while the court is sitting if possible.*

In *R* v *Slough Justices, ex parte Stirling* [1987] Crim LR 576 the 36-hour period expired at 12.53 pm. The case was not heard by the justices until 2.45 pm. The Divisional Court held that the police should have made their application between 10.30 am and 11.30 am, even though this was before the 36-hour time limit had been reached.

In monitoring a person's detention, officers should be mindful of whether a warrant for further detention may be required and, if it is, consider whether a court will be available to hear the application. If a court will not be available then consideration should be given to making an earlier application. The process the magistrates go through in deciding the merits of the application also provides some safeguards in that the person's continued detention has been considered by the courts and therefore may reduce the likelihood of the defence suggesting that detention was not justified.

Further Warrants of Detention

Under s. 44 of the 1984 Act, the process for further warrants follows the same procedure as for the initial warrant, with the exception that the application *must be* made before the expiry of the extension given in the previous warrant.

Once the period of detention that has been authorised under the warrant has expired, and no other applications have been made, the detained person must be charged or released with or without bail.

15.6 Charging

A custody officer must decide whether there is sufficient evidence to charge a person when he/she is first brought to the police station (s. 37(1) of the 1984 Act) and when an officer informs them that he/she considers there is sufficient evidence to prosecute the detained person successfully (Code C, para. 16.1). If the custody officer decides that there is sufficient evidence to charge, then he/she must charge that person or release him/her without charge. (Similarly, if the custody officer considers that detention is not required, or is no longer required in order to obtain or secure evidence, the person should be released with or without bail attached to the release (s. 37(2)).)

Where a detained person is not in a fit state to be charged or released in accordance with s. 34(7) (for instance because he/she is drunk), he/she may be kept in custody until fit (but medical care may have to be considered).

(See also the provisions relating to drunk drivers in **Road Traffic, chapter 5**.)

Even where there is sufficient evidence to prosecute successfully, the detained person may be released without charge because it is felt that a charge is not in the public interest or the person has been cautioned or a decision has not yet been made about prosecuting the person. In this case, the person must be informed when he/she is released that the decision to prosecute has not yet been made (s. 37(8)).

In cases where a person is bailed without being charged, the custody officer cannot impose conditions on that bail (s. 47(1A)).

If a decision is taken to charge the detained person, Code C, para. 16 sets out the procedures to be followed by the custody officer. When a detained person is charged with, or informed that he/she may be prosecuted for an offence, para. 16.2 requires him/her to be cautioned. The caution varies slightly from that when arrested or interviewed (**see General Police Duties, chapter 2**) and is as follows:

> *You do not have to say anything. But it may harm your defence if you do not mention now something which you later rely on in court. Anything you do say may be given in evidence.*

At the time a person is charged, he/she shall be given a written notice as set out in Code C, para. 16 and a record shall be made of anything the person says when charged (para. 16.7). Where the person being charged is a juvenile or is mentally disordered or mentally impaired, the appropriate adult should be present and the notice given to him/her.

Once the person has been charged with or informed that he/she may be prosecuted for an offence, fingerprints can be taken if it is a recordable offence and he/she has not had his/her fingerprints taken during the course of the investigation (s. 61(3)(b)) (**see chapter 16**). Photographs may also be taken. However, unlike the power to take fingerprints which can be taken by force (s. 117), there is no power to force the person to have his/her photograph taken (Code D, para. 4.3).

If fingerprints are taken, the person must be informed of the reason why and that those prints may be used for a speculative search concerning other crimes (**see para. 16.5**). The reasons should also be recorded in the custody record, along with confirmation that the detained person has been given the required information. If the person's photograph is taken, this should also be recorded in the custody record. If a person is cleared of the charge, the fingerprints are destroyed (**see para. 16.5**); the person must be informed of this fact and that he/she can request to be present when they are destroyed (s. 63A).

Once a person has been charged or informed that he/she may be prosecuted for an offence (which does not include the service of the Notice of Intended Prosecution under ss. 1 and 2 of the Road Traffic Offenders Act 1988; **see Road Traffic, chapter 3**), generally the person cannot be questioned or spoken to about the matter. Code C, paras 16.4 and 16.5 set out occasions where further investigation involving the person may be allowed and para. 16.8 sets out the procedure to be adopted. It should only be in these circumstances that the custody officer allows any further inquiries involving the detained person to be made. Paragraphs 16.4 and 16.5 deal with:

- written statements made by other people which the investigating officers may wish to show to another person charged;

- questions necessary for the purpose of preventing or minimising harm or loss to some other person or to the public or for clearing up an ambiguity in a previous answer or statement;

- where it is in the interests of justice that the person should have put to him/her — and have an opportunity to comment on — information concerning the offence which has come to light since he/she was charged or informed that he/she might be prosecuted.

15.7 Cautioning

There are occasions where a person for whom there is sufficient evidence to charge may be cautioned as an alternative method of disposing with the case. *R v Chief Constable of the Lancashire Constabulary, ex parte Atkinson* (1998) 162 JP 275 is a case which considered the level of evidence required before a caution can be considered. There the court said that, provided it was clear that there had been an admission of guilt, it was not necessary, for the purposes of administering a caution, to show that the admission had been obtained in circumstances which satisfied the Codes of Practice. That was not to say that police authorities would not be well advised to take precautions which would satisfy the Code, but it did not follow that in every case there had to be a formal interview. However, police officers would be well advised to take precautions that would satisfy Code C. It would be both fairer and more reliable for a formal interview to take place.

Guidance as to the use of cautioning is provided by Home Office Circular 18/94 and the relevant sections are reproduced in **appendix 4**.

The guidelines should be considered carefully in all cases as any decision can be challenged by judicial review (**see para. 2.6.4**).

Sections 65 and 66 of the Crime and Disorder Act 1998 have made new provisions for reprimands and warnings for children and young persons which are currently being piloted and are due to be brought fully into force in April 2000 (**see chapter 7**).

15.8 Bail

If the person is charged then the custody officer has to decide whether the person is going to be bailed to appear at court or whether bail will be refused and the person kept in custody until the next available court. This is a review of the person's detention and therefore the person or his/her solicitor should be given an opportunity to make representations to the custody officer. The review should be conducted with regard to Code C, paras 15.1 to 15.6.

For a full discussion of bail, **see chapter 5**.

15.9 Custody Officer's Checklist

The following provides a guide to be followed when a person is brought to the police station. The PACE Code of Practice C applies throughout and custody officers should be conversant with its contents.

Throughout the period of detention of a person there are occasions where information must be given to that person. The Codes do allow these requirements to be delayed in certain circumstances, i.e. the detained person is violent or likely to become violent, or is incapable of understanding what is being said or is in need of urgent medical treatment (Code C para. 1.8). If the detained person is not informed at the time, he/she must be informed as soon as practicable. Where the person is incapable of understanding what is being said because of a language or hearing barrier, action must be taken to obtain an interpreter so that the information can be relayed to the detained person (Code C para. 3.6).

Initial Action when Commencing Custody Officer's Duties

- Ensure a poster as set out in Code C, para. 6.3 and Note 6H is displayed in the charge room and copies of the Codes of Practice are readily available (para. 1.2).

- Ensure cells that might be used comply with paras 8.2 and 8.4.

- Ensure that suitable blankets etc. will be available (para. 8.3).

- If video cameras are installed in the custody areas, notices of such cameras must be prominently displayed (para. 3.5A). (Any request to turn the cameras off shall be refused.) Any audio or video recording made in the custody area does not form part of the custody record (para. 2.1).

On Arrival of the Arrested Person (including people transferred from other police stations)

- Begin custody record (para. 2.1).

- Inform the arrested person of his/her rights (para. 3.1).

- If an appropriate adult is present or required, follow the guidance in para. 3.11.

- Provide the detained person with a written notice setting out his/her rights (para. 3.2 and Note 3B).

- Ask the person to sign the custody record to acknowledge receipt of the notice or note refusal to sign in the custody record (para. 3.2).

When making records concerning a detained person, all entries must be made in the custody record unless otherwise specified (para. 2.1). Action taken by a person must be noted in the custody record with the person's name and rank, except for officers dealing with persons detained under the Prevention of Terrorism (Temporary Provisions) Act 1989 (para. 2.2).

Special Groups

- If the person is deaf or there is doubt over his/her hearing or understanding of English refer to para. 3.6 and paras 13.1 to 13.11 of Code C (use of interpreters).

- If the person is blind or seriously visually impaired or is unable to read, refer to para. 3.14 and Note 3F.

- If the detained person could be a juvenile (para. 1.5), obtain the services of an appropriate adult.

- If the person is mentally impaired (for people that fall in to this group, see Note 1G), obtain the services of an appropriate adult.

Decision to Authorise Detention? (see para. 15.4.7)

- Arresting officer to give the reasons of arrest (in the presence of the arrested person (para. 3.4).

- Record any comment made by that person in response to the arresting officer's account (para. 3.4).

- Make a decision whether to authorise detention or release with or without bail (para. 3.4).

- Note any comment made by the detained person (para. 3.4).

If detention is authorised, record the reasons in the custody record and inform the detained person of the decision (para. 3.4). (If the detained person is violent, likely to become violent or incapable of understanding what is being said (but if due to hearing/language barriers consider para. 3.6), or is in need of urgent medical treatment he/she *must* be informed as soon as practicable (para. 1.8 and s. 37(6) of the 1984 Act).

If the person has already been in custody for the offence for which he/she has been arrested, it will be necessary to confirm that the person still has time left within his/her 'detention period'. The review clock is also relevant in terms of when the next review is due. (If the person has been arrested for an offence for which he/she has been bailed and there is 'new evidence', the detention clock starts again (s. 41(9)).)

New evidence can be described as evidence that was not in existence at the time of arrest or when the detained person was granted bail (e.g. the results of fingerprint analysis sent off for comparison).

Ascertain whether Detained Person requires Legal Advice

- Ask the detained person if he/she wants legal advice (para. 3.5) and point out that legal advice is free (para. 6.1).

- Ask the detained person to sign the custody record to indicate whether he/she requires legal advice and ensure he/she signs it in the right place (para. 3.5).

- If legal advice is requested it must be given unless Annex B to Code C applies or delay would hinder the investigation (para. 6.6). If any delay occurs, record the reason (para. 1.1A).

- If delay is not authorised, the custody officer must act without delay to secure the provision of legal advice (para. 6.5).

- If the offer of legal advice is declined, point out the right to speak to a solicitor on the phone (para. 6.5).

- If legal advice is still declined, ask the detained person for reasons why and record any reasons given in the custody record (if during interview this can be recorded in the interview record) (para. 6.5). Once it is clear that the detained person does not wish to have any contact with a legal adviser, the custody officer should cease to ask why (para. 6.5).

When complying with the need to provide legal advice the following should be considered:

- For the treatment of the detained person once he/she has requested legal advice, see para. 6.6.

- Remember that this is a continuing right that can be exercised at any time during police detention (para. 6.1).

- Note 6B provides guidance on how much choice the detained person has in choosing a solicitor.

- For those persons who can provide legal advice under the Codes of Practice, see para. 6.12. Refer to paras 6.13 and 6.14 if refusing an adviser access.

- If a solicitor arrives to provide legal advice, inform the detained person unless Annex B applies (para. 6.15).

- If the detained person cannot understand the solicitor because of a language barrier refer to para. 13.9 (people who can act as interpreters).

- Consultation with a solicitor must be in private (para. 6.1) with the exception of those detained on terrorism charges.

Right to Inform Third Party

- Contact must be made with a juvenile's appropriate adult (para. 3.7).

- For detained persons who are citizens of independent commonwealth countries or foreign nationals, see paras 7.1 to 7.5.

Ascertain whether the detained person wants a third party informed of his/her detention. Should the detained person at any stage request that a person be informed of his/her arrest, consider whether this right should be delayed. This right can only be delayed in circumstances outlined in Annex B to Code C, otherwise paras 5.1 to 5.3 and 5.8 must be followed. If the detained person has no one to contact, see Note 5C for guidance.

The detained person has the right to send letters and make phone calls (paras 5.6 to 5.8) but this can be delayed (para. 5.6).

If a person inquires about a detained person, refer to para. 5.5 and Note 5D.

Visits are covered by para. 5.4 and Note 5B.

Searching

The searching of a detained person is very important. It may lead to the discovery of new evidence, it may also avoid people being injured or even escaping from police detention. The law governing the searching of people on arrest and searches under warrant is discussed elsewhere (**see General Police Duties, chapter 2**).

Section 54 of the Police and Criminal Evidence Act 1984 details the duties and powers relating to the searching of detained persons.

> *(1) The custody officer at a police station shall ascertain and record or cause to be recorded everything which a person has with him when he is—*
> *(a) brought to the station after being arrested elsewhere or after being committed to custody by an order or sentence of a court; or*
> *(b) arrested at the station or detained there, as a person falling within section 34(7), under section 37 above.*
> *(2) In the case of an arrested person the record shall be made as part of his custody record.*
> *(3) Subject to subsection (4) below, a custody officer may seize and retain any such thing or cause any such thing to be seized and retained.*
> *(4) Clothes and personal effects may only be seized if the custody officer—*
> *(a) believes that the person from whom they are seized may use them—*
> *(i) to cause physical injury to himself or any other person;*
> *(ii) to damage property;*
> *(iii) to interfere with evidence; or*
> *(iv) to assist him to escape; or*
> *(b) has reasonable grounds for believing that they may be evidence relating to an offence.*
> *(5) Where anything is seized, the person from whom it is seized shall be told the reason for the seizure unless he is—*
> *(a) violent or likely to become violent; or*
> *(b) incapable of understanding what is said to him.*
> *(6) Subject to subsection (7) below, a person maybe searched if the custody officer considers it necessary to enable him to carry out his duty under subsection (1) above and to the extent that the custody officer considers necessary for that purpose.*
> *(7) An intimate search may not be conducted under this section.*
> *(8) A search under this section shall be carried out by a constable.*
> *(9) The constable carrying out a search shall be of the same sex as the person searched.*

Keynote

Section 54 places a duty on a custody officer to ascertain and make a record of what property a person has with him/her when:

- arrested and brought to the station;

- committed to police custody by order of the court;

- arrested at the station;

- detained after surrendering to bail;

- arrested after failing to surrender to bail.

The custody officer must also consider what property the detained person might have in his/her possession for an unlawful or harmful purpose while in custody. The safekeeping of any property taken from the detained person and kept at the police station, is the responsibility of the custody officer.

The custody officer must record in the custody record, all property brought to the police station or which was taken from the detained person at the time of arrest (Code C, para. 4.4). The only exceptions to this requirement are items which, by virtue of their nature, quantity or size, it was not practicable to bring to the police station (Code C, Note 4B).

The Search

While the custody officer has a duty to ascertain what property a person has with them (often by means of searching the person), there is also a need to consider the rights of that detained person. The custody officer may authorise a constable to search a detained person, or may search the detained person themselves in order to ascertain what property the detained person has with them (s. 54(6)). Therefore the custody officer may only authorise a search to the extent that he/she considers necessary to comply with this duty. In order to safeguard the rights of the detained person there are three levels to which searches can be conducted:

- searches that do not involve the removal of more than the detained person's outer clothing;
- strip searches;
- intimate searches.

Each of these is examined below.

If the detained person is not going to be placed in a cell and is only going to be kept in detention for a short period, the custody officer has the option not to search (Code C, Note 4A). If no search is conducted the custody record should be endorsed 'not searched'. The duty to ascertain what property a person has with them is a continuing duty and therefore the custody officer can have the person searched at a later time if he/she feels it is necessary to comply with his/her responsibility under the 1984 Act or the Codes.

The extent of the search is determined by the custody officer on the basis of what he/she honestly believes is necessary in order to comply with the above duties. Both the decision to search the detained person and the extent of the search must be decided on the facts of the case in question. Force standing orders are not an automatic right to search all detained persons (*Brazil* v *Chief Constable of Surrey* [1983] Crim LR 483). A custody officer can authorise a strip search but an intimate search can only be authorised by an officer of the rank of superintendent or above (see below).

Searches that do not involve the removal of more than the detained person's outer clothing
In effect this is any search that does not become a strip search or an intimate search. This type of search applies to almost every person coming before the custody officer unless Code C, Note 4A applies. Typically this will involve emptying out all items that are in the person's pockets, removing jewellery and the searching of other areas that can be conducted without the need to remove more than outer garments such as coats and possibly items such as jumpers. This type of authorisation would also lend itself to a 'pat down' of the detained person. If there is any doubt as to whether the search goes beyond one that falls into this category, it is suggested that it should be treated as a strip search.

Strip searches
Strip searches are dealt with in Code C, Annex A. A strip search is a search involving the removal of more than outer clothing. Although a person's mouth may be examined during a strip search, the examination of any other body orifice would amount to an intimate search.

A strip search may take place only if the custody officer reasonably considers that the detained person might have concealed an article which he/she would not be allowed to keep, such as those items which the detained person may use to:

- cause harm to himself/herself or others;
- damage property;
- effect an escape; or
- which might be evidence of an offence; *and*

that if such an item were found it would be necessary to remove it.

Reasons for the search, the extent of the search, details of the people present and the results of the search must be recorded in the custody record (Annex A, para. 12). The search must be conducted in accordance with Annex A, para. 11.

Intimate searches
Intimate searches are dealt with in Code C, Annex A. An intimate search is a search which consists of the physical examination of a person's body orifices other than the mouth. Such searches can only be carried out in two circumstances and then only if they are authorised by an officer of the rank of superintendent or above.

The circumstances mentioned above are that the authorising officer has reasonable grounds for believing:

- that an article which could cause physical injury to the detained person or others at the police station has been concealed; or
- that the detained person has concealed a Class A drug which he/she intended to supply to another or to export.

Not only must the authorising officer have reasonable grounds for believing that one or both of the above grounds are satisfied but he/she must also believe that an intimate search is the only practicable means of removing an item.

The custody officer must record which parts of the person's body were searched, who carried out the search, who was present, the reasons for the search and its result.

Conduct of a search
The manner in which a search must be conducted is set out in Code C, paras 4.1 to 4.4. Some relevant practical matters are set out below:

- Before the search begins the detained person should be informed of the reasons for the search, unless it is impracticable to do so (*Brazil* v *Chief Constable of Surrey* [1983] Crim LR 483).

- The search must be conducted by an officer (s. 54(8) of the 1984 Act) of the same sex (s. 54(9)) and Code C, para. 4.1.

- Reasonable force may be used (s. 117 of the 1984 Act and Code C, para. 8.9).

- The custody officer should specify the level of the search to be conducted.

- Reference to Code A, para. 3.1 may be useful when considering how to conduct the search: 'Every reasonable effort must be made to reduce to the minimum the embarrassment that a person being searched may experience.'

- For cases where the intimate search has been authorised to search for a concealed Class A drug which the detained person intended to supply to another or to export:

  - The search may only be carried out by a registered medical practitioner or registered nurse.

  - The search must take place at a hospital, surgery or other medical premises.

  - No person of the opposite sex who is not a medical practitioner or nurse should be present.

  - A minimum of two people, other than the person searched, must be present during the search.

What property can be retained?

Once a person has been searched and the custody officer has ascertained what property the detained person has with him/her, a decision must be made as to what property will be returned to the detained person and what property will be retained by the police.

The basic position is that, with the exception of articles subject to legal privilege (**see chapter 10**), all property in the possession of a detained person may be retained by the police. However, in the case of clothing and personal items (as defined by Code C, para. 4.3), these may only be retained if the custody officer believes that the item(s) may be used by the detained person to:

- cause harm to himself/herself or others;
- damage to property;
- effect an escape; or
- that they might be evidence of an offence.

Where personal items are retained by the custody officer, he/she must inform the person of the reasons why they have been retained.

It is suggested that the custody officer may authorise the seizure of an article of clothing under s. 54(4)(b) of the 1984 Act, where he/she has reasonable grounds for believing that such clothing may be evidence relating to an offence. For instance, if the detained person is wearing a pair of trainers of the same type as those which are reasonably believed to have made impressions at the scene of a recent burglary and the detained person has a burglary record then, unless the custody officer knows of other facts clearly putting the suspect at some other place at the time of the offence, he/she is plainly justified in having those shoes forensically examined. However, it is submitted that this does not authorise the custody officer to seize footwear on the off-chance that some officer or some other police force may have obtained impressions at a burglary site which might match the trainers of the detained person.

Where it is necessary to retain items of clothing that the detained person is wearing replacement clothing of a reasonable standard of comfort and cleanliness must be provided (Code C, para. 8.5). What is 'reasonable' clothing will be a question of fact. At the time of writing there is no available case law on this point. It is also important to make a record of any offer of replacement clothing (Code C, para. 8.11).

Where the person is searched and a record of his/her property is made, the detained person should be allowed to check the property list and be invited to sign the list as correct. If he/she declines, this should be recorded in the custody record (Code C, para. 4.4).

Unless the property has been seized and retained as evidence under s. 22 of the 1984 Act, it must be returned to the detained person on his/her release.

Juveniles

Juveniles are provided with the additional safeguard of an appropriate adult to look out for their interests while in police detention. The Codes of Practice state that where a juvenile or a mentally disordered/mentally handicapped person is the subject of a strip search or an intimate search, in most cases, an appropriate adult must be present. The Codes do not make any mention of this requirement for an ordinary search and therefore searches other than strip and intimate searches may be conducted without an appropriate adult being present. Where an appropriate adult is required:

- the appropriate adult may be of the opposite sex;

- where there is a risk of serious harm to the detained person or to others the search may be conducted without the appropriate adult being present;

- a search of a juvenile may take place in the absence of the appropriate adult only if the juvenile signifies in the presence of the appropriate adult that he/she prefers the search to be done in his/her absence and the appropriate adult agrees. In such cases a record shall be made of the juvenile's decision and signed by the appropriate adult.

Well-being of Detained Person

The custody officer should be mindful at all times for the well-being of the detained person.

Code C, para. 12.2 provides a requirement for a detained person to have a rest period:

In any period of 24 hours a detained person must be allowed a continuous period of at least 8 hours for rest, free from questioning, travel or any interruption by police officers in connection with the investigation concerned. This period should normally be at night. The period of rest may not be interrupted or delayed, except at the request of the person, his appropriate adult or his legal representative, unless there are reasonable grounds for believing that it would:
> *(i)   involve a risk of harm to persons or serious loss of, or damage to, property; or*
> *(ii)   delay unnecessarily the person's release from custody; or*
> *(iii) otherwise prejudice the outcome of the investigation.*

Keynote

The period of 24 hours runs from the time the person is arrested and not the time of his/her arrival at the police station (para. 12.2).

If a complaint is made by or on behalf of the detained person, or the person is treated improperly, follow Code C, para. 9.1.

If the detained person:

- appears to be suffering from a physical illness or mental disorder;
- is injured;

- fails to respond normally to questions or conversation;
- otherwise appears to be in need of medical attention;
- requests a medical examination;

follow Code C, paras 9.1 to 9.9.

If the detained person is suffering from an infectious disease, see Code C, para. 9.3.

At least two light meals and one main meal shall be offered in any period of 24 hours. Drinks should be provided at meal times and upon reasonable request between meal times (Code C, para. 8.6). Meals should so far as practicable be offered at recognised meal times (Code C, Note 8C).

Brief outdoor exercise must be given if practicable (Code C, para. 8.7).

Other Events involving the Detained Person

- Where the detained person is delivered to the custody of another officer, the fact must be recorded (Code C, para. 12.9). Any refusal to hand over the detained person must also be recorded with the reasons why (para. 12.9).

- When handing over the custody of a detained person to another police officer, the custody officer ceases to have responsibility for ensuring that the detained person is treated in accordance with the Codes of Practice and the responsibility passes to the person to whom the detained person is handed (s. 39(2)).

- When the detained person is returned to the care of the custody officer, the person returning the detained person must report to the custody officer as to the manner in which the Codes of Practice have been complied with (s. 39(3)). This information must be recorded in the custody record along with any reported breaches of the Codes.

If a police officer wishes to interview, or conduct enquiries which require the presence of a detained person, the custody officer is responsible for deciding whether to deliver him/her into his/her custody (Code C, para. 12.1). In considering this decision, the custody officer should bear in mind the following factors:

- Whether the person is in need of a rest period (Code C, para. 12.2).

- Whether the detained person is unfit through drink or drugs (Code C, para. 12.3 and Note 12B).

- Whether the right of access to legal advice is being complied with as required by Code C, paras 6.1 to 6.17).

If the detained person is to be interviewed, the custody officer should consider the following questions under Code C:

- Will the interview room be adequately heated, lit and ventilated? (para. 12.4)

- Is seating available in the interview room? (para. 12.5)

- If an interpreter is required, will he/she be available for the interview? (paras 13.2 and 13.5)

- Where the detained person is a juvenile or a person who is mentally disordered or impaired, whether suspected or not, do not hand over the detained person to the interviewing officer without an appropriate adult being present unless para. 11.1 or Annex C applies (para. 11.14).

- Allow private consultation with a legal adviser (para. 6.1).

- Allow visits (para. 5.4).

- Transfer to another station or court (para. 2.3).

- Release either with or without bail.

(Paragraph 2.3 requires the time of release to be recorded. This is relevant in calculating any period of detention which may still be remaining if the person has been bailed and periods in police detention also count towards the period a person serves in custody.)

Code C, para. 8.9 reiterates s. 117 of the 1984 Act concerning the use of force that can be used on a detained person. 'Reasonable force' may be used if necessary for the following purposes:

- to secure compliance with reasonable instructions, including instructions given in pursuance of the provisions of a Code of Practice; or

- to prevent escape, injury, damage to property or the destruction of evidence.

A further important duty is placed upon a custody officer where a person is to be handed over to prison custody. The custody officer must complete a form in respect of every prisoner handed over for prison custody who is reasonably suspected of:

- being likely to try to escape;
- being associated with a dangerous gang who may attempt rescue;
- against whom other serious charges may be brought;
- being of a violent nature;
- any other reason which may help the governor in deciding whether this prisoner represents a special security risk, e.g. having suicidal tendencies, being ill, being liable to take drugs into prison etc.

15.10 Special Groups and Appropriate Adults

In cases where the detained person is a juvenile or a person who is mentally handicapped or appears to be suffering from mental disorder, the custody officer must inform an appropriate adult as soon as possible (this must be done in the case of a juvenile regardless of whether he/she is held incommunicado (Code C, para. 3.7). In the case of a juvenile who is the subject of a supervision order, the person supervising the juvenile should also be informed. If the custody officer has any doubt as to the mental state or capacity of a person detained, an appropriate adult should be called (Code C, Note 1G).

A juvenile is any person who is under the age of 17 or who appears to be under the age of 17 until it is established that he/she is 17 or over (Code C, para. 1.5).

Note 1G defines 'mental disorder' as having the same meaning as in s. 1(2) of the Mental Health Act 1983, as 'mental illness, arrested or incomplete development of mind, psychopathic disorder and any other disorder or disability of mind'. For the purposes of the Codes 'mental disorder' and 'mental handicap' are dealt with similarly throughout. Paragraph 1.4 also provides that:

> If an officer has any suspicion, or is told in good faith, that a person of any age may be mentally disordered or mentally handicapped, or mentally incapable of understanding the significance of questions put to him or his replies, then that person shall be treated as a mentally disordered or mentally handicapped person for the purposes of this code.

An appropriate adult is defined by para. 1.7 as:

> (a) in the case of a juvenile:
>   (i)   his parent or guardian (or, if he is in care, the care authority or voluntary organisation . . .;
>   (ii)   a social worker; or
>   (iii) failing either of the above, another responsible adult aged 18 or over who is not a police officer or employed by the police.
> (b) in the case of a person who is mentally disordered or mentally handicapped:
>   (i)   a relative, guardian or other person responsible for his care or custody;
>   (ii)   someone who has experience of dealing with mentally disordered or mentally impaired persons but who is not a police officer or employed by the police (such as an approved social worker as defined by the Mental Health Act 1983 or a specialist social worker); or
>   (iii) failing either of the above, some other responsible adult aged 18 or over who is not a police officer or employed by the police.

Keynote

The role of the appropriate adult is to assist and advise the detained person. Care should be taken when considering the suitability of an appropriate adult. Code C, Note 1E gives guidance for choosing the appropriate adult. Evidence obtained whilst a person is in custody where the person called as an appropriate adult does not have that person's best interests in mind or is not capable of assisting them could be excluded.

In *R* v *Aspinall*, *The Times*, 4 February 1999, the Court of Appeal emphasised the importance of appropriate adults. There it was held that an appropriate adult played a significant role in respect of a vulnerable person whose condition rendered him/her liable to provide information which was unreliable, misleading or self-incriminating.

It is also important to consider the welfare of the appropriate adult. This is demonstrated by the case of *Leach* v *Chief Constable of Gloucestershire Constabulary* [1999] 1 All ER 215. Here L was asked by a police officer to attend police interviews of a murder suspect who was also thought to be mentally disordered, as an 'appropriate adult' per the requirement of the PACE Codes. She was told only that the suspect was a 52-year-old male, and was not informed of the nature of the case. The suspect was in fact Frederick West, who was being questioned in connection with murders committed in particularly harrowing and traumatic circumstances. For many weeks L acted as an appropriate adult, accompanying the officer and suspect to murder scenes and on many occasions being left alone in a locked cell with the suspect. She claimed to be suffering from post-traumatic distress and psychological injury as well as a stroke as a result of her experiences. The Court of Appeal said that the Fred West case was notorious amongst modern crimes and it was forseeable that psychiatric harm might arise. Whilst there was no requirement to pre-select or warn appropriate adults as to the nature of the case, however in some cases, counselling or trained help should be offered.

CHAPTER SIXTEEN

IDENTIFICATION

16.1 Introduction

A critical issue in the investigation and prosecution of offences is the identification of the offender and this, like all other facts in issue, must be proved beyond a reasonable doubt. Many different methods of identification exist but the main feature which must be considered in relation to each is its *reliability*.

16.2 Code D

Identification evidence is governed by Code D of the PACE Codes of Practice (**see appendix 6**).

Generally, the methods of identification covered by Code D can be divided into two:

- occasions where the identity of the suspect is known; and
- occasions where the identity of the suspect is not known.

Although a breach of Code D (or any of the other Codes of Practice) will not automatically result in the evidence being excluded (*R v Khan* [1997] Crim LR 584), the judge or magistrate(s) will consider the effects of any breach on the fairness of any subsequent proceedings. The Codes are intended to provide protection to suspects and, if it is felt that the breach of Code D has resulted in unfairness or other prejudicial effect on the defendant, the court may exclude the related evidence under s. 78 of the Police and Criminal Evidence Act 1984 (**see chapter 13**).

16.3 Check 'This'

Conversely, even if Code D is followed, that is no guarantee that evidence obtained will be admissible. In each case the ultimate purpose of any identification procedure should be borne in mind and the 'this' list used elsewhere in the series (**see General Police Duties and Road Traffic**) should be applied to any proposed procedure by asking:

How reliable is *this* piece of evidence in proving, or disproving, *this* person's involvement in *this* offence?

This approach should be adopted even if the provisions of Code D are followed. A good example of a situation where such an approach may have helped is *R* v *Hickin* [1996] Crim LR 584. This case was decided under the old Codes of Practice before it was necessary to obtain a first description from a witness. In the case, a group of some 14 suspects were arrested following an attack on two men at night. Clearly it would have been impracticable to arrange identification parades or group identifications for each suspect at that time, thereby allowing for a direct confrontation (**see para. 16.4.3**). However, witnesses could have been asked to provide initial descriptions of suspects before being used in the confrontation. The witnesses' comments at the time of the confrontation could also have been noted and some witnesses might have been asked to remain behind to take part in some later identification parades. As these things were not done, the Court of Appeal held that the identification evidence obtained by the confrontation procedure was unfairly prejudicial, *even though the provisions of Code D had been followed.*

16.4   Methods of Identification

16.4.1   Visual

The visual identification of suspects by witnesses is one of the most common forms of identification; it is also one of the most unreliable. Even under research conditions, the recall of eye witnesses is inconsistent; where the witness sees or experiences the spontaneous commission of a crime, that reliability is reduced even further.

It was for these reasons that the *Turnbull* guidelines (**see chapter 11**) were set out, together with the provisions of Code D (**see appendix 6**).

Problems of reliability in identification can arise even where the person accused is known to the witness. (See, for example *R* v *Conway* (1990) 91 Cr App R 143 where the defendant was accused by two witnesses of a stabbing. Even though the witnesses knew the defendant, his request to appear on an identification parade (**see para. 16.4.3**) should have been acceded to.)

A lot will depend on the individual circumstances of each case but it is essential that these issues are covered in any interview or other evidence gathering process.

'Dock identifications', where the witness's first identification of the accused involves pointing out the person in the dock, are often dramatised by film makers but, in practice, are generally disallowed as being unreliable and unfair.

16.4.2   First Description and Media Releases

The rules for identification differ between cases where the suspect *is known* and those where suspect is *not known*. Code D, Note 2E defines the terms as:

> . . . *a suspect being 'known' means there is sufficient information known to the police to justify the arrest of a particular person for suspected involvement in the offence. A suspect being 'available' means that he is immediately available to take part in the procedure or he will become available within a reasonably short time.*

Keynote

Code D requires that a first description provided of a person suspected of a crime (regardless of the time it was given) must be recorded (para. 2.0). This must also be disclosed to the defence in the pre-trial procedure in all cases and, in particular, before any identification procedures take place. The Code also makes provision for the disclosure of materials previously released to the media in relation to an enquiry and for witnesses to be asked if they have seen such material before the identification procedure.

16.4.3 Identification where Suspect is Known

Where the suspect is known there are four possible methods of identification provided for in Code D. These are:

- identification parades;
- group identification;
- video identification; and
- confrontation.

This list follows the order in which each method should be considered. The first option should be a parade unless it would be unfair, impracticable or unsatisfactory for the reasons set out in Code D (paras 2.4, 2.7 and 2.10), or if the suspect refuses.

Confrontation is the least acceptable form of identification from the list and cannot be used unless none of the others is practicable (see para. 2.13).

When must an Identification Parade be Held?

The Codes give guidance on when an identification parade must or may be held. Code D, para. 2.3 provides that:

> *Whenever a suspect disputes an identification, an identification parade shall be held if the suspect consents unless . . . A parade may also be held if the officer in charge of the investigation considers that it would be useful, and the suspect consents.*

Keynote

The exceptions to holding an identification parade under para. 2.3 are where:

- The identification officer considers that, whether by reason of the unusual appearance of the suspect or for some other reason, it would not be practicable to assemble sufficient people who resembled him/her to make a parade fair.

- A group identification takes place (para. 2.7).

- A video film of a suspect is used (para. 2.10).

Despite the wording of Code D, it has been held that a suspect's right to have an identification parade is not confined to cases where a dispute over identity has already arisen; that right also applies where such a dispute might reasonably be anticipated (*R v Rutherford* (1993) 98 Cr App R 191). Similarly, a suspect's failure to request an identification parade does not mean that the police may proceed without one (*R v Graham* [1994] Crim LR 212).

Any decision to proceed without an identification parade must be capable of justification later to the relevant court. The courts have taken different approaches to justification based on practical difficulties. In an early case, the submissions of the identification officer that it was impracticable to find enough people who sufficiently resembled the defendant were treated fairly dismissively by the trial judge (*R* v *Gaynor* [1988] Crim LR 242). In later cases, however, the courts have been more lenient, accepting that the timescales involved in arranging identification parades may render them 'impracticable' (see *R* v *Jamel* [1993] Crim LR 52 where the court refused an objection by the defence to a group identification). A group identification was used in *Jamel* because a parade using mixed-race volunteers would have taken too long to arrange. All reasonable steps must be taken to investigate the possibility of one identification option before moving on to an alternative, and an offer from a suspect's solicitor to find volunteers to stand on a parade is such a 'reasonable' step (*R* v *Britton and Richards* [1989] Crim LR 144).

Code D, para. 2.3 would seem to make it quite clear when an identification parade is required. However, the Court of Appeal have considered a number of cases recently where identification parades were not held and have given further guidance.

The effect of the Code and the case decisions is that, when a suspect becomes known and disputes his/her identification, the question must be asked whether the witness has provided an actual and complete identification. If the answer is yes then the mandatory requirement of the first sentence of para. 2.3 does not apply. If the answer is no para. 2.3 must be complied with. What is an actual and complete prior identification will depend upon the facts of each individual case.

Other cases have supported this view. In *R* v *Anastasiou* [1998] Crim LR 67 police officers who witnessed an assault were involved in the suspect's arrested. No identification parade was held and the court agreed that the identification of the suspect had occurred unavoidably when he was arrested. No more formal modes of identification were possible. An identification parade at a later date would have added nothing to the identification already made by the police.

In *D* v *DPP*, *The Times*, 7 August 1998, a witness had observed two youths for a continuous period of five to six minutes and then informed the police of what he had seen, describing the age of the youths and the clothes that they were wearing. The court held that there had not been an identification within the terms of the Codes of Practice because the witness had at no stage identified the defendant or the co-accused. He had described only their clothing and their approximate ages and the police, acting on that information, had made the arrests. An identification parade could have served no useful purpose since the clothing would have been changed and those persons used for the parade would have been the same approximate age.

Conduct of Identification Parades

Identification evidence can be crucial to the success of a prosecution, particularly identification parades. There are clear guidelines that must be followed. Where such guidelines are not followed it is likely that the defence will strongly attempt to have the identification parade evidence excluded.

The conduct of identification parades was criticised in the Stephen Lawrence Inquiry. The McPherson report stated that:

IDENTIFICATION

The identification parades were poorly planned. There were clear breaches of the Codes of Practice governing identity parades. In particular witnesses were allowed to be together before parades took place. Witnesses were not properly supervised. Successful identification might well have been compromised by these breaches.

The report also went on to say that the timing of any identification parade during an investigation must also be considered carefully:

where there are a number of suspects and witnesses and where identification evidence may be crucial this can only emphasise the extreme need for careful planning and foresight. . . . The ID parades were delayed until about the middle or end of May partly because of the delay in making the arrests of the suspects. If the arrests had been made earlier it can be said that there would have been more prospect of successful identification, since the passage of time inevitably blunts the memory of the features or look of somebody who has been seen committing a crime.

Annex A to Code D sets out the procedure which must be followed in conducting identification parades.

Although the courts are aware of the many practical difficulties involved in organising and running parades (see e.g. *R* v *Jamel* above), any flaws in the procedure will be considered in the light of their potential impact on the defendant's trial. Serious or deliberate breaches (such as the showing of photographs to witnesses before the parade contrary to para. 2.8), will invariably lead to any evidence so gained being excluded (*R* v *Finley* [1993] Crim LR 50).

So too will breaches which appear to impact on the safeguards imposed by Annex A to separate the functions of investigation and identification (e.g. where the investigating officer becomes involved with the running of the parade in a way which allows him/her to talk to the witnesses (*R* v *Gall* (1989) 90 Cr App R 64).

It is important to follow the guidance in the Codes regardless of what agreement is obtained from the suspect or his/her solicitor. In *R* v *Hutton* [1999] Crim LR 74 at the suggestion of the suspect's solicitor, all the participants in the identification parade wore back to front baseball caps and had the lower part of their faces obscured by material. That identification was the only evidence against the defendant on that count. The court excluded the evidence and did not accept the fact that the decision had been agreed with the solicitor. The court said it was a mistake, whether it arose out of a request made by the defence solicitor or not, to have all participants on the parade masked.

Details of what a witness *does* at an identification parade (e.g. points to a particular person) may be admissible. This is because the action is directly perceived by the person giving evidence, that is, the identification officer or a volunteer on the parade. Details of what a witness *says* at an identification parade may be admissible under the *res gestae* principle following the slightly generous decision of the Court of Appeal in *R* v *McCay* [1990] 1 WLR 645 (**see chapter 11**).

Group Identification

Group identifications, together with video identifications and confrontations, are often considered to be less valuable than identification parades for the simple reason that, if a suspect has to pick out one person from several who look similar, that will be more credible than viewing the suspect among a heterogeneous group.

The procedure for group identification is governed by Annex E to Code D. Whereas an identification parade needs the consent and co-operation of the suspect, the procedure for group identification expressly caters for such methods to be used without the consent — or even the knowledge — of the suspect (see Annex E, para. 2). Covert identification cannot be employed, however, unless the suspect has already refused to co-operate or has failed to attend an identification parade or group identification (see Annex E, para. 33).

Again, each case involving the decision to use a group identification will be assessed on its particular circumstances. A group identification may take place inside or outside; the decision is a matter for the identification officer. A group identification may take place inside a police station but only if this is necessary on grounds of safety, security or practicability (see Annex E, paras 3 and 36).

Video Identification

The procedure for video identification is set out in Annex B to Code D. The option to use a video identification is determined by the view of the *investigating officer*, as opposed to the identification officer. If the investigating officer considers that a video identification would, *in the circumstances*, be the most satisfactory course of action the identification officer *may* show a witness a video film of a suspect (see Code D, para. 2.10).

In conducting the video identification the identification officer should ensure:

- The film includes the suspect and at least eight other people. Only one suspect must be on the film unless there are two suspects of roughly the same appearance (Code D, Annex B, para. 3).

- That the suspect's representative has an opportunity to be present. In the absence of a representative the viewing itself shall be recorded on video (Annex B, para. 8).

- Only one witness sees the film at a time and he/she should be asked to refrain from making a positive identification or otherwise until the entire film has been seen at least twice. There is no limit on how many times the film may be viewed (Annex B, para. 10).

Code D does not apply to films made by closed circuit television cameras or recordings made of a crime scene before any suspect has come to light (*R* v *Jones (M.A.)* (1995) 159 JP 293).

Confrontation

The procedure for confrontation is set out in Annex C to Code D.

This is probably the least persuasive method of identification but is at times the only viable option. Even where the correct procedure has been adhered to, the courts are wary of identification evidence obtained in this way. See, for example, *R* v *Joseph* [1994] Crim LR 48 where the defendant had demanded a confrontation and was subsequently identified by two witnesses. The Court of Appeal still ruled that, under the particular circumstances, the evidence was unreliable and ought to have been excluded at trial. The courts take an even dimmer view where the procedure is deliberately manipulated, for instance where a 'chance' confrontation is staged outside a police station so that the witness bumps into the suspect as he/she is released (*R* v *Nagah* [1991] Crim LR 55), or where an investigating officer arranges his/her own 'confrontation' (see *Powell* v *DPP* [1992] RTR 270).

16.4.4 Identification at the Scene

There are occasions where the identification is made immediately after the alleged offence. This usually happens when the witness is taken round a particular area to try and find the suspect (in which case Code D, paras 2.17 and 2.18 must be complied with). In such cases, where the meeting of the suspect and the witness takes place soon after the event, not all of Code D will apply (although it will still be important to obtain a description of the suspect from the witness prior to any form of identification if this is practicable). These exceptional circumstances were recognised by Lord Lane CJ in *R* v *Oscar* [1991] Crim LR 778 and were again applied by the Court of Appeal in *R* v *Rogers* [1993] Crim LR 386. In *Oscar* the defendant was arrested near the victim's house following an attempted burglary. His clothing matched that described by the victim and he was taken for an immediate confrontation with her, whereupon she identified him as the person she had seen breaking into her house. The Court held that there had been no requirement for an identity parade in that case and Lord Lane pointed out that, in any case, a later parade where the suspect was dressed differently would be of no value at all. In *Rogers* the suspect was found near a crime scene and was confronted by a witness who positively identified him. The Court held that the identification in that case was necessary for an arrest to be made and therefore Code D did not apply (although a later parade could have been carried out).

Careful consideration must be given before a decision to identify a suspect in this manner is used. If there is sufficient evidence to arrest the suspect without using a witnesses identification, then it is likely the courts will find that an identification parade should have been held and the evidence may be excluded.

An example where a street identification was appropriate is *R* v *El-Hannachi* [1998] 2 Cr App R 226. Here an affray took place in the car park of a public house. A witness had seen the man earlier in the pub and she had had an unobstructed view in good light before the attack. The witness described the attackers' clothing to police and then identified a group of men who had been stopped by other officers a short distance away. The court accepted that it was the correct approach. The defendants were not known suspects when they were stopped by the police prior to the witness's identification. The court also accepted that it had not been practicable for a record to have been made of the witness's description, as required by Code D, para. 2.17, prior to the identification.

16.4.5 Identification where Suspect is Not Known

If the suspect is not known, Code D provides for witnesses (including police officers) to be shown photographs or taken to a place where the suspect might be (paras 2.17 and 2.18).

If photographs are to be shown, the procedure set out at Annex D must be followed. Once a witness has made a positive identification from the photographs, no further witnesses should be shown photographs (unless the person identified is eliminated from the enquiry).

Using photographs from police criminal records can affect the judgment of a jury and nothing should be done to draw their attention to the fact that the defendant's photograph was already held by the police (*R v Lamb* (1979) 71 Cr App R 198). This rule does not apply if the jury are already aware of the defendant's previous convictions (*R v Allen* [1996] Crim LR 426).

The showing of a closed circuit television camera film used for security purposes is addressed at para. 2.21A of Code D.

If a film which has been shown to a witness is later lost or unavailable, the witness may give evidence of what he/she saw on that film but the court will have to consider all the relevant circumstances in deciding whether to admit that evidence *and* what weight to attach to it (for a discussion of those circumstances, see *Taylor v Chief Constable of Cheshire* [1986] 1 WLR 1479).

Even if the film or photographs are available for trial, a jury must be warned to exercise considerable care before accepting evidence of such identification (*R v Blenkinsop* [1995] 1 Cr App R 7).

16.4.6 Photographs, Image and Sound Reproduction Generally

The use of photographic and computer-generated images (such as E-Fit) to identify suspects has increased considerably over the last few years. Although the courts will exercise considerable caution when admitting such evidence (see *R v Blenkinsop*, above), these methods of identification are particularly useful. Expert evidence (**see chapter 11**) may be admitted to interpret images on film (see e.g. *R v Stockwell* (1993) 97 Cr App R 260) and police officers who are very familiar with a particular film clip (e.g. of crowd violence at a football match) may be allowed to assist the court in interpreting and explaining events shown within it (see *R v Clare* (1995) 159 JP 142).

E-Fit and other witness-generated images should logically be treated as 'visual statements', in that they represent the witness's recollection of what he/she saw. However, the Court of Appeal has decided that they are not to be so treated (*R v Cook* [1987] QB 417) and therefore the restrictions imposed by the rule against hearsay (**see chapter 11**) will not apply (see also *R v Constantinou* (1989) 91 Cr App R 74 where this ruling was followed in relation to a photofit image).

Voice identification from what a suspect on an identification parade says is dealt with under para. 17 of Annex A to Code D. *R v Gummerson* (1998, unreported) said that PACE Code D related only to *visual* identification.

Generally, a witness may give evidence identifying the defendant's voice (*R v Robb* (1991) 93 Cr App R 161), while expert testimony may be admitted in relation to tape recordings of a voice which is alleged to belong to the defendant. In the latter case, the jury should be allowed to hear the recording(s) so that they can draw their own conclusions (*R v Bentum* (1989) 153 JP 538).

16.5 Fingerprints

16.5.1 Before Conviction

The taking of finger and palm prints is governed by ss. 61 and 63A of the Police and Criminal Evidence Act 1984.

Section 61 provides that:

> *(1)   Except as provided by this section no person's fingerprints may be taken without the appropriate consent.*
>
> *(2)   Consent to the taking of a person's fingerprints must be in writing if it is given at a time when he is at a police station.*

Keynote

Fingerprints of a person detained at a police station may be taken without that person's consent in the following circumstances:

- where an officer of at least the rank of superintendent authorises them to be taken; or

- where the person has been charged or reported for a recordable offence; and

- the person's fingerprints have not already been taken in the course of the investigation of the offence by the police

(s. 61(3)).

A superintendent may only give authority for fingerprints to be taken if he/she has reasonable grounds:

- for suspecting the person is involved in a criminal offence; and

- for believing that the person's fingerprints will tend to confirm or disprove his/her involvement

(s. 61(4)).

The superintendent's authority may be given orally or in writing, but if given orally he/she shall confirm it in writing as soon as is practicable (s. 61(5)).

Where a person's fingerprints are taken without consent that person must be told of the reason before his/her fingerprints are taken and the reason must be recorded as soon as practicable after the fingerprints are taken (s. 61(7)). Where the person is at a police station the reason for taking the fingerprints must be recorded on the custody record (s. 61(8)).

Where a person's fingerprints are taken with or without their consent, at a police station, an officer shall inform him/her that he/she may be subject to a speculative search and record on his/her custody record that the person was so informed as soon as practicable after the fingerprints were taken (s. 61(7A) and (8)).

16.5.2   After Conviction

Section 61(7) provides that:

> *(7)   In a case where by virtue of subsection (3) or (6) above a person's fingerprints are taken without the appropriate consent—*
> *(a)   he shall be told the reason before his fingerprints are taken, and*
> *(b)   the reason shall be recorded as soon as is practicable after the fingerprints are taken.*

Keynote

As with the taking of fingerprints before conviction, where prints are taken without the appropriate consent, the person shall be told the reason before the fingerprints are taken, and the reasons recorded as soon as practicable after the fingerprints are taken (s. 61(7)).

A constable may require a person to attend at a police station to have their fingerprints taken if the person:

- has been convicted of a recordable offence; and

- has not at any time been in police detention for the offence; and

- has not had his/her fingerprints taken either in the course of police investigation of the offence or thereafter.

Such a requirement may be made within one month of conviction (s. 27(1)) of the 1984 Act.

A person who fails to attend in accordance with competent directions may be arrested without warrant (s. 27(2) and (3)).

For the purposes of the requirement under s. 27 the constable must give the person a period of at least seven days within which he/she must attend at a police station. This requirement may direct the person to attend at a specified time of day or between specified times of day.

Section 64 of the 1984 Act provides for the destruction of fingerprints (and other samples) once a person is cleared of the relevant offence or he/she is informed that no prosecution will take place. Although information from samples which are about to be destroyed under s. 64 cannot now be used in the investigation of further offences (s. 64(3B)), this restriction does not appear to apply to fingerprints.

Expert evidence on fingerprints is admissible from suitably qualified individuals who have at least five years' experience in that field.

Whether fingerprint evidence is admissible as evidence tending to prove guilt, depends on:

- the experience and expertise of the witness,
- the number of similar ridge characteristics (if there are fewer than eight ridge characteristics matching the fingerprints of the accused with those found by the police, it is unlikely that a judge would exercise his/her discretion to admit such evidence),
- whether there are dissimilar characteristics,
- the size of print relied on, and
- the quality and clarity of print relied on.

The jury should be warned that expert evidence is not conclusive in itself and that guilt has to be proved in the light of all evidence (*R* v *Buckley*, *The Times*, 12 May 1999).

16.6 Body Samples and Impressions

The taking of samples and impressions is governed by ss. 62 to 63A of the Police and Criminal Evidence Act 1984, together with Code D (paras 5.1 to 5.12) (**see appendix 6**).

Inferences from a defendant's refusal to consent to the taking of certain samples may be drawn by a court.

16.6.1 DNA Profiles

The purpose behind the taking of many samples is to enable the process of DNA profiling. Very basically, this involves an analysis of the sample taken from the suspect (the first sample), an analysis of samples taken from the crime scene or victim (the second sample) and then a comparison of the two. Both the process and the conclusions which might be drawn from the results are set out by Lord Taylor CJ in *R* v *Deen*, *The Times*, 10 January 1994.

The matching process involves creating 'bands' from each sample and then comparing the number of those bands which the two samples share. The more 'matches' that exist between the first and second samples, the less probability there is of that happening by pure chance. A 'good match' between the two samples does not of itself prove that the second sample came from the defendant. In using such samples to prove identification the prosecution will give evidence of:

- the *probability* of such a match happening by chance; and
- the *likelihood* that the person responsible was in fact the defendant.

When applying the 'this' rule (**see para. 16.3**) a jury must consider the second issue, that is, the likelihood of the defendant's being responsible.

The jury's task was set out by Phillips LJ in *R* v *Doheny* [1997] 1 Cr App R 369. In that case, involving a semen sample, his Lordship said:

> If you accept the scientific evidence called by the Crown, that indicates there are probably only four or five white males in the United Kingdom from whom that semen stain could have come. The defendant is one of them. The decision you have to reach, on all the evidence, is whether you are sure that it was the defendant who left that stain or whether it is possible that it is one of that other small group of men who share the same DNA characteristics.

(See also *Blackstone's Criminal Practice*, 1999, section F18.26.)

In most cases there will be other evidence against the defendant, evidence which clearly increases the likelihood of his/her having committed the offence.

16.7 Intimate and Non-intimate Samples

As discussed earlier, there are three key ways to prove a person's involvement in a criminal offence:

- witnesses
- confessions

- scientific evidence.

Given the inherent problems and weaknesses of the first two (**see chapters 6 and 13**), together with the advances being made in scientific procedures, the last of these is becoming more and more important in criminal evidence.

The analysis of intimate and non-intimate samples may provide essential evidence in showing or refuting a person's involvement in an offence.

The police powers to obtain intimate and non-intimate samples are provided by the Police and Criminal Evidence Act 1984 and were extended by amendments made by the Criminal Justice and Public Order Act 1994. Further guidance as to the exercise of these powers is contained within Code D of the PACE Codes of Practice.

16.7.1 Intimate and Non-intimate Samples Defined

Section 65(2) of the 1984 Act provides the definition of intimate and non-intimate samples and states that:

> . . . *'intimate sample' means—*
> *(a)   a sample of blood, semen or any other tissue fluid, urine or pubic hair;*
> *(b)   a dental impression;*
> *(c)   a swab taken from a person's body orifice other than the mouth.*
> . . .
> *'non-intimate sample' means—*
> *(a)   sample of hair other than pubic hair [and includes hair plucked from the root];*
> *(b)   a sample taken from a nail or from under a nail;*
> *(c)   a swab taken from any part of a person's body including the mouth but not any other body orifice;*
> *(d)   saliva*
> *(e)   a footprint or a similar impression of any part of a person's body other than a part of his hand;*
> . . .

Code D, Note 5C sets out advice for taking non-intimate hair samples and provides that:

> *Where hair samples are taken for the purpose of DNA analysis (rather than for other purposes such as making a visual match) the suspect should be permitted a reasonable choice as to what part of the body he wishes the hairs to be taken from. When hairs are plucked they should be plucked individually unless the suspect prefers otherwise and no more should be plucked than the person taking them reasonably considers necessary for a sufficient sample.*

16.7.2 Intimate Samples

Section 62 of the Police and Criminal Evidence Act 1984 sets out police powers to take intimate samples. Code D of the PACE Codes of Practice provides additional guidance as to the exercise of the powers. The provisions of s. 62 together with Code D describe the circumstances and manner in which intimate samples can be taken. These can be understood by considering a number of key issues:

Consent

Before an intimate sample can be taken from a person in police detention, the consent of an officer of the rank of superintendent is necessary, *together with the consent of the person*. Without the consent of *both*, such a sample cannot be taken.

Where a person is not in police detention, an intimate sample may be taken where that person has already provided two (or more) samples in the course of the investigation of the offence, which have proved insufficient for *the same means of analysis*. Should this pre-condition apply then the consent of both a superintendent and the person concerned is necessary, as in the case of a person in police detention.

Note 5E of Code D recognises that a sample may be taken from a person not in police detention, for the purposes of elimination, providing his/her consent is given.

In all cases where an intimate sample is to be taken from a young person aged 14 but under 17, the consent of his/her parents or guardian is also necessary. If the person is a child under 14, the consent of his/her parents or guardian is necessary only.

Grounds for Consent

Regardless of whether the person is in police detention or not, a superintendent may only give his/her authorisation if he/she has reasonable grounds:

• for suspecting the involvement of the person from whom the sample is to be taken in a recordable offence; *and*

• for believing that the sample will tend to confirm or disprove the person's involvement in the offence.

For further discussion on the meaning of 'reasonable grounds to suspect', **see General Police Duties, chapter 2**).

Information to be Given to the Suspect

Where an authorisation has been given and it is proposed to take a sample, an officer shall inform the suspect that the authorisation has been given *and* of the grounds for it being given (including the nature of the offence which the person is suspected of committing). If the person is at a police station then, in addition to the above, an officer must also inform the suspect, before the sample is taken, that the sample may be subject to a 'speculative search'.

(A speculative search is a check made against other samples and information derived from other samples contained in records or held by or on behalf of the police or held in connection with or as a result of an investigation of an offence.)

Paragraph 5.2 of Code D also requires that, before the sample is given, the suspect must be warned that if he/she refuses without good cause, that refusal may harm his/her case if it comes to trial. Where the suspect is in police detention, or is at the police station voluntarily, the officer shall also explain the entitlement to legal advice (as to which, **see chapter 15**).

Recording the Authorisation

A superintendent's authorisation may be given orally but, if so given, it must be confirmed in writing as soon as practicable. The authorisation from the suspect must be given in writing.

Other Information to be Recorded

Where an intimate sample is taken, certain information should be recorded. This information includes:

- the *authorisation* by virtue of which the sample was taken;
- the *grounds* for the authorisation;
- the fact the suspect *consented*;
- where a person is in police detention, the fact that the suspect has been informed that the sample may be subject to a *speculative search*;
- that the *warning* that a refusal may harm the suspect's case has been given.

This information shall be recorded as soon as possible after the sample has been taken. Where a suspect is in police detention the information shall be recorded in the custody record.

Refusal of a Suspect to Give Consent

Where a suspect refuses, without good cause, to provide an intimate sample then, in proceedings against that person for an offence, the court may draw such inferences as appear proper. The court may use such an inference for the purposes of determining:

- guilt;
- whether there is a case to answer;
- whether to commit for trial;
- whether an application to dismiss charges should be granted (where a notice of transfer from a magistrates' court to a Crown Court has been given earlier).

Taking an Intimate Sample

Dental impressions may only be taken by a registered dentist. Intimate samples, other than urine, may only be taken by a registered medical practitioner.

Paragraph 5.12 of Code D sets out the provisions to be followed where clothing needs to removed in circumstances likely to cause embarrassment. These are:

- no person of the opposite sex may be present (other than a medical practitioner or nurse);

- only people whose presence is necessary for the taking of the sample should in fact be present;

- in the case of a mentally disordered person, an appropriate adult of the opposite sex may be present *if specifically requested by the person and the person is readily available*;

- in the case of a juvenile, clothing may only be removed in the absence of an appropriate adult if the person signifies (in the presence of the appropriate adult) that he/she prefers his/her absence and the appropriate adult agrees.

16.7.3   Non-intimate Samples

The taking by police of non-intimate samples is governed by s. 63 of the Police and Criminal Evidence Act 1984. Additional guidance in the exercise of the powers is provided by Code D of the PACE Codes of Practice. The key requirements of these provisions are:

IDENTIFICATION

Consent

A person may consent to the taking of a non-intimate sample. If he/she does so, the consent must be given in writing.

A non-intimate sample may be taken without consent under the following conditions:

- where a person is in police detention or being held in custody by the police under the authority of a court and an officer of the rank of superintendent authorises it to be taken;

- where a person has been charged with a recordable offence (or told he/she is to be reported for such an offence) and has not provided a non-intimate sample in the course of the investigation of the offence *or* where the person *has* had an intimate sample taken but that sample has either proved not suitable for the same means of analysis, or it has proved insufficient;

- where a person has been convicted of a recordable offence.

'Recordable offences' are generally those offences punishable by imprisonment, together with several others designated by statutory instrument.

In order to close a gap in the legislation, the Criminal Evidence (Amendment) Act 1997 was passed, allowing the taking of non-intimate samples without consent in the case of people serving sentences for certain sexual, violent or other specified offences.

The effect of ss. 1 and 2 of the Act is to allow the taking of such samples from people serving a sentence of imprisonment or being detained under a hospital order (under the Mental Health Act 1983) if they were convicted of a recordable offence listed at sch. 1 before 10 April 1995. The provisions also extend to people who were not convicted by reason of their insanity or their unfitness to plead but who were detained at the relevant time under the Mental Health Act 1983.

For the main offences to which these provisions apply **see Crime**.

Grounds for Consent

A superintendent may only give authority for the taking of a non-intimate sample if he/she has reasonable grounds:

- for suspecting the involvement of the person from whom the sample is to be taken in a recordable offence; *and*

- for believing that the sample will tend to confirm *or disprove* the person's involvement in the offence.

Information to be Given to the Suspect

Where an authorisation has been given by a superintendent and it is proposed to take a sample, an officer shall inform the suspect that the authorisation has been given *and* of the grounds for it being given (including the nature of the offence the person is suspected of committing).

Where a non-intimate sample is taken as a result of the suspect being charged, informed he/she is to be reported or following conviction for a recordable offence, he/she must be told of the reason why the sample is to be taken.

IDENTIFICATION

In cases where a person is in police detention, he/she must be informed — before the sample is taken — that the sample may be subject to a 'speculative search' (**see para. 16.7.2**).

Recording the Authorisation

A superintendent's authorisation may be given orally, but if so given, must be confirmed in writing as soon as practicable. The authorisation from the suspect must be given in writing.

Other Information to be Recorded

Where a non-intimate sample is taken as a result of a superintendent's authority, the following information should be recorded:

- the *authorisation* by virtue of which the sample was taken;
- the *grounds* for the authorisation;
- where a person is in police detention the fact that the suspect has been informed that the sample may be subject to a *speculative search*.

This information must be recorded *as soon as possible* after the sample has been taken.

In other cases where a sample is taken without the person's consent, the reason shall be recorded as soon as practicable after the sample is taken.

Where a suspect is in police detention, the information shall be recorded in the custody record.

Use of Force

Paragraph 5.6 of Code D provides that force may be used if necessary to obtain non-intimate samples in the circumstances described. Where force is used, a record should be made of the circumstances and those present at the time.

Taking a Non-intimate Sample

Where clothing needs to be removed in order to take a non-intimate sample, para. 5.12 of the Code D should be applied to prevent embarrassment.

16.7.4 **Power to Require Persons to Attend a Police Station to Provide Samples**

In addition to the powers outlined, s. 63A of the Police and Criminal Evidence Act 1984 also provides for a constable to require a person to attend a police station for samples to be taken. The circumstances under which this requirement can be made are summarised as follows:

When Can the Requirement be Made?

A constable may make the requirement:

- where a person has been charged with a recordable offence or informed that he/she will be reported, or

- where the person has been convicted of a recordable offence

and, in either case, the person has not had a sample taken in the course of the investigation into the offence, or he/she has had a sample taken but it proved either unsuitable for the same means of analysis or the sample was insufficient.

The Period during which a Constable may Make the Requirement

The requirement to attend a police station must be made:

- within one month of the date of charge or of conviction; or
- within one month of the appropriate officer being informed that the sample is not suitable or has proved insufficient for analysis.

In making the requirement the officer:

- shall give the person at least seven days within which the person must attend; and
- may direct the person to attend at a specified time of day or between specified times of day.

Failure to Comply with the Requirement

Should a person fail to comply with the requirement, a constable may arrest the person without a warrant.

An appropriate officer is:

- the officer investigating the offence in the case of a person charged or told he/she will be reported;
- the officer in charge of the police station from which the investigation was conducted in the case of a person convicted.

For the corresponding power to take finger and palm prints, **see para. 16.5**.

16.7.5   **Destruction of Samples**

Where samples are taken in connection with the investigation of an offence, s. 64 of the Police and Criminal Evidence Act 1984 sets out the circumstances where the samples must be destroyed. These are:

- where a person is cleared of that offence;
- it is decided that the person shall not be prosecuted and he/she has not admitted the offence and is dealt with by caution;
- the person is not suspected of having committed the offence.

However, samples will not be destroyed where a person from whom one was taken has been convicted. This allows for all samples in a case to be available for any later miscarriage of justice trial. Where samples are retained because of this proviso (but would otherwise be destroyed) information derived from such samples cannot be used in evidence against the person from whom they are taken or for the purposes of any investigation of an offence (s. 64(3B)). For the situation in relation to finger and palm prints, **see para. 16.5**.

CHAPTER SEVENTEEN

INTERVIEWS

17.1   Introduction

Much police time is spent interviewing witnesses and suspects. Confessions are often seen by the police to be an important part of the prosecution case but have frequently been a source of attack by the defence. The power imbalance between a detained person and his/her custodians has been an issue which has often brought into question the reliability of any confession, particularly as it had, until recently, been the right of an individual detainee to remain silent without any adverse inferences being drawn. The PACE Codes of Practice are intended to provide some protection to people being interviewed by police and lay down guidelines as to how interviews should be conducted. This protection means that confessions may be held to be inadmissible because of:

- the conduct of the interviewing officers (s. 76(2)(a) of the Police and Criminal Evidence Act 1984);

- the unreliability of the confession (s. 76(2)(b)); or

- unfairness in the proceedings (s. 78). It may seem that the balance is in favour of the detained person. However the position now is that, while a person may still remain silent and the rules remain to preserve this right, inferences may now been drawn from a person's silence in some circumstances (**see chapter 11**).

It is not unusual for it to be alleged that officers have fabricated evidence or obtained a confession through trickery or by some kind of oppression. In order to provide safeguards against the risk of evidence from questioning being unreliable or obtained in a manner that breaches an individual's remaining right to silence, there are restrictions and guidelines on police questioning. These rules can be found throughout Code C of the PACE Codes of Practice which is primarily concerned with questioning of persons by police officers. Failure to follow these rules may lead to evidence being excluded and/or disciplinary charges. For conduct that might lead to the exclusion of evidence, **see para. 13.3**. For police disciplinary proceedings, **see General Police Duties, chapter 1**.

17.2 What is an Interview?

Not all discussions between the police and members of the public will be protected or governed by the PACE Codes of Practice. Code C, para. 11.1A defines an interview as:

. . . the questioning of a person regarding his involvement or suspected involvement in a criminal offence or offences which . . . is required to be carried out under caution.

Keynote

If a person is asked questions for reasons *other than obtaining evidence about his/her involvement or suspected involvement in an offence*, this is not an interview (and a caution need not be given). (For the use of cautions, **see para. 17.3.**) This point is confirmed in the case of *R* v *McGuinness* (1998, unreported), where the court confirmed that it was only when a person was suspected of an offence that the caution must be administered before questioning. Consequently, in *R* v *Miller* [1998] Crim LR 209 the court held that asking a person the single question, 'Are these ecstasy tablets?' criminally implicated the person and therefore the conversation was an interview (i.e. it would not be necessary to ask such a question if there were no suspicion that the tablets were a controlled substance).

Guidance on when questions do not amount to an interview is given by Code C, para. 10.1:

. . . [A person] therefore need not be cautioned if questions are put for other purposes, for example, solely to establish his identity or his ownership of any vehicle or to obtain information in accordance with any relevant statutory requirement (see paragraph 10.5C) or in furtherance of the proper and effective conduct of a search (for example to determine the need to search in the exercise of powers of stop and search or to seek cooperation while carrying out a search), or to seek verification of a written record in accordance with paragraph 11.13.

Keynote

Before a person can be interviewed about their involvement in an offence, that person must be cautioned. So it might be said that an interview is any questioning of a person after such time as a caution has been or should have been administered. However, where a person is arrested for an offence, he/she must also be cautioned (**see General Police Duties, chapter 2**).

17.3 The Caution

The wording of the caution can be found in Code C, para. 10.4. The caution was amended after the introduction of the Criminal Justice and Public Order Act 1994 in order to incorporate the limited erosion of the right to silence. The wording of the caution is as follows:

You do not have to say anything. But it may harm your defence if you do not mention when questioned something which you later rely on in court. Anything you do say may be given in evidence.

If a person is questioned without being cautioned when a caution should have been given, any admissions made by that person are likely to be inadmissible in evidence. Conversely, admissions of guilt made by a person who has not been cautioned will be admissible if a caution was not required, so its important to be aware of when to administer a caution and, in cases of doubt, to err on the side of caution. Should an interview be excluded, this may have implications on other evidence obtained as a consequence of the confession (**see para. 13.2.2**).

A caution should be administered to all people who are:

- arrested for an offence, and/or

- where Code C, para. 10.1 applies.

Code C, para. 10.1 provides that:

> *A person whom there are grounds to suspect of an offence must be cautioned before any questions about it (or further questions if it is his answers to previous questions which provide the grounds for suspicion) are put to him regarding his involvement or suspected involvement in that offence if his answers or his silence (i.e. failure or refusal to answer a question or to answer satisfactorily) may be given in evidence to a court in a prosecution. . . .*

Keynote

If a person does not appear to understand the caution, the officer who has given it should go on to explain it in his/her own words (Code C, Note 10C).

The caution must be given where there are 'grounds to suspect the person of an offence'. Normally the 1984 Act and the Codes of Practice refer to 'reasonable grounds', whereas here the reference is simply to 'grounds'. This would suggest that the level of evidence/suspicion needed before a caution is given to a suspect may be *lower* than that needed to arrest the person. This would mean that a person may need to be cautioned when spoken to about offences for which there is no power of arrest or on occasions where there is a power of arrest but the officer's level of suspicion is not sufficient to justify an arrest (**see General Police Duties, chapter 2**).

The courts have given some guidance as to when a caution should be administered. There must be real *grounds* for suspicion; a mere hunch is not sufficient. The grounds have to be such as to lead to suspicion that an offence has been committed by that person. This view is confirmed in *Batley* v *DPP*, *The Times*, 5 March 1998, where the court accepted that, in general terms, where police officers had nothing more than a hunch that an offence was being committed, there would not be enough to activate the Code. However, it was necessary to caution a person before asking questions which went to the very heart of the issue as to whether he/she might be committing an offence, especially since the suspect was being invited to incriminate himself/herself.

Where the questions go beyond issues raised by Code C, para. 10.1 and go to the question of guilt, then this is likely to be an interview for the purposes of the Police and Criminal Evidence Act 1984. In *Crown Prosecution Service* v *O'Shea*, unreported, 1998, police were called to a road traffic accident. O'Shea, the owner of the vehicle, was near the car, exhibiting signs of drunkenness and there was no one else in the vicinity who might have been driving the vehicle. The officer said to O'Shea the words, '*An accident has just happened that is alleged was your fault*'. The court held that it was clear than when the officer had asked O'Shea whether he was driving his vehicle at the time of the accident, the officer had known that he was the owner of the vehicle and therefore the question was not solely to establish whether he was the owner. Accordingly, the thrust of the question was whether he had committed an offence. The defendant's subsequent answer was held to be inadmissible as the PACE Codes of Practice had not been complied with.

O'Shea can be contrasted with *R* v *Maguire* [1989] Crim LR 815 where the court held that Code C does not prevent a police officer from asking questions at or near the scene of the crime to elicit an explanation which if true or accepted, would clear the suspect.

Once a person has been cautioned, consideration of further cautions must be given. The need for additional cautions is provided for by the PACE Codes of Practice. In addition, in *R* v *Miller* [1998] Crim LR 209, the court said that one caution was not necessarily enough, and before other questions are asked of a suspect at a later stage, a further caution may be necessary.

In addition to the duty to caution a suspect, there will be occasions where a person arrested for an offence will have to be given a 'special warning' in interview. Special warnings are concerned with a person's right to silence.

There will be occasions where suspects make unsolicited comments implicating them in an offence before they are suspected of any involvement and therefore before they are cautioned (or further cautioned if already suspected). Such statements are likely to be admissible provided the PACE Codes of Practice are complied with. Code C, para. 11.13 provides that:

> *A written record shall also be made of any comments made by a suspected person, including unsolicited comments, which are outside the context of an interview but which might be relevant to the offence. Any such record must be timed and signed by the maker. Where practicable the person shall be given the opportunity to read that record and to sign it as correct or to indicate the respects in which he considers it inaccurate. Any refusal to sign shall be recorded. [See Note 11D]*

Note 11D provides that:

> *When a suspect agrees to read records of interviews and of other comments and to sign them as correct, he should be asked to endorse the record with the words such as 'I agree that this is a correct record of what was said' and add his signature. Where the suspect does not agree with the record, the officer should record the details of any disagreement and then ask the suspect to read these and then sign them to the effect that they accurately reflect his disagreement. Any refusal to sign when asked to do so shall be recorded.*

Keynote

It is particularly important to record the comment and give the person an opportunity to see what has been recorded and to comment/endorse it.

In *R* v *Miller* (above) the court held that Code C, para. 11.13 requires a written record, timed and signed by the suspect as correct or an opportunity for the suspect to indicate which parts were inaccurate.

If the endorsement cannot be achieved straight away, it is no defence for the prosecution to argue that it was not practicable. This is demonstrated by *Batley* v *DPP*, *The Times*, 5 March 1998 where it was held that as the Code did not require an *immediate* endorsement and no time factor was laid down, there was nothing to constrain the police from returning the next day to get their endorsement.

17.4   Interview of Person Not Under Arrest

If a person has not been arrested then he/she can be interviewed almost anywhere (but an officer intending to interview a person on private property must consider whether he/she is trespassing, **see General Police Duties, chapter 2**). If the interview with a person not under arrest takes place in a police station, Code C, para. 3.15 and Note 1A must be followed.

If the interview is to be with a juvenile, Code C, para. 11.15, gives guidance as to when interviews should take place at a juvenile's place of education. This should only be in exceptional circumstances and with the agreement of the principal or the principal's nominee. The juvenile's parent(s) or person(s) responsible for his/her welfare and the appropriate adult (if a different person) should be notified of the interview and be afforded reasonable time in which to attend. The principal or nominee can act as the appropriate adult where waiting for an appropriate adult would cause unreasonable delay. This is not the case where the juvenile is suspected of an offence against his/her educational establishment.

In cases where the person is not under arrest, certain information must be given to him/her. This is covered by Code C, para. 10.2 which provides that:

Whenever a person who is not under arrest is initially cautioned or is reminded that he is under caution (see paragraph 10.5) he must at the same time be told that he is not under arrest and is not obliged to remain with the officer (see paragraph 3.15).

Keynote

For the situation where a person is a police station voluntarily and not under arrest, see Code C, para. 3.15 (**see General Police Duties, chapter 2**).

17.5   Interview of Person Under Arrest

Any interview of a person who is under arrest must take place at a police station (Code C, para. 11.1) or other authorised place of detention unless waiting until the interview can be conducted at such a place is likely to:

- lead to interference with or harm to evidence connected with an offence or interference with or physical harm to other people; or

- lead to the alerting of other people suspected of having committed an offence but not yet arrested for it; or

- hinder the recovery of property obtained in consequence of the commission of an offence.

Code C requires that interviewing in any of these circumstances shall cease once the relevant risk has been averted or the necessary questions have been put in order to attempt to avert that risk (para. 11.1).

An interview can also be started without an appropriate adult or legal representative being present in limited circumstances (see Code C, paras 11.1 and 6.6 and Annex C).

If a person has been arrested by one police force on behalf of another and the lawful period of detention in respect of that offence has not yet begun (in accordance with s. 41 of the Police and Criminal Evidence Act 1984 (**see para. 15.4.5**), no questions may be put to him/her about the offence while he/she is in transit between the forces except in order to clarify any voluntary statement made by him/her (Code C, para. 14.1).

If a person is in police detention at a hospital, he/she may not be questioned without the agreement of a responsible doctor (Code C, para. 14.2). If an interview does take place, the interviewing officer must inform the custody officer (Note 14A).

If questioning does take place in any of these circumstances it will affect the suspect's 'detention clock' (**see chapter 15**). The Custody officer must be informed of such an interview as it may affect the lawfulness of the suspect's detention (**see para 15.5.1**).

17.6 Person Charged with an Offence

Once a person has been charged with an offence generally he/she cannot be interviewed about the offence unless it is necessary:

- to prevent or minimise harm or loss to some other person or to the public; or

- to clear up an ambiguity in a previous answer or statement; or

- in the interest of justice that the person should have questions put to him/her and have an opportunity to comment on information concerning the offence which has come to light since he/she was charged or informed that he/she might be prosecuted.

It should be noted that the service of the Notice of Intended Prosecution under ss. 1 and 2 of the Road Traffic Offenders Act 1988 (**see Road Traffic, chapter 3**), does not amount to informing a person that he/she may be prosecuted for an offence and so does not preclude further questioning in relation to that offence (Note 16A).

If a person is interviewed for any other reason, the interview is likely to be inadmissible in evidence.

Where a person is interviewed after charge, Code C, para. 16.5 provides that:

> . . . *Before any such questions are put to him, he shall be warned that he does not have to say anything but that anything he does say may be given in evidence and reminded of his rights to legal advice in accordance with paragraph 6.5 above.*

17.7 When Must an Interview be Held?

Code C, para. 16.1 provides that:

> *When an officer considers that there is sufficient evidence to prosecute a detained person, and that there is sufficient evidence for a prosecution to succeed, and that the person has said all that he wishes to say about the offence, he shall without delay (and subject to the following qualification) bring him before the custody officer who shall then be responsible for considering whether or not he should be charged. . . .*

Keynote

It is suggested that, in a case where a suspect has not been interviewed about an offence, Code C, para. 16.1, requires that person to be asked if he/she has anything further to say about the matter, in which case this will be an interview.

This view is supported by the case of *R* v *Pointer* [1997] Crim LR 676 which held that giving a suspect the opportunity to say something more when the officer already has enough evidence to charge is an interview within the definition of Code C, para. 11.1A, and, therefore, an event which attracts the protection of a caution, legal representation and tape recording.

Interviews in these circumstances are conducted to allow the suspect to make any additional comments and for the interviewing officers to follow up on those responses. If the interview is held for any other reason it is likely to be inadmissible. This was the case in *R* v *Pointer* where the court held that there was sufficient evidence to charge prior to the interview and consequently Code C, para. 16.1 had not been complied with.

17.8 Conducting and Recording Interviews

The conduct of officers and the proper treatment of the suspect during an interview are essential if an interview is to be admissible in evidence. If an interview is not conducted properly, confessions made during the interview may be excluded (**see chapter 13**). The PACE Codes of Practice are there to afford suspects proper protection from false confessions and treatment which may lead a court to the conclusion that the confession may not be reliable. It is essential, therefore, that officers are fully aware of the relevant Codes and comply with them. For occasions when evidence may be excluded, **see chapter 13**. For evidential purposes interviews need to be recorded. An accurate record must be made of each interview with a person suspected of an offence, whether or not the interview takes place at a police station Code C, para 11.5(a).

Interviews fall into two main groups:

*   those that are tape recorded; and

*   those where the only record will be made in writing.

If a suspect makes unsolicited comments which are outside the context of an interview but which might be relevant to the offence, those comments should be recorded and Code C, para. 11.13 should be followed (**see para. 13.3**). Code C, paras 11.5 to 11.8 give guidance as to what must be included in the record and when the record should be made.

17.8.1 When Interviews Must Be Taped

The interviewing of suspects is governed by PACE Code of Practice E. Code E, paras 3.1 and 3.4 set out which interviews at a police station must be tape recorded. The most noticeable absence from this list is for interviews about matters which can only be tried summarily. These requirements do not *preclude* other interviews being tape recorded. Investigators may well be advised to tape record interviews concerning summarily only offences as it may be more difficult for the defence to suggest any confession was fabricated. If these interviews are tape recorded, they must follow the requirements of tape recorded interviews (see Code E, Note 3A).

The whole of each interview shall be recorded, including the taking and reading back of any statement (Code E, para. 3.5).

All interviews listed in Code E, para. 3.1 conducted at a police station must be tape recorded *unless* the custody officer authorises the interviewing officer not to tape record the interview. If the custody officer authorises the interview to go ahead without being tape recorded, the interview must be recorded in writing. A custody officer authorising this may have to justify the decision at court and the reasons for his/her decision should be recorded. Code E, para. 3.3 allows the custody officer to make this decision where:

- It is not reasonably practicable to tape record the interview because of:

  - failure of the equipment; or
  - the non-availability of a suitable interview room or recorder; and
  - the custody officer considers on reasonable grounds that the interview should not be delayed until the failure has been rectified or a suitable room or recorder becomes available.

- or it is clear from the outset that no prosecution will ensue.

Further, Code E, para. 3.1 does not apply to:

- certain interviews involving terrorism (Code E, para. 3.2(a));

- an interview with a person suspected on reasonable grounds of an offence under s. 1 of the Official Secrets Act 1911 (Code E, para. 3.2(b));

- people who come within Code C, para. 1.12.

For cases where a person objects to the interview being tape recorded, see Code E, para. 4.5.

17.8.2 Preparation before Interview at Police Station

Preparation is essential before any interview (indeed it is the first step in the PEACE interviewing model). This preparation should include the following points:

- Decide where the interview will be conducted. Consider the availability of a room and the timing of the interview.

- The location must have a seat for the person being interviewed (Code C, para. 12.5) and should be adequately lit, heated and ventilated (Code C, para. 12.4). The detained person must also have adequate clothing (Code C, para. 8.5). (It will be a question of fact as to what amounts to adequate clothing and it is suggested that if the clothing is such as to degrade the detained person or make him/her uncomfortable, it may lead to the confession being held to be unreliable.)

- If the interview is being taped, ensure that there are sufficient tapes for the anticipated length of the interview (or at least until the first break period). If the interview is being recorded in writing, ensure there are enough forms.

- If the interview is being taped, ensure the notice as set out in Code E, para. 4.16 is available.

- In deciding the timing of the interview you will need to consider detainee's rest periods (Code C, para. 12.2) review times and whether the detained person is fit to be interviewed at the proposed time of interview (Code C, para. 12.3). If the detained person is not fit, or he/she is having a rest period, then the interview must be delayed unless Code C, para. 12.2(i) to (iii) or Annex D apply.

- If legal advice has been requested you must arrange for the legal representative to be present at the interview unless Code C, para. 6.6 applies.

- If a person has asked for legal advice and an interview is initiated in the absence of a legal adviser (e.g. where the person has agreed to be interviewed without his/her legal adviser being present or because of the urgent need to interview under Code C, para. 11.1), a record must be made in the interview record (Code C, para. 6.17).

- If an appropriate adult should be present, arrange for his/her attendance. (For the definition of appropriate adult, see Code C, para. 1.7.)

- If an interpreter is needed for the interview, arrange for his/her attendance. Information on obtaining the services of a suitably qualified interpreter for the deaf or for people who do not understand English is given in Code C, Note 3D.

It is also important to draw up an interview plan and to include any relevant areas that may provide a general or specific defence (as to which, **see Crime, chapter 4**).

17.8.3 Starting Interviews

In order to interview a detained person, the interviewing officer must obtain permission from the custody officer. An entry must be made in the custody record to record that the interviewing officer accepts responsibility for the detained person. If the request to hand over the detained person is declined, the custody officer must record this fact and the reasons why on the custody record (Code C, para. 12.9). The responsibility for the detained person at this stage rests with the officer to whom the transfer is made and remains with this person until the detained person is returned to the custody officer (s. 39(2) of the Police and Criminal Evidence Act 1984). Section 39 of the 1984 Act provides that:

> (2) *If this custody officer, in accordance with any code of practise issued under this Act, transfers or permits the transfer of a person in police detention—*
> *(a)   to the custody of a police officer investigating an offence for which that person is in police detention; or*
> *(b)   to the custody of an officer who has charge of that person outside the police station,*
> *the custody officer shall cease in relation to that person to be subject to the duty imposed on him by subsection (1)(a) above; and it shall be the duty of the officer to whom the transfer is made to ensure that he is treated in accordance with the provisions of this Act and of any such codes of practice as are mentioned in subsection (1) above.*

17.8.4   Preliminary Issues for Interviews Not Being Tape Recorded

Before an interview begins the following points must be dealt with:

- Immediately before the commencement of the interview remind the suspect of his/her right to legal advice (Code C, para. 11.2) and make a note of this reminder and any response in the interview record.

- For the interview record, identify all officers present in the interview as required by Code C, para. 12.6.

- If an appropriate adult is present, inform that person of his/her role (Code C, para. 11.16).

- Administer the caution (Code C, para. 10.1) (and re-administer where appropriate, **see para. 17.3**).

17.8.5   Preliminary Issues for Interviews Being Tape Recorded

Before an interview commences the following points must be dealt with:

- Break open tape seals in the presence of the suspect (Code E, para. 4.1).

- Load tapes in the presence of the suspect and set to record (Code E, para. 4.1).

- Inform the suspect about the tape recording in accordance with Code E, para. 4.2.

- Verbally identify all persons present at the interview for the tape.

- Administer the caution (Code E, para. 4.3) (and re-administer where appropriate, **see para. 17.3**).

- Remind the suspect of his/her right to free legal advice (Code E, para. 4.3A and Code C, para 6.5) and ensure that the response is recorded on the tape (for instance a nod of the head would not be picked up by a tape recorder).

17.8.6   What Should be Disclosed to the Solicitor

It is important not to confuse the duty of disclosure to a person once charged with the need to disclose evidence to a suspect before interviewing them. After a person has been charged, and before trial, the rules of disclosure are clear (**see chapter 14**) and almost all material must be disclosed to the defence.

However, this is not necessarily the case at the interview stage of the investigation. There is no specific provision within the Police and Criminal Evidence Act 1984 for the disclosure of any information by the police at the police station, with the exception of the custody record and, in identification cases, the initial description given by the witnesses. Further, there is nothing within the Criminal Justice and Public Order Act 1994 that states that information must be disclosed before an inference from silence can be made. Indeed, in *R* v *Imran* and *Hussein* [1997] Crim LR 754 the court held that it is totally wrong to submit that a defendant should be prevented from lying by being presented with the whole of the evidence against him/her prior to the interview.

In *R* v *Argent* [1997] Crim LR 346 the court dismissed the argument that an inference could not be drawn under s. 34 of the Criminal Justice and Public Order Act 1994 because there had not been full disclosure at the interview. However, the court did recognise that it may be a factor to take into account, but it would be for the jury to decide whether the failure to answer questions was reasonable.

In *R* v *Roble* [1997] Crim LR 449, the court suggested that an inference would not be drawn where a solicitor gave advice to remain silent where, for example, the interviewing officer had disclosed too little of the case for the solicitor usefully to advise his/her client, or where the nature of the offence, or the material in the hands of the police, was so complex or related to matters so long ago that no sensible immediate response was feasible.

There is a balance to be struck between providing the solicitor with enough information to understand the nature of the case against his/her client and keeping back material which, if disclosed, may allow the suspect the opportunity to avoid implicating himself/herself. The disclosure of material may well be a factor which the defendant relies on in showing that the failure to mention possible defences was reasonable. If the officers are not hoping to draw inferences from silence then tactically they may decide not to disclose as much information — it will be a question of fact in each case.

17.8.7 Conduct During Interview

All Interviews

- Code C, para. 11.3 reiterates the fact that officers must not act oppressively.

- If a complaint is made by the suspect the interviewing officer must inform the custody officer and follow Code C, para. 12.8 (if the interview is being tape recorded, leave the tape running (Code E, Note 4H)).

- Officers should only indicate the possible effect of refusing to answer questions or of answering questions if he/she is asked about those possible effects by the suspect *unless this is done as part of a special warning* (see Code C, para. 11.3 and Code E, para 4.3).

- Code C, Note 11B reminds officers of the risks associated with the reliability of interviewing juveniles or people who are mentally disordered or suffering from mental impairment.

At the start of the interview the investigating officer should put to the suspect any significant statement or silence which occurred before his/her arrival at the police station and ask the suspect whether he/she confirms the earlier statement or silence and whether he/she wishes to add anything. Code C, para. 11.2A defines a 'significant' statement or silence. This aspect of the interview is very important in terms of establishing whether the facts are disputed. If they are not disputed at this stage, it is unlikely that they will be challenged at any later court hearing and if challenged the defence will have to explain why this was not done at the time of the interview. If the suspect remains silent in relation to a 'significant silence' it may give rise to an adverse inference being drawn under s. 34 of the Criminal Justice and Public Order Act 1994 if the person raises it in his/her defence at court. (As this is very important issue, it may be necessary to delay the interview until the arrest notes are completed or the officers witnessing the offence/arrest have been consulted to ensure that all matters are put to the suspect at this stage.)

Issues Specific to Tape Recorded Interviews

- If the equipment fails, rectify the fault quickly if possible. If this is not possible, look for an alternative recording machine or room. If none available, seek the authority of the custody officer to continue without the interview being tape recorded (see Code E, para. 4.12).

- If tape breaks, follow Code E, Note 4M.

- When the tapes are removed from the recorder they must be retained (see Code E, para. 4.13).

- If you need to change tapes during interview, follow Code E, para. 4.8.

- If a suspect objects to the interview being tape recorded at any stage of the interview, the procedure in Code E, para. 4.5 must be followed and Note 4G should be taken into account in deciding whether to continue to record the interview on tape.

- If a suspect indicates that he/she wishes to tell the police about matters not connected with the offence(s) being investigated but does not wish this information to be recorded on tape, Code E, para. 4.7 requires this to be dealt with at the conclusion of the formal interview. Any comment by the suspect would still need to be recorded in writing.

Breaks

Breaks from interviewing must be made at recognised meal times (Code C, para. 12.7). Short breaks for refreshment must also be provided at intervals of approximately two hours. Code C, Note 12C gives guidance on how long breaks should be. Code C, para. 12.7 sets out the exceptions to the requirement to provide breaks. These exceptions exist where to break the interview would:

- involve a risk of harm to people or serious loss of, or damage to property;

- delay unnecessarily the person's release from custody; or

- otherwise prejudice the outcome of the investigation.

Any decision to delay a break during an interview must be recorded, with grounds, in the interview record (either on the written record or on the tape) (Code C, para. 12.11).

Solicitors and Legal Advice

A 'solicitor' for the purposes of the Codes of Practice means:

- a solicitor holding a current practising certificate;

- a trainee solicitor;

- a duty solicitor representative or an accredited representative included on the register of representatives maintained by the Legal Aid Board

  (Code C, para. 6.12).

- Where a solicitor is available at the time the interview begins or while it is in progress, the solicitor must be allowed to be present while the person in interviewed (Code C, para. 6.8). (This applies unless the suspect states that he/she does not want the solicitor to be present.)

- If a solicitor arrives at the station to see a suspect, the suspect must be asked whether he/she would like to see the solicitor *regardless of what legal advice has already been received*. The solicitor's attendance and the suspect's decision must be recorded in the custody record (Code C, para. 6.15).

- If the investigating officer considers that a solicitor is acting in such a way that he/she is unable properly to put questions to the suspect, he/she will stop the interview and consult an officer not below the rank of superintendent, if one is readily available, otherwise an officer not below the rank of inspector who is not connected with the investigation to decide whether that solicitor should be excluded from the interview. The interview may also have to be stopped in order to allow another solicitor to be instructed (Code C, para. 6.10). For the proper role of the legal representatives, see Code C, Note 6D.

- If a request for legal advice is made during an interview, the interviewing officer must stop the interview and arrange for legal advice to be provided. If the suspect changes his/her mind again, the interview can continue provided Code C, para. 6.6 is complied with.

It is important to remember that Code C, para. 6.4 reminds officers that they should *not* try and dissuade the detained person from obtaining legal advice.

17.8.8   When Must the Interview be Concluded?

Guidance is provided by Code C, para. 11.4 as to when an interview should be concluded. Paragraph 11.4 states that the interview shall cease if the investigating officer considers that:

- a prosecution should be brought against the detained person, and

- there is sufficient evidence for a prosecution to succeed, and

- the detained person has been asked if he/she has anything further to say about the offence(s) and has indicated that he/she has said all that he/she wishes to say about the offence.

The investigating officer shall then bring detained person before the custody officer for charge.

The interview may continue until the above conditions are satisfied with regard to other offences being investigated (Code C, para. 16.1).

It is important to remember that the interview should not be concluded at the point when there is sufficient evidence to prosecute but when there is sufficient evidence for a prosecution to succeed. Once there is enough evidence to prosecute, it may still be necessary to cover those other points in the interview that may be relevant to the defence case (**see Crime, chapter 4**). If these points are not covered in the interview, the defence may surprise the prosecution case with matters that the prosecution have not covered or with issues that may result in the loss of an inference being drawn from the suspect's silence. This was considered in *R* v *McGuinness* (1998, unreported) where the court held that the words 'sufficient evidence to prosecute' and 'sufficient evidence for a prosecution to succeed' in Code C, para. 11.4 must involve some consideration of any explanation, or lack of one, from the suspect. It would depend on the facts of a case whether the stage where a suspect ought to be charged has been reached. As a word of caution, the court also said that under Code C, paras 16.1 and 11.4 it was not open for a suspect to be questioned beyond the point when he/she ought to have been charged. If the suspect was questioned beyond that point, then the interview was liable to be ruled inadmissible and the content would not be available to support the prosecution case.

17.8.9 Special Groups

As a confession can be very damning evidence against a defendant, it is important to provide safeguards that give all suspects the same level of protection. The PACE Codes of Practice recognise certain groups as being in need of additional protection. These groups include juveniles, people who do not speak English, those suffering from a mental impairment and those who are deaf. Such suspects must not be interviewed without the relevant person being present.

For juveniles and those suffering from a mental impairment (or who appear to be such), an appropriate adult must be present (Code C, para. 11.14).

Under code C, para 13.2, a person capable of acting as interpreter is required where:

* the suspect has difficulty in understanding English;

* the interviewing officer cannot speak the person's own language; and

* the suspect wishes an interpreter to be present.

If the suspect appears to be deaf or there is any doubt about his/her hearing or speaking ability, an interpreter should be found (unless he/she agrees *in writing* to proceed without an interpreter) (Code C, para. 13.5). This requirement also applies in the case of the appropriate adult who appears to be deaf or there is doubt about his/her hearing or speaking ability (Code C, para. 13.6).

There are limited circumstances where an interview may be conducted without an interpreter or appropriate adult being present. These are set out in Code C, para. 11.1 or Annex C. Once those conditions no longer apply, the interview must be suspended until the appropriate person is present.

Where interpreters are required, Code C, paras 13.3 to 13.11 are to be followed.

Taped Interviews and Special Groups

If the suspect is deaf or there is doubt about his/her hearing ability, a contemporaneous written record should be made as well as the tape recording. This record should be the same as where there is no taped record of the interview (Code E, para. 4.4).

17.8.10 Special Warnings

Now that inferences can be drawn from a suspect's silence (albeit in limited circumstances), it is necessary to warn the person of the dangers of remaining silent. For this reason the 'special warning' was introduced (**see para. 11.6.3**). If the special warning is not given, inferences from silence will not be allowed to boost the prosecution case. Code C, paras 10.5A to 10.5C must be followed if any questions are to be put to the arrested suspect about:

- any object, marks or substances found on the him/her, or

- in or on his/her clothing or footwear, or

- otherwise in his/her possession, or

- in the place where he/she was arrested.

These provisions also apply to any questions about why the suspect was:

- at the scene of the offence,

- at or near the time of the offence for which the constable who saw the suspect there arrested him/her, and

- unable to account for his/her presence at or near the scene of the offence.

It must be made clear to the suspect what matters he/she is being asked to answer and the consequences of remaining silent on each occasion.

17.8.11 Conclusion of Interview

All Interviews

- The person interviewed (and the appropriate adult or the suspect's solicitor if present during the interview (Code C, para. 11.11)) must be given an opportunity to read the interview record and to sign it as correct or to indicate the respects in which he/she considers it inaccurate (Code C, para. 11.10). If the person concerned cannot read or refuses to read the record or to sign it, the senior police officer present shall read it to him/her (Code C, para. 11.10). If there is any delay in recording the interview, if practicable, the suspect should still be given an opportunity to read the statement.

- Any refusal to sign the record must be recorded (Code C, para. 11.12).

- If an interpreter has been present at the interview, he/she should be given an opportunity to read the record and certify its accuracy.

- If the person is in police detention, return him/her to the custody officer, informing that officer whether the Codes have been complied with, if any incidents occurred and whether there were any breaches of the Codes (s. 39(3) of the Police and Criminal Evidence Act 1984).

Tape Recorded Interviews

- The person interviewed must be offered the opportunity to clarify anything he/she has said during the interview and to add anything he/she may wish (Code E, para. 4.14). This may be important when the case comes to court and the defence try to explain why certain things were said during the interview.

- Turn off the tape and seal it with a master tape label (Code E, para. 4.15). If the seal on the tape needs to be broken for any reason, follow Code E, para. 6.2 or, if decision has been made not to institute criminal proceedings, follow Code E, para. 6.3.

- Sign the label and ask the suspect and any third party present to sign it also. If the suspect or third party refuses to sign it, an inspector, or if not available a custody officer, shall be called into the interview room and asked to sign it (Code E, para. 4.15).

- Hand the suspect the notice which explains the use which will be made of the tape recording and the arrangement for access to it (Code E, para. 4.16).

- Make a personal notebook entry about the interview as required by Code E, para. 5.1.

- Follow force standing orders or local procedures in relation to tape security whether or not the person is charged (Code E, paras 6.1 and 5.2).

17.9 Statements from Suspects

Statements under caution, particularly of a detained person, are less common than interviews. If a person has been interviewed on tape or an interview has been recorded contemporaneously in writing, a statement under caution should only normally be conducted at the person's express wish (Code C, Note 12A). A statement must not be elicited by the use of oppression (Code C, para. 11.3) (to this end the person should not be required to stand (Code C, para. 12.5)) and, if written at the police station, the statement must be on the correct forms (Code C, para. 12.12). Code C, Annex D sets out how the statement should be taken and matters that must be included in the statement whether it is written by the suspect or a police officer.

When completing the statement, the person must always be invited to write down what he/she wants to say and should be allowed to do so without any prompting, except that a police officer may indicate which matters are material or question any ambiguity in the statement. In the case of a person making a statement in a language other than English, Code C, para. 13.4 provides that:

(a) *the interpreter shall take down the statement in the language in which it is made;*
(b) *the person making the statement shall be invited to sign it; and*
(c) *an official English translation shall be made in due course.*

(In these cases, para. 13.4 means that the person will not be invited to write the statement themselves which is an exception to the guidance in Annex D.)

A juvenile or a person who is mentally disordered or mentally handicapped, *whether suspected or not*, must not be asked to provide or sign a written statement in the absence of the appropriate adult unless Code C, para. 11.1 or Annex C applies (Code C, para. 11.4). Statements made by an accused under caution to the police are confidential. It is clearly implicit in the relationship between the police and the accused that the information, before being used in open court, is used only for the purposes for which it is provided and not for extraneous purposes, such as the media. However, the obligation of confidentiality (which is now included in the Police Code of Conduct; **see General Police Duties, chapter 1**) in respect of such a statement will be brought to an end where the contents of the statement are already in the public domain (*Bann* v *British Broadcasting Corporation and Another* (1998) 148 NLJ 979).

17.10 Interviews on Behalf of Scottish Forces and Vice Versa

The Crown Prosecution Service, in consultation with the Scottish Crown Office, has produced guidelines in relation to the potential admissibility of interview evidence when officers from England and Wales conduct interviews on behalf of Scottish forces and vice versa. These interviews relate to people subject to cross-border arrest as provided by ss. 136–140 of the Criminal Justice and Public Order Act 1994 (**see General Police Duties, chapter 2**).

17.10.1 Suspects in Scotland: Interview Evidence Required for Prosecutions in England and Wales

The PACE Codes of Practice governing interviews of suspects do not apply in Scotland. There is no statutory or common law requirement that an interview should be tape recorded in Scotland. In practice, all interviews conducted by CID officers are tape recorded.

Under the legislation governing prosecutions in Scotland, the suspect is not entitled to legal representation during an interview. Suspects are not warned that a failure to answer questions may harm their defence. Failure to answer questions cannot harm their defence. Interviews under caution are, however, subject to guidelines which incorporate judicial precedent fairness to the accused.

In investigations of any great seriousness, English/Welsh constables should attend in Scotland, arrest the suspect and bring him/her back to their jurisdiction for interview. If such an arrest is made, the arrested person must be taken either to the nearest designed police station in England or a designated police station in a police area in England and Wales in which the offence is being investigated (s. 137(1) and (7)(a) of the 1994 Act).

Scottish officers do not have any statutory or common law powers to detain or arrest a suspect without warrant who is believed to have committed an offence in England and Wales. If there is insufficient evidence for the issue of a warrant, and the case is not sufficiently serious to justify officers travelling to Scotland, Scottish officers can be requested to invite the suspect to attend a police station on a voluntary basis for interview under caution.

INTERVIEWS

When it has not been practicable for an English/Welsh constable to make an arrest, but a constable has gone to Scotland to interview a suspect following arrest or detention by a Scottish constable for Scottish offences, or a person has voluntarily agreed to be interviewed, the English/Welsh constable should comply, insofar as it is practical, with the PACE Codes of Practice, in particular:

- A suspect not under arrest or detention should be told that he/she is not under arrest or detention and that he/she is free to leave.

- A suspect should be told that he/she may seek legal advice and that arrangements are made for legal representation when required. An appropriate adult should also be present when interviewing a youth or a mentally disordered or mentally handicapped person.

- Administer an English/Welsh law caution. When appropriate officers should warn arrested suspects of the consequences of failure or refusal to account for objects, substances or marks (s. 36 of the 1994 Act) and the failure or refusal to account for their presence in a particular place (s. 37).

- Tape record the interview if possible.

- If it is not possible to tape record the interview, a contemporaneous written record of the interview should be made. The suspect must be given the opportunity to read the record and to sign it.

- Also, fingerprints etc. and non-intimate samples may be taken from an arrested or detained person with the authority of an officer of a rank no lower than inspector (s. 18 of the Criminal Procedure (Scotland) Act 1995).

Scottish constables interviewing suspects in Scotland when they are aware that the interview is required for a prosecution in England and Wales, should comply with Scottish law. In addition, insofar as it is practical:

- A suspect should be told that he/she may seek legal advice and that arrangements are made for legal representation when required. A solicitor may be present during any subsequent interview if the suspect requires. An appropriate adult should also be present when interviewing a youth or a mentally disordered or mentally handicapped person.

- When it is certain that the interview evidence will only be used in English/Welsh courts, the English/Welsh caution should be used.

- Tape record the interview if possible.

- If it is not possible to tape record the interview, a written contemporaneous record of the interview should be made. The suspect must be given the opportunity to read the record and to sign it.

English/Welsh officers should assist interviewing Scottish officers by providing a schedule of points to be covered in an interview. This could include a list of appropriate questions.

17.10.2 Suspects in England and Wales: Interview Evidence Required for Prosecutions in Scotland

- English officers do not have any statutory or common law powers to detain or arrest a suspect without warrant who is believed to have committed an offence in Scotland. If there is insufficient evidence for the issue of a warrant, and the case is not sufficiently serious to justify Scottish officers travelling to England or Wales to exercise their cross-border powers under the Act, English or Welsh officers can be requested to invite the suspect to attend an interview on a voluntary basis for interview under caution.

- Where a Scottish officer has attended to interview the suspect, the Scottish form of caution should be given.

- English and Welsh constables interviewing suspects in England/Wales when they are aware that the interview is required for a prosecution in Scotland, should comply with the PACE Codes of Practice, save that a Scottish caution should be used in the following terms: 'You are not obliged to say anything but anything you do say will be noted and may be used in evidence.'

The use of the English/Welsh caution may render the interview inadmissible in Scotland.

Scottish officers should assist the interviewing officers by providing a schedule of points to be covered in an interview and a possible list of appropriate questions.

In all circumstances officers should ensure that suspects fully understand the significance of a caution or warning.

APPENDIX ONE

THE CODE FOR CROWN PROSECUTORS

1 Introduction

1.1   The decision to prosecute an individual is a serious step. Fair and effective prosecution is essential to the maintenance of law and order. But even in a small case, a prosecution has serious implications for all involved – the victim, a witness and a defendant. The Crown Prosecution Service applies the Code for Crown Prosecutors so that it can make fair and consistent decisions about prosecutions.

1.2   The Code contains information that is important to police officers, to others who work in the criminal justice system and to the general public. It helps the Crown Prosecution Service to play its part in making sure that justice is done.

2   General Principles

2.1   Each case is unique and must be considered on its own, but there are general principles that apply in all cases.

2.2   The duty of the Crown Prosecution Service is to make sure that the right person is prosecuted for the right offence and that all relevant facts are given to the court.

2.3   Crown Prosecutors must be fair, independent and objective. They must not let their personal views of the ethnic or national origin, sex, religious beliefs, political views or sexual preference of the offender, victim or witness influence their decisions. They must also not be affected by improper or undue pressure from any source.

3   Review

3.1   Proceedings are usually started by the police. Sometimes they may consult the Crown Prosecution Service before charging a defendant. Each case that the police send to the Crown Prosecution Service is reviewed by a Crown Prosecutor to make sure that it meets the tests set out in this Code. Crown Prosecutors may decide to continue with the original charges, to change the charges or sometimes to stop the proceedings.

3.2   Review, however, is a continuing process so that Crown Prosecutors can take into account any change in circumstances. Wherever possible, they talk to the police first if they are thinking about changing the charges or stopping the proceedings. This gives the police the chance to provide more information that may affect the decision. The Crown Prosecution Service and the police work closely together to reach the right decision, but the final responsibility for the decision rests with the Crown Prosecution Service.

THE CODE FOR CROWN PROSECUTORS

4 The Code Tests

4.1   There are two stages in the decision to prosecute. The first stage is *the evidential test*. If the case does not pass the evidential test, it must not go ahead, no matter how important or serious it may be. If the case does pass the evidential test, Crown Prosecutors must decide if a prosecution is needed in the public interest.

4.2   This second stage is *the public interest test*. The Crown Prosecution Service will only start or continue a prosecution when the case has passed both tests. The evidential test is explained in section 5 and the public interest test is explained in section 6.

5 The Evidential Test

5.1   Crown Prosecutors must be satisfied that there is enough evidence to provide a 'realistic prospect of conviction' against each defendant on each charge. They must consider what the defence case may be and how that is likely to affect the prosecution case.

5.2   A realistic prospect of conviction is an objective test. It means that a jury or bench of magistrates, properly directed in accordance with the law, is more likely than not to convict the defendant of the charge alleged.

5.3   When deciding whether there is enough evidence to prosecute, Crown Prosecutors must consider whether the evidence can be used and is reliable. There will be many cases in which the evidence does not give any cause for concern. But there will also be cases in which the evidence may not be as strong as it first appears. Crown Prosecutors must ask themselves the following questions:

Can the evidence be used in court?

(a)   Is it likely that the evidence will be excluded by the court? There are certain legal rules which might mean that evidence which seems relevant cannot be given at a trial. For example, is it likely that the evidence will be excluded because of the way in which it was gathered or because of the rule against using hearsay as evidence? If so, is there enough other evidence for a realistic prospect of conviction?

Is the evidence reliable?

(b)   Is it likely that a confession is unreliable, for example, because of the defendant's age, intelligence or lack of understanding?
(c)   Is the witness's background likely to weaken the prosecution case? For example, does the witness have any dubious motive that may affect his or her attitude to the case or a relevant previous conviction?
(d)   If the identity of the defendant is likely to be questioned, is the evidence about this strong enough?

5.4   Crown Prosecutors should not ignore evidence because they are not sure that it can be used or is reliable. But they should look closely at it when deciding if there is a realistic prospect of conviction.

6 The Public Interest Test

6.1   In 1951, Lord Shawcross, who was Attorney-General, made the classic statement on public interest, which has been supported by Attorneys-General ever since: 'It has never been the rule in this country – I hope it never will be – that suspected criminal offences must automatically be the subject of prosecution'. (House of Commons Debates, Vol. 483, col. 681, 29 January 1951.)

6.2   The public interest must be considered in each case where there is enough evidence to provide a realistic prospect of conviction. In cases of any seriousness, a prosecution will usually take place unless there are public interest factors tending against prosecution which clearly outweigh those tending in favour. Although there may be public interest factors against prosecution in a particular case, often the prosecution should go ahead and those factors should be put to the court for consideration when sentence is being passed.

6.3   Crown Prosecutors must balance factors for and against prosecution carefully and fairly. Public interest factors that can affect the decision to prosecute usually depend on the seriousness of the offence or the circumstances of the offender. Some factors may increase the need to prosecute but others may suggest that another course of action would be better.

THE CODE FOR CROWN PROSECUTORS

The following lists of some common public interest factors, both for and against prosecution, are not exhaustive. The factors that apply will depend on the facts in each case.

Some common public interest factors in favour of prosecution

6.4 The more serious the offence, the more likely it is that a prosecution will be needed in the public interest. A prosecution is likely to be needed if:

(a) a conviction is likely to result in a significant sentence;
(b) a weapon was used or violence was threatened during the commission of the offence;
(c) the offence was committed against a person serving the public (for example, a police or prison officer, or a nurse);
(d) the defendant was in a position of authority or trust;
(e) the evidence shows that the defendant was a ringleader or an organiser of the offence;
(f) there is evidence that the offence was premeditated;
(g) there is evidence that the offence was carried out by a group;
(h) the victim of the offence was vulnerable, has been put in considerable fear, or suffered personal attack, damage or disturbance;
(i) the offence was motivated by any form of discrimination against the victim's ethnic or national origin, sex, religious beliefs, political views or sexual preference;
(j) there is a marked difference between the actual or mental ages of the defendant and the victim, or if there is any element of corruption;
(k) the defendant's previous convictions or cautions are relevant to the present offence;
(l) the defendant is alleged to have committed the offence whilst under an order of the court;
(m) there are grounds for believing that the offence is likely to be continued or repeated, for example, by a history of recurring conduct; or
(n) the offence, although not serious in itself, is widespread in the area where it was committed.

Some common public interest factors against prosecution

6.5 A prosecution is less likely to be needed if:

(a) the court is likely to impose a very small or nominal penalty;
(b) the offence was committed as a result of a genuine mistake or misunderstanding (these factors must be balanced against the seriousness of the offence);
(c) the loss or harm can be described as minor and was the result of a single incident, particularly if it was caused by a misjudgment;
(d) there has been a long delay between the offence taking place and the date of the trial, unless:
  • the offence is serious;
  • the delay has been caused in part by the defendant;
  • the offence has only recently come to light; or
  • the complexity of the offence has meant that there has been a long investigation;
(e) a prosecution is likely to have a very bad effect on the victim's physical or mental health, always bearing in mind the seriousness of the offence;
(f) the defendant is elderly or is, or was at the time of the offence, suffering from significant mental or physical ill health, unless the offence is serious or there is a real possibility that it may be repeated. The Crown Prosecution Service, where necessary, applies Home Office guidelines about how to deal with mentally disordered offenders. Crown Prosecutors must balance the desirability of diverting a defendant who is suffering from significant mental or physical ill health with the need to safeguard the general public;
(g) the defendant has put right the loss or harm that was caused (but defendants must not avoid prosecution simply because they can pay compensation); or
(h) details may be made public that could harm sources of information, international relations or national security.

6.6 Deciding on the public interest is not simply a matter of adding up the number of factors on each side. Crown Prosecutors must decide how important each factor is in the circumstances of each case and go on to make an overall assessment.

The relationship between the victim and the public interest

6.7 The Crown Prosecution Service acts in the public interest, not just in the interests of any one individual. But Crown Prosecutors must always think very carefully about the interests of the victim, which are an important factor, when deciding where the public interest lies.

Youth offenders

6.8   Crown Prosecutors must consider the interests of a youth when deciding whether it is in the public interest to prosecute. The stigma of a conviction can cause very serious harm to the prospects of a youth offender or a young adult. Young offenders can sometimes be dealt with without going to court. But Crown Prosecutors should not avoid prosecuting simply because of the defendant's age. The seriousness of the offence or the offender's past behaviour may make prosecution necessary.

Police cautions

6.9   The police make the decision to caution an offender in accordance with Home Office guidelines. If the defendant admits the offence, cautioning is the most common alternative to a court appearance. Crown Prosecutors, where necessary, apply the same guidelines and should look at the alternatives to prosecution when they consider the public interest. Crown Prosecutors should tell the police if they think that a caution would be more suitable than a prosecution.

7   Charges

7.1   Crown Prosecutors should select charges which:

(a)   reflect the seriousness of the offending;
(b)   give the court adequate sentencing powers; and
(c)   enable the case to be presented in a clear and simple way.

This means that Crown Prosecutors may not always continue with the most serious charge where there is a choice. Further, Crown Prosecutors should not continue with more charges than are necessary.

7.2   Crown Prosecutors should never go ahead with more charges than are necessary just to encourage a defendant to plead guilty to a few. In the same way, they should never go ahead with a more serious charge just to encourage a defendant to plead guilty to a less serious one.

7.3   Crown Prosecutors should not change the charge simply because of the decision made by the court or the defendant about where the case will be heard.

8   Mode of Trial

8.1   The Crown Prosecution Service applies the current guidelines for magistrates who have to decide whether cases should be tried in the Crown Court when the offence gives the option. (See the 'National Mode of Trial Guidelines' issued by the Lord Chief Justice.) Crown Prosecutors should recommend Crown Court trial when they are satisfied that the guidelines require them to do so.

8.2   Speed must never be the only reason for asking for a case to stay in the magistrates' courts. But Crown Prosecutors should consider the effect of any likely delay if they send a case to the Crown Court, and any possible stress on victims and witnesses if the case is delayed.

9   Accepting Guilty Pleas

9.1   Defendants may want to plead guilty to some, but not all, of the charges. Or they may want to plead guilty to a different, possibly less serious, charge because they are admitting only part of the crime. Crown Prosecutors should only accept the defendant's plea if they think the court is able to pass a sentence that matches the seriousness of the offending. Crown Prosecutors must never accept a guilty plea just because it is convenient.

10   Re-starting a Prosecution

10.1   People should be able to rely on decisions taken by the Crown Prosecution Service. Normally, if the Crown Prosecution Service tells a suspect or defendant that there will not be a prosecution, or that the prosecution has been stopped, that is the end of the matter and the case will not start again. But occasionally there are special reasons why the Crown Prosecution Service will re-start the prosecution, particularly if the case is serious.

10.2   These reasons include:

(a)   rare cases where a new look at the original decision shows that it was clearly wrong and should not be allowed to stand;
(b)   cases which are stopped so that more evidence which is likely to become available in the fairly near future can be collected and prepared. In these cases, the Crown Prosecutor will tell the defendant that the prosecution may well start again;
(c)   cases which are stopped because of a lack of evidence but where more significant evidence is discovered later.

11   Conclusion

11.1   The Crown Prosecution Service is a public service headed by the Director of Public Prosecutions. It is answerable to Parliament through the Attorney-General. The Code for Crown Prosecutors is issued under section 10 of the Prosecution of Offences Act 1985 and is a public document. This is the third edition and it replaces all earlier versions. Changes to the Code are made from time to time and these are also published.

11.2   The Code is designed to make sure that everyone knows the principles that the Crown Prosecution Service applies when carrying out its work. Police officers should take account of the principles of the Code when they are deciding whether to charge a defendant with an offence. By applying the same principles, everyone involved in the criminal justice system is helping the system to treat victims fairly, and to prosecute defendants fairly but effectively.

APPENDIX TWO

CPS NATIONAL CASEWORK GUIDELINES: VISUAL IDENTIFICATION

Rationale for guidelines

1. It has long been recognised that evidence of visual identification must be treated with great care as experience has shown it can, for a number of reasons, be unreliable. The Devlin Report on Evidence of Identification in 1972 stated that 'cases of mistaken identification constituted by far the greatest cause of actual or possible wrong convictions'.

2. The guidelines laid down in *R* v *Turnbull & Others* (1977) 63 Cr App R 132 have largely succeeded in ensuring a consistent approach by the courts to cases where the evidence against an accused depends wholly or substantially on visual identification.

3. The first edition of the Code for Crown Prosecutors listed identification issues as matters to which prosecutors should have particular regard when evaluating the evidence. The present edition of the Code also highlights the reliability of identification evidence when satisfying the evidential test. ***Reliable and admissible identification evidence is an essential feature in every case no matter how minor***.

288

4.   The 1994 Discontinuance Survey revealed that 43% of the cases surveyed were discontinued as a result of insufficient evidence. A quarter of these (11% of the overall discontinuance figure representing 1176 cases) were discontinued as a result of doubts concerning identification evidence.

5.   Furthermore, of those cases prosecuted by the Service, 482 were dropped at the Crown Court because of doubts about identification with a further 483 resulting in judge directed acquittals.

Purpose for guidelines

6.   The purpose of these guidelines is to offer guidance to prosecutors to assist them in

- resolving doubts concerning identification evidence;
- assessing the evidential weight and strength of the identification evidence.

Assessing the quality of visual identification evidence

7.   In summary the recommended approach is as follows.

(1)   Consider whether the evidence of identification is crucial or not crucial to a realistic prospect of conviction.

(2)   If it is not crucial, look at the strength of the other evidence, as well as the identification evidence, before reaching a decision whether to prosecute.

(3)   If the identification evidence is crucial consider:

- what factors have influenced the witness in his or her observation of the suspect?
- what are the surrounding circumstances of the observation?
- what is the reliability of the identifying witness?
- whether the manner of identification is satisfactory?

(4)   Consider whether the identification evidence (whether crucial or not) can be supported by other evidence or circumstances.

(5)   Equally, consider whether the identification evidence is undermined by other evidence or circumstances.

(6)   Consider additional points in recognition cases.

(7)   Look at identification procedures, including circumstances when a parade may be unnecessary.

(8)   Avoid dock identifications.

(9)   Consider the effect of a failure to hold a parade or breaches in the Codes of Practice.

(10)   Ensure disclosure duties are followed.

General approach to identification evidence

8.   Cases involving visual identification fall into two broad categories:

- those where the accuracy of the purported identification is an issue; and
- those cases where the veracity of the witness is an issue.

9.   In the former category are cases where the witness has never seen the suspect before and the quality of the identification is paramount. The latter category will include situations where a witness may be untruthful not only when making a visual identification but also when making an identification in a recognition case. As a first step prosecutors must determine the exact nature of the identification issue.

10.   The police must forward all relevant information about the circumstances of identification and the identifying witness(es). This may include a photograph of the defendant if it will assist your review function.

CPS NATIONAL CASEWORK GUIDELINES: VISUAL IDENTIFICATION

At the very least prosecutors should have a copy of the initial report of the crime, and in appropriate cases a description of the physical appearance and clothing of the suspect when he was first taken into custody. Police should forward copies of all first descriptions given by potential witnesses and recorded in accordance with para 2 of Code D.

11.   Consideration should be given to the importance of identification in relation to the evidence as a whole. For example:

- is there other reliable supporting scientific evidence, such as fingerprint or DNA evidence?
- is there a reliable and admissible confession or part admission?
- is there other direct or circumstantial evidence which connects the suspect with the offence?
- does the case rest entirely on visual identification evidence?

12.   Consideration of the factors in paragraph 11 above will result in an assessment whether the identification evidence is crucial to a realistic prospect of conviction.

Cases where visual identification evidence is not crucial

13.   In cases where *visual* identification evidence is not crucial, a flawed identification need not be fatal **provided that other reliable and admissible evidence exists**. An identification of someone other than the suspect, where a positive identification was reasonable in all the circumstances, may cast doubt on the overall sufficiency of evidence, but this will need to be balanced against the other evidence available.

14.   Where there has been a positive identification, even though that evidence is not crucial, a prosecutor should still look carefully at the strength of the identification evidence in accordance with the steps set out in paragraphs 18–27 below.

Cases where visual identification evidence is crucial

15.   Where the visual identification evidence is crucial, a flawed or a wrong identification is likely to be fatal. Such circumstances will vary from case to case but the most common situations include the following:

- no identification, where the witness provided a good description but failed to identify the suspect either at the scene or on a parade;
- a partial' identification, such as an indication after the parade has concluded;
- a flawed identification where the parade or other identification procedure was in breach of Code D or unlikely to satisfy the court as an 'instant confrontation' (see paragraph 37 below).

- a wrong identification where a person other than the suspect was identified, either on a parade or at the scene.

16.   Every case will depend on its own merits but cases of the type described at paragraph 15 above will seldom be likely to satisfy the evidential sufficiency test.

17.   Where the visual identification evidence is crucial and there is, what appears on the face of the statements, a positive identification, there is still a need to look further at the strength of that identification. This may involve seeking information from the police which is not on the file (see paragraph 20 below).

18.   First, determine the exact nature of the identification issue:

- is it a straightforward visual identification issue?
- is it a case where recognition evidence, rather than identification, is the real issue?
- is the veracity of the identifying witness the principal issue?

19.   This last aspect is not pursued further in these guidelines. Where the defence is likely to be that the witness is lying, for whatever reason, the quality of the identification evidence is not an issue. Witnesses tell lies for a multitude of reasons and if they choose to be untruthful about an identification issue, it is not really an issue of identification quality. Even in these cases, you should assess the veracity of identification witnesses, as you would any other witness, to ensure that any necessary remedial action is taken at the earliest opportunity.

20.   Secondly, consider (by a careful scrutiny of the statements and, if necessary, by seeking further information from the police) the following.

- What factors have caused the witness to identify the suspect (see paragraph 21 below)?
- What are the surrounding circumstances of the identification (see paragraph 22 below)?
- How reliable is the identifying witness (see paragraphs 23–25 below)?
- Is the manner of identification satisfactory (see paragraphs 26–27 below)?

What factors have caused the witness to identify the suspect?

21.   For example:

- is there a particular resemblance of features such as the shape of eyes or nose, colour or type of hair (or absence of hair), colour or shape of beard?
- does the suspect have any distinguishing features, such as a tattoo, a scar or even a particularly distinctive height?
- is there anything distinctive about the suspect's mannerisms, stance, voice or clothing?
- was there a use of a nickname at scene attributable to suspect by other evidence?
- is there a danger that the identification is based on assumption because the suspect is in the company of others common to both scene of incident and scene of identification?
- is the identification simply based on powers of observation and recall?

What are the surrounding circumstances of the identification?

22.   For example:

- how long was the suspect under observation?
- at what distance?
- in what light?
- was the observation impeded?
- had the witness seen the suspect before (and is the real issue therefore one of recognition rather than identification)?
- how long elapsed between the original observation and the subsequent identification to police?
- were there any particular reasons for noting the suspect?

How reliable is the identifying witness?

23.   For example:

- what is the age of the witness (is the witness very young or elderly)? Prosecutors must guard against making unwarranted assumptions about witnesses based on age or perceived disability.
- whether the witness is in possession of all his or her faculties (no suggestion of senility, forgetfulness, poor eyesight, mental instability etc)?
- is there anything else about the witness which may be material? (Are spectacles or contact lenses worn? is the witness long-sighted or short-sighted? a lip reader may have enhanced powers of observation from the necessity of having to observe closely facial features etc.).
- does the first description given to the police (in accordance with Code D) match the appearance of the accused?
- is the witness related to the defendant(s) or other witnesses?

24.   If the identifying witness is a police officer, do not assume that the evidence of identification is stronger than if the witness were a member of the public. [See also Note 2A in Code D].

25.   It is obviously vital that the police provide as much information as possible about any witness who purports to identify a suspect. The police will know the witness; the prosecutor will only have an impression from the statement. The police should provide, or, if necessary, be asked to provide, information about the witness. Elderly witnesses may have deteriorating faculties or be taking medication which could affect the reliability of their evidence. A younger witness who, on the face of things, seems to be a good witness may wear glasses or contact lenses and may not have been wearing spectacles at the relevant time. All these matters must be taken into account when assessing the quality of identification. If this information is not clear from the papers, the prosecutor must ask the police for full details.

CPS NATIONAL CASEWORK GUIDELINES: VISUAL IDENTIFICATION

Is the manner of identification satisfactory?

26.   An identification made on a parade remains the most satisfactory way of dealing with identification issues. Group and video identifications, provided they are carried out in accordance with the requirements of the Code D, will also provide cogent evidence. Confrontation evidence, whilst sometimes unavoidable, does not carry the same weight as identification by other means. This should be borne in mind when considering the quality of identification.

27.   Assessment of whether the manner of identification is satisfactory will include consideration of any reasons to support the decision to rely on a method of identification other than an identification parade: see paragraph 34.

Supporting evidence

28.   The strength of the identification evidence may be improved when other evidence or circumstances which can support the evidence of identification exists, such as:

- identification by another witness;
- similar fact and multiple offences committed by the same person;
- self-incriminating evidence such as admissions or a false alibi;
- deliberate lies relating to a material issue;
- correct identification of other participants in the offence.

29.   There is case law to support each of these examples. Before discontinuing a case because of poor quality identification, prosecutors must examine the surrounding evidence and circumstances to ascertain whether it is capable of supporting the identification evidence.

30.   Remember that the provisions of s. 76(4) of PACE can assist in identifications even when admissions are excluded.

31.   Caution should be exercised against placing more reliance than is appropriate on supporting evidence when the underlying evidence of identification is intrinsically weak. Special caution is required when a defendant admits presence at scene but denies involvement in the offence. A prosecutor would need to ensure that there is sufficient evidence to identify the defendant as a participant (see *R* v *Thornton* (1995) 1 Cr App R 578 and *R* v *Slater* (1995) 1 Cr App R 584).

Recognition evidence

32.   If the case is one where the witness recognises the suspect as someone he or she has seen before, consider:

- how long has the witness known the suspect?
- in what circumstances did they meet?
- how many times has the witness seen the suspect?
- how long ago was the witness's last sighting of the suspect before the incident?
- does the witness know the suspect only by sight or have they spoken?
- does the witness know the name and address of the suspect, and if so, how?
- does the suspect have any particular distinguishing features?
- have the police confirmed the person arrested is the one the witness refers to?

33.   The words in a statement, 'who I now know to be' should always prompt further enquiries to ascertain the answers to the questions posed in paragraph 32 above. Whether the witness' knowledge was gained before or after the incident may have an impact on the evidence and prosecutors should consider the effect it is likely to have.

Identification procedures

34.   The quality of the identification evidence will also be assisted by the circumstances in which the witness actually makes the identification of the suspect (as distinct from the circumstances in which the suspect was observed). This will depend on the propriety of the identification parade or other means of identification in the Codes of Practice.

35.   Consider whether identification procedures have been followed. The police should use the methods in the order set out below:

- a parade;
- a group identification;
- a video film;
- a confrontation.

36.   An identification parade should be held where:

- the suspect disputes identification and consents to a parade
- the witness indicates that he or she is able to identify or might be able to identify the persons responsible for the offence (even if they have seen a photograph or identikit picture, or a video recording of the offence on television).

If both of the above situations apply, an identification parade should be held whether or not the suspect has been charged.

37.   An identification parade need not be held where

- the suspect does not consent to a parade (when one of the other identification methods should be employed);
- the suspect has an unusual appearance;
- it is impracticable to hold a fair parade;
- there has been an 'instant confrontation' within minutes of the offence and in close proximity to the scene; [but note the conflicting authorities on this point].
- the witness has been taken to the scene in accordance with the terms of paragraph 2.17 of Code D;
- in some circumstances, the issue is one of recognition and no useful purpose would be served.

38.   The good faith of the officer is likely to be an issue at any trial and prosecutors will need to explore with the police whether the failure to hold a parade was, in all the circumstances, reasonable.

Dock identifications

39.   Reliance should not be placed on dock identifications. The only possible exception is a recognition case where a parade was neither essential under Code D nor of any real value.

Effect of failure to hold a parade or breaches of the Codes of Practice

40.   The existence of a breach of the Codes of Practice does not mean that the case should be discontinued automatically. The importance of the breach and its effect on the fairness of the identification must be considered carefully.

APPENDIX THREE

DISCLOSURE: CRIMINAL PROCEDURE AND INVESTIGATIONS ACT 1996: CODE OF PRACTICE UNDER PART II

Introduction

1.1   This code of practice is issued under part II of the Criminal Procedure and Investigations Act 1996 ('the Act'). It applies in respect of criminal investigations conducted by police officers which begin on or after the day on which this code comes into effect. Persons other than police officers who are charged with the duty of conducting an investigation as defined in the Act are to have regard to the relevant provisions of the code, and should take these into account in applying their own operating procedures.

1.2   This code does not apply to persons who are not charged with the duty of conducting an investigation as defined in the Act.

1.3   Nothing in this code applies to material intercepted in obedience to a warrant issued under section 2 of the Interception of Communications Act 1985, or to any copy of that material as defined in section 10 of that Act.

1.4   This code extends only to England and Wales.

Definitions

2.1   In this code:

- a *criminal investigation* is an investigation conducted by police officers with a view to it being ascertained whether a person should be charged with an offence, or whether a person charged with an offence is guilty of it. This will include

  - investigations into crimes that have been committed;

  - investigations whose purpose is to ascertain whether a crime has been committed, with a view to the possible institution of criminal proceedings; and

- investigations which begin in the belief that a crime may be committed, for example when the police keep premises or individuals under observation for a period of time, with a view to the possible institution of criminal proceedings;

- charging a person with an offence includes prosecution by way of summons;

- an *investigator* is any police officer involved in the conduct of a criminal investigation. All investigators have a responsibility for carrying out the duties imposed on them under this code, including in particular recording information, and retaining records of information and other material;

- the *officer in charge of an investigation* is the police officer responsible for directing a criminal investigation. He is also responsible for ensuring that proper procedures are in place for recording information, and retaining records of information and other material, in the investigation;

- the *disclosure officer* is the person responsible for examining material retained by the police during the investigation; revealing material to the prosecutor during the investigation and any criminal proceedings resulting from it, and certifying that he has done this; and disclosing material to the accused at the request of the prosecutor;

- the *prosecutor* is the authority responsible for the conduct of criminal proceedings on behalf of the Crown. Particular duties may in practice fall to individuals acting on behalf of the prosecuting authority;

- *material* is material of any kind, including information and objects, which is obtained in the course of a criminal investigation and which may be relevant to the investigation;

- material may be *relevant to an investigation* if it appears to an investigator, or to the officer in charge of an investigation, or to the disclosure officer, that it has some bearing on any offence under investigation or any person being investigated, or on the surrounding circumstances of the case, unless it is incapable of having any impact on the case;

- *sensitive material* is material which the disclosure officer believes, after consulting the officer in charge of the investigation, it is not in the public interest to disclose;

- references to *primary prosecution disclosure* are to the duty of the prosecutor under section 3 of the Act to disclose material which is in his possession or which he has inspected in pursuance of this code, and which in his opinion might undermine the case against the accused;

- references to *secondary prosecution disclosure* are to the duty of the prosecutor under section 7 of the Act to disclose material which is in his possession or which he has inspected in pursuance of this code, and which might reasonably be expected to assist the defence disclosed by the accused in a defence statement given under the Act;

- references to the disclosure of material to a person accused of an offence include references to the disclosure of material to his legal representative;

- references to police officers and to the chief officer of police include those employed in a police force as defined in section 3(3) of the Prosecution of Offences Act 1985.

General responsibilities

3.1   The functions of the investigator, the officer in charge of an investigation and the disclosure officer are separate. Whether they are undertaken by one, two or more persons will depend on the complexity of the case and the administrative arrangements within each police force. Where they are undertaken by more than one person, close consultation between them is essential to the effective performance of the duties imposed by this code.

3.2   The chief officer of police for each police force is responsible for putting in place arrangements to ensure that in every investigation the identity of the officer in charge of an investigation and the disclosure officer is recorded.

DISCLOSURE: CODE OF PRACTICE

3.3   The officer in charge of an investigation may delegate tasks to another investigator or to civilians employed by the police force, but he remains responsible for ensuring that these have been carried out and for accounting for any general policies followed in the investigation. In particular, it is an essential part of his duties to ensure that all material which may be relevant to an investigation is retained, and either made available to the disclosure officer or (in exceptional circumstances) revealed directly to the prosecutor.

3.4   In conducting an investigation, the investigator should pursue all reasonable lines of inquiry, whether these point towards or away from the suspect. What is reasonable in each case will depend on the particular circumstances.

3.5   If the officer in charge of an investigation believes that other persons may be in possession of material that may be relevant to the investigation, and if this has not been obtained under paragraph 3.4 above, he should ask the disclosure officer to inform them of the existence of the investigation and to invite them to retain the material in case they receive a request for its disclosure. The disclosure officer should inform the prosecutor that they may have such material. However, the officer in charge of an investigation is not required to make speculative enquiries of other persons: there must be some reason to believe that they may have relevant material. That reason may come from information provided to the police by the accused or from other inquiries made or from some other source.

3.6   If, during a criminal investigation, the officer in charge of an investigation or disclosure officer for any reason no longer has responsibility for the functions falling to him, either his supervisor or the police officer in charge of criminal investigations for the police force concerned must assign someone else to assume that responsibility. That person's identity must be recorded, as with those initially responsible for these functions in each investigation.

Recording of information

4.1   If material which may be relevant to the investigation consists of information which is not recorded in any form, the officer in charge of an investigation must ensure that it is recorded in a durable or retrievable form (whether in writing, on video or audio tape, or on computer disk).

4.2   Where it is not practicable to retain the initial record of information because it forms part of a larger record which is to be destroyed, its contents should be transferred as a true record to a durable and more easily-stored form before that happens.

4.3   Negative information is often relevant to an investigation. If it may be relevant it must be recorded. An example might be a number of people present in a particular place at a particular time who state that they saw nothing unusual.

4.4   Where information which may be relevant is obtained, it must be recorded at the time it is obtained or as soon as practicable after that time. This includes, for example, information obtained in house-to-house enquiries, although the requirement to record information promptly does not require an investigator to take a statement from a potential witness where it would not otherwise be taken.

Retention of material

(a)   Duty to retain material

5.1   The investigator must retain material obtained in a criminal investigation which may be relevant to the investigation. This includes not only material coming into the possession of the investigator (such as documents seized in the course of searching premises) but also material generated by him (such as interview records). Material may be photographed, or retained in the form of a copy rather than the original, if the original is perishable, or was supplied to the investigator rather than generated by him and is to be returned to its owner.

5.2   Where material has been seized in the exercise of the powers of seizure conferred by the Police and Criminal Evidence Act 1984, the duty to retain it under this code is subject to the provisions on the retention of seized material in section 22 of that Act.

5.3   If the officer in charge of an investigation becomes aware as a result of developments in the case that material previously examined but not retained (because it was not thought to be relevant) may now be relevant to the investigation, he should, wherever practicable, take steps to obtain it or ensure that it is retained for further inspection or for production in court if required.

5.4   The duty to retain material includes in particular the duty to retain material falling into the following categories, where it may be relevant to the investigation:

- crime reports (including crime report forms, relevant parts of incident report books or police officers' notebooks);

- custody records;

- records which are derived from tapes of telephone messages (for example, 999 calls) containing descriptions of an alleged offence or offender;

- final versions of witness statements (and draft versions where their content differs from the final version), including any exhibits mentioned (unless these have been returned to their owner on the understanding that they will be produced in court if required);

- interview records (written records, or audio or video tapes, of interviews with actual or potential witnesses or suspects);

- communications between the police and experts such as forensic scientists, reports of work carried out by experts, and schedules of scientific material prepared by the expert for the investigator, for the purposes of criminal proceedings;

- any material casting doubt on the reliability of a confession;

- any material casting doubt on the reliability of a witness;

- any other material which may fall within the test for primary prosecution disclosure in the Act.

5.5   The duty to retain material falling into these categories does not extend to items which are purely ancillary to such material and possess no independent significance (for example, duplicate copies of records or reports).

(b)   Length of time for which material is to be retained

5.6   All material which may be relevant to the investigation must be retained until a decision is taken whether to institute proceedings against a person for an offence.

5.7   If a criminal investigation results in proceedings being instituted, all material which may be relevant must be retained at least until the accused is acquitted or convicted or the prosecutor decides not to proceed with the case.

5.8   Where the accused is convicted, all material which may be relevant must be retained at least until:

- the convicted person is released from custody, or discharged from hospital, in cases where the court imposes a custodial sentence or a hospital order;

- six months from the date of conviction, in all other cases.

If the court imposes a custodial sentence or hospital order and the convicted person is released from custody or is discharged from hospital earlier than six months from the date of conviction, all material which may be relevant must be retained at least until six months from the date of conviction.

5.9   If an appeal against conviction is in progress when the release or discharge occurs, or at the end of the period of six months specified in paragraph 5.8, all material which may be relevant must be retained until the appeal is determined. Similarly, if the Criminal Cases Review Commission is considering an application at that point in time, all material which may be relevant must be retained at least until the Commission decides not to refer the case to the Court of Appeal, or until the Court determines the appeal resulting from the reference by the Commission.

5.10   Material need not be retained by the police as required in paragraph 5.8 if it was seized and is to be returned to its owner.

Preparation of material for prosecutor

(a)   Introduction

6.1   The officer in charge of the investigation, the disclosure officer or an investigator may seek advice from the prosecutor about whether any particular item of material may be relevant to the investigation.

6.2   Material which may be relevant to an investigation, which has been retained in accordance with this code, and which the disclosure officer believes will not form part of the prosecution case, must be listed on a schedule.

6.3   Material which the disclosure officer does not believe is sensitive must be listed on a schedule of non-sensitive material. The schedule must include a statement that the disclosure officer does not believe the material is sensitive.

6.4   Any material which is believed to be sensitive must be either listed on a schedule of sensitive material or, in exceptional circumstances, revealed to the prosecutor separately.

6.5   Paragraphs 6.6 to 6.11 below apply to both sensitive and non-sensitive material. Paragraphs 6.12 to 6.14 apply to sensitive material only.

(b)   Circumstances in which a schedule is to be prepared

6.6   The disclosure officer must ensure that a schedule is prepared in the following circumstances:

–   the accused is charged with an offence which is triable only on indictment;

–   the accused is charged with an offence which is triable either way, and it is considered either that the case is likely to be tried on indictment or that the accused is likely to plead not guilty at a summary trial;

–   the accused is charged with a summary offence, and it is considered that he is likely to plead not guilty.

6.7   In respect of either way and summary offences, a schedule may not be needed if a person has admitted the offence, or if a police officer witnessed the offence and that person has not denied it.

6.8   If it is believed that the accused is likely to plead guilty at a summary trial, it is not necessary to prepare a schedule in advance. If, contrary to this belief, the accused pleads not guilty at a summary trial, or the offence is to be tried on indictment, the disclosure officer must ensure that a schedule is prepared as soon as is reasonably practicable after that happens.

(c)   Way in which material is to be listed on schedule

6.9   The disclosure officer should ensure that each item of material is listed separately on the schedule, and is numbered consecutively. The description of each item should make clear the nature of the item and should contain sufficient detail to enable the prosecutor to decide whether he needs to inspect the material before deciding whether or not it should be disclosed.

6.10   In some enquiries it may not be practicable to list each item of material separately. For example, there may be many items of a similar or repetitive nature. These may be listed in a block and described by quantity and generic title.

6.11   Even if some material is listed in a block, the disclosure officer must ensure that any items among that material which might meet the test for primary prosecution disclosure are listed and described individually.

(d)   Treatment of sensitive material

6.12   Subject to paragraph 6.13 below, the disclosure officer must list on a sensitive schedule any material which he believes it is not in the public interest to disclose, and the reason for that belief. The schedule must include a statement that the disclosure officer believes the material is sensitive. Depending on the circumstances, examples of such material may include the following among others:

- material relating to national security;

- material received from the intelligence and security agencies;

- material relating to intelligence from foreign sources which reveals sensitive intelligence gathering methods;

- material given in confidence;

- material which relates to the use of a telephone system and which is supplied to an investigator for intelligence purposes only;

- material relating to the identity or activities of informants, or under-cover police officers, or other persons supplying information to the police who may be in danger if their identities are revealed;

- material revealing the location of any premises or other place used for police surveillance, or the identity of any person allowing a police officer to use them for surveillance;

- material revealing, either directly or indirectly, techniques and methods relied upon by a police officer in the course of a criminal investigation, for example covert surveillance techniques, or other methods of detecting crime;

- material whose disclosure might facilitate the commission of other offences or hinder the prevention and detection of crime;

- internal police communications such as management minutes;

- material upon the strength of which search warrants were obtained;

- material containing details of persons taking part in identification parades;

- material supplied to an investigator during a criminal investigation which has been generated by an official of a body concerned with the regulation or supervision of bodies corporate or of persons engaged in financial activities, or which has been generated by a person retained by such a body;

- material supplied to an investigator during a criminal investigation which relates to a child or young person and which has been generated by a local authority social services department, an Area Child Protection Committee or other party contacted by an investigator during the investigation.

6.13   In exceptional circumstances, where an investigator considers that material is so sensitive that its revelation to the prosecutor by means of an entry on the sensitive schedule is inappropriate, the existence of the material must be revealed to the prosecutor separately. This will apply where compromising the material would be likely to lead directly to the loss of life, or directly threaten national security.

6.14   In such circumstances, the responsibility for informing the prosecutor lies with the investigator who knows the detail of the sensitive material. The investigator should act as soon as is reasonably practicable after the file containing the prosecution case is sent to the prosecutor. The investigator must also ensure that the prosecutor is able to inspect the material so that he can assess whether it needs to be brought before a court for a ruling on disclosure.

Revelation of material to prosecutor

7.1   The disclosure officer must give the schedules to the prosecutor. Wherever practicable this should be at the same time as he gives him the file containing the material for the prosecution case (or as soon as is reasonably practicable after the decision on mode of trial or the plea, in cases to which paragraph 6.8 applies).

7.2   The disclosure officer should draw the attention of the prosecutor to any material an investigator has retained (whether or not listed on a schedule) which may fall within the test for primary prosecution disclosure in the Act, and should explain why he has come to that view.

7.3   At the same time as complying with the duties in paragraphs 7.1 and 7.2, the disclosure officer must give the prosecutor a copy of any material which falls into the following categories (unless such material has already been given to the prosecutor as part of the file containing the material for the prosecution case):

–   records of the first description of a suspect given to the police by a potential witness, whether or not the description differs from that of the alleged offender;

–   information provided by an accused person which indicates an explanation for the offence with which he has been charged;

–   any material casting doubt on the reliability of a confession;

–   any material casting doubt on the reliability of a witness;

–   any other material which the investigator believes may fall within the test for primary prosecution disclosure in the Act.

7.4   If the prosecutor asks to inspect material which has not already been copied to him, the disclosure officer must allow him to inspect it. If the prosecutor asks for a copy of material which has not already been copied to him, the disclosure officer must give him a copy. However, this does not apply where the disclosure officer believes, having consulted the officer in charge of the investigation, that the material is too sensitive to be copied and can only be inspected.

7.5   If material consists of information which is recorded other than in writing, whether it should be given to the prosecutor in its original form as a whole, or by way of relevant extracts recorded in the same form, or in the form of a transcript, is a matter for agreement between the disclosure officer and the prosecutor.

Subsequent action by disclosure officer

8.1   At the time a schedule of non-sensitive material is prepared, the disclosure officer may not know exactly what material will form the case against the accused, and the prosecutor may not have given advice about the likely relevance of particular items of material. Once these matters have been determined, the disclosure officer must give the prosecutor, where necessary, an amended schedule listing any additional material:

–   which may be relevant to the investigation,

–   which does not form part of the case against the accused,

–   which is not already listed on the schedule, and

–   which he believes is not sensitive,

unless he is informed in writing by the prosecutor that the prosecutor intends to disclose the material to the defence.

8.2   After a defence statement has been given, the disclosure officer must look again at the material which has been retained and must draw the attention of the prosecutor to any material which might reasonably be expected to assist the defence disclosed by the accused; and he must reveal it to him in accordance with paragraphs 7.4 and 7.5 above.

8.3   Section 9 of the Act imposes a continuing duty on the prosecutor, for the duration of criminal proceedings against the accused, to disclose material which meets the tests for disclosure (subject to public interest considerations). To enable him to do this, any new material coming to light should be treated in the same way as the earlier material.

DISCLOSURE: CODE OF PRACTICE

Certification by disclosure officer

9.1 The disclosure officer must certify to the prosecutor that, to the best of his knowledge and belief, all material which has been retained and made available to him has been revealed to the prosecutor in accordance with this code. He must sign and date the certificate. It will be necessary to certify not only at the time when the schedule and accompanying material is submitted to the prosecutor, but also when material which has been retained is reconsidered after the accused has given a defence statement.

Disclosure of material to accused

10.1 If material has not already been copied to the prosecutor, and he requests its disclosure to the accused on the ground that:

- it falls within the test for primary or secondary prosecution disclosure, or

- the court has ordered its disclosure after considering an application from the accused,

the disclosure officer must disclose it to the accused.

10.2 If material has been copied to the prosecutor, and it is to be disclosed, whether it is disclosed by the prosecutor or the disclosure officer is a matter for agreement between the two of them.

10.3 The disclosure officer must disclose material to the accused either by giving him a copy or by allowing him to inspect it. If the accused person asks for a copy of any material which he has been allowed to inspect, the disclosure officer must give it to him, unless in the opinion of the disclosure officer that is either not practicable (for example because the material consists of an object which cannot be copied, or because the volume of material is so great), or not desirable (for example because the material is a statement by a child witness in relation to a sexual offence).

10.4 If material which the accused has been allowed to inspect consists of information which is recorded other than in writing, whether it should be given to the accused in its original form or in the form of a transcript is a matter for the discretion of the disclosure officer. If the material is transcribed, the disclosure officer must ensure that the transcript is certified to the accused as a true record of the material which has been transcribed.

10.5 If a court concludes that it is in the public interest that an item of sensitive material must be disclosed to the accused, it will be necessary to disclose the material if the case is to proceed. This does not mean that sensitive documents must always be disclosed in their original form: for example, the court may agree that sensitive details still requiring protection should be blocked out, or that documents may be summarised, or that the prosecutor may make an admission about the substance of the material under section 10 of the Criminal Justice Act 1967.

APPENDIX FOUR

NATIONAL STANDARDS FOR CAUTIONING (REVISED)

Aims

1. The purposes of a formal caution are—

— to deal quickly and simply with less serious offenders;
— to divert them from unnecessary appearance in the criminal courts; and
— to reduce the chances of their re-offending.

Note 1A A caution is not a form of sentence. It may not be made conditional upon the satisfactory completion of a specific task such as reparation or the payment of compensation to the victim. Only the courts may impose such requirements.

Decision to caution

2. A formal caution is a serious matter. It is recorded by the police; it should influence them in their decision whether or not to institute proceedings if the person should offend again; and it may be cited in any subsequent court proceedings. In order to safeguard the offender's interests, the following conditions must be met before a caution can be administered—

— there must be *evidence of the offender's guilt* sufficient to give a realistic prospect of conviction;
— the offender must *admit the offence*;
— the offender (or, in the case of a juvenile, his parents or guardian) must understand the significance of a caution and give *informed consent* to being cautioned.

Note 2A Where the evidence does not meet the required standard, a caution cannot be administered.

Note 2B A caution will not be appropriate where a person does not make a clear and reliable admission of the offence (for example if intent is denied or there are doubts about his mental health or intellectual capacity).

Note 2C If an offence is committed by a juvenile under the age of 14, it is necessary to establish that he knew that what he did was seriously wrong.

Note 2D In practice consent to the caution should not be sought until it has been decided that cautioning is the correct course. The significance of the caution must be explained: that is, that a record will be kept of the caution, that the fact of a previous caution may influence the decision whether or not to prosecute if the person should offend again, and that it may be cited if the person should subsequently be found guilty of an offence by a court. In the case of a juvenile this explanation must be given to the offender in the presence of his parents or guardian, or other appropriate adult. The special needs of other vulnerable groups should also be catered for, in accordance with the Code of Practice for the Detention, Treatment and Questioning of Persons by Police Officers.

Public interest considerations

3.   If the first two of the above requirements are met, consideration should be given to whether a caution is in the public interest. The police should take into account the public interest principles described in the Code for Crown Prosecutors.

Note 3A   There should be a presumption in favour of not prosecuting certain categories of offender, such as elderly people or those who suffer from some sort of mental illness or impairment, or a severe physical illness. Membership of these groups does not, however, afford absolute protection against prosecution, which may be justified by the seriousness of the offence.

Note 3B   Two factors should be considered in relation to the offender's attitude towards his offence: the wilfulness with which it was committed and his subsequent attitude. A practical demonstration of regret, such as apologising to the victim and/or offering to put matters right as far as he is able, may support the use of a caution.

Note 3C   The experience and circumstances of offenders involved in group offences can vary greatly, as can their degree of involvement. Although consistency and equity are important considerations in the decision whether to charge or caution, each offender should be considered separately. Different disposals may be justified.

Views of the victim

4.   Before a caution can be administered it is desirable that the victim should normally be contacted to establish—

— his or her view about the offence;
— the nature and extent of any harm or loss, and their significance relative to the victim's circumstances;
— whether the offender has made any form of reparation or paid compensation.

Note 4A   If a caution is being, or likely to be, considered its significance should be explained to the victim.

Note 4B   In some cases where cautioning might otherwise be appropriate, prosecution may be required in order to protect the victim from further attention from the offender.

Note 4C   If the offender has made some form of reparation or paid compensation, and the victim is satisfied, it may no longer be necessary to prosecute in cases where the possibility of the court's awarding compensation would otherwise have been a major determining factor. *Under no circumstances should police officers become involved in negotiating or awarding reparation or compensation.*

Administration of a caution

5.   A formal caution should be administered in person by a police officer, and wherever practicable at a police station. A juvenile must always be cautioned in the presence of a parent, guardian or other appropriate adult. Members of other vulnerable groups must be treated in accordance with Code of Practice C.

Note 5A.   The officer administering the caution should be in uniform and normally of the rank of inspector or above. In some cases, however, a Community Liaison Officer or Community Constable might be more appropriate, or in the inspector's absence the use of a sergeant might be justified. Chief Officers may therefore wish to consider nominating suitable 'cautioning officers'.

Note 5B   Where the person is elderly, infirm or otherwise vulnerable, a caution may be administered less formally, perhaps at the offender's home and in the presence of a friend or relative or other appropriate adult.

Recording cautions

6.   All formal cautions should be recorded and records kept as directed by the Secretary of State. The use of cautioning should also be monitored on a force-wide basis.

Note 6A   Formal cautions should be cited in court if they are relevant to the offence under consideration. In presenting antecedents, care should be taken to distinguish between cautions and convictions, which should usually be listed on separate sheets of paper.

APPENDIX FIVE

PACE CODE OF PRACTICE FOR THE DETENTION, TREATMENT AND QUESTIONING OF PERSONS BY POLICE OFFICERS (CODE C)

1. General

1.1   All persons in custody must be dealt with expeditiously, and released as soon as the need for detention has ceased to apply.

1.1A   A custody officer is required to perform the functions specified in this code as soon as is practicable. A custody officer shall not be in breach of this code in the event of delay provided that the delay is justifiable and that every reasonable step is taken to prevent unnecessary delay. The custody record shall indicate where a delay has occurred and the reason why. [See Note 1H]

1.2   This code of practice must be readily available at all police stations for consultation by police officers, detained persons and members of the public.

1.3   The notes for guidance included are not provisions of this code, but are guidance to police officers and others about its application and interpretation. Provisions in the annexes to this code are provisions of this code.

1.4   If an officer has any suspicion, or is told in good faith, that a person of any age may be mentally disordered or mentally handicapped, or mentally incapable of understanding the significance of questions put to him or his replies, then that person shall be treated as a mentally disordered or mentally handicapped person for the purposes of this code. [See Note 1G]

1.5   If anyone appears to be under the age of 17 then he shall be treated as a juvenile for the purposes of this code in the absence of clear evidence to show that he is older.

1.6   If a person appears to be blind or seriously visually handicapped, deaf, unable to read, unable to speak or has difficulty orally because of a speech impediment, he should be treated as such for the purposes of this code in the absence of clear evidence to the contrary.

1.7   In this code 'the appropriate adult' means:
   (a)   in the case of a juvenile:

(i)   his parent or guardian (or, if he is in care, the care authority or voluntary organisation. The term 'in care' is used in this code to cover all cases in which a juvenile is 'looked after' by a local authority under the terms of the Children Act 1989);

(ii)   a social worker;

(iii)   failing either of the above, another responsible adult aged 18 or over who is not a police officer or employed by the police.

(b)   in the case of a person who is mentally disordered or mentally handicapped:

(i)   a relative, guardian or other person responsible for his care or custody;

(ii)   someone who has experience of dealing with mentally disordered or mentally handicapped people but is not a police officer or employed by the police (such as an approved social worker as defined by the Mental Health Act 1983 or a specialist social worker); or

(iii)   failing either of the above, some other responsible adult aged 18 or over who is not a police officer or employed by the police.

[See Note 1E]

1.8   Whenever this code requires a person to be given certain information he does not have to be given it if he is incapable at the time of understanding what is said to him or is violent or likely to become violent or is in urgent need of medical attention, but he must be given it as soon as practicable.

1.9   Any reference to a custody officer in this code includes an officer who is performing the functions of a custody officer.

1.10   Subject to paragraph 1.12, this code applies to people who are in custody at police stations in England and Wales whether or not they have been arrested for an offence and to those who have been removed to a police station as a place of safety under sections 135 and 136 of the Mental Health Act 1983. Section 15 (reviews and extensions of detention) however applies solely to people in police detention, for example those who have been brought to a police station under arrest for an offence or have been arrested at a police station for an offence after attending there voluntarily.

1.11   People in police detention include anyone taken to a police station after being arrested under section 14 of the Prevention of Terrorism (Temporary Provisions) Act 1989 or under paragraph 6 of schedule 5 to that Act by an examining officer who is a constable.

1.12   This code does not apply to the following groups of people in custody:

(i)   people who have been arrested by officers from a police force in Scotland exercising their powers of detention under section 137(2) of the Criminal Justice and Public Order Act 1994 (cross border powers of arrest etc.);

(ii)   people arrested under section 3(5) of the Asylum and Immigration Appeals Act 1993 for the purpose of having their fingerprints taken;

(iii)   people who have been served a notice advising them of their detention under powers contained in the Immigration Act 1971;

(iv)   convicted or remanded prisoners held in police cells on behalf of the Prison Service under the Imprisonment (Temporary Provisions) Act 1980;

but the provisions on conditions of detention and treatment in sections 8 and 9 of this code must be considered as the minimum standards of treatment for such detainees.

Notes for Guidance

1A   Although certain sections of this code (e.g. section 9 – treatment of detained persons) apply specifically to people in custody at police stations, those there voluntarily to assist with an investigation should be treated with no less consideration (e.g. offered refreshments at appropriate times) and enjoy an absolute right to obtain legal advice or communicate with anyone outside the police station.

1B   This code does not affect the principle that all citizens have a duty to help police officers to prevent crime and discover offenders. This is a civic rather than a legal duty; but when a police officer is trying to discover whether, or by whom, an offence has been committed he is entitled to question any person from whom he thinks useful information can be obtained, subject to the restrictions imposed by this code. A person's declaration that he is unwilling to reply does not alter this entitlement.

1C   A person, including a parent or guardian, should not be an appropriate adult if he is suspected of involvement in the offence in question, is the victim, is a witness, is involved in the investigation or has received admissions prior to attending to act as the appropriate adult. If the parent of a juvenile is estranged from the juvenile, he should not be asked to act as the appropriate adult if the juvenile expressly and specifically objects to his presence.

1D   If a juvenile admits an offence to or in the presence of a social worker other than during the time that the social worker is acting as the appropriate adult for that juvenile, another social worker should be the appropriate adult in the interest of fairness.

1E   In the case of people who are mentally disordered or mentally handicapped, it may in certain circumstances be more satisfactory for all concerned if the appropriate adult is someone who has experience or training in their care rather than a relative lacking such qualifications. But if the person himself prefers a relative to a better qualified stranger or objects to a particular person as the appropriate adult, his wishes should if practicable be respected.

1EE   A person should always be given an opportunity, when an appropriate adult is called to the police station, to consult privately with a solicitor in the absence of the appropriate adult if they wish to do so.

1F   A solicitor or lay visitor who is present at the police station in that capacity may not act as the appropriate adult.

1G   The generic term 'mental disorder' is used throughout this code. 'Mental disorder' is defined in section 1(2) of the Mental Health Act 1983 as 'mental illness, arrested or incomplete development of mind, psychopathic disorder and any other disorder or disability of mind'. It should be noted that 'mental disorder' is different from 'mental handicap' although the two are dealt with similarly throughout this code. Where the custody officer has any doubt as to the mental state or capacity of a person detained an appropriate adult should be called.

1H   Paragraph 1.1A is intended to cover the kinds of delays which may occur in the processing of detained persons because, for example, a large number of suspects are brought into the police station simultaneously to be placed in custody, or interview rooms are all being used, or where there are difficulties in contacting an appropriate adult, solicitor or interpreter.

1I   It is important that the custody officer reminds the appropriate adult and the detained person of the right to legal advice and records any reasons for waiving it in accordance with section 6 of this code.

2.   Custody records

2.1   A separate custody record must be opened as soon as practicable for each person who is brought to a police station under arrest or is arrested at the police station having attended there voluntarily. All information which has to be recorded under this code must be recorded as soon as practicable in the custody record unless otherwise specified. Any audio or video recording made in the custody area is not part of the custody record.

2.2   In the case of any action requiring the authority of an officer of a specified rank, his name and rank must be noted in the custody record. The recording of names does not apply to officers dealing with people detained under the Prevention of Terrorism (Temporary Provisions) Act 1989. Instead the record shall state the warrant or other identification number and duty station of such officers.

2.3   The custody officer is responsible for the accuracy and completeness of the custody record and for ensuring that the record or a copy of the record accompanies a detained person if he is transferred to another police station. The record shall show the time of and reason for transfer and the time a person is released from detention.

2.4   A solicitor or appropriate adult must be permitted to consult the custody record of a person detained as soon as practicable after their arrival at the police station. When a person leaves police detention or is taken before a court, he or his legal representative or his appropriate adult shall be supplied on request with a copy of the custody record as soon as practicable. This entitlement lasts for 12 months after his release.

2.5   The person who has been detained, the appropriate adult, or the legal representative shall be permitted to inspect the original custody record after the person has left police detention provided they give reasonable notice of their request. A note of any such inspection shall be made in the custody record.

2.6   All entries in custody records must be timed and signed by the maker. In the case of a record entered on a computer this shall be timed and contain the operator's identification. Warrant or other identification numbers shall be used rather than names in the case of detention under the Prevention of Terrorism (Temporary Provisions) Act 1989.

2.7   The fact and time of any refusal by a person to sign a custody record when asked to do so in accordance with the provisions of this code must itself be recorded.

3.   Initial action

(a)   Detained persons: normal procedure

3.1   When a person is brought to a police station under arrest or is arrested at the police station having attended there voluntarily, the custody officer must tell him clearly of the following rights and of the fact that they are continuing rights which may be exercised at any stage during the period in custody.
   (i)   the right to have someone informed of his arrest in accordance with section 5 below;
   (ii)   the right to consult privately with a solicitor and the fact that independent legal advice is available free of charge; and
   (iii)   the right to consult these codes of practice.
[See Note 3E]

3.2   In addition the custody officer must give the person a written notice setting out the above three rights, the right to a copy of the custody record in accordance with paragraph 2.4 above and the caution in the terms prescribed in section 10 below. The notice must also explain the arrangements for obtaining legal advice. The custody officer must also give the person an additional written notice briefly setting out his entitlements while in custody. [See Notes 3A and 3B] The custody officer shall ask the person to sign the custody record to acknowledge receipt of these notices and any refusal to sign must be recorded on the custody record.

3.3   A citizen of an independent Commonwealth country or a national of a foreign country (including the Republic of Ireland) must be informed as soon as practicable of his rights of communication with his High Commission, Embassy or Consulate. [See Section 7]

3.4   The custody officer shall note on the custody record any comment the person may make in relation to the arresting officer's account but shall not invite comment. If the custody officer authorises a person's detention he must inform him of the grounds as soon as practicable and in any case before that person is then questioned about any offence. The custody officer shall note any comment the person may make in respect of the decision to detain him but, again, shall not invite comment. The custody officer shall not put specific questions to the person regarding his involvement in any offence, nor in respect of any comments he may make in response to the arresting officer's account or the decision to place him in detention. Such an exchange is likely to constitute an interview as defined by paragraph 11.1A and would require the associated safeguards included in section 11. [See also paragraph 11.13 in respect of unsolicited comments.]

3.5   The custody officer shall ask the detained person whether at this time he would like legal advice (see paragraph 6.5). The person shall be asked to sign the custody record to confirm his decision. The custody officer is responsible for ensuring that in confirming any decision the person signs in the correct place.

3.5A   If video cameras are installed in the custody area, notices which indicate that cameras are in use shall be prominently displayed. Any request by a detained person or other person to have video cameras switched off shall be refused.

(b)   Detained persons: special groups

3.6   If the person appears to be deaf or there is doubt about his hearing or speaking ability or ability to understand English, and the custody officer cannot establish effective communication, the custody officer must as soon as practicable call an interpreter and ask him to provide the information required above. [See Section 13]

3.7   If the person is a juvenile, the custody officer must, if it is practicable, ascertain the identity of a person responsible for his welfare. That person may be his parent or guardian (or, if he is in care, the care authority or voluntary organisation) or any other person who has, for the time being, assumed responsibility for his welfare. That person must be informed as soon as practicable that the juvenile has been arrested, why he has been arrested and where he is detained. This right is in addition to the juvenile's right in section 5 of the code not to be held incommunicado. [See Note 3C]

3.8   In the case of a juvenile who is known to be subject to a supervision order, reasonable steps must also be taken to notify the person supervising him.

3.9   If the person is a juvenile, is mentally handicapped or appears to be suffering from a mental disorder, then the custody officer must, as soon as practicable, inform the appropriate adult (who in the case of a juvenile may or may not be a person responsible for his welfare, in accordance with paragraph 3.7 above) of the grounds for his detention and his whereabouts, and ask the adult to come to the police station to see the person.

3.10   It is imperative that a mentally disordered or mentally handicapped person who has been detained under section 136 of the Mental Health Act 1983 shall be assessed as soon as possible. If that assessment is to take place at the police station, an approved social worker and a registered medical practitioner shall be called to the police station as soon as possible in order to interview and examine the person. Once the person has been interviewed and examined and suitable arrangements have been made for his treatment or care, he can no longer be detained under section 136. The person should not be released until he has been seen by both the approved social worker and the registered medical practitioner.

3.11   If the appropriate adult is already at the police station, then the provisions of paragraphs 3.1 to 3.5 above must be complied with in his presence. If the appropriate adult is not at the police station when the provisions of paragraphs 3.1 to 3.5 above are complied with, then these provisions must be complied with again in the presence of the appropriate adult once that person arrives.

3.12   The person shall be advised by the custody officer that the appropriate adult (where applicable) is there to assist and advise him and that he can consult privately with the appropriate adult at any time.

3.13   If, having been informed of the right to legal advice under paragraph 3.11 above, either the appropriate adult or the person detained wishes legal advice to be taken, then the provisions of section 6 of this code apply. [See Note 3G]

3.14   If the person is blind or seriously visually handicapped or is unable to read, the custody officer should ensure that his solicitor, relative, the appropriate adult or some other person likely to take an interest in him (and not involved in the investigation) is available to help in checking any documentation. Where this code requires written consent or signification then the person who is assisting may be asked to sign instead if the detained person so wishes. [See Note 3F]

(c)   Persons attending a police station voluntarily

3.15   Any person attending a police station voluntarily for the purpose of assisting with an investigation may leave at will unless placed under arrest. If it is decided that he should not be allowed to leave then he must be informed at once that he is under arrest and brought before the custody officer, who is responsible for ensuring that he is notified of his rights in the same way as other detained persons. If he is not placed under arrest but is cautioned in accordance with section 10 below, the officer who gives the caution must at the same time inform him that he is not under arrest, that he is not obliged to remain at the police station but that if he remains at the police station he may obtain free and independent legal advice if he wishes. The officer shall point out that the right to legal advice includes the right to speak with a solicitor on the telephone and ask him if he wishes to do so.

3.16   If a person who is attending the police station voluntarily (in accordance with paragraph 3.15) asks about his entitlement to legal advice, he shall be given a copy of the notice explaining the arrangements for obtaining legal advice. [See paragraph 3.2]

(d)   Documentation

3.17   The grounds for a person's detention shall be recorded, in his presence if practicable.

3.18   Action taken under paragraphs 3.6 to 3.14 shall be recorded.

PACE CODE OF PRACTICE (CODE C)

Notes for Guidance

3A   The notice of entitlements is intended to provide detained persons with brief details of their entitlements over and above the statutory rights which are set out in the notice of rights. The notice of entitlements should list the entitlements contained in this code, including visits and contact with outside parties (including special provisions for Commonwealth citizens and foreign nationals), reasonable standards of physical comfort, adequate food and drink, access to toilets and washing facilities, clothing, medical attention, and exercise where practicable. It should also mention the provisions relating to the conduct of interviews, the circumstances in which an appropriate adult should be available to assist the detained person and his statutory rights to make representation whenever the period of his detention is reviewed.

3B   In addition to the notices in English, translations should be available in Welsh, the main ethnic minority languages and the principal European languages whenever they are likely to be helpful.

3C   If the juvenile is in the care of a local authority or voluntary organisation but is living with his parents or other adults responsible for his welfare then, although there is no legal obligation on the police to inform them, they as well as the authority or organisation should normally be contacted unless suspected of involvement in the offence concerned. Even if a juvenile in care is not living with his parents, consideration should be given to informing them as well.

3D   Most local authority Social Services Departments can supply a list of interpreters who have the necessary skills and experience to interpret for the deaf at police interviews. The local Community Relations Council may be able to provide similar information in cases where the person concerned does not understand English. [See Section 13]

3E   The right to consult the codes of practice under paragraph 3.1 above does not entitle the person concerned to delay unreasonably any necessary investigative or administrative action while he does so. Procedures requiring the provision of breath, blood or urine specimens under the terms of the Road Traffic Act 1988 need not be delayed.

3F   Blind or seriously visually handicapped persons may be unwilling to sign police documents. The alternative of their representative signing on their behalf seeks to protect the interests of both police and detained people.

3G   The purpose of paragraph 3.13 is to protect the rights of a juvenile, mentally disordered or mentally handicapped person who may not understand the significance of what is being said to him. If such a person wishes to exercise the right to legal advice the appropriate action should be taken straightaway and not delayed until the appropriate adult arrives.

4.   Detained persons' property

(a)   Action

4.1   The custody officer is responsible for:
    (a)   ascertaining:
        (i)   what property a detained person has with him when he comes to the police station (whether on arrest, re-detention on answering to bail, commitment to prison custody on the order or sentence of a court, lodgement at the police station with a view to his production in court from such custody, arrival at a police station on transfer from detention at another police station or from hospital or on detention under section 135 or 136 of the Mental Health Act 1983);
        (ii)   what property he might have acquired for an unlawful or harmful purpose while in custody;
    (b)   the safekeeping of any property which is taken from him and which remains at the police station. To these ends the custody officer may search him or authorise his being searched to the extent that he considers necessary (provided that a search of intimate parts of the body or involving the removal of more than outer clothing may only be made in accordance with Annex A to this code). A search may only be carried out by an officer of the same sex as the person searched. [See Note 4A]

4.2   A detained person may retain clothing and personal effects at his own risk unless the custody officer considers that he may use them to cause harm to himself or others, interfere with evidence, damage property or effect an escape or they are needed as evidence. In this event the custody officer may withhold such articles as he considers necessary. If he does so he must tell the person why.

4.3   Personal effects are those items which a person may lawfully need or use or refer to while in detention but do not include cash and other items of value.

(b)   Documentation

4.4   The custody officer is responsible for recording all property brought to the police station which a detained person had with him, or had taken from him on arrest. The detained person shall be allowed to check and sign the record of property as correct. Any refusal to sign should be recorded.

4.5   If a detained person is not allowed to keep any article of clothing or personal effects the reason must be recorded.

Notes for Guidance

4A   Section 54(1) of PACE and paragraph 4.1 require a detained person to be searched where it is clear that the custody officer will have continuing duties in relation to that person or where that person's behaviour or offence makes an inventory appropriate. They do not require *every* detained person to be searched. Where, for example, it is clear that a person will only be detained for a short period and is not to be placed in a cell, the custody officer may decide not to search him. In such a case the custody record will be endorsed 'not searched', paragraph 4.4 will not apply, and the person will be invited to sign the entry. Where the person detained refuses to sign, the custody officer will be obliged to ascertain what property he has on him in accordance with paragraph 4.1.

4B   Paragraph 4.4 does not require the custody officer to record on the custody record property in the possession of the person on arrest, if by virtue of its nature, quantity or size, it is not practicable to remove it to the police station.

4C   Paragraph 4.4 above is not to be taken as requiring that items of clothing worn by the person be recorded unless withheld by the custody officer in accordance with paragraph 4.2.

5.   Right not to be held incommunicado

(a)   Action

5.1   Any person arrested and held in custody at a police station or other premises may on request have one person known to him or who is likely to take an interest in his welfare informed at public expense of his whereabouts as soon as practicable. If the person cannot be contacted the person who has made the request may choose up to two alternatives. If they too cannot be contacted the person in charge of detention or of the investigation has discretion to allow further attempts until the information has been conveyed. [See Notes 5C and 5D]

5.2   The exercise of the above right in respect of each of the persons nominated may be delayed only in accordance with Annex B to this code.

5.3   The above right may be exercised on each occasion that a person is taken to another police station.

5.4   The person may receive visits at the custody officer's discretion. [See Note 5B]

5.5   Where an enquiry as to the whereabouts of the person is made by a friend, relative or person with an interest in his welfare, this information shall be given, if he agrees and if Annex B does not apply. [See Note 5D]

5.6   Subject to the following condition, the person shall be supplied with writing materials on request and allowed to speak on the telephone for a reasonable time to one person [See Notes 5A and 5E]. Where an officer of the rank of inspector or above considers that the sending of a letter or the making of a telephone call may result in:
   (a)   any of the consequences set out in the first and second paragraphs of Annex B and the person is detained in connection with an arrestable or a serious arrestable offence, for which purpose, any reference to a serious arrestable offence in Annex B includes an arrestable offence; or
   (b)   either of the consequences set out in paragraph 8 of Annex B and the person is detained under the Prevention of Terrorism (Temporary Provisions) Act 1989;

that officer can deny or delay the exercise of either or both these privileges. However, nothing in this section permits the restriction or denial of the rights set out in paragraphs 5.1 and 6.1.

5.7   Before any letter or message is sent, or telephone call made, the person shall be informed that what he says in any letter, call or message (other than in the case of a communication to a solicitor) may be read or listened to as appropriate and may be given in evidence. A telephone call may be terminated if it is being abused. The costs can be at public expense at the discretion of the custody officer.

(b)   Documentation

5.8   A record must be kept of:
    (a)   any request made under this section and the action taken on it;
    (b)   any letters, messages or telephone calls made or received or visits received; and
    (c)   any refusal on the part of the person to have information about himself or his whereabouts given to an outside enquirer. The person must be asked to countersign the record accordingly and any refusal to sign shall be recorded.

Notes for Guidance

5A   An interpreter may make a telephone call or write a letter on a person's behalf.

5B   In the exercise of his discretion the custody officer should allow visits where possible in the light of the availability of sufficient manpower to supervise a visit and any possible hindrance to the investigation.

5C   If the person does not know of anyone to contact for advice or support or cannot contact a friend or relative, the custody officer should bear in mind any local voluntary bodies or other organisations who might be able to offer help in such cases. But if it is specifically legal advice that is wanted, then paragraph 6.1 below will apply.

5D   In some circumstances it may not be appropriate to use the telephone to disclose information under paragraphs 5.1 and 5.5 above.

5E   The telephone call at paragraph 5.6 is in addition to any communication under paragraphs 5.1 and 6.1.

6.   Right to legal advice

(a)   Action

6.1   Subject to the provisos in Annex B all people in police detention must be informed that they may at any time consult and communicate privately, whether in person, in writing or by telephone with a solicitor, and that independent legal advice is available free of charge from the duty solicitor. [See paragraph 3.1 and Note 6B and Note 6J]

6.2   [Not Used]

6.3   A poster advertising the right to have legal advice must be prominently displayed in the charging area of every police station. [See Note 6H]

6.4   No police officer shall at any time do or say anything with the intention of dissuading a person in detention from obtaining legal advice.

6.5   The exercise of the right of access to legal advice may be delayed only in accordance with Annex B to this code. Whenever legal advice is requested (and unless Annex B applies) the custody officer must act without delay to secure the provision of such advice to the person concerned. If, on being informed or reminded of the right to legal advice, the person declines to speak to a solicitor in person, the officer shall point out that the right to legal advice includes the right to speak with a solicitor on the telephone and ask him if he wishes to do so. If the person continues to waive his right to legal advice the officer shall ask him the reasons for doing so, and any reasons shall be recorded on the custody record or the interview record as appropriate. Reminders of the right to legal advice must be given in accordance with paragraphs 3.5, 11.2, 15.3, 16.4 and 16.5 of this code and paragraphs 2.15(ii) and 5.2 of Code D. Once it is clear that a person neither wishes to speak to a solicitor in person nor by telephone he should cease to be asked his reasons. [See Note 6K]

6.6   A person who wants legal advice may not be interviewed or continue to be interviewed until he has received it unless:
    (a)   Annex B applies; or
    (b)   an officer of the rank of superintendent or above has reasonable grounds for believing that:
        (i)   delay will involve an immediate risk of harm to persons or serious loss of, or damage to, property; or
        (ii)   where a solicitor, including a duty solicitor, has been contacted and has agreed to attend, awaiting his arrival would cause unreasonable delay to the process of investigation; or
    (c)   the solicitor nominated by the person, or selected by him from a list:
        (i)   cannot be contacted; or
        (ii)   has previously indicated that he does not wish to be contacted; or
        (iii)   having been contacted, has declined to attend;
and the person has been advised of the Duty Solicitor Scheme but has declined to ask for the duty solicitor, or the duty solicitor is unavailable. (In these circumstances the interview may be started or continued without further delay provided that an officer of the rank of Inspector or above has given agreement for the interview to proceed in those circumstances – See Note 6B.)
    (d)   the person who wanted legal advice changes his mind.
In these circumstances the interview may be started or continued without further delay provided that the person has given his agreement in writing or on tape to being interviewed without receiving legal advice and that an officer of the rank of inspector or above, having inquired into the person's reasons for his change of mind, has given authority for the interview to proceed. Confirmation of the person's agreement, his change of mind, his reasons where given and the name of the authorising officer shall be recorded in the taped or written interview record at the beginning or re-commencement of interview. [See Note 6I]

6.7   Where 6.6(b)(i) applies, once sufficient information to avert the risk has been obtained, questioning must cease until the person has received legal advice unless 6.6(a), (b)(ii), (c) or (d) apply.

6.8   Where a person has been permitted to consult a solicitor and the solicitor is available (i.e. present at the station or on his way to the station or easily contactable by telephone) at the time the interview begins or is in progress, the solicitor must be allowed to be present while he is interviewed.

6.9   The solicitor may only be required to leave the interview if his conduct is such that the investigating officer is unable properly to put questions to the suspect. [See Notes 6D and 6E]

6.10   If the investigating officer considers that a solicitor is acting in such a way, he will stop the interview and consult an officer not below the rank of superintendent, if one is readily available, and otherwise an officer not below the rank of inspector who is not connected with the investigation. After speaking to the solicitor, the officer who has been consulted will decide whether or not the interview should continue in the presence of that solicitor. If he decides that it should not, the suspect will be given the opportunity to consult another solicitor before the interview continues and that solicitor will be given an opportunity to be present at the interview.

6.11   The removal of a solicitor from an interview is a serious step and, if it occurs, the officer of superintendent rank or above who took the decision will consider whether the incident should be reported to the Law Society. If the decision to remove the solicitor has been taken by an officer below the rank of superintendent, the facts must be reported to an officer of superintendent rank or above who will similarly consider whether a report to the Law Society would be appropriate. Where the solicitor concerned is a duty solicitor, the report should be both to the Law Society and to the Legal Aid Board.

6.12   In Codes of Practice issued under the Police and Criminal Evidence Act 1984, 'solicitor' means a solicitor who holds a current practising certificate, a trainee solicitor, a duty solicitor representative or an accredited representative included on the register of representatives maintained by the Legal Aid Board. If a solicitor wishes to send a non-accredited or probationary representative to provide advice on his behalf, then that person shall be admitted to the police station for this purpose unless an officer of the rank of inspector or above considers that such a visit will hinder the investigation of crime and directs otherwise. (Hindering the investigation of a crime does not include giving proper legal advice to a detained person in accordance with Note 6D.) Once admitted to the police station, the provisions of paragraphs 6.6 to 6.10 apply.

6.13   In exercising his discretion under paragraph 6.12, the officer should take into account in particular whether the identity and status of the non-accredited or probationary representative have been [satisfactorily] established; whether he is of suitable character to provide legal advice (a person with a criminal record is unlikely to be suitable unless the conviction was for a minor offence and is not of recent date); and any other matters in any written letter of authorisation provided by the solicitor on whose behalf the clerk or legal executive is attending the police station. [See Note 6F]

6.14   If the inspector refuses access to a non-accredited or probationary representative or a decision is taken that such a person should not be permitted to remain at an interview, he must forthwith notify a solicitor on whose behalf the non-accredited or probationary representative was to have acted or was acting, and give him an opportunity to make alternative arrangements. The detained person must also be informed and the custody record noted.

6.15   If a solicitor arrives at the station to see a particular person, that person must (unless Annex B applies) be informed of the solicitor's arrival whether or not he is being interviewed and asked whether he would like to see him. This applies even if the person concerned has already declined legal advice or having requested it, subsequently agreed to be interviewed without having received advice. The solicitor's attendance and the detained person's decision must be noted in the custody record.

(b)   Documentation

6.16   Any request for legal advice and the action taken on it shall be recorded.

6.17   If a person has asked for legal advice and an interview is begun in the absence of a solicitor or his representative (or the solicitor or his representative has been required to leave an interview), a record shall be made in the interview record.

Notes for Guidance

6A   In considering whether paragraph 6.6(b) applies, the officer should where practicable ask the solicitor for an estimate of the time that he is likely to take in coming to the station, and relate this information to the time for which detention is permitted, the time of day (i.e. whether the period of rest required by paragraph 12.2 is imminent) and the requirements of other investigations in progress. If the solicitor says that he is on his way to the station or that he will set off immediately, it will not normally be appropriate to begin an interview before he arrives. If it appears that it will be necessary to begin an interview before the solicitor's arrival he should be given an indication of how long the police would be able to wait before paragraph 6.6(b) applies so that he has an opportunity to make arrangements for legal advice to be provided by someone else.

6B   A person who asks for legal advice should be given an opportunity to consult a specific solicitor or another solicitor from that solicitor's firm or the duty solicitor. If advice is not available by these means, or he does not wish to consult the duty solicitor, the person should be given an opportunity to choose a solicitor from a list of those willing to provide legal advice. If this solicitor is unavailable, he may choose up [to] two alternatives. If these attempts to secure legal advice are unsuccessful, the custody officer has discretion to allow further attempts until a solicitor has been contacted and agrees to provide legal advice. Apart from carrying out his duties under Note 6B, a police officer must not advise the suspect about any particular firm of solicitors.

6C   [Not Used]

6D   A detained person has a right to free legal advice and to be represented by a solicitor. The solicitor's only role in the police station is to protect and advance the legal rights of his client. On occasions this may require the solicitor to give advice which has the effect of his client avoiding giving evidence which strengthens a prosecution case. The solicitor may intervene in order to seek clarification or to challenge an improper question to his client or the manner in which it is put, or to advise his client not to reply to particular questions, or if he wishes to give his client further legal advice. Paragraph 6.9 will only apply if the solicitor's approach or conduct prevents or unreasonably obstructs proper questions being put to the suspect or his response being recorded. Examples of unacceptable conduct include answering questions on a suspect's behalf or providing written replies for him to quote.

6E   In a case where an officer takes the decision to exclude a solicitor, he must be in a position to satisfy the court that the decision was properly made. In order to do this he may need to witness what is happening himself.

6F   If an officer of at least the rank of inspector considers that a particular solicitor or firm of solicitors is persistently sending non-accredited or probationary representatives who are unsuited to provide legal advice, he should inform an officer of at least the rank of superintendent, who may wish to take the matter up with the Law Society.

6G   Subject to the constraints of Annex B, a solicitor may advise more than one client in an investigation if he wishes. Any question of a conflict of interest is for the solicitor under his professional code of conduct. If, however, waiting for a solicitor to give advice to one client may lead to unreasonable delay to the interview with another, the provisions of paragraph 6.6(b) may apply.

6H   In addition to the poster in English advertising the right to legal advice, a poster or posters containing translations into Welsh, the main ethnic minority languages and the principal European languages should be displayed wherever they are likely to be helpful and it is practicable to do so.

6I   Paragraph 6.6(d) requires the authorisation of an officer of the rank of inspector or above, to the continuation of an interview, where a person who wanted legal advice changes his mind. It is permissible for such authorisation to be given over the telephone, if the authorising officer is able to satisfy himself as to the reason for the person's change of mind and is satisfied that it is proper to continue the interview in those circumstances.

6J   Where a person chooses to speak to a solicitor on the telephone, he should be allowed to do so in private unless this is impractical because of the design and layout of the custody area or the location of telephones.

6K   A person is not obliged to give reasons for declining legal advice and should not be pressed if he does not wish to do so.

7.   Citizens of Independent Commonwealth countries or foreign nationals

(a)   Action

7.1   Any citizen of an independent Commonwealth country or a national of a foreign country (including the Republic of Ireland) may communicate at any time with his High Commission, Embassy or Consulate. He must be informed of this right as soon as practicable. He must also be informed as soon as practicable of his right, upon request to have his High Commission, Embassy or Consulate told of his whereabouts and the grounds for his detention. Such a request should be acted upon as soon as practicable.

7.2   If a person is detained who is a citizen of an independent Commonwealth or foreign country with which a bilateral consular convention or agreement is in force requiring notification of arrest, the appropriate High Commission, Embassy or Consulate shall be informed as soon as practicable, subject to paragraph 7.4 below. The countries to which this applies as at 1 January 1995 are listed in Annex F.

7.3   Consular officers may visit one of their nationals who is in police detention to talk to him and, if required, to arrange for legal advice. Such visits shall take place out of the hearing of a police officer.

7.4   Notwithstanding the provisions of consular conventions, where the person is a political refugee (whether for reasons of race, nationality, political opinion or religion) or is seeking political asylum, a consular officer shall not be informed of the arrest of one of his nationals or given access or information about him except at the person's express request.

(b)   Documentation

7.5   A record shall be made when a person is informed of his rights under this section and of any communications with a High Commission, Embassy or Consulate.

Note for Guidance

7A   The exercise of the rights in this section may not be interfered with even though Annex B applies.

PACE CODE OF PRACTICE (CODE C)

8. Conditions of Detention

(a) Action

8.1   So far as is practicable, not more than one person shall be detained in each cell.

8.2   Cells in use must be adequately heated, cleaned and ventilated. They must be adequately lit, subject to such dimming as is compatible with safety and security to allow people detained overnight to sleep. No additional restraints shall be used within a locked cell unless absolutely necessary, and then only suitable handcuffs. In the case of a mentally handicapped or mentally disordered person, particular care must be taken when deciding whether to use handcuffs. [See Annex E paragraph 13]

8.3   Blankets, mattresses, pillows and other bedding supplied shall be of a reasonable standard and in a clean and sanitary condition. [See Note 8B]

8.4   Access to toilet and washing facilities must be provided.

8.5   If it is necessary to remove a person's clothes for the purposes of investigation, for hygiene or health reasons or for cleaning, replacement clothing of a reasonable standard of comfort and cleanliness shall be provided. A person may not be interviewed unless adequate clothing has been offered to him.

8.6   At least two light meals and one main meal shall be offered in any period of 24 hours. [See Note 8C] Drinks should be provided at meal times and upon reasonable request between meal times. Whenever necessary, advice shall be sought from the police surgeon on medical or dietary matters. As far as practicable, meals provided shall offer a varied diet and meet any special dietary needs or religious beliefs that the person may have; he may also have meals supplied by his family or friends at his or their own expense. [See Note 8B]

8.7   Brief outdoor exercise shall be offered daily if practicable.

8.8   A juvenile shall not be placed in a police cell unless no other secure accommodation is available and the custody officer considers that it is not practicable to supervise him if he is not placed in a cell or the custody officer considers that a cell provides more comfortable accommodation than other secure accommodation in the police station. He may not be placed in a cell with a detained adult.

8.9   Reasonable force may be used if necessary for the following purposes:
    (i)   to secure compliance with reasonable instructions, including instructions given in pursuance of the provisions of a code of practice; or
    (ii)   to prevent escape, injury, damage to property or the destruction of evidence.

8.10   People detained shall be visited every hour, and those who are drunk, at least every half hour. A person who is drunk shall be roused and spoken to on each visit. [See Note 8A] Should the custody officer feel in any way concerned about the person's condition, for example because he fails to respond adequately when roused, then the officer shall arrange for medical treatment in accordance with paragraph 9.2 of this code.

(b) Documentation

8.11   A record must be kept of replacement clothing and meals offered.

8.12   If a juvenile is placed in a cell, the reason must be recorded.

Notes for Guidance

8A   Whenever possible juveniles and other persons at risk should be visited more frequently.

8B   The provisions in paragraphs 8.3 and 8.6 respectively regarding bedding and a varied diet are of particular importance in the case of a person detained under the Prevention of Terrorism (Temporary Provisions) Act 1989, immigration detainees and others who are likely to be detained for an extended period.

8C   Meals should so far as practicable be offered at recognised meal times.

9. Treatment of Detained Persons

(a)   General

9.1   If a complaint is made by or on behalf of a detained person about his treatment since his arrest, or it comes to the notice of any officer that he may have been treated improperly, a report must be made as soon as practicable to an officer of the rank of inspector or above who is not connected with the investigation. If the matter concerns a possible assault or the possibility of the unnecessary or unreasonable use of force then the police surgeon must also be called as soon as practicable.

(b)   Medical Treatment

9.2   The custody officer must immediately call the police surgeon (or, in urgent cases, – for example, where a person does not show signs of sensibility or awareness, – must send the person to hospital or call the nearest available medical practitioner) if a person brought to a police station or already detained there:
  (a)   appears to be suffering from physical illness or a mental disorder; or
  (b)   is injured; or
  (c)   [Not Used]
  (d)   fails to respond normally to questions or conversation (other than through drunkenness alone); or
  (e)   otherwise appears to need medical attention.
This applies even if the person makes no request for medical attention and whether or not he has already had medical treatment elsewhere (unless brought to the police station direct from hospital). It is not intended that the contents of this paragraph should delay the transfer of a person to a place of safety under section 136 of the Mental Health Act 1983 where that is applicable. Where an assessment under that Act is to take place at the police station, the custody officer has discretion not to call the police surgeon so long as he believes that the assessment by a registered medical practitioner can be undertaken without undue delay. [See Note 9A]

9.3   If it appears to the custody officer, or he is told, that a person brought to the police station under arrest may be suffering from an infectious disease of any significance he must take steps to isolate the person and his property until he has obtained medical directions as to where the person should be taken, whether fumigation should take place and what precautions should be taken by officers who have been or will be in contact with him.

9.4   If a detained person requests a medical examination the police surgeon must be called as soon as practicable. He may in addition be examined by a medical practitioner of his own choice at his own expense.

9.5   If a person is required to take or apply any medication in compliance with medical directions, but prescribed before the person's detention, the custody officer should consult the police surgeon prior to the use of the medication. The custody officer is responsible for the safekeeping of any medication and for ensuring that the person is given the opportunity to take or apply medication which the police surgeon has approved. However no police officer may administer medicines which are also controlled drugs subject to the Misuse of Drugs Act 1971 for this purpose. A person may administer a controlled drug to himself only under the personal supervision of the police surgeon. The requirement for personal supervision will have been satisfied if the custody officer consults the police surgeon (this may be done by telephone) and both the police surgeon and the custody officer are satisfied that, in all the circumstances, self administration of the controlled drug will not expose the detained person, police officers or anyone to the risk of harm or injury. If so satisfied, the police surgeon may authorise the custody officer to permit the detained person to administer the controlled drug. If the custody officer is in any doubt, the police surgeon should be asked to attend. Such consultation should be noted in the custody record.

9.6   If a detained person has in his possession or claims to need medication relating to a heart condition, diabetes, epilepsy or a condition of comparable potential seriousness then, even though paragraph 9.2 may not apply, the advice of the police surgeon must be obtained.

(c)   Documentation

9.7   A record must be made of any arrangements made for an examination by a police surgeon under paragraph 9.1 above and of any complaint reported under that paragraph together with any relevant remarks by the custody officer.

9.8   A record must be kept of any request for a medical examination under paragraph 9.4, of the arrangements for any examination made, and of any medical directions to the police.

9.9   Subject to the requirements of section 4 above the custody record shall include not only a record of all medication that a detained person has in his possession on arrival at the police station but also a note of any such medication he claims he needs but does not have with him.

Notes for Guidance

9A   The need to call a police surgeon need not apply to minor ailments or injuries which do not need attention. However, all such ailments or injuries must be recorded in the custody record and any doubt must be resolved in favour of calling the police surgeon.

9B   It is important to remember that a person who appears to be drunk or behaving abnormally may be suffering from illness or the effects of drugs or may have sustained injury (particularly head injury) which is not apparent, and that someone needing or addicted to certain drugs may experience harmful effects within a short time of being deprived of their supply. Police should therefore always call the police surgeon when in any doubt, and act with all due speed.

9C   If a medical practitioner does not record his clinical findings in the custody record, the record must show where they are recorded.

10.   Cautions

(a)   When a caution must be given

10.1   A person whom there are grounds to suspect of an offence must be cautioned before any questions about it (or further questions if it is his answers to previous questions which provide the grounds for suspicion) are put to him regarding his involvement or suspected involvement in that offence if his answers or his silence (i.e. failure or refusal to answer a question or to answer satisfactorily) may be given in evidence to a court in a prosecution. He therefore need not be cautioned if questions are put for other purposes, for example, solely to establish his identity or his ownership of any vehicle or to obtain information in accordance with any relevant statutory requirement (see paragraph 10.5C) or in furtherance of the proper and effective conduct of a search (for example to determine the need to search in the exercise of powers of stop and search or to seek cooperation while carrying out a search), or to seek verification of a written record in accordance with paragraph 11.13.

10.2   Whenever a person who is not under arrest is initially cautioned or is reminded that he is under caution (see paragraph 10.5) he must at the same time be told that he is not under arrest and is not obliged to remain with the officer (see paragraph 3.15).

10.3   A person must be cautioned upon arrest for an offence unless:
    (a)   it is impracticable to do so by reason of his condition or behaviour at the time; or
    (b)   he has already been cautioned immediately prior to arrest in accordance with paragraph 10.1 above.

(b)   Action: general

10.4   The caution shall be in the following terms:

'You do not have to say anything. But it may harm your defence if you do not mention when questioned something which you later rely on in court. Anything you do say may be given in evidence.'

Minor deviations do not constitute a breach of this requirement provided that the sense of the caution is preserved. [See Note 10C]

10.5   When there is a break in questioning under caution the interviewing officer must ensure that the person being questioned is aware that he remains under caution. If there is any doubt the caution should be given again in full when the interview resumes. [See Note 10A]

Special warnings under sections 36 and 37 of the Criminal Justice and Public Order Act 1994

10.5A   When a suspect who is interviewed after arrest fails or refuses to answer certain questions, or to answer them satisfactorily, after due warning, a court or jury may draw such inferences as appear proper under sections 36 and 37 of the Criminal Justice and Public Order Act 1994. This applies when:

(a)   a suspect is arrested by a constable and there is found on his person, or in or on his clothing or footwear, or otherwise in his possession, or in the place where he was arrested, any objects, marks or substances, or marks on such objects, and the person fails or refuses to account for the objects, marks or substances found; or

(b)   an arrested person was found by a constable at a place at or about the time the offence for which he was arrested, is alleged to have been committed, and the person fails or refuses to account for his presence at that place.

10.5B   For an inference to be drawn from a suspect's failure or refusal to answer a question about one of these matters or to answer it satisfactorily, the interviewing officer must first tell him in ordinary language:

(a)   what offence he is investigating;

(b)   what fact he is asking the suspect to account for;

(c)   that he believes this fact may be due to the suspect's taking part in the commission of the offence in question;

(d)   that a court may draw a proper inference if he fails or refuses to account for the fact about which he is being questioned;

(e)   that a record is being made of the interview and that it may be given in evidence if he is brought to trial.

10.5C   Where, despite the fact that a person has been cautioned, failure to cooperate may have an effect on his immediate treatment, he should be informed of any relevant consequences and that they are not affected by the caution. Examples are when his refusal to provide his name and address when charged may render him liable to detention, or when his refusal to provide particulars and information in accordance with a statutory requirement, for example, under the Road Traffic Act 1988, may amount to an offence or may make him liable to arrest.

(c)   Juveniles, the mentally disordered and the mentally handicapped

10.6   If a juvenile or a person who is mentally disordered or mentally handicapped is cautioned in the absence of the appropriate adult, the caution must be repeated in the adult's presence.

(d)   Documentation

10.7   A record shall be made when a caution is given under this section, either in the officer's pocket book or in the interview record as appropriate.

Notes for Guidance

10A   In considering whether or not to caution again after a break, the officer should bear in mind that he may have to satisfy a court that the person understood that he was still under caution when the interview resumed.

10B   [Not Used]

10C   If it appears that a person does not understand what the caution means, the officer who has given it should go on to explain it in his own words.

10D   [Not Used]

11.   Interviews: general

(a)   Action

11.1A   An interview is the questioning of a person regarding his involvement or suspected involvement in a criminal offence or offences which, by virtue of paragraph 10.1 of Code C, is required to be carried out under caution. Procedures undertaken under section 7 of the Road Traffic Act 1988 do not constitute interviewing for the purpose of this code.

PACE CODE OF PRACTICE (CODE C)

11.1   Following a decision to arrest a suspect he must not be interviewed about the relevant offence except at a police station or other authorised place of detention unless the consequent delay would be likely:

(a)   to lead to interference with or harm to evidence connected with an offence or interference with or physical harm to other people; or

(b)   to lead to the alerting of other people suspected of having committed an offence but not yet arrested for it; or

(c)   to hinder the recovery of property obtained in consequence of the commission of an offence.

Interviewing in any of these circumstances shall cease once the relevant risk has been averted or the necessary questions have been put in order to attempt to avert that risk.

11.2   Immediately prior to the commencement or re-commencement of any interview at a police station or other authorised place of detention, the interviewing officer shall remind the suspect of his entitlement to free legal advice and that the interview can be delayed for him to obtain legal advice (unless the exceptions in paragraph 6.6 or Annex C apply). It is the responsibility of the interviewing officer to ensure that all such reminders are noted in the record of interview.

11.2A   At the beginning of an interview carried out in a police station, the interviewing officer, after cautioning the suspect, shall put to him any significant statement or silence which occurred before his arrival at the police station, and shall ask him whether he confirms or denies that earlier statement or silence and whether he wishes to add anything. A 'significant' statement or silence is one which appears capable of being used in evidence against the suspect, in particular a direct admission of guilt, or failure or refusal to answer a question or to answer it satisfactorily, which might give rise to an inference under part III of the Criminal Justice and Public Order Act 1994.

11.3   No police officer may try to obtain answers to questions or to elicit a statement by the use of oppression. Except as provided for in paragraph 10.5C, no police officer shall indicate, except in answer to a direct question, what action will be taken on the part of the police if the person being interviewed answers questions, makes a statement or refuses to do either. If the person asks the officer directly what action will be taken in the event of his answering questions, making a statement or refusing to do either, then the officer may inform the person what action the police propose to take in that event provided that action is itself proper and warranted.

11.4   As soon as a police officer who is making enquiries of any person about an offence believes that a prosecution should be brought against him and that there is sufficient evidence for it to succeed, he should ask the person if he has anything further to say. If the person indicates that he has nothing more to say the officer shall without delay cease to question him about that offence. This should not, however, be taken to prevent officers in revenue cases or acting under the confiscation provisions of the Criminal Justice Act 1988 or the Drug Trafficking [Act 1994] from inviting suspects to complete a formal question and answer record after the interview is concluded.

(b)   Interview records

11.5   (a)   An accurate record must be made of each interview with a person suspected of an offence, whether or not the interview takes place at a police station.

(b)   The record must state the place of the interview, the time it begins and ends, the time the record is made (if different), any breaks in the interview and the names of all those present; and must be made on the forms provided for this purpose or in the officer's pocket-book or in accordance with the code of practice for the tape-recording of police interviews with suspects (Code E).

(c)   The record must be made during the course of the interview, unless in the investigating officer's view this would not be practicable or would interfere with the conduct of the interview, and must constitute either a verbatim record of what has been said or, failing this, an account of the interview which adequately and accurately summarises it.

11.6   The requirement to record the names of all those present at an interview does not apply to police officers interviewing people detained under the Prevention of Terrorism (Temporary Provisions) Act 1989. Instead the record shall state the warrant or other identification number and duty station of such officers.

11.7   If an interview record is not made during the course of the interview it must be made as soon as practicable after its completion.

11.8   Written interview records must be timed and signed by the maker.

11.9   If an interview record is not completed in the course of the interview the reason must be recorded in the officer's pocket book.

11.10   Unless it is impracticable the person interviewed shall be given the opportunity to read the interview record and to sign it as correct or to indicate the respects in which he considers it inaccurate. If the interview is tape-recorded the arrangements set out in Code E apply. If the person concerned cannot read or refuses to read the record or to sign it, the senior police officer present shall read it over to him and ask him whether he would like to sign it as correct (or make his mark) or to indicate the respects in which he considers it inaccurate. The police officer shall then certify on the interview record itself what has occurred. [See Note 11D]

11.11   If the appropriate adult or the person's solicitor is present during the interview, he shall also be given an opportunity to read and sign the interview record (or any written statement taken down by a police officer).

11.12   Any refusal by a person to sign an interview record when asked to do so in accordance with the provisions of the code must itself be recorded.

11.13   A written record shall also be made of any comments made by a suspected person, including unsolicited comments, which are outside the context of an interview but which might be relevant to the offence. Any such record must be timed and signed by the maker. Where practicable the person shall be given the opportunity to read that record and to sign it as correct or to indicate the respects in which he considers it inaccurate. Any refusal to sign shall be recorded. [See Note 11D]

(c)   Juveniles, mentally disordered people and mentally handicapped people

11.14   A juvenile or a person who is mentally disordered or mentally handicapped, whether suspected or not, must not be interviewed or asked to provide or sign a written statement in the absence of the appropriate adult unless paragraph 11.1 or Annex C applies.

11.15   Juveniles may only be interviewed at their places of education in exceptional circumstances and then only where the principal or his nominee agrees. Every effort should be made to notify both the parent(s) or other person responsible for the juvenile's welfare and the appropriate adult (if this is a different person) that the police want to interview the juvenile and reasonable time should be allowed to enable the appropriate adult to be present at the interview. Where awaiting the appropriate adult would cause unreasonable delay and unless the interviewee is suspected of an offence against the educational establishment, the principal or his nominee can act as the appropriate adult for the purposes of the interview.

11.16   Where the appropriate adult is present at an interview, he should be informed that he is not expected to act simply as an observer; and also that the purposes of his presence are, first, to advise the person being questioned and to observe whether or not the interview is being conducted properly and fairly, and secondly, to facilitate communication with the person being interviewed.

Notes for Guidance

11A   [Not Used]

11B   It is important to bear in mind that, although juveniles or people who are mentally disordered or mentally handicapped are often capable of providing reliable evidence, they may, without knowing or wishing to do so, be particularly prone in certain circumstances to provide information which is unreliable, misleading or self-incriminating. Special care should therefore always be exercised in questioning such a person, and the appropriate adult should be involved, if there is any doubt about a person's age, mental state or capacity. Because of the risk of unreliable evidence it is also important to obtain corroboration of any facts admitted whenever possible.

11C   It is preferable that a juvenile is not arrested at his place of education unless this is unavoidable. Where a juvenile is arrested at his place of education, the principal or his nominee must be informed.

11D   When a suspect agrees to read records of interviews and of other comments and to sign them as correct, he should be asked to endorse the record with words such as 'I agree that this is a correct record of what was said' and add his signature. Where the suspect does not agree with the record, the officer should record the details of any disagreement and then ask the suspect to read these details and then sign them to the effect that they accurately reflect his disagreement. Any refusal to sign when asked to do so shall be recorded.

12. Interviews in police stations

(a) Action

12.1   If a police officer wishes to interview, or conduct enquiries which require the presence of a detained person, the custody officer is responsible for deciding whether to deliver him into his custody.

12.2   In any period of 24 hours a detained person must be allowed a continuous period of at least 8 hours for rest, free from questioning, travel or any interruption by police officers in connection with the investigation concerned. This period should normally be at night. The period of rest may not be interrupted or delayed, except at the request of the person, his appropriate adult or his legal representative, unless there are reasonable grounds for believing that it would:
  (i)   involve a risk of harm to persons or serious loss of, or damage to, property; or
  (ii)   delay unnecessarily the person's release from custody; or
  (iii)   otherwise prejudice the outcome of the investigation.
If a person is arrested at a police station after going there voluntarily, the period of 24 hours runs from the time of his arrest and not the time of arrival at the police station. Any action which is required to be taken in accordance with section 8 of this code, or in accordance with medical advice or at the request of the detained person, his appropriate adult or his legal representative, does not constitute an interruption to the rest period such that a fresh period must be allowed.

12.3   A detained person may not be supplied with intoxicating liquor except on medical directions. No person, who is unfit through drink or drugs to the extent that he is unable to appreciate the significance of questions put to him and his answers, may be questioned about an alleged offence in that condition except in accordance with Annex C. [See Note 12B]

12.4   As far as practicable interviews shall take place in interview rooms which must be adequately heated, lit and ventilated.

12.5   People being questioned or making statements shall not be required to stand.

12.6   Before the commencement of an interview each interviewing officer shall identify himself and any other officers present by name and rank to the person being interviewed, except in the case of persons detained under the Prevention of Terrorism (Temporary Provisions) Act 1989 when each officer shall identify himself by his warrant or other identification number and rank rather than his name.

12.7   Breaks from interviewing shall be made at recognised meal times. Short breaks for refreshment shall also be provided at intervals of approximately two hours, subject to the interviewing officer's discretion to delay a break if there are reasonable grounds for believing that it would:
  (i)   involve a risk of harm to people or serious loss of, or damage to, property;
  (ii)   delay unnecessarily the person's release from custody; or
  (iii)   otherwise prejudice the outcome of the investigation.

[See Note 12C]

12.8   If in the course of the interview a complaint is made by the person being questioned or on his behalf concerning the provisions of this code then the interviewing officer shall:
  (i)   record it in the interview record; and
  (ii)   inform the custody officer, who is then responsible for dealing with it in accordance with section 9 of this code.

(b) Documentation

12.9   A record must be made of the time at which a detained person is not in the custody of the custody officer, and why; and of the reason for any refusal to deliver him out of that custody.

12.10   A record must be made of any intoxicating liquor supplied to a detained person, in accordance with paragraph 12.3 above.

12.11   Any decision to delay a break in an interview must be recorded, with grounds, in the interview record.

12.12   All written statements made at police stations under caution shall be written on the forms provided for the purpose.

12.13   All written statements made under caution shall be taken in accordance with Annex D to this code.

Notes for Guidance

12A   If the interview has been contemporaneously recorded and the record signed by the person interviewed in accordance with paragraph 11.10 above, or has been tape recorded, it is normally unnecessary to ask for a written statement. Statements under caution should normally be taken in these circumstances only at the person's express wish. An officer may, however, ask him whether or not he wants to make such a statement.

12B   The police surgeon can give advice about whether or not a person is fit to be interviewed in accordance with paragraph 12.3 above.

12C   Meal breaks should normally last at least 45 minutes and shorter breaks after two hours should last at least 15 minutes. If the interviewing officer delays a break in accordance with paragraph 12.7 of this code and prolongs the interview, a longer break should then be provided. If there is a short interview, and a subsequent short interview is contemplated, the length of the break may be reduced if there are reasonable grounds to believe that this is necessary to avoid any of the consequences in paragraph 12.7(i) to (iii).

13.   Interpreters

(a)   General

13.1   Information on obtaining the services of a suitably qualified interpreter for the deaf or for people who do not understand English is given in Note for Guidance 3D.

(b)   Foreign languages

13.2   Except in accordance with paragraph 11.1 or unless Annex C applies, a person must not be interviewed in the absence of a person capable of acting as interpreter if:
    (a)   he has difficulty in understanding English;
    (b)   the interviewing officer cannot himself speak the person's own language; and
    (c)   the person wishes an interpreter to be present.

13.3   The interviewing officer shall ensure that the interpreter makes a note of the interview at the time in the language of the person being interviewed for use in the event of his being called to give evidence, and certifies its accuracy. He shall allow sufficient time for the interpreter to make a note of each question and answer after each has been put or given and interpreted. The person shall be given an opportunity to read it or have it read to him and sign it as correct or to indicate the respects in which he considers it inaccurate. If the interview is tape-recorded the arrangements set out in Code E apply.

13.4   In the case of a person making a statement in a language other than English:
    (a)   the interpreter shall take down the statement in the language in which it is made;
    (b)   the person making the statement shall be invited to sign it; and
    (c)   an official English translation shall be made in due course.

(c)   Deaf people and people with a speech handicap

13.5   If a person appears to be deaf or there is doubt about his hearing or speaking ability, he must not be interviewed in the absence of an interpreter unless he agrees in writing to be interviewed without one or paragraph 11.1 or Annex C applies.

13.6   An interpreter shall also be called if a juvenile is interviewed and the parent or guardian present as the appropriate adult appears to be deaf or there is doubt about his hearing or speaking ability, unless he agrees in writing that the interview should proceed without one or paragraph 11.1 or Annex C applies.

13.7 The interviewing officer shall ensure that the interpreter is given an opportunity to read the record of the interview and to certify its accuracy in the event of his being called to give evidence.

(d) Additional rules for detained persons

13.8 All reasonable attempts should be made to make clear to the detained person that interpreters will be provided at public expense.

13.9 Where paragraph 6.1 applies and the person concerned cannot communicate with the solicitor, whether because of language, hearing or speech difficulties, an interpreter must be called. The interpreter may not be a police officer when interpretation is needed for the purposes of obtaining legal advice. In all other cases a police officer may only interpret if he first obtains the detained person's (or the appropriate adult's) agreement in writing or if the interview is tape-recorded in accordance with Code E.

13.10 When a person is charged with an offence who appears to be deaf or there is doubt about his hearing or speaking ability or ability to understand English, and the custody officer cannot establish effective communication, arrangements must be made for an interpreter to explain as soon as practicable the offence concerned and any other information given by the custody officer.

(e) Documentation

13.11 Action taken to call an interpreter under this section and any agreement to be interviewed in the absence of an interpreter must be recorded.

Note for Guidance

13A If the interpreter is needed as a prosecution witness at the person's trial, a second interpreter must act as the court interpreter.

14. Questioning: special restrictions

14.1 If a person has been arrested by one police force on behalf of another and the lawful period of detention in respect of that offence has not yet commenced in accordance with section 41 of the Police and Criminal Evidence Act 1984 no questions may be put to him about the offence while he is in transit between the forces except in order to clarify any voluntary statement made by him.

14.2 If a person is in police detention at a hospital he may not be questioned without the agreement of a responsible doctor. [See Note 14A]

Note for Guidance

14A If questioning takes place at a hospital under paragraph 14.2 (or on the way to or from a hospital) the period concerned counts towards the total period of detention permitted.

15. Reviews and extensions of detention

(a) Action

15.1 The review officer is responsible under section 40 of the Police and Criminal Evidence Act 1984 (or, in terrorist cases, under Schedule 3 to the Prevention of Terrorism (Temporary Provisions) Act 1989) for determining whether or not a person's detention continues to be necessary. In reaching a decision he shall provide an opportunity to the detained person himself to make representations (unless he is unfit to do so because of his condition or behaviour) or to his solicitor or the appropriate adult if available at the time. Other people having an interest in the person's welfare may make representations at the review officer's discretion.

15.2 The same people may make representations to the officer determining whether further detention should be authorised under section 42 of the Act or under Schedule 3 to the 1989 Act. [See Note 15A]

15.2A After hearing any representations, the review officer or officer determining whether further detention should be authorised shall note any comment the person may make if the decision is to keep him in detention. The officer shall not put specific questions to the suspect regarding his involvement in any offence, nor in respect of any comments he may make in response to the decision to keep him in detention. Such an exchange is likely to constitute an interview as defined by paragraph 11.1A and would require the associated safeguards included in section 11. [See also paragraph 11.13]

(b) Documentation

15.3   Before conducting a review the review officer must ensure that the detained person is reminded of his entitlement to free legal advice (see paragraph 6.5). It is the responsibility of the review officer to ensure that all such reminders are noted in the custody record.

15.4   The grounds for and extent of any delay in conducting a review shall be recorded.

15.5   Any written representations shall be retained.

15.6   A record shall be made as soon as practicable of the outcome of each review and application for a warrant of further detention or its extension.

Notes for Guidance

15A   If the detained person is likely to be asleep at the latest time when a review of detention or an authorisation of continued detention may take place, the appropriate officer should bring it forward so that the detained person may make representations without being woken up.

15B   An application for a warrant of further detention or its extension should be made between 10am and 9pm, and if possible during normal court hours. It will not be practicable to arrange for a court to sit specially outside the hours of 10am to 9pm. If it appears possible that a special sitting may be needed (either at a weekend, Bank/Public Holiday or on a weekday outside normal court hours but between 10am and 9pm) then the clerk to the justices should be given notice and informed of this possibility, while the court is sitting if possible.

15C   If in the circumstances the only practicable way of conducting a review is over the telephone then this is permissible, provided that the requirements of section 40 of the Police and Criminal Evidence Act 1984 or of schedule 3 to the Prevention of Terrorism (Temporary Provisions) Act 1989 are observed. However, a review to decide whether to authorise a person's continued detention under section 42 of the 1984 Act must be done in person rather than over the telephone.

16. Charging of detained persons

(a) Action

16.1   When an officer considers that there is sufficient evidence to prosecute a detained person, and that there is sufficient evidence for a prosecution to succeed, and that the person has said all that he wishes to say about the offence, he shall without delay (and subject to the following qualification) bring him before the custody officer who shall then be responsible for considering whether or not he should be charged. When a person is detained in respect of more than one offence it is permissible to delay bringing him before the custody officer until the above conditions are satisfied in respect of all the offences (but see paragraph 11.4). Any resulting action should be taken in the presence of the appropriate adult if the person is a juvenile or mentally disordered or mentally handicapped.

16.2   When a detained person is charged with or informed that he may be prosecuted for an offence he shall be cautioned in the following terms:

'You do not have to say anything. But it may harm your defence if you do not mention now something which you later rely on in court. Anything you do say may be given in evidence.'

16.3   At the time a person is charged he shall be given a written notice showing particulars of the offence with which he is charged and including the name of the officer in the case (in terrorist cases, the officer's warrant or other identification number instead), his police station and the reference number for the case. So far as possible the particulars of the charge shall be stated in simple terms, but they shall also show the precise offence in law with which he is charged. The notice shall begin with the following words:

'You are charged with the offence(s) shown below. You do not have to say anything. But it may harm your defence if you do not mention now something which you later rely on in court. Anything you do say may be given in evidence.'

If the person is a juvenile or is mentally disordered or mentally handicapped the notice shall be given to the appropriate adult.

16.4   If at any time after a person has been charged with or informed that he may be prosecuted for an offence, a police officer wishes to bring to the notice of that person any written statement made by another person or the content of an interview with another person, he shall hand to that person a true copy of any such written statement or bring to his attention the content of the interview record, but shall say or do nothing to invite any reply or comment save to warn him that he does not have to say anything but that anything he does say may be given in evidence and to remind him of his right to legal advice in accordance with paragraph 6.5 above. If the person cannot read then the officer may read it to him. If the person is a juvenile or mentally disordered or mentally handicapped the copy shall also be given to, or the interview record brought to the attention of, the appropriate adult.

16.5   Questions relating to an offence may not be put to a person after he has been charged with that offence, or informed that he may be prosecuted for it, unless they are necessary for the purpose of preventing or minimising harm or loss to some other person or to the public or for clearing up an ambiguity in a previous answer or statement, or where it is in the interests of justice that the person should have put to him and have an opportunity to comment on information concerning the offence which has come to light since he was charged or informed that he might be prosecuted. Before any such questions are put to him, he shall be warned that he does not have to say anything but that anything he does say may be given in evidence and reminded of his right to legal advice in accordance with paragraph 6.5 above. [See Note 16A]

16.6   Where a juvenile is charged with an offence and the custody officer authorises his continued detention he must try to make arrangements for the juvenile to be taken into the care of a local authority to be detained pending appearance in court unless he certifies that it is impracticable to do so, or, in the case of a juvenile of at least 12 years of age, no secure accommodation is available and there is a risk to the public of serious harm from that juvenile, in accordance with section 38(6) of the Police and Criminal Evidence Act 1984, as amended by section 59 of the Criminal Justice Act 1991 and section 24 of the Criminal Justice and Public Order Act 1994. [See Note 16B]

(b)   Documentation

16.7   A record shall be made of anything a detained person says when charged.

16.8   Any questions put after charge and answers given relating to the offence shall be contemporaneously recorded in full on the forms provided and the record signed by that person or, if he refuses, by the interviewing officer and any third parties present. If the questions are tape-recorded the arrangements set out in Code E apply.

16.9   If it is not practicable to make arrangements for the transfer of a juvenile into local authority care in accordance with paragraph 16.6 above the custody officer must record the reasons and make out a certificate to be produced before the court together with the juvenile.

Notes for Guidance

16A   The service of the Notice of Intended Prosecution under sections 1 and 2 of the Road Traffic Offenders Act 1988 does not amount to informing a person that he may be prosecuted for an offence and so does not preclude further questioning in relation to that offence.

16B   Except as provided for in 16.6 above, neither a juvenile's behaviour nor the nature of the offence with which he is charged provides grounds for the custody officer to decide that it is impracticable to seek to arrange for his transfer to the care of the local authority. Similarly, the lack of secure local authority accommodation shall not make it impracticable for the custody officer to transfer him. The availability of secure accommodation is only a factor in relation to a juvenile aged 12 or over when the local authority accommodation would not be adequate to protect the public from serious harm from the juvenile. The obligation to transfer a juvenile to local authority accommodation applies as much to a juvenile charged during the daytime as it does to a juvenile to be held overnight, subject to a requirement to bring the juvenile before a court under section 46 of the Police and Criminal Evidence Act 1984.

PACE CODE OF PRACTICE (CODE C)

ANNEX A
INTIMATE AND STRIP SEARCHES [SEE PARAGRAPH 4.1]

A. INTIMATE SEARCH

1.   An 'intimate search' is a search which consists of the physical examination of a person's body orifices other than the mouth.

(a) Action

2.   Body orifices other than the mouth may be searched only if an officer of the rank of superintendent or above has reasonable grounds for believing:

    (a)   that an article which could cause physical injury to the detained person or others at the police station has been concealed; or

    (b)   that the person has concealed a Class A drug which he intended to supply to another or to export; and

    (c)   that in either case an intimate search is the only practicable means of removing it.

The reasons why an intimate search is considered necessary shall be explained to the person before the search takes place.

3.   An intimate search may only be carried out by a registered medical practitioner or registered nurse, unless an officer of at least the rank of superintendent considers that this is not practicable and the search is to take place under sub-paragraph 2(a) above.

4.   An intimate search under sub-paragraph 2(a) above may take place only at a hospital, surgery, other medical premises or police station. A search under sub-paragraph 2(b) may take place only at a hospital, surgery or other medical premises.

5.   An intimate search at a police station of a juvenile or a mentally disordered or mentally handicapped person may take place only in the presence of an appropriate adult of the same sex (unless the person specifically requests the presence of a particular adult of the opposite sex who is readily available). In the case of a juvenile the search may take place in the absence of the appropriate adult only if the juvenile signifies in the presence of the appropriate adult that he prefers the search to be done in his absence and the appropriate adult agrees. A record shall be made of the juvenile's decision and signed by the appropriate adult.

6.   Where an intimate search under sub-paragraph 2(a) above is carried out by a police officer, the officer must be of the same sex as the person searched. Subject to paragraph 5 above, no person of the opposite sex who is not a medical practitioner or nurse shall be present, nor shall anyone whose presence is unnecessary but a minimum of two people, other than the person searched, must be present during the search. The search shall be conducted with proper regard to the sensitivity and vulnerability of the person in these circumstances.

(b) Documentation

7.   In the case of an intimate search the custody officer shall as soon as practicable record which parts of the person's body were searched, who carried out the search, who was present, the reasons for the search and its result.

8.   If an intimate search is carried out by a police officer, the reason why it was impracticable for a suitably qualified person to conduct it must be recorded.

B. STRIP SEARCH

9.   A strip search is a search involving the removal of more than outer clothing.

(a) Action

10.   A strip search may take place only if it is considered necessary to remove an article which a person would not be allowed to keep, and the officer reasonably considers that the person might have concealed such an article. Strip searches shall not be routinely carried out where there is no reason to consider that articles have been concealed.

The conduct of strip searches

11.   The following procedures shall be observed when strip searches are conducted:
    (a)   a police officer carrying out a strip search must be of the same sex as the person searched;
    (b)   the search shall take place in an area where the person being searched cannot be seen by anyone who does not need to be present, nor by a member of the opposite sex (except an appropriate adult who has been specifically requested by the person being searched);
    (c)   except in cases of urgency, where there is a risk of serious harm to the person detained or to others, whenever a strip search involves exposure of intimate parts of the body, there must be at least two people present other than the person searched, and if the search is of a juvenile or a mentally disordered or mentally handicapped person, one of the people must be the appropriate adult. Except in urgent cases as above, a search of a juvenile may take place in the absence of the appropriate adult only if the juvenile signifies in the presence of the appropriate adult that he prefers the search to be done in his absence and the appropriate adult agrees. A record shall be made of the juvenile's decision and signed by the appropriate adult. The presence of more than two people, other than an appropriate adult, shall be permitted only in the most exceptional circumstances;
    (d)   the search shall be conducted with proper regard to the sensitivity and vulnerability of the person in these circumstances and every reasonable effort shall be made to secure the person's co-operation and minimise embarrassment. People who are searched should not normally be required to have all their clothes removed at the same time, for example, a man shall be allowed to put on his shirt before removing his trousers, and a woman shall be allowed to put on her blouse and upper garments before further clothing is removed;
    (e)   where necessary to assist the search, the person may be required to hold his or her arms in the air or to stand with his or her legs apart and to bend forward so that a visual examination may be made of the genital and anal areas provided that no physical contact is made with any body orifice;
    (f)   if, during a search, articles are found, the person shall be asked to hand them over. If articles are found within any body orifice other than the mouth, and the person refuses to hand them over, their removal would constitute an intimate search, which must be carried out in accordance with the provisions of part A of this Annex;
    (g)   a strip search shall be conducted as quickly as possible, and the person searched allowed to dress as soon as the procedure is complete.

(b)   Documentation

12.   A record shall be made on the custody record of a strip search including the reason it was considered necessary to undertake it, those present and any result.

ANNEX B
DELAY IN NOTIFYING ARREST OR ALLOWING ACCESS TO LEGAL ADVICE

A.   Persons detained under the Police and Criminal Evidence Act 1984

(a)   Action

1.   The rights set out in sections 5 or 6 of the code or both may be delayed if the person is in police detention in connection with a serious arrestable offence, has not yet been charged with an offence and an officer of the rank of superintendent or above has reasonable grounds for believing that the exercise of either right:
    (i)   will lead to interference with or harm to evidence connected with a serious arrestable offence or interference with or physical injury to other people; or
    (ii)   will lead to the alerting of other people suspected of having committed such an offence but not yet arrested for it; or
    (iii)   will hinder the recovery of property obtained as a result of such an offence.
[See Note B3]

2.   These rights may also be delayed where the serious arrestable offence is either:
    (i)   a drug trafficking offence and the officer has reasonable grounds for believing that the detained person has benefited from drug trafficking, and that the recovery of the value of that person's proceeds of drug trafficking will be hindered by the exercise of either right or;
    (ii)   an offence to which part VI of the Criminal Justice Act 1988 (covering confiscation orders) applies and the officer has reasonable grounds for believing that the detained person has benefited from the

offence, and that the recovery of the value of the property obtained by that person from or in connection with the offence, or if the pecuniary advantage derived by him from or in connection with it, will be hindered by the exercise of either right.

3.   Access to a solicitor may not be delayed on the grounds that he might advise the person not to answer any questions or that the solicitor was initially asked to attend the police station by someone else, provided that the person himself then wishes to see the solicitor. In the latter case the detained person must be told that the solicitor has come to the police station at another person's request, and must be asked to sign the custody record to signify whether or not he wishes to see the solicitor.

4.   These rights may be delayed only for as long as is necessary and, subject to paragraph 9 below, in no case beyond 36 hours after the relevant time as defined in section 41 of the Police and Criminal Evidence Act 1984. If the above grounds cease to apply within this time, the person must as soon as practicable be asked if he wishes to exercise either right, the custody record must be noted accordingly, and action must be taken in accordance with the relevant section of the code.

5.   A detained person must be permitted to consult a solicitor for a reasonable time before any court hearing.

(b)   Documentation

6.   The grounds for action under this Annex shall be recorded and the person informed of them as soon as practicable.

7.   Any reply given by a person under paragraphs 4 or 9 must be recorded and the person asked to endorse the record in relation to whether he wishes to receive legal advice at this point.

B.   Persons detained under the Prevention of Terrorism (Temporary Provisions) Act 1989

(a)   Action

8.   The rights set out in sections 5 or 6 of this code or both may be delayed if paragraph 1 above applies or if an officer of the rank of superintendent or above has reasonable grounds for believing that the exercise of either right:
    (a)   will lead to interference with the gathering of information about the commission, preparation or instigation of acts of terrorism; or
    (b)   by alerting any person, will make it more difficult to prevent an act of terrorism or to secure the apprehension, prosecution or conviction of any person in connection with the commission, preparation or instigation of an act of terrorism.

9.   These rights may be delayed only for as long as is necessary and in no case beyond 48 hours from the time of arrest. If the above grounds cease to apply within this time, the person must as soon as practicable be asked if he wishes to exercise either right, the custody record must be noted accordingly, and action must be taken in accordance with the relevant section of this code.

10.   Paragraphs 3 and 5 above apply.

(b)   Documentation

11.   Paragraphs 6 and 7 above apply.

Notes for Guidance

B1   Even if Annex B applies in the case of a juvenile, or a person who is mentally disordered or mentally handicapped, action to inform the appropriate adult (and the person responsible for a juvenile's welfare, if that is a different person) must nevertheless be taken in accordance with paragraph 3.7 and 3.9 of this code.

B2   In the case of Commonwealth citizens and foreign nationals see Note 7A.

B3   Police detention is defined in section 118(2) of the Police and Criminal Evidence Act 1984.

B4   The effect of paragraph 1 above is that the officer may authorise delaying access to a specific solicitor only if he has reasonable grounds to believe that that specific solicitor will, inadvertently or otherwise, pass on a message from the detained person or act in some other way which will lead to any of the three results in paragraph 1 coming about. In these circumstances the officer should offer the detained person access to a solicitor (who is not the specific solicitor referred to above) on the Duty Solicitor Scheme.

B5   The fact that the grounds for delaying notification of arrest under paragraph 1 above may be satisfied does not automatically mean that the grounds for delaying access to legal advice will also be satisfied.

ANNEX C
VULNERABLE SUSPECTS: URGENT INTERVIEWS AT POLICE STATIONS

1.   When an interview is to take place in a police station or other authorised place of detention if, and only if, an officer of the rank of superintendent or above considers that delay will lead to the consequences set out in paragraph 11.1(a) to (c) of this Code:
   (a)   a person heavily under the influence of drink or drugs may be interviewed in that state; or
   (b)   a juvenile or a person who is mentally disordered or mentally handicapped may be interviewed in the absence of the appropriate adult; or
   (c)   a person who has difficulty in understanding English or who has a hearing disability may be interviewed in the absence of an interpreter.

2.   Questioning in these circumstances may not continue once sufficient information to avert the immediate risk has been obtained.

3.   A record shall be made of the grounds for any decision to interview a person under paragraph 1 above.

Note for Guidance

C1   The special groups referred to in this Annex are all particularly vulnerable. The provisions of the Annex, which override safeguards designed to protect them and to minimise the risk of interviews producing unreliable evidence, should be applied only in exceptional cases of need.

ANNEX D
WRITTEN STATEMENTS UNDER CAUTION [SEE PARAGRAPH 12.13]

(a)   Written by a person under caution

1.   A person shall always be invited to write down himself what he wants to say.

2.   Where the person wishes to write it himself, he shall be asked to write out and sign, before writing what he wants to say, the following:

  I make this statement of my own free will. I understand that I do not have to say anything but that it may harm my defence if I do not mention when questioned something which I later rely on in court. This statement may be given in evidence.

3.   Any person writing his own statement shall be allowed to do so without any prompting except that a police officer may indicate to him which matters are material or question any ambiguity in the statement.

(b)   Written by a police officer

4.   If a person says that he would like someone to write it for him, a police officer shall write the statement, but, before starting, he must ask him to sign, or make his mark, to the following:

  'I, ..., wish to make a statement. I want someone to write down what I say. I understand that I need not say anything but that it may harm my defence if I do not mention when questioned something which I later rely on in court. This statement may be given in evidence.'

5.   Where a police officer writes the statement, he must take down the exact words spoken by the person making it and he must not edit or paraphrase it. Any questions that are necessary (e.g. to make it more intelligible) and the answers given must be recorded contemporaneously on the statement form.

6.   When the writing of a statement by a police officer is finished the person making it shall be asked to read it and to make any corrections, alterations or additions he wishes. When he has finished reading it he shall be asked to write and sign or make his mark on the following certificate at the end of the statement:

'I have read the above statement, and I have been able to correct, alter or add anything I wish. This statement is true. I have made it of my own free will.'

7.   If the person making the statement cannot read, or refuses to read it, or to write the above mentioned certificate at the end of it or to sign it, the senior police officer present shall read it to him and ask him whether he would like to correct, alter or add anything and to put his signature or make his mark at the end. The police officer shall then certify on the statement itself what has occurred.

ANNEX E
SUMMARY OF PROVISIONS RELATING TO MENTALLY DISORDERED AND MENTALLY HANDICAPPED PEOPLE

1.   If an officer has any suspicion, or is told in good faith, that a person of any age may be mentally disordered or mentally handicapped, or mentally incapable of understanding the significance of questions put to him or his replies, then that person shall be treated as mentally disordered or mentally handicapped for the purposes of this code. [See paragraph 1.4]

2.   In the case of a person who is mentally disordered or mentally handicapped, 'the appropriate adult' means:
  (a)   a relative, guardian or some other person responsible for his care or custody;
  (b)   someone who has experience of dealing with mentally disordered or mentally handicapped people but is not a police officer or employed by the police; or
  (c)   failing either of the above, some other responsible adult aged 18 or over who is not a police officer or employed by the police.
[See paragraph 1.7(b)]

3.   If the custody officer authorises the detention of a person who is mentally handicapped or appears to be suffering from a mental disorder he must as soon as practicable inform the appropriate adult of the grounds for the person's detention and his whereabouts, and ask the adult to come to the police station to see the person. If the appropriate adult is already at the police station when information is given as required in paragraphs 3.1 to 3.5 the information must be given to the detained person in the appropriate adult's presence. If the appropriate adult is not at the police station when the provisions of 3.1 to 3.5 are complied with then these provisions must be complied with again in the presence of the appropriate adult once that person arrives. [See paragraphs 3.9 and 3.11]

4.   If the appropriate adult, having been informed of the right to legal advice, considers that legal advice should be taken, the provisions of section 6 of the code apply as if the mentally disordered or mentally handicapped person had requested access to legal advice. [See paragraph 3.13 and Note E2]

5.   If a person brought to a police station appears to be suffering from mental disorder or is incoherent other than through drunkenness alone, or if a detained person subsequently appears to be mentally disordered, the custody officer must immediately call the police surgeon or, in urgent cases, send the person to hospital or call the nearest available medical practitioner. It is not intended that these provisions should delay the transfer of a person to a place of safety under section 136 of the Mental Health Act 1983 where that is applicable. Where an assessment under that Act is to take place at the police station, the custody officer has discretion not to call the police surgeon so long as he believes that the assessment by a registered medical practitioner can be undertaken without undue delay. [See paragraph 9.2]

6.   It is imperative that a mentally disordered or mentally handicapped person who has been detained under section 136 of the Mental Health Act 1983 should be assessed as soon as possible. If that assessment is to take place at the police station, an approved social worker and a registered medical practitioner should be called to the police station as soon as possible in order to interview and examine the person. Once the person has been interviewed and examined and suitable arrangements have been made for his treatment or care, he can no longer be detained under section 136. The person shall not be released until he has been seen by both the approved social worker and the registered medical practitioner. [See paragraph 3.10]

7.   If a mentally disordered or mentally handicapped person is cautioned in the absence of the appropriate adult, the caution must be repeated in the appropriate adult's presence. [See paragraph 10.6]

8.   A mentally disordered or mentally handicapped person must not be interviewed or asked to provide or sign a written statement in the absence of the appropriate adult unless the provisions of paragraph 11.1 or Annex C of this code apply. Questioning in these circumstances may not continue in the absence of the appropriate adult once sufficient information to avert the risk has been obtained. A record shall be made of the grounds for any decision to begin an interview in these circumstances. [See paragraphs 11.1 and 11.14 and Annex C]

9.   Where the appropriate adult is present at an interview, he should be informed that he is not expected to act simply as an observer; and also that the purposes of his presence are, first, to advise the person being interviewed and to observe whether or not the interview is being conducted properly and fairly, and, secondly to facilitate communication with the person being interviewed. [See paragraph 11.16]

10.   If the detention of a mentally disordered or mentally handicapped person is reviewed by a review officer or a superintendent, the appropriate adult must, if available at the time, be given an opportunity to make representations to the officer about the need for continuing detention. [See paragraphs 15.1 and 15.2]

11.   If the custody officer charges a mentally disordered or mentally handicapped person with an offence or takes such other action as is appropriate when there is sufficient evidence for a prosecution this must be done in the presence of the appropriate adult. The written notice embodying any charge must be given to the appropriate adult. [See paragraphs 16.1 to 16.3]

12.   An intimate or strip search of a mentally disordered or mentally handicapped person may take place only in the presence of the appropriate adult of the same sex, unless the person specifically requests the presence of a particular adult of the opposite sex. A strip search may take place in the absence of an appropriate adult only in cases of urgency where there is a risk of serious harm to the person detained or to others. [See Annex A, paragraphs 5 and 11(c)]

13.   Particular care must be taken when deciding whether to use handcuffs to restrain a mentally disordered or mentally handicapped person in a locked cell. [See paragraph 8.2]

Notes for Guidance

E1   In the case of mentally disordered or mentally handicapped people, it may in certain circumstances be more satisfactory for all concerned if the appropriate adult is someone who has experience or training in their care rather than a relative lacking such qualifications. But if the person himself prefers a relative to a better qualified stranger or objects to a particular person as the appropriate adult, his wishes should if practicable be respected. [See Note 1E]

E2   The purpose of the provision at paragraph 3.13 is to protect the rights of a mentally disordered or mentally handicapped person who does not understand the significance of what is being said to him. If the person wishes to exercise the right to legal advice, the appropriate action should be taken and not delayed until the appropriate adult arrives. [See Note 3G] A mentally disordered or mentally handicapped person should always be given an opportunity, when an appropriate adult is called to the police station, to consult privately with a solicitor in the absence of the appropriate adult if he wishes to do so. [See Note 1EE].

E3   It is important to bear in mind that although mentally disordered or mentally handicapped [people are] often capable of providing reliable evidence, they may, without knowing or wishing to do so, be particularly prone in certain circumstances to provide information which is unreliable, misleading or self-incriminating. Special care should therefore always be exercised in questioning such a person, and the appropriate adult involved, if there is any doubt about a person's mental state or capacity. Because of the risk of unreliable evidence, it is important to obtain corroboration of any facts admitted whenever possible. [See Note 11B]

E4   Because of the risks referred to in Note E3, which the presence of the appropriate adult is intended to minimise, officers of superintendent rank or above should exercise their discretion to authorise the commencement of an interview in the adult's absence only in exceptional cases, where it is necessary to avert an immediate risk of serious harm. [See paragraph 11.1 and Annex C and Note C1]

PACE CODE OF PRACTICE (CODE C)

ANNEX F
COUNTRIES WITH WHICH BILATERAL CONSULAR CONVENTIONS OR AGREEMENTS REQUIRING NOTIFICATION OF THE ARREST AND DETENTION OF THEIR NATIONALS ARE IN FORCE AS AT 1 JANUARY 1995

Armenia
Austria
Azerbaijan
Belarus
Belgium
Bosnia-Hercegovina
Bulgaria
China*
Croatia
Cuba
Czech Republic
Denmark
Egypt
France
Georgia
German Federal Republic
Greece
Hungary
Kazakhstan

Kyrgyzstan
Macedonia
Mexico
Moldova
Mongolia
Norway
Poland
Romania
Russia
Slovak Republic
Slovenia
Spain
Sweden
Tajikistan
Turkmenistan
Ukraine
USA
Uzbekistan
Yugoslavia

*Police are required to inform Chinese officials of arrest/detention in the Manchester consular district only. This comprises Derbyshire, Durham, Greater Manchester, Lancashire, Merseyside, North, South and West Yorkshire, and Tyne and Wear.

PACE CODE OF PRACTICE FOR THE IDENTIFICATION OF PERSONS BY POLICE OFFICERS (CODE D)

1. General

1.1   This code of practice must be readily available at all police stations for consultation by police officers, detained persons and members of the public.

1.2   The notes for guidance included are not provisions of this code, but are guidance to police officers and others about its application and interpretation. Provisions in the Annexes to the code are provisions of this code.

1.3   If an officer has any suspicion, or is told in good faith, that a person of any age may be mentally disordered or mentally handicapped, or mentally incapable of understanding the significance of questions put to him or his replies, then that person shall be treated as a mentally disordered or mentally handicapped person for the purposes of this code.

1.4   If anyone appears to be under the age of 17 then he shall be treated as a juvenile for the purposes of this code in the absence of clear evidence to show that he is older.

1.5   If a person appears to be blind or seriously visually handicapped, deaf, unable to read, unable to speak or has difficulty orally because of a speech impediment, he shall be treated as such for the purposes of this code in the absence of clear evidence to the contrary.

1.6   In this code the term 'appropriate adult' has the same meaning as in paragraph 1.7 of Code C, and the term 'solicitor' has the same meaning as in paragraph 6.12 of Code C.

1.7   Any reference to a custody officer in this code includes an officer who is performing the functions of a custody officer.

1.8   Where a record is made under this code of any action requiring the authority of an officer of a specified rank, his name (except in the case of enquiries linked to the investigation of terrorism, in which case the officer's warrant or other identification number shall be given) and rank must be included in the record.

1.9   All records must be timed and signed by the maker. Warrant or other identification numbers shall be used rather than names in the case of detention under the Prevention of Terrorism (Temporary Provisions) Act 1989.

1.10   In the case of a detained person records are to be made in his custody record unless otherwise specified.

1.11   In the case of any procedure requiring a suspect's consent, the consent of a person who is mentally disordered or mentally handicapped is only valid if given in the presence of the appropriate adult; and in the case of a juvenile the consent of his parent or guardian is required as well as his own (unless he is under 14, in which case the consent of his parent or guardian is sufficient in its own right). [See Note 1E]

1.12   In the case of a person who is blind or seriously visually handicapped or unable to read, the custody officer shall ensure that his solicitor, relative, the appropriate adult or some other person likely to take an interest in him (and not involved in the investigation) is available to help in checking any documentation. Where this code requires written consent or signification, then the person who is assisting may be asked to sign instead if the detained person so wishes. [See Note 1F]

1.13   In the case of any procedure requiring information to be given to or sought from a suspect, it must be given or sought in the presence of the appropriate adult if the suspect is mentally disordered, mentally handicapped or a juvenile. If the appropriate adult is not present when the information is first given or sought, the procedure must be repeated in his presence when he arrives. If the suspect appears to be deaf or there is doubt about his hearing or speaking ability or ability to understand English, and the officer cannot establish effective communication, the information must be given or sought through an interpreter.

1.14   Any procedure in this code involving the participation of a person (whether as a suspect or a witness) who is mentally disordered, mentally handicapped or a juvenile must take place in the presence of the appropriate adult; but the adult must not be allowed to prompt any identification of a suspect by a witness.

1.15   Subject to paragraph 1.16 below, nothing in this code affects any procedure under:
    (i)   Sections 4 to 11 of the Road Traffic Act 1988 or sections 15 and 16 of the Road Traffic Offenders Act 1988; or
    (ii)   paragraph 18 of schedule 2 to the Immigration Act 1971; or
    (iii)   the Prevention of Terrorism (Temporary Provisions) Act 1989, section 15(9), paragraph 8(5) of schedule 2, and paragraph 7(5) of schedule 5.

1.16   Notwithstanding paragraph 1.15, the provisions of section 3 below on the taking of fingerprints, and of section 5 below on the taking of body samples, do apply to people detained under section 14 of, or paragraph 6 of schedule 5 to, the Prevention of Terrorism (Temporary Provisions) Act 1989. (In the case of fingerprints, section 61 of PACE is modified by section 15(10) of, and paragraph 7(6) of schedule 5 to, the 1989 Act.) In the case of samples, sections 62 and 63 of PACE are modified by section 15(11) of and paragraph 7(6A) of Schedule 5 to the 1989 Act. The effect of both of these modifications is to allow fingerprints and samples to be taken in terrorist cases to help determine whether a person is or has been involved in terrorism, as well as where there are reasonable grounds for suspecting that person's involvement in a particular offence. There is, however, no statutory requirement (and, therefore, no requirement under paragraph 3.4 below) to destroy fingerprints or body samples taken in terrorist cases, no requirement to tell the people from whom these were taken that they will be destroyed, and no statutory requirement to offer such people an opportunity to witness the destruction of their fingerprints.

1.17   In this code, references to photographs, negatives and copies include reference to images stored or reproduced through any medium.

1.18   The code does not apply to those groups of people listed in paragraph 1.12 of Code C.

Notes for Guidance

1A   A person, including a parent or guardian, should not be the appropriate adult if he is suspected of involvement in the offence, is the victim, is a witness, is involved in the investigation or has received admissions prior to attending to act as the appropriate adult. If the parent of a juvenile is estranged from the juvenile, he should not be asked to act as the appropriate adult if the juvenile expressly and specifically objects to his presence.

1B   If a juvenile admits an offence to or in the presence of, a social worker other than during the time that the social worker is acting as the appropriate adult for that juvenile, another social worker should be the appropriate adult in the interest of fairness.

1C   In the case of people who are mentally disordered or mentally handicapped, it may in certain circumstances be more satisfactory for all concerned if the appropriate adult is someone who has experience or training in their care rather than a relative lacking such qualifications. But if the person himself prefers a relative to a better-qualified stranger, or objects to a particular person as the appropriate adult, his wishes should if practicable be respected.

1D   A solicitor or lay visitor who is present at the station in that capacity may not act as the appropriate adult.

1E   For the purposes of paragraph 1.11 above, the consent required to be given by a parent or guardian may be given, in the case of a juvenile in the care of a local authority or voluntary organisation, by that authority or organisation.

1F   Persons who are blind, seriously visually handicapped or unable to read may be unwilling to sign police documents. The alternative of their representative signing on their behalf seeks to protect the interests of both police and suspects.

1G   Further guidance about fingerprints and body samples is given in Home Office circulars.

1H   The generic term 'mental disorder' is used throughout this code. 'Mental disorder' is defined in section 1(2) of the Mental Health Act 1983 as 'mental illness, arrested or incomplete development of mind, psychopathic disorder and any other disorder or disability of mind'. It should be noted that 'mental disorder' is different from 'mental handicap' although the two are dealt with similarly throughout this code. Where the custody officer has any doubt as to the mental state or capacity of a person detained an appropriate adult should be called.

2.   Identification by witnesses

2.0   A record shall be made of the description of the suspect as first given by a potential witness. This must be done before the witness takes part in the forms of identification listed in paragraph 2.1 or Annex D of this code. The record may be made or kept in any form provided that details of the description as first given by the witness can accurately be produced from it in a written form which can be provided to the suspect or his solicitor in accordance with this code. A copy shall be provided to the suspect or his solicitor before any procedures under paragraph 2.1 of this code are carried out. [See Note 2D]

(a) Cases where the suspect is known

2.1   In a case which involves disputed identification evidence, and where the identity of the suspect is known to the police and he is available (See Note 2E), the methods of identification by witnesses which may be used are:
  (i)   a parade;
  (ii)   a group identification;
  (iii)   a video film;
  (iv)   a confrontation.

2.2   The arrangements for, and conduct of, these types of identification shall be the responsibility of an officer in uniform not below the rank of inspector who is not involved with the investigation ('the identification officer'). No officer involved with the investigation of the case against the suspect may take any part in these procedures.

Identification Parade
2.3   Whenever a suspect disputes an identification, an identification parade shall be held if the suspect consents unless paragraphs 2.4 or 2.7 or 2.10 apply. A parade may also be held if the officer in charge of the investigation considers that it would be useful, and the suspect consents.

2.4   A parade need not be held if the identification officer considers that, whether by reason of the unusual appearance of the suspect or for some other reason, it would not be practicable to assemble sufficient people who resembled him to make a parade fair.

2.5   Any parade must be carried out in accordance with Annex A. A video recording or colour photograph shall be taken of the parade.

2.6   If a suspect refuses or, having agreed, fails to attend an identification parade or the holding of a parade is impracticable, arrangements must if practicable be made to allow the witnesses an opportunity of seeing him in a group identification, a video identification, or a confrontation (see below).

Group Identification
2.7   A group identification takes place where the suspect is viewed by a witness amongst an informal group of people. The procedure may take place with the consent and co-operation of a suspect or covertly where a suspect has refused to co-operate with an identification parade or a group identification or has failed to attend. A group identification may also be arranged if the officer in charge of the investigation considers, whether because of fear on the part of the witness or for some other reason, that it is, in the circumstances, more satisfactory than a parade.

2.8   The suspect should be asked for his consent to a group identification and advised in accordance with paragraphs 2.15 and 2.16 of this code. However, where consent is refused the identification officer has the discretion to proceed with a group identification if it is practicable to do so.

2.9   A group identification shall be carried out in accordance with Annex E. A video recording or colour photograph shall be taken of the group identification in accordance with Annex E.

Video Film Identification
2.10   The identification officer may show a witness a video film of a suspect if the investigating officer considers, whether because of the refusal of the suspect to take part in an identification parade or group identification or other reasons, that this would in the circumstances be the most satisfactory course of action.

2.11   The suspect should be asked for his consent to a video identification and advised in accordance with paragraphs 2.15 and 2.16. However, where such consent is refused the identification officer has the discretion to proceed with a video identification if it is practicable to do so.

2.12   A video identification must be carried out in accordance with Annex B.

Confrontation
2.13   If neither a parade, a group identification nor a video identification procedure is arranged, the suspect may be confronted by the witness. Such a confrontation does not require the suspect's consent, but may not take place unless none of the other procedures are practicable.

2.14   A confrontation must be carried out in accordance with Annex C.

Notice to Suspect
2.15   Before a parade takes place or a group identification or video identification is arranged, the identification officer shall explain to the suspect:
>   (i)   the purposes of the parade or group identification or video identification;
>   (ii)   that he is entitled to free legal advice (see paragraph 6.5 of Code C);
>   (iii)   the procedures for holding it (including his right to have a solicitor or friend present);
>   (iv)   where appropriate the special arrangements for juveniles;
>   (v)   where appropriate the special arrangements for mentally disordered and mentally handicapped people;
>   (vi)   that he does not have to take part in a parade, or co-operate in a group identification, or with the making of a video film and, if it is proposed to hold a group identification or video identification, his entitlement to a parade if this can practicably be arranged;
>   (vii)   if he does not consent to take part in a parade or co-operate in a group identification or with the making of a video film, his refusal may be given in evidence in any subsequent trial and police may proceed covertly without his consent or make other arrangements to test whether a witness identifies him;
>   (vii)a   that if he should significantly alter his appearance between the taking of any photograph at the time of his arrest or after charge and any attempt to hold an identification procedure, this may be given in evidence if the case comes to trial; and the officer may then consider other forms of identification;
>   (vii)b   that a video or photograph may be taken of him when he attends for any identification procedure;
>   (viii)   whether the witness had been shown photographs, photofit, identikit or similar pictures by the police during the investigation before the identity of the suspect became known; [See Note 2B]
>   (ix)   that if he changes his appearance before a parade it may not be practicable to arrange one on the day in question or subsequently and, because of his change of appearance, the identification officer may then consider alternative methods of identification;

(x)   that he or his solicitor will be provided with details of the description of the suspect as first given by any witnesses who are to attend the parade, group identification, video identification or confrontation.

2.16   This information must also be contained in a written notice which must be handed to the suspect. The identification officer shall give the suspect a reasonable opportunity to read the notice, after which he shall be asked to sign a second copy of the notice to indicate whether or not he is willing to take part in the parade or group identification or co-operate with the making of a video film. The signed copy shall be retained by the identification officer.

(b)   Cases where the identity of the suspect is not known

2.17   A police officer may take a witness to a particular neighbourhood or place to see whether he can identify the person whom he said he saw on the relevant occasion. Before doing so, where practicable a record shall be made of any description given by the witness of the suspect. Care should be taken not to direct the witness's attention to any individual.

2.18   A witness must not be shown photographs, photofit, identikit or similar pictures if the identity of the suspect is known to the police and he is available to stand on an identification parade. If the identity of the suspect is not known, the showing of such pictures to a witness must be done in accordance with Annex D. [See paragraph 2.15(viii) and Note 2E]

(c)   Documentation

2.19   The identification officer shall make a record of the parade, group identification or video identification on the forms provided.

2.20   If the identification officer considers that it is not practicable to hold a parade, he shall tell the suspect why and record the reason.

2.21   A record shall be made of a person's refusal to co-operate in a parade, group identification or video identification.

(d)   Showing films and photographs of incidents

2.21A   Nothing in this code inhibits an investigating officer from showing a video film or photographs of an incident to the public at large through the national, or local media, or to police officers, for the purposes of recognition and tracing suspects. However when such material is shown to potential witnesses (including police officers [see Note 2A] for the purpose of obtaining identification evidence, it shall be shown on an individual basis so as to avoid any possibility of collusion, and the showing shall, as far as possible, follow the principles for Video Film Identification (see paragraph 2.10) or Identification by Photographs (see paragraph 2.18) as appropriate).

2.21B   Where such a broadcast or publication is made a copy of the material released by the police to the media for the purposes of recognising or tracing the suspect shall be kept and the suspect or his solicitor should be allowed to view such material before any procedures under paragraph 2.1 of this code are carried out [see Notes 2D and 2E] provided it is practicable to do so and would not unreasonably delay the investigation. Each witness who is involved in the procedure shall be asked by the investigating officer after they have taken part whether they have seen any broadcast or published films or photographs relating to the offence and their replies shall be recorded.

Notes for Guidance

2A   Except for the provision of Annex D paragraph 1, a police officer who is a witness for the purposes of this part of the code is subject to the same principles and procedures as a civilian witness.

2B   Where a witness attending an identification parade has previously been shown photographs or photofit, identikit or similar pictures, it is the responsibility of the officer in charge of the investigation to make the identification officer aware that this is the case.

2C   [Not Used]

2D   Where it is proposed to show photographs to a witness in accordance with Annex D, it is the responsibility of the officer in charge of the investigation to confirm to the officer responsible for supervising and directing the showing that the first description of the suspect given by that witness has been recorded. If this description has not been recorded, the procedure under Annex D must be postponed. (See Annex D paragraph 1A)

2E   References in this section to a suspect being 'known' means there is sufficient information known to the police to justify the arrest of a particular person for suspected involvement in the offence. A suspect being 'available' means that he is immediately available to take part in the procedure or he will become available within a reasonably short time.

3.   Identification by fingerprints

(a)   Action

3.1   A person's fingerprints may be taken only with his consent or if paragraph 3.2 applies. If he is at a police station consent must be in writing. In either case the person must be informed of the reason before they are taken and that they will be destroyed as soon as practicable if paragraph 3.4 applies. He must be told that he may witness their destruction if he asks to do so within five days of being cleared or informed that he will not be prosecuted.

3.2   Powers to take fingerprints without consent from any person over the age of ten years are provided by sections 27 and 61 of the Police and Criminal Evidence Act 1984. These provide that fingerprints may be taken without consent:
    (a)   from a person detained at a police station if an officer of at least the rank of superintendent has reasonable grounds for suspecting that the fingerprints will tend to confirm or disprove his involvement in a criminal offence and the officer authorises the fingerprints to be taken;
    (b)   from a person detained at a police station who has been charged with a recordable offence or informed that he will be reported for such an offence and he has not previously had his fingerprints taken in relation to that offence;
    (c)   from a person convicted of a recordable offence. Section 27 of the Police and Criminal Evidence Act 1984 provides power to require such a person to attend a police station for the purposes of having his fingerprints taken if he has not been in police detention for the offence nor had his fingerprints taken in the course of the investigation of the offence or since conviction.
Reasonable force may be used if necessary to take a person's fingerprints without his consent.

3.2A   A person whose fingerprints are to be taken with or without consent shall be informed beforehand that his prints may be subject of a speculative search against other fingerprints. [See Note 3B]

3.3   [Not Used]

3.4   The fingerprints of a person and all copies of them taken in that case must be destroyed as soon as practicable if:
    (a)   he is prosecuted for the offence concerned and cleared; or
    (b)   he is not prosecuted (unless he admits the offence and is cautioned for it).
An opportunity of witnessing the destruction must be given to him if he wishes and if, in accordance with paragraph 3.1, he applies within five days of being cleared or informed that he will not be prosecuted.

3.5   When fingerprints are destroyed, access to relevant computer data shall be made impossible as soon as it is practicable to do so.

3.6   References to fingerprints include palm prints.

(b)   Documentation

3.7   A record must be made as soon as possible of the reason for taking a person's fingerprints without consent and of their destruction. If force is used a record shall be made of the circumstances and those present.

3.8   A record shall be made when a person has been informed under the terms of paragraph 3.2A that his fingerprints may be subject of a speculative search.

PACE CODE OF PRACTICE (CODE D)

Notes for Guidance

3A   References to recordable offences in this code relate to those offences for which convictions may be recorded in national police records. (See section 27(4) of the Police and Criminal Evidence Act 1984.) The recordable offences to which this code applies at the time when the code was prepared, are any offences which carry a sentence of imprisonment on conviction (irrespective of the period, or the age of the offender or actual sentence passed) and non-imprisonable offences under section 1 of the Street Offences Act 1959 (loitering or soliciting for purposes of prostitution), section 43 of the Telecommunications Act 1984 (improper use of public telecommunications system), section 25 of the Road Traffic Act 1988 (tampering with motor vehicles), section 1 of the Malicious Communications Act 1988 (sending letters etc. with intent to cause distress or anxiety) and section 139(1) of the Criminal Justice Act 1988 (having article with a blade or point in a public place).

3B   A speculative search means that a check may be made against other fingerprints contained in records held by or on behalf of the police or held in connection with or as a result of an investigation of an offence.

4.   Photographs

(a)   Action

4.1   The photograph of a person who has been arrested may be taken at a police station only with his written consent or if paragraph 4.2 applies. In either case he must be informed of the reason for taking it and that the photograph will be destroyed if paragraph 4.4 applies. He must be told that if he should significantly alter his appearance between the taking of the photograph and any attempt to hold an identification procedure this may be given in evidence if the case comes to trial. He must be told that he may witness the destruction of the photograph or be provided with a certificate confirming its destruction if he applies within five days of being cleared or informed that he will not be prosecuted.

4.2   The photograph of a person who has been arrested may be taken without consent if:
    (i)   he is arrested at the same time as other people, or at a time when it is likely that other people will be arrested, and a photograph is necessary to establish who was arrested, at what time and at what place; or
    (ii)   he has been charged with, or reported for a recordable offence and has not yet been released or brought before a court [see Note 3A]; or
    (iii)   he is convicted of such an offence and his photograph is not already on record as a result of (i) or (ii). There is no power of arrest to take a photograph in pursuance of this provision which applies only where the person is in custody as a result of the exercise of another power (e.g. arrest for fingerprinting under section 27 of the Police and Criminal Evidence Act 1984); or
    (iv)   an officer of at least the rank of superintendent authorises it, having reasonable grounds for suspecting the involvement of the person in a criminal offence and where there is identification evidence in relation to that offence.

4.3   Force may not be used to take a photograph.

4.4   Where a person's photograph has been taken in accordance with this section, the photograph, negatives and all copies taken in that particular case must be destroyed if:
    (a)   he is prosecuted for the offence and cleared unless he has a previous conviction for a recordable offence; or
    (b)   he has been charged but not prosecuted (unless he admits the offence and is cautioned for it or he has a previous conviction for a recordable offence).
An opportunity of witnessing the destruction or a certificate confirming the destruction must be given to him if he so requests, provided that, in accordance with paragraph 4.1, he applies within five days of being cleared or informed that he will not be prosecuted. [See Note 4B]

(b)   Documentation

4.5   A record must be made as soon as possible of the reason for taking a person's photograph under this section without consent and of the destruction of any photographs.

Notes for Guidance

4A   The admissibility and value of identification evidence may be compromised if a potential witness in an identification procedure views any photographs of the suspect otherwise than in accordance with the provisions of this code.

4B   This paragraph is not intended to require the destruction of copies of a police gazette in cases where, for example, a remand prisoner has escaped from custody, or a person in custody is suspected of having committed offences in other force areas, and a photograph of the person concerned is circulated in a police gazette for information.

5.   Identification by body samples and impressions

(a)   Action

Intimate samples
5.1   Intimate samples may be taken from a person in police detention only:
        (i)   if an officer of the rank of superintendent or above has reasonable grounds to believe that such an impression or sample will tend to confirm or disprove the suspect's involvement in a recordable offence and gives authorisation for a sample to be taken; and
        (ii)   with the suspect's written consent.

5.1A   Where two or more non-intimate samples have been taken from a person in the course of an investigation of an offence and the samples have proved unsuitable or insufficient for a particular form of analysis and that person is not in police detention, an intimate sample may be taken from him if a police officer of at least the rank of superintendent authorises it to be taken, and the person concerned gives his written consent. [See Note 5B and Note 5E]

5.2   Before a person is asked to provide an intimate sample he must be warned that if he refuses without good cause, his refusal may harm his case if it comes to trial. [See Note 5A] If he is in police detention and not legally represented, he must also be reminded of his entitlement to have free legal advice (see paragraph 6.5 of Code C) and the reminder must be noted in the custody record. If paragraph 5.1A above applies and the person is attending a police station voluntarily, the officer shall explain the entitlement to free legal advice as provided for in accordance with paragraph 3.15 of Code C.

5.3   Except for samples of urine, intimate samples or dental impressions may be taken only by a registered medical or dental practitioner as appropriate.

Non-intimate samples
5.4   A non-intimate sample may be taken from a detained person only with his written consent or if paragraph 5.5 applies.

5.5   A non-intimate sample may be taken from a person without consent in accordance with the provisions of section 63 of the Police and Criminal Evidence Act 1984, as amended by section 55 of the Criminal Justice and Public Order Act 1994. The principal circumstances provided for are as follows:
        (i)   if an officer of the rank of superintendent or above has reasonable grounds to believe that the sample will tend to confirm or disprove the person's involvement in a recordable offence and gives authorisation for a sample to be taken; or
        (ii)   where the person has been charged with a recordable offence or informed that he will be reported for such an offence; and he has not had a non-intimate sample taken from him in the course of the investigation or if he has had a sample taken from him, it has proved unsuitable or insufficient for the same form of analysis [See Note 5B]; or
        (iii)   if the person has been convicted of a recordable offence after the date on which this code comes into effect. Section 63A of the Police and Criminal Evidence Act 1984, as amended by section 56 of the Criminal Justice and Public Order Act 1994, describes the circumstances in which a constable may require a person convicted of a recordable offence to attend a police station in order that a non-intimate sample may be taken.

5.6   Where paragraph 5.5 applies, reasonable force may be used if necessary to take non-intimate samples.

(b)   Destruction

5.7   [Not Used]

PACE CODE OF PRACTICE (CODE D)

5.8   Except in accordance with paragraph 5.8A below, where a sample or impression has been taken in accordance with this section it must be destroyed as soon as practicable if:
    (a)   the suspect is prosecuted for the offence concerned and cleared; or
    (b)   he is not prosecuted (unless he admits the offence and is cautioned for it).

5.8A   In accordance with section 64 of the Police and Criminal Evidence Act 1984 as amended by section 57 of the Criminal Justice and Public Order Act 1994 samples need not be destroyed if they were taken for the purpose of an investigation of an offence for which someone has been convicted, and from whom a sample was also taken. [See Note 5F]

(c)   Documentation

5.9   A record must be made as soon as practicable of the reasons for taking a sample or impression and of its destruction. If force is used a record shall be made of the circumstances and those present. If written consent is given to the taking of a sample or impression, the fact must be recorded in writing.

5.10   A record must be made of the giving of a warning required by paragraph 5.2 above. A record shall be made of the fact that a person has been informed under the terms of paragraph 5.11A below that samples may be subject of a speculative search.

(d)   General

5.11   The terms intimate and non-intimate samples are defined in section 65 of the Police and Criminal Evidence Act 1984, as amended by section 58 of the Criminal Justice and Public Order Act 1994, as follows:
    (a)   'intimate sample' means a dental impression or a sample of blood, semen or any other tissue fluid, urine, or pubic hair, or a swab taken from a person's body orifice other than the mouth;
    (b)   'non-intimate sample' means:
      (i)   a sample of hair (other than pubic hair) which includes hair plucked with the root [See Note 5C];
      (ii)   a sample taken from a nail or from under a nail;
      (iii)   a swab taken from any part of a person's body including the mouth but not any other body orifice;
      (iv)   saliva;
      (v)   a footprint or similar impression of any part of a person's body other than a part of his hand.

5.11A   A person from whom an intimate or non-intimate sample is to be taken shall be informed beforehand that any sample taken may be the subject of a speculative search. [See Note 5D]

5.11B   The suspect must be informed, before an intimate or non-intimate sample is taken, of the grounds on which the relevant authority has been given, including where appropriate the nature of the suspected offence.

5.12   Where clothing needs to be removed in circumstances likely to cause embarrassment to the person, no person of the opposite sex who is not a medical practitioner or nurse shall be present, (unless in the case of a juvenile or a mentally disordered or mentally handicapped person, that person specifically requests the presence of an appropriate adult of the opposite sex who is readily available) nor shall anyone whose presence is unnecessary. However, in the case of a juvenile this is subject to the overriding proviso that such a removal of clothing may take place in the absence of the appropriate adult only if the person signifies in the presence of the appropriate adult that he prefers the search to be done in his absence and the appropriate adult agrees.

Notes for Guidance

5A   In warning a person who is asked to provide an intimate sample in accordance with paragraph 5.2, the following form of words may be used:

'You do not have to [provide this sample] [allow this swab or impression to be taken], but I must warn you that if you refuse without good cause, your refusal may harm your case if it comes to trial.'

342

PACE CODE OF PRACTICE (CODE D)

5B An insufficient sample is one which is not sufficient either in quantity or quality for the purpose of enabling information to be provided for the purpose of a particular form of analysis such as DNA analysis. An unsuitable sample is one which, by its nature, is not suitable for a particular form of analysis.

5C Where hair samples are taken for the purpose of DNA analysis (rather than for other purposes such as making a visual match) the suspect should be permitted a reasonable choice as to what part of the body he wishes the hairs to be taken from. When hairs are plucked they should be plucked individually unless the suspect prefers otherwise and no more should be plucked than the person taking them reasonably considers necessary for a sufficient sample.

5D A speculative search means that a check may be made against other samples and information derived from other samples contained in records or held by or on behalf of the police or held in connection with or as a result of an investigation of an offence.

5E Nothing in paragraph 5.1A prevents intimate samples being taken for elimination purposes with the consent of the person concerned but the provisions of paragraph 1.11, relating to the role of the appropriate adult, should be applied.

5F The provisions for the retention of samples in 5.8A allow for all samples in a case to be available for any subsequent miscarriage of justice investigation. But such samples – and the information derived from them – may not be used in the investigation of any offence or in evidence against the person who would otherwise be entitled to their destruction.

ANNEX A
IDENTIFICATION PARADES

(a) General

1. A suspect must be given a reasonable opportunity to have a solicitor or friend present, and the identification officer shall ask him to indicate on a second copy of the notice whether or not he so wishes.

2. A parade may take place either in a normal room or in one equipped with a screen permitting witnesses to see members of the parade without being seen. The procedures for the composition and conduct of the parade are the same in both cases, subject to paragraph 7 below (except that a parade involving a screen may take place only when the suspect's solicitor, friend or appropriate adult is present or the parade is recorded on video).

2A Before the parade takes place the suspect or his solicitor shall be provided with details of the first description of the suspect by any witnesses who are to attend the parade. The suspect or his solicitor should also be allowed to view any material released to the media by the police for the purpose of recognising or tracing the suspect, provided it is practicable to do so and would not unreasonably delay the investigation.

(b) Parades involving prison inmates

3. If an inmate is required for identification, and there are no security problems about his leaving the establishment, he may be asked to participate in a parade or video identification.

4. A parade may be held in a Prison Department establishment, but shall be conducted as far as practicable under normal parade rules. Members of the public shall make up the parade unless there are serious security or control objections to their admission to the establishment. In such cases, or if a group or video identification is arranged within the establishment, other inmates may participate. If an inmate is the suspect, he shall not be required to wear prison uniform for the parade unless the other people taking part are other inmates in uniform or are members of the public who are prepared to wear prison uniform for the occasion.

(c) Conduct of the parade

5. Immediately before the parade, the identification officer must remind the suspect of the procedures governing its conduct and caution him in the terms of paragraph 10.4 of Code C.

6. All unauthorised people must be excluded from the place where the parade is held.

7.   Once the parade has been formed, everything afterwards in respect of it shall take place in the presence and hearing of the suspect and of any interpreter, solicitor, friend or appropriate adult who is present (unless the parade involves a screen, in which case everything said to or by any witness at the place where the parade is held must be said in the hearing and presence of the suspect's solicitor, friend or appropriate adult or be recorded on video).

8.   The parade shall consist of at least eight people (in addition to the suspect) who so far as possible resemble the suspect in age, height, general appearance and position in life. One suspect only shall be included in a parade unless there are two suspects of roughly similar appearance in which case they may be paraded together with at least twelve other people. In no circumstances shall more than two suspects be included in one parade and where there are separate parades they shall be made up of different people.

9.   Where all members of a similar group are possible suspects, separate parades shall be held for each member of the group unless there are two suspects of similar appearance when they may appear on the same parade with at least twelve other members of the group who are not suspects. Where police officers in uniform form an identification parade, any numerals or other identifying badges shall be concealed.

10.   When the suspect is brought to the place where the parade is to be held, he shall be asked by the identification officer whether he has any objection to the arrangements for the parade or to any of the other participants in it. The suspect may obtain advice from his solicitor or friend, if present, before the parade proceeds. Where practicable, steps shall be taken to remove the grounds for objection. Where it is not practicable to do so, the officer shall explain to the suspect why his objections cannot be met.

11.   The suspect may select his own position in the line. Where there is more than one witness, the identification officer must tell the suspect, after each witness has left the room, that he can if he wishes change position in the line. Each position in the line must be clearly numbered, whether by means of a numeral laid on the floor in front of each parade member or by other means.

12.   The identification officer is responsible for ensuring that, before they attend the parade, witnesses are not able to:
>   (i)   communicate with each other about the case or overhear a witness who has already seen the parade;
>   (ii)   see any member of the parade;
>   (iii)   on that occasion see or be reminded of any photograph or description of the suspect or be given any other indication of his identity; or
>   (iv)   on that occasion, see the suspect either before or after the parade.

13.   The officer conducting a witness to a parade must not discuss with him the composition of the parade, and in particular he must not disclose whether a previous witness has made any identification.

14.   Witnesses shall be brought in one at a time. Immediately before the witness inspects the parade, the identification officer shall tell him that the person he saw may or may not be on the parade and if he cannot make a positive identification he should say so but that he should not make a decision before looking at each member of the parade at least twice. The officer shall then ask him to look at each member of the parade at least twice, taking as much care and time as he wishes. When the officer is satisfied that the witness has properly looked at each member of the parade, he shall ask him whether the person he himself saw on an earlier relevant occasion is on the parade.

15.   The witness should make an identification by indicating the number of the person concerned.

16.   If the witness makes an identification after the parade has ended the suspect and, if present, his solicitor, interpreter or friend shall be informed. Where this occurs, consideration should be given to allowing the witness a second opportunity to identify the suspect.

17.   If a witness wishes to hear any parade member speak, adopt any specified posture or see him move, the identification officer shall first ask whether he can identify any persons on the parade on the basis of appearance only. When the request is to hear members of the parade speak, the witness shall be reminded that the participants in the parade have been chosen on the basis of physical appearance only. Members of the parade may then be asked to comply with the witness's request to hear them speak, to see them move or to adopt any specified posture.

17A.   Where video films or photographs have been released to the media by the police for the purpose of recognising or tracing the suspect, the investigating officer shall ask each witness after the parade whether he has seen any broadcast or published films or photographs relating to the offence and shall record his reply.

18.   When the last witness has left, the identification officer shall ask the suspect whether he wishes to make any comments on the conduct of the parade.

(d)   Documentation

19.   A colour photograph or a video film of the parade shall be taken. A copy of the photograph or video film shall be supplied on request to the suspect or his solicitor within a reasonable time.

20.   The photograph or video film taken in accordance with paragraph 19 and held by the police shall be destroyed or wiped clean at the conclusion of the proceedings unless the person concerned is convicted or admits the offence and is cautioned for it.

21.   If the identification officer asks any person to leave a parade because he is interfering with its conduct the circumstances shall be recorded.

22.   A record must be made of all those present at a parade whose names are known to the police.

23.   If prison inmates make up a parade the circumstances must be recorded.

24.   A record of the conduct of any parade must be made on the forms provided.

ANNEX B
VIDEO IDENTIFICATION

(a)   General

1.   Where a video parade is to be arranged the following procedures must be followed.

2.   Arranging, supervising and directing the making and showing of a video film to be used in a video identification must be the responsibility of an identification officer or identification officers who have no direct involvement with the relevant case.

3.   The film must include the suspect and at least eight other people who so far as possible resemble the suspect in age, height, general appearance and position in life. Only one suspect shall appear on any film unless there are two suspects of roughly similar appearance in which case they may be shown together with at least twelve other people.

4.   The suspect and other people shall as far as possible be filmed in the same positions or carrying out the same activity and under identical conditions.

5.   Provisions must be made for each person filmed to be identified by number.

6.   If police officers are filmed, any numerals or other identifying badges must be concealed. If a prison inmate is filmed either as a suspect or not, then either all or none of the people filmed should be in prison uniform.

7.   The suspect and his solicitor, friend, or appropriate adult must be given a reasonable opportunity to see the complete film before it is shown to witnesses. If he has a reasonable objection to the video film or any of its participants, steps shall, if practicable be taken to remove the grounds for objection. If this is not practicable the identification officer shall explain to the suspect and/or his representative why his objections cannot be met and record both the objection and the reason on the forms provided.

8.   The suspect's solicitor, or where one is not instructed the suspect himself, where practicable shall be given reasonable notification of the time and place that it is intended to conduct the video identification in order that a representative may attend on behalf of the suspect. The suspect himself may not be present

when the film is shown to the witness(es). In the absence of a person representing the suspect the viewing itself shall be recorded on video. No unauthorised people may be present.

8A. Before the video identification takes place the suspect or his solicitor shall be provided with details of the first description of the suspect by any witnesses who are to attend the parade. The suspect or his solicitor should also be allowed to view any material released to the media by the police for the purpose of recognising or tracing the suspect, provided it is practicable to do so and would not unreasonably delay the investigation.

(b) Conducting the Video Identification

9. The identification officer is responsible for ensuring that, before they see the film, witnesses are not able to communicate with each other about the case or overhear a witness who has seen the film. He must not discuss with the witness the composition of the film and must not disclose whether a previous witness has made any identification.

10. Only one witness may see the film at a time. Immediately before the video identification takes place the identification officer shall tell the witness that the person he saw may or may not be on the video film. The witness should be advised that at any point he may ask to see a particular part of the tape again or to have a particular picture frozen for him to study. Furthermore, it should be pointed out that there is no limit on how many times he can view the whole tape or any part of it. However, he should be asked to refrain from making a positive identification or saying that he cannot make a positive identification until he has seen the entire film at least twice.

11. Once the witness has seen the whole film at least twice and has indicated that he does not want to view it or any part of it again, the identification officer shall ask the witness to say whether the individual he saw in person on an earlier occasion has been shown on the film and, if so, to identify him by number. The identification officer will then show the film of the person identified again to confirm the identification with the witness.

12. The identification officer must take care not to direct the witness's attention to any one individual on the video film, or give any other indication of the suspect's identity. Where a witness has previously made an identification by photographs, or a photofit, identikit or similar picture has been made, the witness must not be reminded of such a photograph or picture once a suspect is available for identification by other means in accordance with this code. Neither must he be reminded of any description of the suspect.

12A Where video films or photographs have been released to the media by the police for the purpose of recognising or tracing the suspect, the investigating officer shall ask each witness after the parade whether he has seen any broadcast or published films or photographs relating to the offence and shall record his reply.

(c) Tape Security and Destruction

13. It shall be the responsibility of the identification officer to ensure that all relevant tapes are kept securely and their movements accounted for. In particular, no officer involved in the investigation against the suspect shall be permitted to view the video film prior to it being shown to any witness.

14. Where a video film has been made in accordance with this section all copies of it held by the police must be destroyed if the suspect:
    (a) is prosecuted for the offence and cleared; or
    (b) is not prosecuted (unless he admits the offence and is cautioned for it).
An opportunity of witnessing the destruction must be given to him if he so requests within five days of being cleared or informed that he will not be prosecuted.

(d) Documentation

15. A record must be made of all those participating in or seeing the video whose names are known to the police.

16. A record of the conduct of the video identification must be made on the forms provided.

PACE CODE OF PRACTICE (CODE D)

ANNEX C
CONFRONTATION BY A WITNESS

1.   The identification officer is responsible for the conduct of any confrontation of a suspect by a witness.

2.   Before the confrontation takes place, the identification officer must tell the witness that the person he saw may or may not be the person he is to confront and that if he cannot make a positive identification he should say so.

2A   Before the confrontation takes place, the suspect or his solicitor shall be provided with details of the first description of the suspect given by any witness who is to attend the confrontation. The suspect or his solicitor should also be allowed to view any material released by the police to the media for the purposes of recognising or tracing the suspect provided that it is practicable to do so and would not unreasonably delay the investigation.

3.   The suspect shall be confronted independently by each witness, who shall be asked 'Is this the person?' Confrontation must take place in the presence of the suspect's solicitor, interpreter or friend, unless this would cause unreasonable delay.

4.   The confrontation should normally take place in the police station, either in a normal room or in one equipped with a screen permitting a witness to see the suspect without being seen. In both cases the procedures are the same except that a room equipped with a screen may be used only when the suspect's solicitor, friend or appropriate adult is present or the confrontation is recorded on video.

5.   Where video films or photographs have been released to the media by the police for the purposes of recognising or tracing the suspect, the investigating officer shall ask each witness after the procedure whether he has seen any broadcast or published films or photographs relating to the offence and shall record his reply.

ANNEX D
SHOWING OF PHOTOGRAPHS

(a)   Action

1.   An officer of the rank of sergeant or above shall be responsible for supervising and directing the showing of photographs. The actual showing may be done by a constable or a civilian police employee.

1A   The officer must confirm that the first description of the suspect given by the witness has been recorded before the witness is shown the photographs. If he is unable to confirm that the description has been recorded, he shall postpone the showing.

2.   Only one witness shall be shown photographs at any one time. He shall be given as much privacy as practicable and shall not be allowed to communicate with any other witness in the case.

3.   The witness shall be shown not less than twelve photographs at a time, which shall, as far as possible, all be of a similar type.

4.   When the witness is shown the photographs, he shall be told that the photograph of the person he saw may or may not be amongst them. He shall not be prompted or guided in any way but shall be left to make any selection without help.

5.   If a witness makes a positive identification from photographs, then, unless the person identified is otherwise eliminated from enquiries, other witnesses shall not be shown photographs. But both they and the witness who has made the identification shall be asked to attend an identification parade or group or video identification if practicable unless there is no dispute about the identification of the suspect.

6.   Where the use of a photofit, identikit or similar picture has led to there being a suspect available who can be asked to appear on a parade, or participate in a group or video group identification, the picture shall not be shown to other potential witnesses.

7.   Where a witness attending an identification parade has previously been shown photographs or photofit, identikit or similar pictures (and it is the responsibility of the officer in charge of the investigation to make

347

the identification officer aware that this is the case) then the suspect and his solicitor must be informed of this fact before the identity parade takes place.

8.   None of the photographs used shall be destroyed, whether or not an identification is made, since they may be required for production in court. The photographs shall be numbered and a separate photograph taken of the frame or part of the album from which the witness made an identification as an aid to reconstituting it.

(b)   Documentation

9.   Whether or not an identification is made, a record shall be kept of the showing of photographs and of any comment made by the witness.

ANNEX E
GROUP IDENTIFICATION

(a)   General

1.   The purpose of the provisions of this Annex is to ensure that as far as possible, group identifications follow the principles and procedures for identification parades so that the conditions are fair to the suspect in the way they test the witness's ability to make an identification.

2.   Group identifications may take place either with the suspect's consent and co-operation or covertly without his consent.

3.   The location of the group identification is a matter for the identification officer, although he may take into account any representations made by the suspect, appropriate adult, his solicitor or friend. The place where the group identification is held should be one where other people are either passing by, or waiting around informally, in groups such that the suspect is able to join them and be capable of being seen by the witness at the same time as others in the group. Examples include people leaving an escalator, pedestrians walking through a shopping centre, passengers on railway and bus stations waiting in queues or groups or where people are standing or sitting in groups in other public places.

4.   If the group identification is to be held covertly, the choice of locations will be limited by the places where the suspect can be found and the number of other people present at that time. In these cases, suitable locations might be along regular routes travelled by the suspect, including buses or trains, or public places he frequents.

5.   Although the number, age, sex, race and general description and style of clothing of other people present at the location cannot be controlled by the identification officer, in selecting the location he must consider the general appearance and number of people likely to be present. In particular, he must reasonably expect that over the period the witness observes the group, he will be able to see, from time to time, a number of others (in addition to the suspect) whose appearance is broadly similar to that of the suspect.

6.   A group identification need not be held if the identification officer believes that because of the unusual appearance of the suspect, none of the locations which it would be practicable to use satisfy the requirements of paragraph 5 necessary to make the identification fair.

7.   Immediately after a group identification procedure has taken place (with or without the suspect's consent), a colour photograph or a video should be taken of the general scene, where this is practicable, so as to give a general impression of the scene and the number of people present. Alternatively, if it is practicable, the group identification may be video recorded.

8.   If it is not practicable to take the photograph or video film in accordance with paragraph 7, a photograph or film of the scene should be taken later at a time determined by the identification officer, if he considers that it is practicable to do so.

9.   An identification carried out in accordance with this code remains a group identification notwithstanding that at the time of being seen by the witness the suspect was on his own rather than in a group.

10.   The identification officer need not be in uniform when conducting a group identification.

11.   Before the group identification takes place the suspect or his solicitor should be provided with details of the first description of the suspect by any witnesses who are to attend the identification. The suspect or his solicitor should also be allowed to view any material released by the police to the media for the purposes of recognising or tracing the suspect provided that it is practicable to do so and would not unreasonably delay the investigation.

12.   Where video films or photographs have been released to the media by the police for the purposes of recognising or tracing the suspect, the investigating officer shall ask each witness after the procedure whether he has seen any broadcast or published films or photographs relating to the offence and shall record his reply.

(b)   Identification with the consent of the suspect

13.   A suspect must be given a reasonable opportunity to have a solicitor or friend present. The identification officer shall ask him to indicate on a second copy of the notice whether or not he so wishes.

14.   The witness, identification officer and suspect's solicitor, appropriate adult, friend or any interpreter for the witness, if present may be concealed from the sight of the persons in the group which they are observing if the identification officer considers that this facilitates the conduct of the identification.

15.   The officer conducting a witness to a group identification must not discuss with the witness the forthcoming group identification and in particular he must not disclose whether a previous witness has made any identification.

16.   Anything said to or by the witness during the procedure regarding the identification should be said in the presence and hearing of the identification officer and, if present, the suspect's solicitor, appropriate adult, friend or any interpreter for the witness.

17.   The identification officer is responsible for ensuring that before they attend the group identification witnesses are not able to:
      (i)   communicate with each other about the case or overhear a witness who has already been given an opportunity to see the suspect in the group;
      (ii)   on that occasion see the suspect; or
      (iii)   on that occasion see or be reminded of any photographs or description of the suspect or be given any other indication of his identity.

18.   Witnesses shall be brought to the place where they are to observe the group one at a time. Immediately before the witness is asked to look at the group, the identification officer shall tell him that the person he saw may or may not be in the group and if he cannot make a positive identification he should say so. The witness shall then be asked to observe the group in which the suspect is to appear. The way in which the witness should do this will depend on whether the group is moving or stationary.

Moving group
19.   When the group in which the suspect is to appear is moving, for example, leaving an escalator, the provisions of paragraphs 20 to 23 below should be followed.

20.   If two or more suspects consent to a group identification, each should be the subject of separate identification procedures. These may however be conducted consecutively on the same occasion.

21.   The identification officer shall tell the witness to observe the group and ask him to point out any person he thinks he saw on the earlier relevant occasion. When the witness makes such an indication the officer shall, if it is practicable, arrange for the witness to take a closer look at the person he has indicated and ask him whether he can make a positive identification. If this is not practicable, the officer shall ask the witness how sure he is that the person he has indicated is the relevant person.

22.   The witness should continue to observe the group for the period which the identification officer reasonably believes is necessary in the circumstances for the witness to be able to make comparisons between the suspect and other persons of broadly similar appearance to the suspect in accordance with paragraph 5.

23.   Once the identification officer has informed the witness in accordance with paragraph 21, the suspect should be allowed to take any position in the group he wishes.

Stationary groups

24. When the group in which the suspect is to appear is stationary, for example, people waiting in a queue, the provisions of paragraphs 25 to 28 below should be followed.

25. If two or more suspects consent to a group identification, each should be the subject of separate identification procedures unless they are of broadly similar appearance when they may appear in the same group. Where separate group identifications are held, the groups must be made up of different persons.

26. The suspect may take any position in the group he wishes. Where there is more than one witness, the identification officer must tell the suspect, out of the sight and hearing of any witness, that he can if he wishes change his position in the group.

27. The identification officer shall ask the witness to pass along or amongst the group and to look at each person in the group at least twice, taking as much care and time as is possible according to the circumstances, before making an identification. When he has done this, the officer shall ask him whether the person he saw on an earlier relevant occasion is in the group and to indicate any such person by whatever means the identification officer considers appropriate in the circumstances. If this is not practicable, the officer shall ask the witness to point out any person he thinks he saw on the earlier relevant occasion.

28. When the witness makes an indication in accordance with paragraph 27, the officer shall, if it is practicable, arrange for the witness to take a closer look at the person he has indicated and ask him whether he can make a positive identification. If this is not practicable, the officer shall ask the witness how sure he is that the person he has indicated is the relevant person.

All Cases

29. If the suspect unreasonably delays joining the group, or having joined the group, deliberately conceals himself from the sight of the witness, the identification officer may treat this as a refusal to co-operate in a group identification.

30. If the witness identifies a person other than the suspect, an officer should inform that person what has happened and ask if they are prepared to give their name and address. There is no obligation upon any member of the public to give these details. There shall be no duty to record any details of any other member of the public present in the group or at the place where the procedure is conducted.

31. When the group identification has been completed, the identification officer shall ask the suspect whether he wishes to make any comments on the conduct of the procedure.

32. If he has not been previously informed the identification officer shall tell the suspect of any identifications made by the witnesses.

(c) Identification without suspect's consent

33. Group identifications held covertly without the suspect's consent should so far as is practicable follow the rules for conduct of group identification by consent.

34. A suspect has no right to have a solicitor, appropriate adult or friend present as the identification will, of necessity, take place without the knoweldge of the suspect.

35. Any number of suspects may be identified at the same time.

(d) Identifications in police stations

36. Group identifications should only take place in police stations for reasons of safety, security, or because it is impracticable to hold them elsewhere.

37. The group identification may take place either in a room equipped with a screen permitting witnesses to see members of the group without being seen, or anywhere else in the police station that the identification officer considers appropriate.

38. Any of the additional safeguards applicable to identification parades should be followed if the identification officer considers it is practicable to do so in the circumstances.

(e)   Identifications involving prison inmates

39.   A group identification involving a prison inmate may only be arranged in the prison or at a police station.

40.   Where a group identification takes place involving a prison inmate, whether in a prison or in a police station, the arrangements should follow those in paragraphs 36 to 38 of this Annex. If a group identification takes place within a prison other inmates may participate. If an inmate is the suspect he should not be required to wear prison uniform for the group identification unless the other persons taking part are wearing the same uniform.

(f)   Documentation

41.   Where a photograph or video film is taken in accordance with paragraph 7 or 8, a copy of the photograph or video film shall be supplied on request to the suspect or his solicitor within a reasonable time.

42.   If the photograph or film includes the suspect, it and all copies held by the police shall be destroyed or wiped clean at the conclusion of the proceedings unless the person is convicted or admits the offence and is cautioned for it.

43.   A record of the conduct of any group identification must be made on the forms provided. This shall include anything said by the witness or the suspect about any identifications or the conduct of the procedure and any reasons why it was not practicable to comply with any of the provisions of this code governing the conduct of group identifications.

APPENDIX SEVEN

PACE CODE OF PRACTICE ON TAPE RECORDING OF INTERVIEWS WITH SUSPECTS (CODE E)

1. General

1.1   This code of practice must be readily available for consultation by police officers, detained persons and members of the public at every police station to which an order made under section 60(1)(b) of the Police and Criminal Evidence Act 1984 applies.

1.2   The notes for guidance included are not provisions of this code. They form guidance to police officers and others about its application and interpretation.

1.3   Nothing in this code shall be taken as detracting in any way from the requirements of the Code of Practice for the Detention, Treatment and Questioning of Persons by Police Officers (Code C). [See Note 1A]

1.4   This code does not apply to those groups of people listed in paragraph 1.12 of Code C.

1.5   In this code the term 'appropriate adult' has the same meaning as in paragraph 1.7 of Code C; and the term 'solicitor' has the same meaning as in paragraph 6.12 of Code C.

Notes for Guidance

1A   As in Code C, references to custody officers include those carrying out the functions of a custody officer.

2. Recording and the sealing of master tapes

2.1   Tape recording of interviews shall be carried out openly to instil confidence in its reliability as an impartial and accurate record of the interview. [See Note 2A]

2.2   One tape, referred to in this code as the master tape, will be sealed before it leaves the presence of the suspect. A second tape will be used as a working copy. The master tape is either one of the two tapes used in a twin deck machine or the only tape used in a single deck machine. The working copy is either the second tape used in a twin deck machine or a copy of the master tape made by a single deck machine. [See Notes 2B and 2C]

PACE CODE OF PRACTICE (CODE E)

Notes for Guidance

2A   Police Officers will wish to arrange that, as far as possible, tape recording arrangements are unobtrusive. It must be clear to the suspect, however, that there is no opportunity to interfere with the tape recording equipment or the tapes.

2B   The purpose of sealing the master tape before it leaves the presence of the suspect is to establish his confidence that the integrity of the tape is preserved. Where a single deck machine is used the working copy of the master tape must be made in the presence of the suspect and without the master tape having left his sight. The working copy shall be used for making further copies where the need arises. The recorder will normally be capable of recording voices and have a time coding or other security device.

2C   Throughout this code any reference to 'tapes' shall be construed as 'tape', as appropriate, where a single deck machine is used.

3.   Interviews to be tape recorded

3.1   Subject to paragraph 3.2 below, tape recording shall be used at police stations for any interview:
   (a)   with a person who has been cautioned in accordance with section 10 of Code C in respect of an indictable offence (including an offence triable either way) [see Notes 3A and 3B];
   (b)   which takes place as a result of a police officer exceptionally putting further questions to a suspect about an offence described in sub-paragraph (a) above after he has been charged with, or informed he may be prosecuted for, that offence [see Note 3C]; or
   (c)   in which a police officer wishes to bring to the notice of a person, after he has been charged with, or informed he may be prosecuted for an offence described in sub-paragraph (a) above, any written statement made by another person, or the content of an interview with another person [see Note 3D].

3.2   Tape recording is not required in respect of the following:
   (a)   an interview with a person arrested under section 14(1)(a) or schedule 5 paragraph 6 of the Prevention of Terrorism (Temporary Provisions) Act 1989 or an interview with a person being questioned in respect of an offence where there are reasonable grounds for suspecting that it is connected to terrorism or was committed in furtherance of the objectives of an organisation engaged in terrorism. This sub-paragraph applies only where the terrorism is connected with the affairs of Northern Ireland or is terrorism of any other description except terrorism connected solely with the affairs of the United Kingdom or any part of the United Kingdom other than Northern Ireland. 'Terrorism' has the meaning given by section 20(1) of the Prevention of Terrorism (Temporary Provisions) Act 1989 [see Notes 3E, 3F, 3G and 3H];
   (b)   an interview with a person suspected on reasonable grounds of an offence under section 1 of the Official Secrets Act 1911 [see Note 3H].

3.3   The custody officer may authorise the interviewing officer not to tape record the interview:
   (a)   where it is not reasonably practicable to do so because of failure of the equipment or the non-availability of a suitable interview room or recorder and the authorising officer considers on reasonable grounds that the interview should not be delayed until the failure has been rectified or a suitable room or recorder becomes available [see Note 3J]; or
   (b)   where it is clear from the outset that no prosecution will ensue.
In such cases the interview shall be recorded in writing and in accordance with section 11 of Code C. In all cases the custody officer shall make a note in specified terms of the reasons for not tape recording. [See Note 3K]

3.4   Where an interview takes place with a person voluntarily attending the police station and the police officer has grounds to believe that person has become a suspect (i.e. the point at which he should be cautioned in accordance with paragraph 10.1 of Code C) the continuation of the interview shall be tape recorded, unless the custody officer gives authority in accordance with the provisions of paragraph 3.3 above for the continuation of the interview not to be recorded.

3.5   The whole of each interview shall be tape recorded, including the taking and reading back of any statement.

PACE CODE OF PRACTICE (CODE E)

Notes for Guidance

3A   Nothing in this code is intended to preclude tape recording at police discretion of interviews at police stations with persons cautioned in respect of offences not covered by paragraph 3.1, or responses made by interviewees after they have been charged with, or informed they may be prosecuted for, an offence, provided that this code is complied with.

3B   Attention is drawn to the restrictions in paragraph 12.3 of Code C on the questioning of persons unfit through drink or drugs to the extent that they are unable to appreciate the significance of questions put to them or of their answers.

3C   Circumstances in which a suspect may be questioned about an offence after being charged with it are set out in paragraph 16.5 of Code C.

3D   Procedures to be followed when a person's attention is drawn after charge to a statement made by another person are set out in paragraph 16.4 of Code C. One method of bringing the content of an interview with another person to the notice of a suspect may be to play him a tape recording of that interview.

3E   Section 14(1)(a) of the Prevention of Terrorism (Temporary Provisions) Act 1989, permits the arrest without warrant of a person reasonably suspected to be guilty of an offence under section 2, 8, 10 or 11 of the Act.

3F   Section 20(1) of the Prevention of Terrorism (Temporary Provisions) Act 1989 says 'terrorism means the use of violence for political ends, and includes any use of violence for the purpose of putting the public or any section of the public in fear'.

3G   It should be noted that the provisions of paragraph 3.2 apply only to those suspected of offences connected with terrorism connected with Northern Ireland, or with terrorism of any other description other than terrorism connected solely with the affairs of the United Kingdom or any part of the United Kingdom other than Northern Ireland, or offences committed in furtherance of such terrorism. Any interviews with those suspected of offences connected with terrorism of any other description or in furtherance of the objectives of an organisation engaged in such terrorism should be carried out in compliance with the rest of this code.

3H   When it only becomes clear during the course of an interview which is being tape recorded that the interviewee may have committed an offence to which paragraph 3.2 applies the interviewing officer should turn off the tape recorder.

3J   Where practicable, priority should be given to tape recording interviews with persons who are suspected of more serious offences.

3K   A decision not to tape record an interview for any reason may be the subject of comment in court. The authorising officer should therefore be prepared to justify his decision in each case.

4.   The interview

(a)   Commencement of interviews

4.1   When the suspect is brought into the interview room the police officer shall without delay, but in the sight of the suspect, load the tape recorder with clean tapes and set it to record. The tapes must be unwrapped or otherwise opened in the presence of the suspect. [See Note 4A]

4.2   The police officer shall then tell the suspect formally about the tape recording. He shall say:
   (a)   that the interview is being tape recorded;
   (b)   his name and rank and the name and rank of any other police officer present except in the case of enquiries linked to the investigation of terrorism where warrant or other identification numbers shall be stated rather than names;
   (c)   the name of the suspect and any other party present (e.g. a solicitor);
   (d)   the date, time of commencement and place of the interview; and
   (e)   that the suspect will be given a notice about what will happen to the tapes.
[See Note 4B]

4.3 The police officer shall then caution the suspect in the following terms:

You do not have to say anything. But it may harm your defence if you do not mention when questioned something which you later rely on in court. Anything you do say may be given in evidence.

Minor deviations do not constitute a breach of this requirement provided that the sense of the caution is preserved. [See Note 4C].

4.3A The police officer shall remind the suspect of his right to free and independent legal advice and that he can speak to a solicitor on the telephone in accordance with paragraph 6.5 of Code C.

4.3B The police officer shall then put to the suspect any significant statement or silence (i.e. failure or refusal to answer a question or to answer it satisfactorily) which occurred before the start of the tape-recorded interview, and shall ask him whether he confirms or denies that earlier statement or silence or whether he wishes to add anything. A 'significant' statement or silence means one which appears capable of being used in evidence against the suspect, in particular a direct admission of guilt, or failure or refusal to answer a question or to answer it satisfactorily, which might give rise to an inference under Part III of the Criminal Justice and Public Order Act 1994.

Special warnings under Sections 36 and 37 of the Criminal Justice and Public Order Act 1994
4.3C When a suspect who is interviewed after arrest fails or refuses to answer certain questions, or to answer them satisfactorily, after due warning, a court or jury may draw a proper inference from this silence under sections 36 and 37 of the Criminal Justice and Public Order Act 1994. This applies when:
(a) a suspect is arrested by a constable and there is found on his person, or in or on his clothing or footwear, or otherwise in his possession, or in the place where he was arrested, any objects, marks or substances, or marks on such objects, and the person fails or refuses to account for the objects, marks or substances found; or
(b) an arrested person was found by a constable at a place at or about the time the offence for which he was arrested, is alleged to have been committed, and the person fails or refuses to account for his presence at that place.

4.3D For an inference to be drawn from a suspect's failure or refusal to answer a question about one of these matters or to answer it satisfactorily, the interviewing officer must first tell him in ordinary language:
(a) what offence he is investigating;
(b) what fact he is asking the suspect to account for;
(c) that he believes this fact may be due to the suspect's taking part in the commission of the offence in question;
(d) that a court may draw a proper inference from his silence if he fails or refuses to account for the fact about which he is being questioned;
(e) that a record is being made of the interview and may be given in evidence if he is brought to trial.

4.3E Where, despite the fact that a person has been cautioned, failure to co-operate may have an effect on his immediate treatment, he should be informed of any relevant consequences and that they are not affected by the caution. Examples are when his refusal to provide his name and address when charged may render him liable to detention, or when his refusal to provide particulars and information in accordance with a statutory requirement, for example, under the Road Traffic Act 1988, may amount to an offence or may make him liable to arrest.

(b) Interviews with the deaf

4.4 If the suspect is deaf or there is doubt about his hearing ability, the police officer shall take a contemporaneous note of the interview in accordance with the requirements of Code C, as well as tape record it in accordance with the provisions of this code. [See Notes 4E and 4F]

(c) Objections and complaints by the suspect

4.5 If the suspect raises objections to the interview being tape recorded either at the outset or during the interview or during a break in the interview, the police officer shall explain the fact that the interview is being tape recorded and that the provisions of this code require that the suspect's objections should be recorded on tape. When any objections have been recorded on tape or the suspect has refused to have his objections recorded, the police officer may turn off the recorder. In this eventuality he shall say that he is turning off the recorder and give his reasons for doing so and then turn it off. The police officer shall then make a written record of the interview in accordance with section 11 of Code C. If, however, the police officer reasonably considers that he may proceed to put questions to the suspect with the tape recorder still on, he may do so. [See Note 4G]

4.6   If in the course of an interview a complaint is made by the person being questioned, or on his behalf, concerning the provisions of this code or of Code C, then the officer shall act in accordance with paragraph 12.8 of Code C. [See Notes 4H and 4J]

4.7   If the suspect indicates that he wishes to tell the police officer about matters not directly connected with the offence of which he is suspected and that he is unwilling for these matters to be recorded on tape, he shall be given the opportunity to tell the police officer about these matters after the conclusion of the formal interview.

(d)   Changing tapes

4.8   When the recorder indicates that the tapes have only a short time left to run, the police officer shall tell the suspect that the tapes are coming to an end and round off that part of the interview. If the police officer wishes to continue the interview but does not already have a second set of tapes, he shall obtain a set. The suspect shall not be left unattended in the interview room. The police officer will remove the tapes from the tape recorder and insert the new tapes which shall be unwrapped or otherwise opened in the suspect's presence. The tape recorder shall then be set to record on the new tapes. Care must be taken, particularly when a number of sets of tapes have been used, to ensure that there is no confusion between the tapes. This may be done by marking the tapes with an identification number immediately they are removed from the tape recorder.

(e)   Taking a break during interview

4.9   When a break is to be taken during the course of an interview and the interview room is to be vacated by the suspect, the fact that a break is to be taken, the reason for it and the time shall be recorded on tape. The tapes shall then be removed from the tape recorder and the procedures for the conclusion of an interview set out in paragraph 4.14 below followed.

4.10   When a break is to be a short one and both the suspect and a police officer are to remain in the interview room the fact that a break is to be taken, the reasons for it and the time shall be recorded on tape. The tape recorder may be turned off; there is, however, no need to remove the tapes and when the interview is recommenced the tape recording shall be continued on the same tapes. The time at which the interview recommences shall be recorded on tape.

4.11   When there is a break in questioning under caution the interviewing officer must ensure that the person being questioned is aware that he remains under caution and of his right to legal advice. If there is any doubt the caution must be given again in full when the interview resumes. [See Notes 4K and 4L]

(f)   Failure of recording equipment

4.12   If there is a failure of equipment which can be rectified quickly, for example by inserting new tapes, the appropriate procedures set out in paragraph 4.8 shall be followed, and when the recording is resumed the officer shall explain what has happened and record the time the interview recommences. If, however, it will not be possible to continue recording on that particular tape recorder and no replacement recorder or recorder in another interview room is readily available, the interview may continue without being tape recorded. In such circumstances the procedures in paragraphs 3.3 above for seeking the authority of the custody officer will be followed. [See Note 4M]

(g)   Removing tapes from the recorder

4.13   Where tapes are removed from the recorder in the course of an interview, they shall be retained and the procedures set out in paragraph 4.15 below followed.

(h)   Conclusion of interview

4.14   At the conclusion of the interview, the suspect shall be offered the opportunity to clarify anything he has said and to add anything he may wish.

4.15 At the conclusion of the interview, including the taking and reading back of any written statement, the time shall be recorded and the tape recorder switched off. The master tape shall be sealed with a master tape label and treated as an exhibit in accordance with the force standing orders. The police officer shall sign the label and ask the suspect and any third party present to sign it also. If the suspect or third party refuses to sign the label, an officer of at least the rank of inspector, or if one is not available the custody officer, shall be called into the interview room and asked to sign it. In the case of enquiries linked to the investigation of terrorism, an officer who signs the label shall use his warrant or other identification number.

4.16 The suspect shall be handed a notice which explains the use which will be made of the tape recording and the arrangements for access to it and that a copy of the tape shall be supplied as soon as practicable if the person is charged or informed that he will be prosecuted.

Notes for Guidance

4A The police officer should attempt to estimate the likely length of the interview and ensure that the appropriate number of clean tapes and labels with which to seal the master copies are available in the interview room.

4B It will be helpful for the purpose of voice identification if the officer asks the suspect and any other people present to identify themselves.

4C If it appears that a person does not understand what the caution means, the officer who has given it should go on to explain it in his own words.

4D [Not Used]

4E This provision is intended to give the deaf equivalent rights of first hand access to the full interview record as other suspects.

4F The provisions of paragraphs 13.2, 13.5 and 13.9 of Code C on interpreters for the deaf or for interviews with suspects who have difficulty in understanding English continue to apply. In a tape recorded interview there is no requirement on the interviewing officer to ensure that the interpreter makes a separate note of interview as prescribed in section 13 of Code C.

4G The officer should bear in mind that a decision to continue recording against the wishes of the suspect may be the subject of comment in court.

4H Where the custody officer is called immediately to deal with the complaint, wherever possible the tape recorder should be left to run until the custody officer has entered the interview room and spoken to the person being interviewed. Continuation or termination of the interview should be at the discretion of the interviewing officer pending action by an inspector under paragraph 9.1 of Code C.

4I [Not Used]

4J Where the complaint is about a matter not connected with this code of practice or Code C, the decision to continue with the interview is at the discretion of the interviewing officer. Where the interviewing officer decides to continue with the interview the person being interviewed shall be told that the complaint will be brought to the attention of the custody officer at the conclusion of the interview. When the interview is concluded the interviewing officer must, as soon as practicable, inform the custody officer of the existence and nature of the complaint made.

4K In considering whether to caution again after a break, the officer should bear in mind that he may have to satisfy a court that the person understood that he was still under caution when the interview resumed.

4L The officer should bear in mind that it may be necessary to show to the court that nothing occurred during a break in an interview or between interviews which influenced the suspect's recorded evidence. The officer should consider, therefore, after a break in an interview or at the beginning of a subsequent interview summarising on tape the reason for the break and confirming this with the suspect.

4M If one of the tapes breaks during the interview it should be sealed as a master tape in the presence of the suspect and the interview resumed where it left off. The unbroken tape should be copied and the original sealed as a master tape in the suspect's presence, if necessary after the interview. If equipment for copying the unbroken tape is not readily available, both tapes should be sealed in the suspect's presence and the interview begun again. If the tape breaks when a single deck machine is being used and the machine is one where a broken tape cannot be copied on available equipment, the tape should be sealed as a master tape in the suspect's presence and the interview begun again.

5. After the interview

5.1 The police officer shall make a note in his notebook of the fact that the interview has taken place and has been recorded on tape, its time, duration and date and the identification number of the master tape.

5.2 Where no proceedings follow in respect of the person whose interview was recorded the tapes must nevertheless be kept securely in accordance with paragraph 6.1 and Note 6A.

Note for Guidance

5A Any written record of a tape recorded interview shall be made in accordance with national guidelines approved by the Secretary of State.

6. Tape security

6.1 The officer in charge of each police station at which interviews with suspects are recorded shall make arrangements for master tapes to be kept securely and their movements accounted for on the same basis as other material which may be used for evidential purposes, in accordance with force standing orders. [See Note 6A]

6.2 A police officer has no authority to break the seal on a master tape which is required for criminal proceedings. If it is necessary to gain access to the master tape, the police officer shall arrange for its seal to be broken in the presence of a representative of the Crown Prosecution Service. The defendant or his legal adviser shall be informed and given a reasonable opportunity to be present. If the defendant or his legal representative is present he shall be invited to reseal and sign the master tape. If either refuses or neither is present this shall be done by the representative of the Crown Prosecution Service. [See Notes 6B and 6C]

6.3 Where no criminal proceedings result it is the responsibility of the chief officer of police to establish arrangements for the breaking of the seal on the master tape, where this becomes necessary.

Notes for Guidance

6A This section is concerned with the security of the master tape which will have been sealed at the conclusion of the interview. Care should, however, be taken of working copies of tapes since their loss or destruction may lead unnecessarily to the need to have access to master tapes.

6B If the tape has been delivered to the Crown Court for their keeping after committal for trial the crown prosecutor will apply to the chief clerk of the Crown Court centre for the release of the tape for unsealing by the crown prosecutor.

6C Reference to the Crown Prosecution Service or to the crown prosecutor in this part of the code shall be taken to include any other body or person with a statutory responsibility for prosecution for whom the police conduct any tape recorded interviews.

APPENDIX EIGHT

FLOW CHARTS

FLOW CHARTS

Strip Searches

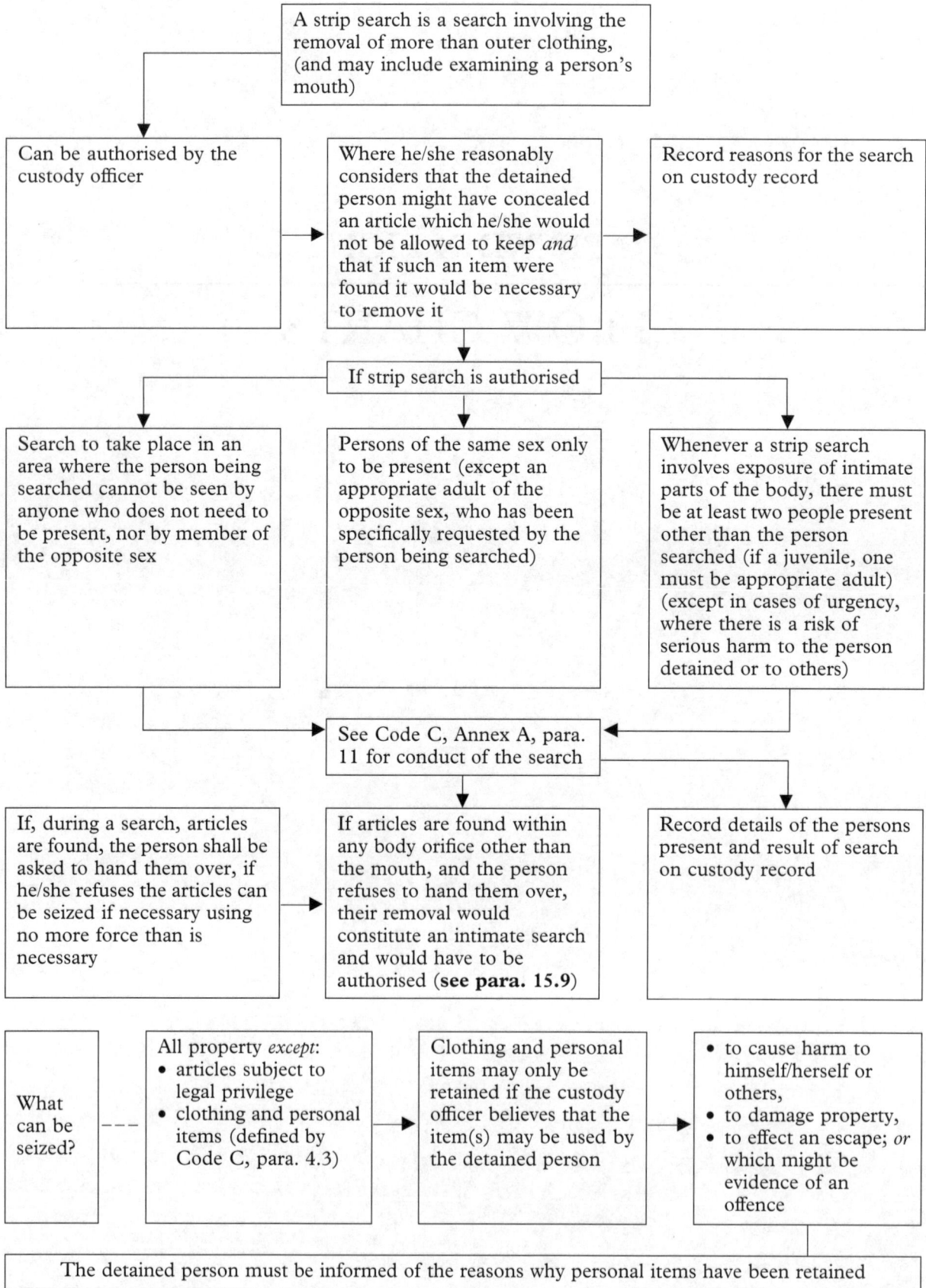

A strip search is a search involving the removal of more than outer clothing, (and may include examining a person's mouth)

| Can be authorised by the custody officer | Where he/she reasonably considers that the detained person might have concealed an article which he/she would not be allowed to keep *and* that if such an item were found it would be necessary to remove it | Record reasons for the search on custody record |

If strip search is authorised

| Search to take place in an area where the person being searched cannot be seen by anyone who does not need to be present, nor by member of the opposite sex | Persons of the same sex only to be present (except an appropriate adult of the opposite sex, who has been specifically requested by the person being searched) | Whenever a strip search involves exposure of intimate parts of the body, there must be at least two people present other than the person searched (if a juvenile, one must be appropriate adult) (except in cases of urgency, where there is a risk of serious harm to the person detained or to others) |

See Code C, Annex A, para. 11 for conduct of the search

| If, during a search, articles are found, the person shall be asked to hand them over, if he/she refuses the articles can be seized if necessary using no more force than is necessary | If articles are found within any body orifice other than the mouth, and the person refuses to hand them over, their removal would constitute an intimate search and would have to be authorised (**see para. 15.9**) | Record details of the persons present and result of search on custody record |

| What can be seized? | All property *except*:
• articles subject to legal privilege
• clothing and personal items (defined by Code C, para. 4.3) | Clothing and personal items may only be retained if the custody officer believes that the item(s) may be used by the detained person | • to cause harm to himself/herself or others,
• to damage property,
• to effect an escape; *or* which might be evidence of an offence |

The detained person must be informed of the reasons why personal items have been retained

Intimate Searches

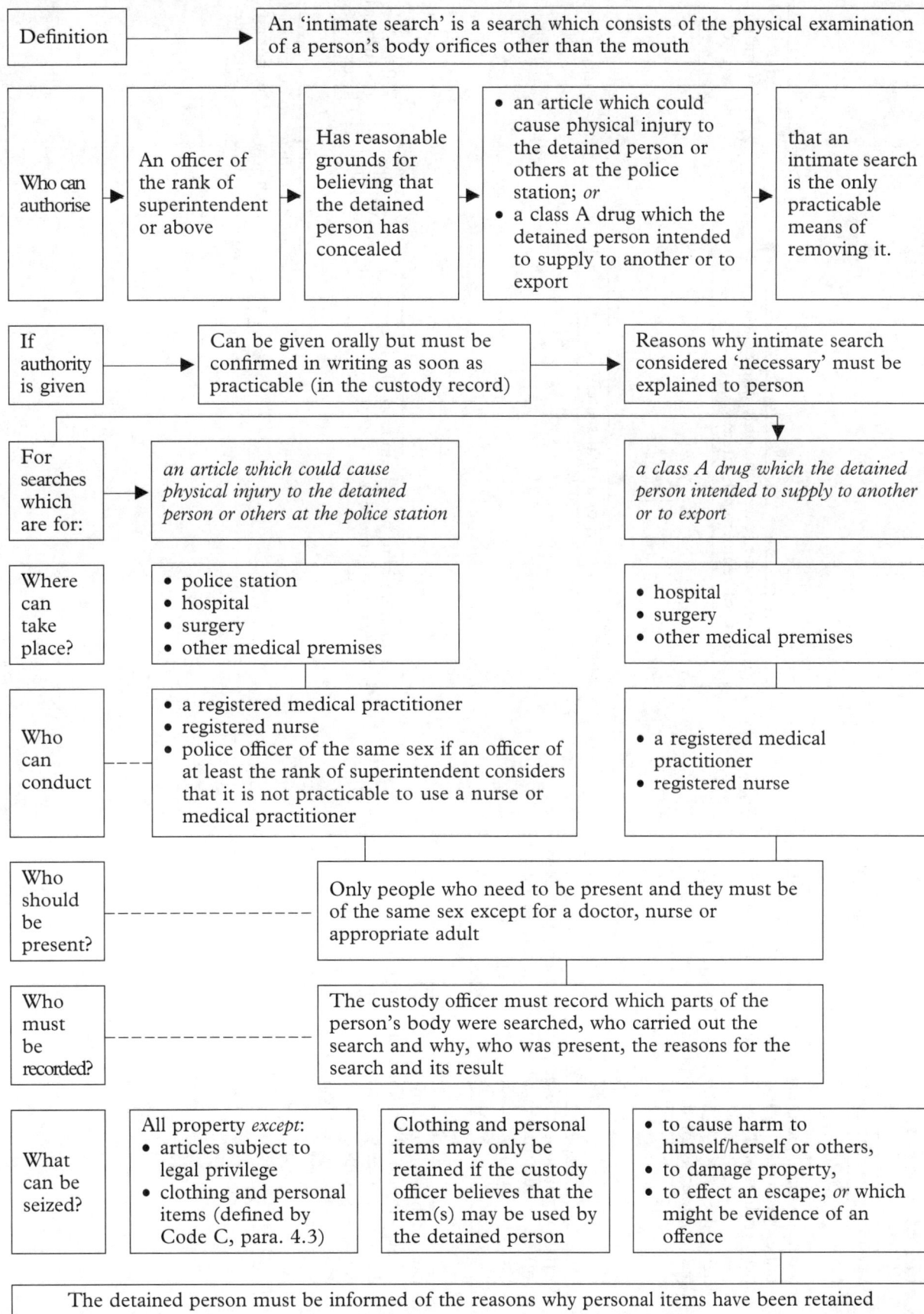

Definition	An 'intimate search' is a search which consists of the physical examination of a person's body orifices other than the mouth

Who can authorise	An officer of the rank of superintendent or above	Has reasonable grounds for believing that the detained person has concealed	• an article which could cause physical injury to the detained person or others at the police station; *or* • a class A drug which the detained person intended to supply to another or to export	that an intimate search is the only practicable means of removing it.

If authority is given	Can be given orally but must be confirmed in writing as soon as practicable (in the custody record)	Reasons why intimate search considered 'necessary' must be explained to person

For searches which are for:	*an article which could cause physical injury to the detained person or others at the police station*	*a class A drug which the detained person intended to supply to another or to export*
Where can take place?	• police station • hospital • surgery • other medical premises	• hospital • surgery • other medical premises
Who can conduct	• a registered medical practitioner • registered nurse • police officer of the same sex if an officer of at least the rank of superintendent considers that it is not practicable to use a nurse or medical practitioner	• a registered medical practitioner • registered nurse

Who should be present?	Only people who need to be present and they must be of the same sex except for a doctor, nurse or appropriate adult
Who must be recorded?	The custody officer must record which parts of the person's body were searched, who carried out the search and why, who was present, the reasons for the search and its result

What can be seized?	All property *except*: • articles subject to legal privilege • clothing and personal items (defined by Code C, para. 4.3)	Clothing and personal items may only be retained if the custody officer believes that the item(s) may be used by the detained person	• to cause harm to himself/herself or others, • to damage property, • to effect an escape; *or* which might be evidence of an offence

The detained person must be informed of the reasons why personal items have been retained

Level of Search

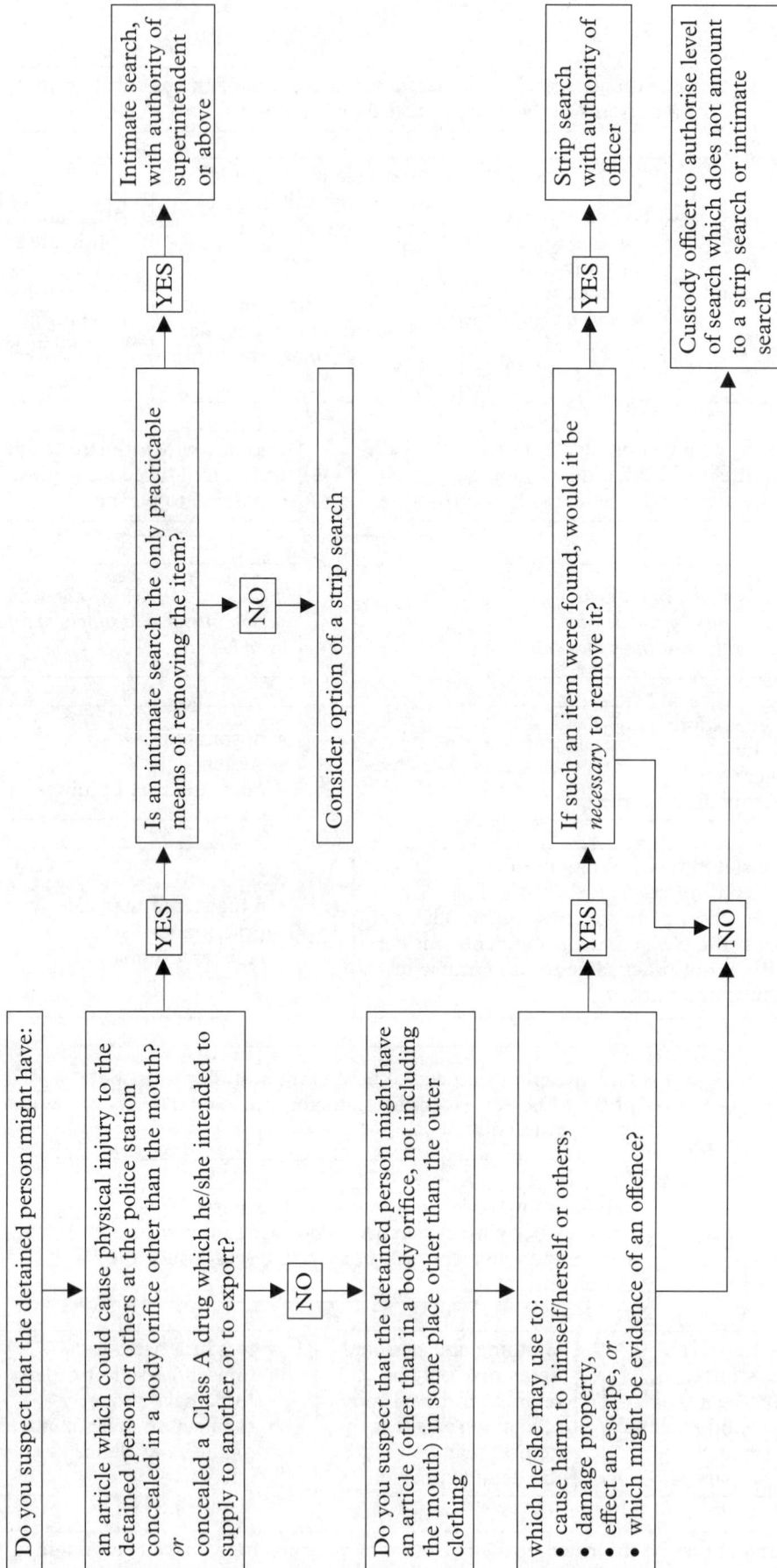

Do you suspect that the detained person might have:

→ an article which could cause physical injury to the detained person or others at the police station concealed in a body orifice other than the mouth?

or

concealed a Class A drug which he/she intended to supply to another or to export?

YES → Is an intimate search the only practicable means of removing the item?

YES → Intimate search, with authority of superintendent or above

NO → Consider option of a strip search

NO → Do you suspect that the detained person might have an article (other than in a body orifice, not including the mouth) in some place other than the outer clothing

→ which he/she may use to:
- cause harm to himself/herself or others,
- damage property,
- effect an escape, *or*
- which might be evidence of an offence?

YES → If such an item were found, would it be *necessary* to remove it?

YES → Strip search with authority of officer

NO → Custody officer to authorise level of search which does not amount to a strip search or intimate search

Medical Care of Detained Persons

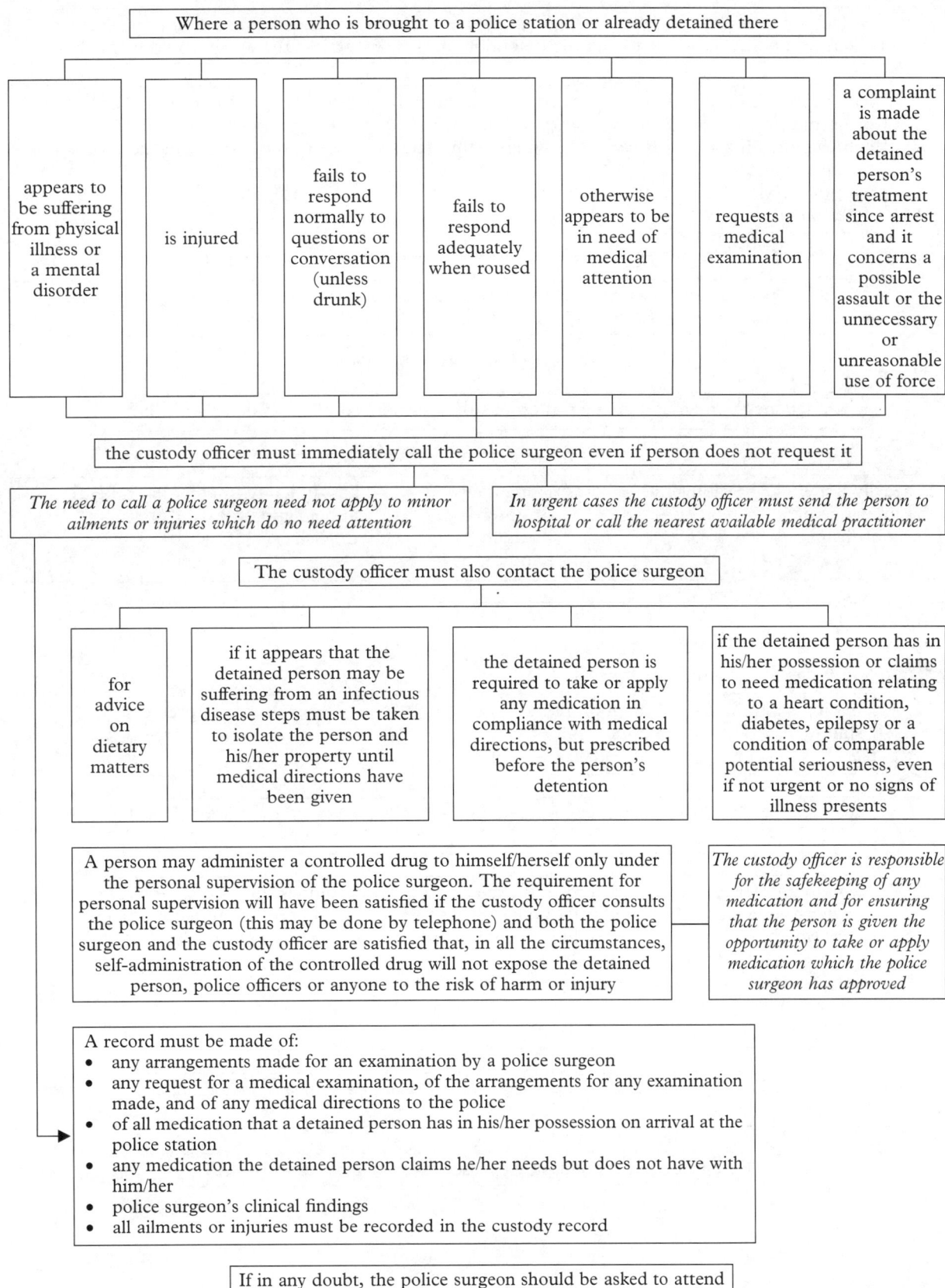

> Where a person who is brought to a police station or already detained there

appears to be suffering from physical illness or a mental disorder	is injured	fails to respond normally to questions or conversation (unless drunk)	fails to respond adequately when roused	otherwise appears to be in need of medical attention	requests a medical examination	a complaint is made about the detained person's treatment since arrest and it concerns a possible assault or the unnecessary or unreasonable use of force

> the custody officer must immediately call the police surgeon even if person does not request it

The need to call a police surgeon need not apply to minor ailments or injuries which do no need attention

In urgent cases the custody officer must send the person to hospital or call the nearest available medical practitioner

> The custody officer must also contact the police surgeon

for advice on dietary matters	if it appears that the detained person may be suffering from an infectious disease steps must be taken to isolate the person and his/her property until medical directions have been given	the detained person is required to take or apply any medication in compliance with medical directions, but prescribed before the person's detention	if the detained person has in his/her possession or claims to need medication relating to a heart condition, diabetes, epilepsy or a condition of comparable potential seriousness, even if not urgent or no signs of illness presents

A person may administer a controlled drug to himself/herself only under the personal supervision of the police surgeon. The requirement for personal supervision will have been satisfied if the custody officer consults the police surgeon (this may be done by telephone) and both the police surgeon and the custody officer are satisfied that, in all the circumstances, self-administration of the controlled drug will not expose the detained person, police officers or anyone to the risk of harm or injury

The custody officer is responsible for the safekeeping of any medication and for ensuring that the person is given the opportunity to take or apply medication which the police surgeon has approved

A record must be made of:
- any arrangements made for an examination by a police surgeon
- any request for a medical examination, of the arrangements for any examination made, and of any medical directions to the police
- of all medication that a detained person has in his/her possession on arrival at the police station
- any medication the detained person claims he/her needs but does not have with him/her
- police surgeon's clinical findings
- all ailments or injuries must be recorded in the custody record

> If in any doubt, the police surgeon should be asked to attend

FLOW CHARTS

Urgent Interviews prior to the Attendance of an Appropriate Adult

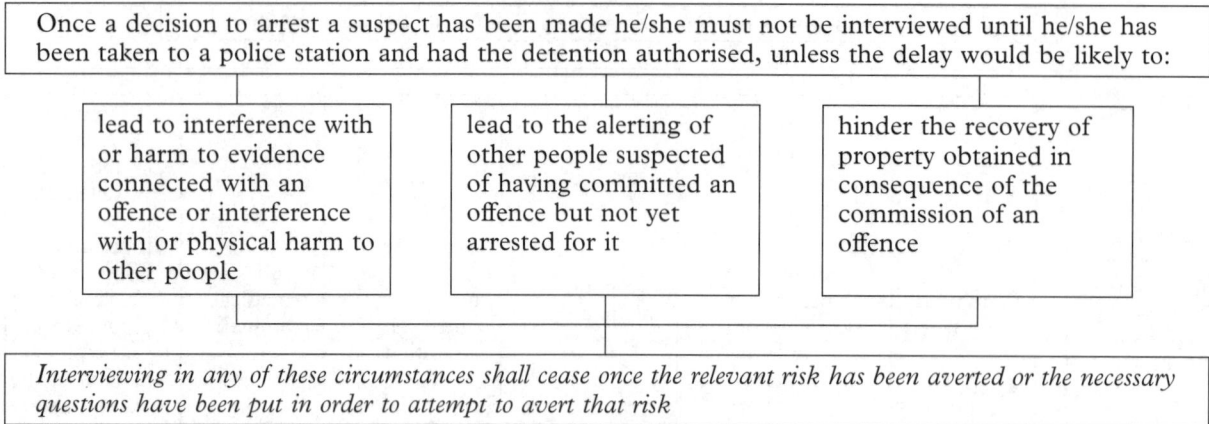

Once a decision to arrest a suspect has been made he/she must not be interviewed until he/she has been taken to a police station and had the detention authorised, unless the delay would be likely to:

lead to interference with or harm to evidence connected with an offence or interference with or physical harm to other people	lead to the alerting of other people suspected of having committed an offence but not yet arrested for it	hinder the recovery of property obtained in consequence of the commission of an offence

Interviewing in any of these circumstances shall cease once the relevant risk has been averted or the necessary questions have been put in order to attempt to avert that risk

VULNERABLE SUSPECTS

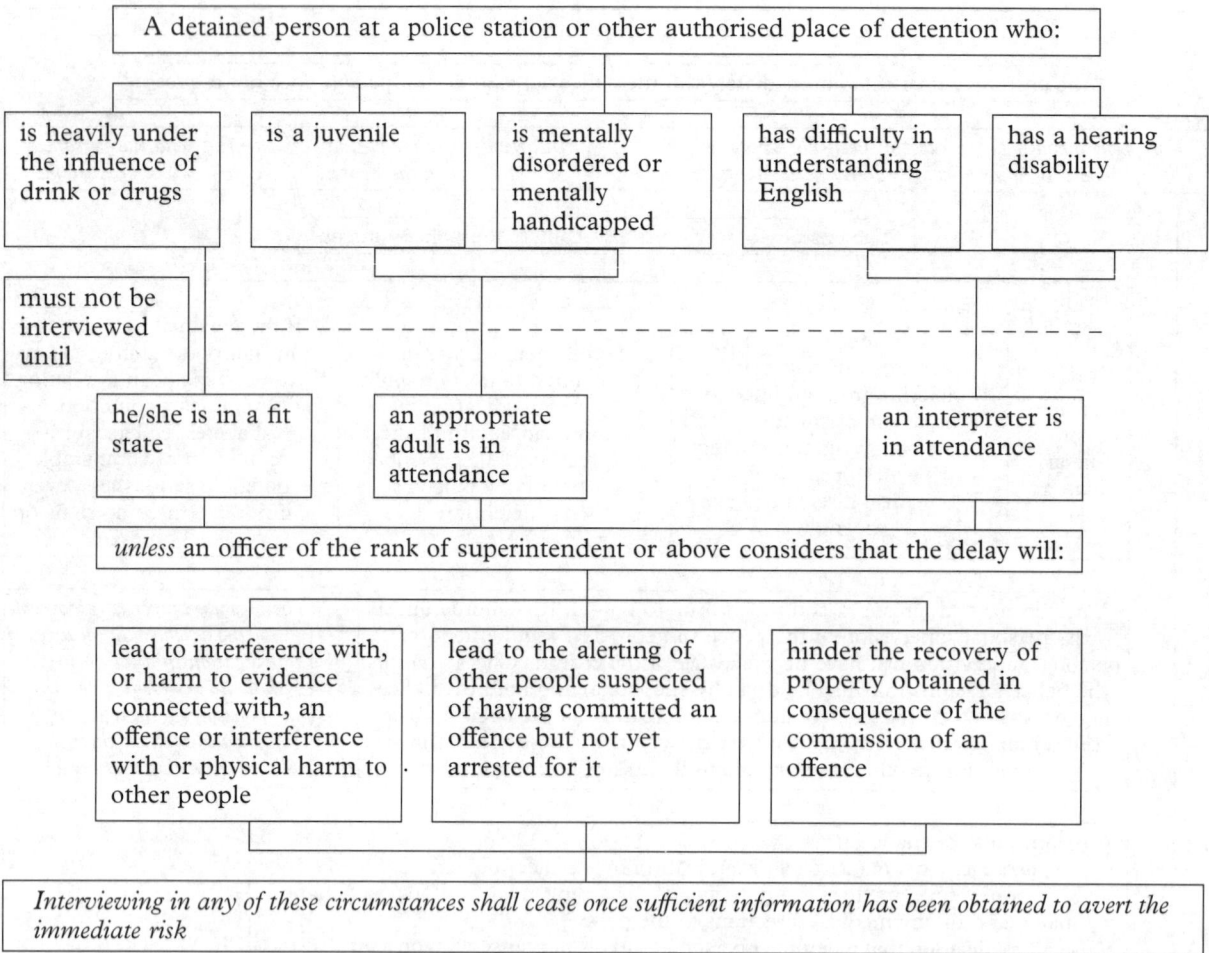

A detained person at a police station or other authorised place of detention who:

is heavily under the influence of drink or drugs	is a juvenile	is mentally disordered or mentally handicapped	has difficulty in understanding English	has a hearing disability

must not be interviewed until

- -

he/she is in a fit state	an appropriate adult is in attendance	an interpreter is in attendance

unless an officer of the rank of superintendent or above considers that the delay will:

lead to interference with, or harm to evidence connected with, an offence or interference with or physical harm to other people	lead to the alerting of other people suspected of having committed an offence but not yet arrested for it	hinder the recovery of property obtained in consequence of the commission of an offence

Interviewing in any of these circumstances shall cease once sufficient information has been obtained to avert the immediate risk

This procedure should only be used in *exceptional cases of need*

INDEX

INDEX

INDEX